THE MADNESS OF WOMEN

Why are women more likely to be positioned or diagnosed as mad than men?

If madness is a social construction, a gendered label, as many feminist critics would argue, how can we understand and explain women's prolonged misery and distress? In turn, can we prevent or treat women's distress, in a non-pathologising women centred way? *The Madness of Women* addresses these questions through a rigorous exploration of the myths and realities of women's madness.

Drawing on academic and clinical experience, including case studies and in-depth interviews, as well as on the now extensive critical literature in the field of mental health, Jane Ussher presents a critical multifactorial analysis of women's madness that both addresses the notion that madness is a myth, and yet acknowledges the reality and multiple causes of women's distress. Topics include:

- The genealogy of women's madness – incarceration of difficult or deviant women
- Regulation through treatment
- Deconstructing depression, PMS and borderline personality disorder
- Madness as a reasonable response to objectification and sexual violence
- Women's narratives of resistance

This book will be of great interest to students and scholars of psychology, gender studies, sociology, women's studies, cultural studies, counselling and nursing.

Jane M. Ussher is Professor of Women's Health Psychology, and director of Gender Culture and Health Research, at the University of Western Sydney, Australia. She is author of a number of books. Her current research focuses on women's sexual and reproductive health, with particular emphasis on premenstrual experiences, gendered issues in caring, and sexuality and fertility in the context of cancer.

WOMEN AND PSYCHOLOGY
Series Editor: Jane Ussher
School of Psychology, University of Western Sydney

This series brings together current theory and research on women and psychology. Drawing on scholarship from a number of different areas of psychology, it bridges the gap between abstract research and the reality of women's lives by integrating theory and practice, research and policy.

Each book addresses a 'cutting edge' issue of research, covering such topics as post-natal depression, eating disorders, theories, and methodologies.

The series provides accessible and concise accounts of key issues in the study of women and psychology, and clearly demonstrates the centrality of psychology to debates within women's studies or feminism.

The Series Editor would be pleased to discuss proposals for new books in the series.

GENDER, LANGUAGE AND DISCOURSE
Anne Weatherall

THE SCIENCE/FICTION OF SEX
Annie Potts

THE PSYCHOLOGICAL DEVELOPMENT OF GIRLS
AND WOMEN
Sheila Greene

JUST SEX?
Nicola Gavey

WOMAN'S RELATIONSHIP WITH HERSELF
Helen O'Grady

GENDER TALK
Susan A. Speer

BEAUTY AND MISOGYNY
Sheila Jeffreys

BODY WORK
Sylvia K. Blood

MANAGING THE MONSTROUS FEMININE
Jane M. Ussher

THE CAPACITY TO CARE
Wendy Hollway

SANCTIONING PREGNANCY
Harriet Gross and Helen Pattison

ACCOUNTING FOR RAPE
Irina Anderson and Kathy Doherty

THE SINGLE WOMAN
Jill Reynolds

MATERNAL ENCOUNTERS
Lisa Baraitser

WOMEN AND DEPRESSION
Michelle N. Lafrance

UNDERSTANDING THE EFFECTS OF CHILD SEXUAL ABUSE
Sam Warner

THE GENDERED UNCONSCIOUS
Louise Gyler

THE MADNESS OF WOMEN

Myth and Experience

Jane M. Ussher

Routledge
Taylor & Francis Group

LONDON AND NEW YORK

First published 2011 by Routledge
27 Church Road, Hove, East Sussex BN3 2FA

Simultaneously published in the USA and Canada
by Routledge
270 Madison Avenue, New York, NY 10016

Routledge is an imprint of the Taylor & Francis Group, an Informa business

Copyright © 2011 Psychology Press

Typeset in Times by Garfield Morgan, Swansea, West Glamorgan
Printed and bound in Great Britain by TJ International Ltd, Padstow, Cornwall
Cover design by Anú Design

This publication has been produced with paper manufactured to strict environmental
standards and with pulp derived from sustainable forests.

British Library Cataloguing in Publication Data
A catalogue record for this book is available from the British Library

Library of Congress Cataloging in Publication Data
Ussher, Jane M., 1961-
The madness of women : myth and experience / Jane M. Ussher.
p. cm.
Includes bibliographical references and index.
ISBN 978-0-415-33927-8 (hb) – ISBN 978-0-415-33928-5 (pb)
1. Women–Mental health. 2. Women–Psychology. I. Title.
RC451.4.W6U868 2011
616.890082–dc22
2010041202

ISBN: 978-0-415-33927-8 (hbk)
ISBN: 978-0-415-33928-5 (pbk)

FOR JANETTE PERZ, WHO KEEPS ME SANE,
MOST OF THE TIME

CONTENTS

ACKNOWLEDGEMENTS

This book has been many years in gestation, drawing on research conducted in both the UK and Australia, as well as personal experience of what is known as 'madness'. I am grateful to all of the women who gave generously of their time in being interviewed about their lived experiences of distress, in both continents. I would also like to acknowledge my mother, and thank her for showing me that it is possible to face the abyss of despair and survive. Janette Perz collaborated on the research projects examining women's experience of premenstrual syndrome (PMS) and women at midlife, and the Gender and Therapy Referrals Study, from which many of the interviews are drawn, as well as making insightful comments on drafts of the manuscript, talking with me about the ideas, and ensuring that I stopped working before I got too tired. Janette also took responsibility for the management of our current research projects and PhD students when I was on sabbatical, for which I am eternally grateful. I couldn't have done the research, or the writing, without her. Michelle Rousseau provided support and insight at a personal level at the early stages of writing, and showed me the value of an empowering model of therapy. Nicola Gavey, Michelle LaFrance, and Ann Weatherall made many constructive suggestions as reviewers of the manuscript (as did an anonymous reviewer). Nicola also contributed to my thinking through her editorial comments on a paper I submitted to *Feminism and Psychology*, from which sections of Chapter 2 are drawn, as did Dave Pilgrim in his capacity of editor on a chapter I contributed to *The Sage handbook of mental health*, part of which is included in Chapter 2. Colleagues and PhD students within the Gender, Culture and Health Research group at University of Western Sydney provide me with a stimulating and supportive environment to work in – as well as facilitating my writing by carrying on so effectively when I was on leave. In particular, I thank Tim Wong, Emilee Gilbert and Yasmin Hawkins. As well as Marlee King, whose honours thesis research on positive experiences of PMS is reported in Chapter 5. Lynn Christie and Coral O'Toole provided ongoing friendship and encouragement, and a space that allowed me to switch off. And Barney was my constant companion when I was writing, as well as being always available for walks when I wasn't.

I would like to acknowledge my appreciation of those organisations and grant giving bodies who funded the research projects on which this book is based: Economic and Social Sciences Research Council (ESRC, UK); Australian Research Council (ARC); Nepean Division of General Practitioners; and University of Western Sydney (UWS). I am also grateful to UWS for granting me six months' sabbatical to complete the writing. Permission for reprinting a fragment of the poem Mad Skywriting, previously published in the anthology, S. Chapadjiev (ed) (2008) Live through this: On creativity and self-destruction. New York, Seven Stories Press, was received from Bonfire Madigan Shive; www.bonfiremadigan.com; www.theicarusproject.net. Diagnostic Criteria for Major Depressive Disorder are reprinted with permission from the American Psychiatric Association (2000) *Diagnostic and statistical manual of mental disorders*, Fourth Edition, Text Revision (© Copyright 2000), Washington, DC: American Psychiatric Association.

In this book I draw on some work previously published and am grateful to the following for permission to reproduce this material here:

Ussher, J.M. (2011) Gender matters: Differences in depression between women and men, in D. Pilgrim, A. Rogers and B. Pescosolido (eds) *The Sage handbook of mental health and illness*. London: Sage, pp. 103–126.

Ussher, J.M. (2010) Are we medicalizing women's misery? A critical review of women's higher rates of reported depression. *Feminism and Psychology*, **20**(1): 9–35.

Ussher, J.M. and J. Perz (2010) Disruption of the silenced-self: The case of premenstrual syndrome, in D.C. Jack and A. Ali (eds) *The depression epidemic: International perspectives on women's self-silencing and psychological distress.* Oxford: Oxford University Press, pp. 435–456.

Perz, J. and J.M. Ussher (2009) Connectedness, communication and reciprocity in lesbian relationships: Implications for women's construction and experience of PMS, in P.L. Hammack and B.J. Cohler (eds) *The story of sexual identity: Narrative perspectives on gay and lesbian identity.* New York: Oxford University Press, pp. 223–250.

Perz, J. and J.M. Ussher (2008) 'The horror of this living decay': Women's negotiation and resistance of medical discourses around menopause and midlife. *Women's Studies International Forum*, **31**: 293–299.

Ussher, J.M. and J. Perz (2008) Empathy, egalitarianism and emotion work in the relational negotiation of PMS: The experience of lesbian couples. *Feminism and Psychology*, **18**(1): 87–111.

Ussher, J.M. (2005) Unravelling women's madness: Beyond positivism and constructivism and towards a material-discursive-intrapsychic approach, in R. Menzies, D.E. Chunn and W. Chan (eds) *Women, madness and the law: A feminist reader*. London: Glasshouse, pp. 19–41.

1

THE MADNESS OF WOMEN

Myth or experience?

Philip Martin writes:

> Woman and madness share the same territory . . . they may be said
> to enter a concentric relationship around a central point occupied by
> a fundamental male normality. Like some insidious virus, insanity
> therefore invades the mythology of woman, finding there a semiotic
> fund that it may use for the purpose of self-definition.[1, p.42]

Paula Caplan writes:

> An official announcement [reads that] . . . nearly half of all
> American's experience a psychiatric disorder . . . does that mean
> no one is normal . . .? Or [do] we live in such a crazy-making, sick,
> impersonal society that it does serious psychological damage to
> half of us? . . . Should we be calling [women] the mentally ill . . . or
> society's wounded?[2, p.6]

For centuries, women have occupied a unique place in the annals of
insanity. Women outnumber men in diagnoses of madness, from the
'hysteria' of the eighteenth and nineteenth centuries, to 'neurotic' and mood
disorders in the twentieth and twenty-first. Women are also more likely to
receive psychiatric 'treatment', ranging from hospitalisation in an asylum,[i]
accompanied by restraint, electro-convulsive therapy (ECT) and psycho-
surgery, to psychological therapy and psychotropic drug treatments today.
Why is this so? Some would say that women *are* more mad than men, with
psychiatric treatment a beneficent force that sets out to cure the disordered
female mind. I proffer an alternative explanation – that women are subjected to misdiagnosis and mistreatment by experts whose own pecuniary
interests can be questioned, as can their use (or abuse) of power. This is not
to deny the reality of women's experience of prolonged misery or distress,
which undoubtedly exists. However, if we examine the roots of this distress,
in the context of women's lives, it can be conceptualised as a reasonable

1

response, not a reflection of pathology within. This book exposes the myths of women's madness, by revealing the flaws within the 'regimes of truth',[4] put forward by the many experts who populate this field. I also explore the function of these supposed truths – the regulation of women deemed mad – and give voice to the lived experience of these same women, who remind us that madness not only is an academic debate, but also can be the defining point in a life; a diagnosis many women resist and escape in order to survive.

This is a subject that has always been close to my own heart. As I have discussed previously,[5–6] my own mother was marked as 'mad' for many years when I was a child. While she had always thought that her formal diagnosis was depression, a request to examine her medical records 30 years after the event revealed that she had been labelled 'psychotic'. This finally explained why she was treated with enforced hospitalisation, ECT, and a cocktail of drugs, including the 'chemical cosh' Largactile (chlorpromazine) for symptoms of deep unhappiness and despair. It also explained why those providing such 'treatment' were so reluctant to allow her to come off the drugs, providing no advice and support when she tried to do so herself. My mother's madness occurred in the context of looking after four young children in straitened circumstances, with no support from family, friends or husband. Her 'madness' was an understandable response to her situation; she did not have the psychological, social or financial resources to respond in any other way. And while she may have been experiencing abject misery, psychotic she was not. However, once she was formally diagnosed, and had entered the psychiatric system, she was irrevocably marked with the mantle of madness, and subjected to treatments that dulled her mind, annihilated her short-term memory, and left her unable to care for herself, never mind four young dependents. Her madness may have been erased – the extreme despair transformed into a deadening ache – but so was her very self. She was a mere remnant of the mother I had known, with vacant eyes, listless slow movements, and seemingly endless tears – at least until she began to fight back, gradually coming off the drugs, taking up paid work outside the home, then developing friendships and a life of her own.[ii]

My awareness of madness began in the shadow of my mother's despair. I grew up afraid of it, not understanding what was happening to her, and distressed by the vulnerability and incoherence she displayed after her many 'treatments', particularly ECT. The electric shocks that were fired into her brain did more than erase misery and memory: they left her a physical and psychological wreck – a frightening sight to a pubescent child. My greatest fear was that she would die, and that I would be left to care for my younger siblings permanently. The anger I felt towards those who could leave her in such a state – far worse than the unhappiness she experienced before she turned to them for help – fuels me to this day. When I realised that my mother was going to survive, and saw that, finally, she had begun to recover, I developed a new fear: that one day I would become mad myself. Whether it was in my blood, or lurking in my mind, I did not know, but I was determined to avoid this wretched state. I studied psychology, which gave me academic insight into the subject I feared the most. By becoming an 'expert' I imagined that I might be immune. I also decided to live a life that was very different from my mother's – no children to drag me down (as I had feared), no financial dependence on a man; instead, a life of work and play that was full to the extreme, leaving little space for despondency. If only it were so easy. If it were, I wouldn't need to write this book, as we could solve the conundrum of women's madness with a busy schedule and the avoidance of solitary reflection (or avoidance of motherhood).

The madness I have experienced has never been formally diagnosed – it didn't need to be, as I recognised it well enough myself, and could access therapeutic support by paying for it privately, rather than entering a system within which I might drown (or be damned). I have known the depths of despair that many speak of as 'depression', even if I haven't been officially labelled with that term. I have known the anguish and turmoil of inter-minable dark nights when I have imagined ending it all to make the pain go away. I have known the agitation of seemingly endless anxiety, when my mind is full of fear, and my heart is beating so fast I feel as if my chest will burst. And I have known the feelings of relief – if not euphoria – when the misery and tension finally abate, when life seems worth living again. I have experienced this excruciating pit of hopelessness a number of times during my adult life, primarily precipitated by events at work, which is ironic, given my belief that a fulfilling career would keep me sane. Yet the experience that I have had of madness, and of the machinations of experts I was determined to avoid, provided knowledge and power which influenced the course and outcome of my misery, allowing me to avoid the stigma of being publically positioned as 'mad', at least until I wrote these words. My mother did not have that knowledge or power when I was a child. We may not always be able to prevent women's madness, but by understanding it we gain the power to ameliorate it in ways that do not cause additional pain or suffering (or cause 'side effects' – the iatrogenic symptoms which can be worse than the problem being treated). We can also avoid the trap of inappropriately attributing distress to pathology within the woman, effectively dismissing her voice and her views through bestowing a psychiatric diagnosis, when her emotions are often an understandable response to her situation.

I have begun with a reflexive account of my own experience, and of that of my mother, because this analysis is not about madness as 'other', a shameful experience that should remain silenced. Madness is a spectre that haunts all women. No woman is immune from psychiatric diagnosis; no woman is immune from the distress (or the ascription of deviance) that can lead to this diagnosis. 'Why *madness*?' you might say. 'Why not talk of mental illness, or indeed, the diagnostic categories established by modern psychiatry?' The term 'mental illness' is problematic, as it suggests an internal pathology that can be incontrovertibly categorised and cured by biomedicine; a disease state that occurs within the individual and is separate from culture, values and politics. Notions of 'mental illness' also serve to absolve the individual of all responsibility for their feelings or actions, implying a passive sick role and reliance on the doctor for a biochemical cure.[9] At the same time, as many of the anti-psychiatrists of the 1960s and 1970s argued, physical illness can be located in 'underlying pathologies in the individual organism',[10, p.345] whereas 'the mind is not an organ or part of the body [and] cannot be diseased in the same way as the body can'.[11, p.94] And while it has been claimed that diagnosis of *all* illness 'is, like beauty, in the eye of the beholder',[12, p.106] social norms and subjective judgement are central to the diagnosis of disorders of the mind. The use of the term 'madness' reminds us of this fact.

Deconstructing madness: acknowledging women's distress

I will at times, however, refer to specific diagnostic categories, because they form part of the language within which we are taught to understand our distress (or our social deviance). But this will always be with a critical eye, recognising that diagnostic categories are social constructions reflecting beliefs about madness and sanity in a particular place at a particular point in time. Unlike many in the 'psy-professions',[13]iii I do not accept these diagnostic categories as unquestioned truth, assuming that they refer to some 'real' disorder that has been uncovered by scientific sleuthing. Rather, they reflect the interests of particular groups of experts, who reify their right to regulate those deemed mad through the diagnosis of an ever increasing array of pathological conditions, supported by the *Diagnostic and statistical manual of mental disorders* (DSM),iv the bible of psychiatry first developed by the American Psychiatric Association in 1954, and now in its fourth edition.[15]v

In this vein, I draw on the work of the French philosopher Michel Foucault, who argued that power is irrevocably connected to knowledge, which in turn has a regulatory function – for example, through categorising what is normal and abnormal; what is 'mad' and what is 'sane'.[16] Foucault argued that discursive representations and practicesvi 'systematically form the objects of which they speak',[18, p.49] actively constructing realities in specific ways, and normalising particular forms of social control.[14] In this view, discourses produce identities, subject positions, and 'institutional sites' from which a person can speak or be addressed, as subjectivity is not conceptualised as coming from within, but rather as constructed within language and cultural practices.[19, p.28] Therefore, representations of madness encapsulated within the DSM not only define the boundaries of what it means to have a 'disordered' mind, but also function to construct the subject position 'mad woman', legitimising the right of particular experts to speak about and treat her condition, and defining which particular 'truths' are accepted as explanations for her disordered state. For rather than accepting science, medicine and the 'psy-professions' as disciplines that objectively analyse and reveal reality, they are seen to simply construct and support particular 'truths' that serve the interests of those in power. In the context of madness in the twenty-first century, this means positioning the problem solely within the woman, and legitimising bio-psychiatry and Big Pharma – the drug companies which profit from the now ubiquitous biochemical 'cures'.

While I may question the veracity of the accounts in the DSM, I do recognise the reality of the distress that gets classified as 'symptoms' of the various diagnostic disorders applied to women. The existence of what has been described as an 'extra-discursive reality'[20] is compatible with a feminist Foucaultian analysis of women's madness, through the adoption of a critical realist standpoint, which acknowledges that realities 'exist and act independently of our descriptions, but we can only know them under particular circumstances', in the words of Roy Bhaskar. He continues: 'the relations between the "real material" object and the practices of its production are complex: there is never a moment of "reality" which is comprehensible outside a framework of discursive practices which render it possible and transformable'.[21, p.250] Critical realism allows us to recognise women's lived experience of misery or prolonged distress as well as the material and intrapsychic concomitants of this distress, while acknowledging that it is known as 'madness' (or as one of the diagnostic categories reified in the DSM) only because of the discourses which circulate in a particular culture at a particular point in time. The use of the term 'madness' in this book thus serves to remind us of its function as signifier of pathology, without reifying psychiatric diagnosis, or the positioning of women's distress as 'illness'.

In recent years, 'mad' has also been a term embraced by those who fall under the mantle of psychiatry – those most affected by the stigma of having a 'disordered' mind. *Mad Pride*vii founder Simon Barnett says 'everybody knows what "mad" means, whereas they don't know what a "mental health service user" is',[22] and *Mad Pride* members declare that they 'reclaim the word mad and any other stigmatizing term of abuse – crazy, loony etc'.[23] So what is madness? Thomas Szasz, who has long been critical of the power and prejudices of psychiatry, defines madness thus:

> The term 'madness' refers to a potpourri of emotions and behaviours, expressed verbally or more often non-verbally, composed of a variety of ingredients, any one of which may be dominant in any one case. The ingredients are anger, aggression, fear, frustration, confusion, exhaustion, isolation, conceit (megalomania, narcissism, self-dramatization), cowardliness, and difficulty getting on with others.[24, p.12]

5

The authors of the *Diagnostic and statistical manual of mental disorders* use the terminology 'mental disorder', which is defined as 'a clinically significant syndrome or pattern that is associated with distress or disability or with significantly increased risk of suffering, death, pain disability, or an important loss of freedom' considered as a 'manifestation of a behavioral, psychological, or biological dysfunction in the individual', which is not 'an expectable and culturally sanctioned response'.[25, p.xx] Implicit in each of these definitions is the notion of individual distress and social disturbance – with the concept of 'dysfunction' reminding us that madness is always culturally defined, leaving room for subjective interpretation of that which is deemed 'madness' (and thus conversely, of that which is deemed sane).

It is also useful to reflect on R.D. Laing's view that 'madness need not be all breakdown. It may also be break through. It is potentially liberation and renewal as well as enslavement and existential death'.[26, p.47] Sometimes in the depths of our despair we can see and speak the truth of our situation. Indeed, madness may be a reasonable response to an untenable situation; the result of living in an insane world. However, this is not to say that madness is an existential experience that will always be embraced. Take Susanna Kaysen's account of madness in her autobiographical novel *Girl, interrupted*, where she eloquently describes the dulling of perception, the slowing of reflexes and the general torpor where 'experience is thick'.[27, p.116]

> Insanity comes in two basic varieties: slow and fast. I'm not talking about onset or duration. I mean the quality of the insanity, the day to day business of being nuts. There are a lot of names: depression, catatonia, mania, anxiety, agitation. They don't tell you much. The predominant quality of the slow form is viscosity. Experience is thick. Perceptions are thickened and dulled. Time is slow, dripping slowly through the clogged filter of thickened perception. The body temperature is low. The pulse is sluggish. The immune system is half asleep. The organism is torpid and brackish. Even the reflexes are diminished, as if the lower leg couldn't be bothered to jerk itself out of its stupor when the knee is tapped. . . . Which is worse, overload or underload? Luckily, I never had to choose. One or the other would assert itself, rush or dribble, through me, and pass on.
>
> Pass on to where? Back to my cells to lurk like a virus waiting for the next opportunity? Out into the ether of the world to wait for the circumstances that would provoke its reappearance? Endogenous or exogenous, nature or nurture – it's the great mystery of mental illness.[27, pp.116–119]

In this book, I explore this 'great mystery' through examining the discursive construction and lived experience of women's madness at the beginning of

6

the twenty-first century, as well as tracing the genealogy of our current practices in the prejudices and policies of the past. I explore competing expert explanations for women's greater propensity to be diagnosed as mad, the 'regimes of knowledge'[13, p.11] that define what can be known, and what solutions are offered as 'treatment'. This includes biomedical theories that locate women's madness in the reproductive body (their raging hormones); psychological theories focusing on women's disordered minds (their cognitions or attachment style); and socio-cultural theories that blame women's social environment (poverty, inequality and abuse). I also explore feminist social constructionist theories that dismiss the very notion of madness itself, and argue that psychiatric diagnosis and treatment simply acts to pathologise and regulate femininity; the view that by defining what is mad we define what it is to be sane, or more specifically, the boundaries of behaviour for the 'good woman'.

This will provide insight into how and why women are more likely to be positioned as mad than men – more likely to be diagnosed as having a range of 'disorders', which include: mood disorder (depression or dysthymic disorder); anxiety disorder (panic attacks, agoraphobia and specific phobia, or generalised anxiety disorder); somatoform disorder (conversion disorder or pain disorder); factitious disorder; dissociative identity or depersonalisation disorder; eating disorders; many of the sleep disorders (primary insomnia, nightmare disorder, and sleep disorders related to another disorder); adjustment disorder; borderline, histrionic or dependent personality disorder,[28] and post-traumatic stress disorder (PTSD).[29] It is a sobering list of supposed female maladies. I not only challenge the legitimacy of these 'disorders' as objective diagnostic categories, but also explore how and why women come to experience distress and then see themselves as mad, accepting these diagnostic categories as explanations for their distress (or their supposed deviance), through a process of subjectification.

Drawing on Foucault, Nikolas Rose describes subjectification as

> regimes of knowledge through which human beings have come to recognise themselves as certain kinds of creatures, the strategies of regulation and tactics of action to which these regimes of knowledge have been connected, and the correlative relations that human beings have established within themselves, in taking themselves as subjects.[13, p.11]

It is through this process of subjectification that truths about women's madness are reproduced and lived by women: the fictions framed as facts that serve to regulate women's experience of distress, and through this process, our very experience of what it is to be 'woman'. In this analysis of subjectification I also draw on positioning theory, which posits that identity

7

is constructed and negotiated in relation to the subject positions taken up by an individual, or the positions within which they are put by others.[30]

As Bronwyn Davies and Rom Harré[31] outline in their seminal paper on positioning theory:

> Positioning as we will use it is the discursive process whereby selves are located in conversations as observably and subjectively coherent participants in jointly produced story lines. There can be interactive positioning in which what one person says positions another. And there can be reflexive positioning in which one positions oneself. . . . One lives one's life in terms of one's ongoingly produced self, whoever might be responsible for its production.[31, p.48]

I explore how and why women take up the subject position 'mad' (or are positioned as such by others), and the implications of this positioning, in particular, how women are treated by health professionals, their families, and their partners. Finally, I examine how women resist the spectre of psychopathology that haunts us all and how they survive the distress that is deemed madness. This will provide insight into ways in which women deal with distress without being positioned as 'Other', as inherently flawed simply for being born woman (or for performing the script of femininity as we are told to do).

The genealogy of women's madness

Through examining the genealogy of current discourses and discursive practices,[4; 32] Foucault demonstrated the continuity between past and present, and the culturally located nature of particular beliefs and regulatory techniques. If we look to accounts of hysteria, the most commonly diagnosed 'female malady' of the eighteenth and nineteenth centuries, we can trace the genealogy of the 'regimes of truth' which define and regulate women's madness today. While hysteria was first described by the ancient Greeks, appearing in the writings of Plato and Hippocrates, it was in the seventeenth century that it emerged as one of the most common diseases treated by medics. Thus Thomas Sydenham commented that 'the frequency of hysteria is no less remarkable than the multiformity of the shapes which it puts on. Few of the maladies of miserable mortality are not imitated by it'.[33, p.85] Sydenham was also the first to see hysteria as a disorder of the mind expressed through the body,[34, p.109] when previously it had been deemed a disorder of the body that troubles the mind.[35] While the causes of this nebulous disorder were widened to include the nervous system in the late eighteenth century, allowing men to receive a diagnosis of hysteria,[36, p.15] it was always considered to be a 'woman's disease', a disorder linked to the essence of femininity itself. For example, in the Edinburgh infirmary in the eighteenth century, 98 per cent of hysteria cases were women.[36, p.16] Equally, while Jean-Martin Charcot, who has been described as heralding the modern epidemic of hysteria in the late nineteenth century, treated 90 male hysterics, approximately 900 women were diagnosed as such at the hospital where he worked.[36, p.33] Indeed, Thomas Laycock,[37] in 1840, described hysteria as a woman's 'natural state', whereas it was deemed a 'morbid state' in a man.[38, p.206] Otto Weininger, in 1903,[39] asserted that 'hysteria is the organic crisis of the organic mendacity of woman'.[34, p.115] The British physician Edward Tilt argued in 1881 that 'mutability is characteristic of hysteria because it is characteristic of women', a sentiment echoed in 1883 by the French physician Auguste Fabre, who declared 'all women are hysterical and . . . every woman carries with her the seeds of hysteria. Hysteria . . . is a temperament, and what constitutes the temperament of a woman is rudimentary hysteria'.[40, pp.286–287]

Nineteenth century physicians were highly critical of this feminine 'temperament', describing hysterical women as difficult, narcissistic, impressionable, suggestible, egocentric and labile.[38, p.202] The affluent hysteric was characterised as an idle, self-indulgent and deceitful woman, 'craving for sympathy',[38, p.205] who had an 'unnatural' desire for privacy and independence,[41] and was 'personally and morally repulsive, idle, intractable, and manipulative'.[3, p.133] Some went as far as to describe such women as 'evil', with the physician Silas Weir Mitchell declaring that 'a hysterical girl is a vampire who sucks the blood of the healthy people around her'.[38, p.207; 42, p.266] In contrast, women suffering from the 'nervous disorder' of neurasthenia,viii which shared many of the symptoms of hysteria, were described as having a 'refined and unselfish nature', and as being 'just the kind of woman one likes to meet'.[3, p.134] The neurasthenic was 'sensible, not over sensitive or emotional, exhibiting a proper amount of illness [with] a willingness to perform their share of work quietly and to the best of their ability', in the words of one nineteenth century physician.[44, p.851] Politeness and compliance on the part of the patient was clearly of the essence, as is arguably still the case today, when 'difficult' women are diagnosed with borderline personality disorder,[45] as is discussed in Chapter 3.

By the late nineteenth century, as Carol Smith-Rosenberg has argued, 'every known human ill'[38, p.202] was attributed to hysteria, meaning that the diagnosis ceased to mean anything at all.[46, p.220] Women diagnosed with hysteria could exhibit symptoms of depression, rage, nervousness, the tendency to tears and chronic tiredness, eating disorders, speech disturbances, paralysis, palsies and limps, or complain of disabling pain. Many women also exhibited a hysterical 'fit', which could either come on gradually, or could occur suddenly, mimicking an epileptic seizure.[38, p.201] Indeed, hysteria has been described by Roy Porter as a 'veritable joker in the taxonomic pack',[47, p.226] and by Lesegne as the 'wastebasket of medicine',[34, xi] largely because of its nebulous and multifarious nature. Hysteria has also been described as a 'mimetic disorder' because it mimics culturally permissible expressions of distress – hysterical limps, paralyses and palsies were accepted symptoms of illness in the nineteenth century, but have virtually disappeared today, as they no longer stand as a 'sickness stylistics for expressing inner pain'.[47, p.229] As Edward Shorter argues,[48] the symptoms that are accepted as legitimate signs of illness or madness, the 'symptom pool', are particular and peculiar to a specific culture, at a particular point in time. By deeming certain symptoms 'illegitimate', culture encourages patients not to develop them in order to avoid being positioned as 'undeserving', as not having a 'real' medical problem. There is thus, Shorter declares, 'great pressure on the unconscious mind to produce only legitimate symptoms'.[48, p.x]

At the beginning of the twenty-first century the 'legitimate' symptoms of madness are laid out for all to see in the *Diagnostic and statistical manual of mental disorders* of the American Psychiatric Association.[15] As new diagnoses are added with each edition (and others, such as hysteria or homosexuality, removed),[49] details of the necessary symptoms for diagnosis are circulated through interactions with the psy-professions, or through pharmaceutical company advertising, media discussion of madness, and 'self-help' diagnostic websites. Is it surprising that so many women self-diagnose with these disorders, and then come forward for professional confirmation of their pathological state? Their distress is no less real than that of the women diagnosed as hysterics in the nineteenth century. However, the myriad disorders with which we are now diagnosed are no less mimetic than hysteria was then: we signal our psychic pain, our deep distress, through culturally sanctioned 'symptoms', which allows our distress to be positioned as 'real'. Or we are told by others that we have a problem, and are then effectively positioned within the realm of psychiatric diagnosis and treatment, with all the regulation and subjugation that this entails.

Contemporary feminist critics have focused on the diagnostic category of anorexia nervosa as the successor to hysteria, seeing it as the modern manifestation of a 'female malady'.[3; 50–51] This is a persuasive argument: hysteria and anorexia nervosa are diagnoses predominantly ascribed to women; the 'typical patient' is often described as wilful or immature in both contexts; and each has been conceptualised as a feminine 'disorder', tied to the enactment of archetypal femininity.[50–51] Anorexia nervosa is not, however, the only female malady to afflict women today; nor is it the only diagnostic category to be contested, or located in cultural constructions of femininity. Depression is presently the diagnostic category widely accepted as a 'woman's problem', described as a 'menace to mood and national productivity',[52, p.109] and the most common diagnosis applied to women's distress.[ix] Diagnosis of depression is primarily the reason why women significantly outnumber men in first admission rates for psychiatric treatment, and in register studies where incidence of madness is calculated by contact with services.[see 56]x The fact that women are twice as likely as men to be prescribed psychotropic medication,[58-60] in particular selective serotonin reuptake inhibitors (SSRIs),[61]xi and twice as likely to be given ECT, is also largely attributable to diagnoses of depression.[xii]

For this reason, in this book I focus substantial critical attention on the construction and experience of this particular diagnostic category. However, depression is not the only 'disorder' wherein women predominate, as outlined above. I thus turn my gaze onto three other manifestations of madness ascribed to significant proportions of the female population: borderline personality disorder (BPD), post-traumatic stress disorder (PTSD) and premenstrual dysphoric disorder (PMDD). While my arguments can be generalised to other 'female maladies' (such as anorexia or anxiety disorders), these three psychiatric disorders are ideal exemplars of the pathologisation of women's reasonable response to restricted and repressive lives. For as the women diagnosed as hysterics in the nineteenth century might have experienced distress or debilitating fatigue in response to an oppressive and restrictive social or relational context, or more specifically, to violence and sexual abuse, so might the women diagnosed with depression, PMDD, BPD or PTSD today. This does not mean these women are mad. Drawing on interviews conducted as part of my own research (see Table 1.1), as well as previously published literary, autobiographical and research accounts, I explore women's experience of distress and of the diagnosis of 'symptoms' that come to be positioned as these particular manifestations of madness. I also critically examine the discursive construction of these disorders, in particular the role that they play in pathologising women's reasonable response to the material inequities of their lives. I then examine the interrelationship of these three irrevocably interconnected levels of analysis, adopting what I have previously described as a material-discursive-intrapsychic (MDI) model,[64] within a critical realist epistemological framework.[xiii]

As well as recognising the reality of somatic, psychological, and social experience, but conceptualising this reality as constructed and mediated by culture, language and politics,[21] as noted above, in a critical realist framework both qualitative and quantitative research methodologies are accepted, without one being privileged above the other.[65] This allows for the acknowledgement of research findings from a range of perspectives without the necessity of having to reconcile competing epistemological assumptions,[66] and without the truth claims that often underpin positivist research being accepted. Thus a broad body of research, ranging from

11

Table 1.1 Details of research studies described in this book

Title of study	Participants
PMS and Relationships Study	Survey of 321 women self-presenting as PMS sufferers; interviews with 60 women and 25 partners (10 women; 15 men)
Positive Premenstrual Experiences Study	Focus group interviews with 47 women
Women at Midlife Study	Interviews with 21 women at midlife
Gender and Therapy Referrals Study	Survey of 22 general practitioners and 23 allied health professionals (AHPs; psychologists); interviews with 4 GPs and 4 AHPs
Long Term Effects of Child Sexual Abuse Study	Survey of 369 women who had experienced child sexual abuse, and 238 women who had not; narrative interviews with 25 women who had experienced child sexual abuse.

See Appendix for full details of the research, including details of the funding bodies and research teams.

large scale epidemiological studies to single case designs, can be used to provide insight into women's diagnosis of madness and experience of distress – whether this is categorised as depression, PMDD, BPD or any of the other myriad 'disorders' in the DSM. More specifically, the material-discursive-intrapsychic model allows for acknowledgement of the irrevocable interconnections between the material conditions of women's lives; their embodied and intrapsychic experience; and the discursive construction of deviance or distress as 'madness', in relation to broader cultural narratives of femininity and psychopathology. This is an approach that addresses the demand for recognition that 'what is social is also psychic and also somatic, or bodily', in the words of Victoria Grace.[67, p.273]

What about men?

Madness is not solely a 'woman's problem'. All of the emotions and behaviour that serve as signifiers of madness – including distress, anger and misery – are experienced by both women and men, and psychiatric diagnosis is also applied to both. However, madness is a gendered experience, with 'symptoms' judged differently in women and men, and certain diagnostic categories more likely to be applied to women. Indeed, madness is still signified by femininity, whether it occurs in women or men, which is one of the reasons why distressed men often eschew psychological diagnosis or treatment, as they do not want to be seen to be 'like a woman'.[68] While

I agree with Joan Busfield that it is important to look at *gender* and madness,[43] and I applaud the renewed interest in the mental health of men by many researchers and policy makers,[e.g. 68–70]xiv my focus in this book is unashamedly on women. Why? Because I want to explore constructions of *women's* madness, the ways *women* are treated by the psy-professions, and *women's* lived experiences of distress and psychiatric diagnosis. However, my analysis does have implications for men. It has been argued that unravelling the reasons behind women's higher rates of experiences such as depression may provide insights into the nature and aetiology of depression per se.[56; 71] Unravelling women's madness also provides insights into the gendered nature of social and familial life, the consequences of inequality and discrimination for both women and men, and the gendered patterns in certain aspects of psychological processing which occur within a relational and cultural context. Equally, examining the construction and treatment of madness provides insights into the cultural construction of what it means to be 'woman' and 'man', as madness is often defined as deviation from archetypal gendered roles.

Structure of the book

The outline of the book is as follows: in Chapter 2, I critically examine the regimes of knowledge that define women's madness today, focusing on expert explanations for women's higher rates of reported depression, from a biomedical, psychological and socio-cultural standpoint. One of the common features of these different approaches is the adoption of a positivist-realist epistemological standpoint, the limitations of which are outlined in detail. In Chapter 3, I examine the feminist social constructionist argument that madness is a label that serves to pathologise femininity and women's social deviance. The role of bio-psychiatry and 'Big Pharma' in medicalising women's lives comes under particular scrutiny here. This chapter ends with an exploration of some of the limitations of a social constructivist approach, and the ways in which a critical realist framework and a material-discursive-intrapsychic (MDI) model can reconcile discip-linary divides. Chapters 4 and 5 use the MDI model to explore the con-struction, experience and consequences of women's madness, drawing on two areas as detailed case studies. First, woman as object, not subject, with a focus on sexual violence and abuse, including a critique of the diagnosis of sexually abused women as having BPD or PTSD. Second, an examination of the construction of premenstrual change as a psychiatric syndrome, PMDD, and women's lived experience of premenstrual distress in a relational con-text. The final chapter examines women's survival and resistance to regimes of truth associated with madness, as well as the implications of an MDI analysis for interventions and preventative practices which aim to reduce women's distress. This analysis demonstrates that women's madness is both

13

a myth – a culturally constructed label for distress or deviance – and a real experience for many women, a reflection of deep discontent in response to the context of their lives.

2

THE DAUGHTER OF HYSTERIA

Depression as a 'woman's problem'?

- Depressed mood most of the day, nearly every day, as indicated by either subjective report (e.g., feels sad or empty) or observation made by others (e.g., appears tearful). (In children and adolescents, this may be characterized as an irritable mood)
- Markedly diminished interest or pleasure in all, or almost all, activities most of the day, nearly every day (as indicated by subjective account or observation made by others)
- Significant weight loss when not dieting or weight gain (e.g., a change of more than 5% of body weight in a month), or decrease or increase in appetite nearly every day
- Insomnia or hypersomnia nearly every day
- Psychomotor agitation or retardation nearly every day
- Fatigue or loss of energy nearly every day
- Feelings of worthlessness or excessive or inappropriate guilt (which may be delusional) nearly every day (not merely self-reproach about being sick)
- Diminished ability to think or concentrate, or indecisiveness, nearly every day (either by subjective judgement or as observed by others)
- Recurrent thoughts of death (not just fear of dying), recurrent suicidal ideation without a specific plan, or a suicide attempt or a specific plan for committing suicide.

Criteria for Major Depressive Episode, *Diagnostic and statistical manual of mental disorders* (DSM-IV)[1, p.356]

In the current era of psychiatric nosology, women's madness is manifested, or so we are told, as higher levels of the psychiatric disorder 'major depression', characterised by the symptoms outlined above. Any woman who experiences five or more of these 'symptoms' over a two-week period, and says that she has felt 'down and miserable' for most of this time, or has lost interest in her usual activities, is liable to be told that she has a depressive illness.[e.g. 2] I begin this chapter by examining the epidemiological statistics, the evidence put forward to support the view that women are more likely to experience this supposed 'illness' than men. I then critically examine the regimes of knowledge that variously locate depression in women's bodies, women's minds or in their social environment. While this substantial body of research is positioned as objective science, presenting competing theories of the aetiology of gender differences in depression, in reality it plays a major role in the ongoing construction of women's distress as madness, through reifying distress as a pathological condition, which serves to legitimise bio-psychiatric intervention. In this vein, I deconstruct the very definition of depression itself, as well as critically examine the vested interests of those perpetuating a medicalised analysis of women's distress – in particular Big Pharma. I also question the epistemological assumptions adopted by the majority of researchers in this field, who are not the neutral scientific observers they claim to be. Their adoption of a positivist-realist standpoint serves to reify the notion of depression as 'thing' within the woman; it negates the complexity of women's subjective experience of distress, and strips 'depression' of its cultural and political context, by emphasising the role of embodied or psychological 'dysfunctions'.

Epidemiological evidence for gender differences in depression

If we look to epidemiological research, the evidence that women are more likely to experience 'depressive illness' would appear to be indisputable.[i] First, researchers have examined lifetime occurrence in non-clinical contexts, by recruiting a representative sample of the population and asking whether they have ever experienced depression. Across various studies it has been reported that women outnumber men at a rate of two to one.[3–8] However, disparities as high as four to one have been reported.[9][ii] Second, studies examining incidence rates in the previous twelve months report that women are between 1.3 and 3.8 times more likely than men to have experienced depression and anxiety.[4][iii] This is illustrated in Table 2.1, where the findings of recent large scale population surveys conducted in the USA, the UK and Australia are reported.

These statistics may seem incontrovertible, demonstrating that women *are* more mad than men – if by madness we mean depression or anxiety. The majority of experts concur, with bio-psychiatrists, psychologists and socio-cultural theorists accepting this epidemiological evidence, and proffering competing explanations for gender differences in depression. However, it is not that simple. Paula Treichler has argued that these epidemiological statistics are 'bad science infected by rumor and fantasy',[17, p.391] which give the impression that diseases such as depression are an 'unmediated epidemiological phenomenon'.[18, p.109] This suggests that we should question the validity of these statistical 'facts', and at the same time, the very definition of depression (or madness) itself. Before elaborating upon this social constructionist critique, I examine each of the expert accounts in

Table 2.1 Gender differences in depression and anxiety: 12-month incidence

Percentage of the population of men	Percentage of the population of women	Ratio*	
Depression 7.7 Anxiety 11.8	Depression 12.9 Anxiety 22.6	1.7 1.9	USA, 1993, National Comorbidity Study, 8,098 respondents[12]
Depression 7.1	Depression 12.5	1.8	Worldwide, 1999, 25,900 respondents[6]
Depression 4.2 Anxiety 7	Depression 7.4 Anxiety 12	1.8 1.7	Australian Bureau of Statistics, 1997, 10,600 adults[17]
Depression 2 Anxiety 4 Mixed anxiety and depression 7	Depression 3 Anxiety 5 Mixed anxiety and depression 11	1.5 1.3 1.6	UK Govt statistics, 2000, 8,886 respondents[11]
Depression 3.1 Anxiety 10.8	Depression 5.1 Anxiety 17.9	1.6 1.7	Australian Bureau of Statistics, 2008, 20,789 respondents[16]
Depression 2.2 Anxiety 2.8	Depression 7.5 Anxiety 10.7	3.4 3.8	Australian community based survey, 2008, 7,485 respondents[18]
Depression 2 Anxiety 4 Mixed anxiety and depression 7	Depression 3 Anxiety 5 Mixed anxiety and depression 11	1.5 1.3 1.6	UK Govt statistics, 2000, 8,886 respondents[11]

* The ratio indicates the magnitude of increased likelihood of depression or anxiety experienced by women, in comparison to men.

turn, starting with the biomedical view that women's madness originates in the reproductive body, beginning with the age-old opinion that women's madness was located in the wandering womb, the precursor to the 'raging hormone' theories that circulate today.

The madness of woman: a problem peculiar to her sex?

In 1848, Thomas Coutts Morison declared:

It is generally understood that mental alienation is of more frequent occurrence among females than amongst men . . . because there exists in the female a variety of causes, as disorders of the menstrual function, pregnancy, parturition, and suckling; which are, of course, peculiar to sex.[19]

17

In 1801, the *Encyclopaedia Britannica* defined hysteric affection:

> HYSTERIC AFFECTION, or *Passion*, (formed of νςερα 'womb'); a disease in women, also called *suffocation of the womb*, and vulgarly *fits of the mother*. It is a spasmodico-convulsive affection of the nervous system, proceeding from the womb.[20, p.16]

Across history, women's greater propensity to madness has been attributed to the reproductive body – with women's reproductive organs deemed to be 'pre-eminent' in all aspects of her psyche and physical well-being. As one mid nineteenth century physician declared: 'They exercise a controlling influence upon her entire system, and entail upon her many painful and dangerous diseases. They are the source of her peculiarities, the centre of her sympathies, and the seat of her diseases'.[21, p.7; 22, p.183] Thus medical officer John Haslam explained women's preponderance in the Bethlem asylum during this period as due to the 'natural processes which women undergo',[iv] claiming that 'insanity' is 'often connected with menstruation' and 'parturition'.[24, p.215] Similarly, George Man Burrows concluded that 'many circumstances in the physical and moral condition of women, from the epoch of puberty to the critical period, would lead us to conclude that more women than men become insane in every country and every place'. These 'circumstances' included 'women being exposed to more natural causes of physical excitation and irritation than men', as well as 'menstruation, parturition and all its consequences'.[25, p.243] Similarly, menopause was described as 'a critical and dangerous time for women',[26, p.15] a time when 'the nervous system is so unhinged that the management of the mental and moral fibres often taxes the ingenuity of the medical confident'.[26, p.101] These pronouncements follow in the Hippocratic tradition of locating pathological behaviour in the womb, characterised by the disorder 'hysteria', which derives from the Greek term for the womb νςερα (ustera).[27]

While Hippocrates may have first coined the term 'hysteria', it was Plato who memorably attributed women's disorders to the 'wandering womb', in *Timaeus*, published in 91CE. Plato saw the womb as 'an animal which longs to generate children', claiming that it could be found 'straying about in the body and cutting off the passages of breath . . . [where] it impedes respiration and brings the sufferer into the extremist anguish'.[28, p.10] During the Restoration and up until the eighteenth century, even healthy women were considered to be simply a 'walking womb'.[27, p.149] However, at the end of the eighteenth century the link between the womb and madness became established as scientific 'fact', which, as Michel Foucault notes, resulted in 'the entire female body' being 'riddled' by 'a perpetual possibility of hysteria'.[29, p.154] This served to legitimise medical management of all errant women, described by Foucault as a 'process whereby the feminine body was analysed – qualified and disqualified – as being thoroughly saturated with sexuality; whereby it was integrated into medical practices, by reasons of a pathology intrinsic to it'.[30, p.104]

In addition to menstruation, parturition and menopause, a gamut of ailments were purported to be the root cause of hysteria and neurasthenia, including menstrual pain and irregularity, absence of pregnancy, uterine disorders, and vaginal infections.[22, p.206] Some physicians extended their analysis to the whole reproductive system: 'not only the uterus and ovaries, but also the bladder, rectum, vagina, clitoris, labia, perineum, and the now so fashionable fallopian tubes all join in producing local or reflex neurosis'.[31, p.131] The other aspect of female corporality blamed for hysteria (and by implication, for women's madness) was sexuality, reflecting the nineteenth century view that female desire was morally dangerous.[32, p.105] On the one hand, the 'necessary' suppression of women's sexuality, 'in compliance with the usages of society',[33] was seen as a cause of hysteria, while at the same time, hysteria among lower class women was attributed to the base sexuality which was believed to characterise their class, with prostitutes assumed to be at particular risk.[22, p.207] Sexual excess among married middle class women was also considered problematic, as was masturbation, leading to clitoridectomy (surgical removal of the clitoris) being put forward as a recommended treatment. Here is an extract from the writings of A.J. Bloch, an American surgeon, describing how he diagnosed and treated an 'obscure nervous disorder' in a female patient, a child, who had been previously observed masturbating by her mother:

> To assure myself . . . that masturbation really existed as represented, and in order to be able to define if such were true, the pleasure centre, I determined to put the child to a practical test. Having her undressed and put on the bed, I first touched the external orifice of the vagina, and then the labia minora, without any appreciable excitement on the part of the child. However as soon as I reached the clitoris, the true phenomena developed. The legs were thrown widely open, the face became pale, the breathing short and rapid, the body twitching with excitement, slight groans would come from the patient.[34, p.3]

After inducing orgasm in his patient, which confirmed his diagnosis that the 'clitoris was responsible' for her 'disorder', Dr. Bloch declared that he 'decided to excise this organ' which he achieved forthwith. 'I dissected up the clitoris and amputated it almost to its attachment to the pubes. Haemorrhage was controlled by simple pressure, the denuded surfaces of the labiae minorae were brought together with two silk sutures'. He concludes by declaring that the 'cure is complete' as 'the nervous condition has entirely disappeared'.[34, p.4]

This is not an isolated case. Many women were subjected to clitoridectomy, as well as removal of the ovaries, as a treatment for the nebulous disorder of hysteria, or other similar 'nervous complaints'. Jean-Martin Charcot treated women with an ovarian compressor,[v] a 'heavy leather and metal belt strapped onto the patient and often left as long as three days'.[35, p.33] The revocation of Sigmund Freud's seduction theory in 1897 can be seen as operating within the same vein – women's sexuality, damaged or otherwise, is assumed to be making her mad. In 1896 Freud argued that repressed childhood sexual abuse caused hysteria, with symptoms 'derivatives of memories that are operating unconsciously'. He also argued that fathers were the 'seducers' in most instances. However, in 1897 the 'seduction theory' was abandoned, to be replaced with a theory that placed emphasis on the patient's unconscious desires, and on sexual and oedipal fantasy. The reasons for the withdrawal of the theory were that Freud believed that his initial theory did not lead to therapeutic success; it also suggested that the incidence of paternal sexual abuse was improbably vast, and Freud claimed it was impossible to distinguish between truth and fantasy in the accounts of hysterics.[35, p.40] Women's distress was thus attributed to pathology within, allowing the reality and magnitude of child sexual abuse to remain largely unacknowledged for a further 100 years.[vi]

Notions of the wandering womb may seem laughable today, and hysteria is all but a defunct diagnostic category. However, the location of women's madness in the sexual or reproductive body is not a historical anachronism. The Hippocratic tradition is maintained by the biomedical monopoly over health and illness, that results in bio-psychiatry having jurisdiction over women's madness,[36] and raging hormones being positioned as to blame.

Raging hormones and reproductive debilitation

The National Institute of Mental Health (NIMH) reported in 2008:

> The biological and hormonal changes that occur during puberty likely contribute to the high rates of depression in adolescent girls.[37, p.9]

Angold and colleagues claimed in 1999:

> In later life (after age 55), the female excess of depressions diminishes; mostly because of falling rates in women at a time when their oestrogen levels are again low.[38, p.1044]

Current bio-psychiatric theories of depression focus either on genetic determinants,[39] or on neuro-chemical 'imbalance',[40] as the psychiatrists Klein and Wender[41, p.87] declare:

the majority of cases of depression and manic-depressive illness appear to be genetically transmitted and chemically produced. Stated differently, the disorders seem to be hereditary and what is inherited is a tendency towards abnormal chemical functioning . . . in the brain.[cited by 42, p.75]

In this vein, it has been argued that genetic differences between women and men are the explanation for women's higher rates of depression.[vii] However, a meta-analysis of four community and two twin studies, containing 20,000 participants, did not find any consistent gender difference in heritability,[39] leading to the conclusion that 'the relative importance of genetic effects in major depression is the same in women and men'.[8, p.166]

An alternative strand of bio-psychiatric theorising can be traced to the pronouncements of Plato, or to the nineteenth century prelates who proselytised about hysteria. Today, the focus is on reproductive hormones, exemplified by the comments of Mary Seaman,[47, p.1645] in a review of hormonal causes of 'psychopathology', that 'evolutionary imperatives' have given 'female hormones' not only a 'special neuro-protective role but also a stress mediating role' which acts to shield women from psychosis, but make them 'more vulnerable than men to depression and anxiety'. In a similar vein, John Studd has argued that dysregulation of the 'sex hormones' oestrogen and progesterone are to blame for women's depression:

> The excess of depression in women compared with men occurs at times of great hormonal fluctuations – at the time of puberty, in the postnatal period, and premenstrually – and it is worst in the few years before menstrual cycles end. At this time the worsening symptoms of premenstrual tension with age blend with the worst years of the climacteric. These wretchedly depressed women in their 40s usually respond well to oestrogen treatment rather than to the psychoactive drugs that remain the first line treatment of psychiatrists.[48, p.977]

Justification for this view is located in the fact that gender differences in diagnoses of depression emerge at puberty, and appear to be reduced post-menopause. Prior to adolescence, boys outnumber girls over the whole gamut of mental health diagnoses, including conduct disorders, language and speech disorders, autism and Asperger syndrome, attention deficit hyperactivity disorder, as well as enuresis and encopresis (bedwetting and soiling).[49–50] In preadolescence, boys also outnumber girls in community studies of depressive symptoms,[51–52] and in rates of diagnosed depressive disorders.[53] Post-adolescence, however, this gender imbalance is reversed.[viii] This suggests that adolescence may be an important turning point in women's mental health.

In the minds of many experts, it is the biological event of puberty that is deemed to be the key factor, which is reminiscent of the advice given to mothers in the late nineteenth century, when adolescence was described as 'naturally a time of restlessness and nerve irritability' for girls. A 'period of storm and stress' and of 'brooding, depression and morbid intro-spection'.[56, cited by 22, p.186] This view would initially appear to be supported by epidemiological research. The 1993 US National Comorbidity Survey reported that the increased rate of female depression occurred at ages 10–14,[12] whereas other studies are more precise, specifying age 13,[57] or achievement of pubertal status, rather than simple chronological age.[52] And while girls' propensity to report depression appears to increase at mid-puberty, boys are less likely to report depression post-puberty, which has led to the conclusion that 'the transition to mid-puberty appeared transiently to protect boys from depression'.[52, p.59] At the same time, there is inconsistent evidence as to the continuity of gender differences in report-ing of depression across the adult lifespan. On the one hand it has been concluded that 'there is evidence for a female preponderance of depression in older age groups',[8, p.165] a conclusion based on a review of 34 com-munity studies,[58] and a substantial study looking at depression in indi-viduals aged 65 and over across different European countries.[59] However, two large scale population studies conducted in the USA[12] and the UK[60] in the 1990s reported that gender differences in depression do not persist after 55 years of age, 'due an absolute fall in female prevalences',[60, p.16] with the size and representativeness of these population reviews leading psychiatric reviewer Paul Bebbington to conclude that 'considerable weight' should be placed on the findings.[61, p.2]ix This may appear to confirm the essentialist view that women's madness is tied to the reproductive body, to the physiological changes that accompany fecundity, support-ing the conclusion that 'the female prevalence in depression is linked to women's reproductive years'.[62, p.25] However, the evidence for this view-point is more equivocal than this confident statement would suggest, as is outlined below.

Resisting biological determinism: rejecting raging biomedical explanations for women's madness

Rachel Liebert writes:

> The hormonal discourse constructs women as biologically and innately inferior, if not dangerous . . . naturalizes patriarchal authority, and the institutions (such as heterosexual marriage, heteronormativity, house-wifery and protectionist sex 'education') that this brings into practice.[63, p.279]

There have always been dissenters to the view that women's madness is located in the body. The seventeenth century physician Thomas Willis stated that while diseases of 'unknown nature and origins', including madness, were blamed on the 'bad influence of the uterus', this organ is 'for the most part, not responsible at all'.[29, p.138] His contemporary, Thomas Sydnenham, was more specific, stating that hysteria was the result of social conditions that enslaved women.[32, p.103] In the nineteenth century the British psychiatrist Henry Maudsley adopted a similar view, claiming that hysteria resulted from women having fewer outlets for their nervous energy:

> The range of activities of women is so limited, and their available paths in life so few, compared with those men have in the present social arrangements, that they have not, like men, vicarious outlets for feelings in a variety of healthy aims and pursuits.[64, p.450]x

The French psychiatrist Philippe Pinel agreed that hysteria was the product of a restrictive and rigid bourgeois family life; however, he believed that 'neurosis' in women was also encouraged by 'lascivious reading'.[27, p.101] Even Silas Wier Mitchell, who described hysterical women as 'vampires', acknowledged that this disorder could be caused by 'the daily fret and wearisomeness of their lives which . . . lack . . . distinct occupations and aims'.[66, p.14]

Thus the 'symptoms' experienced by women diagnosed as hysterics could be framed as reasonable responses to an untenable social situation – young middle class women secluded from the world and courted prior to marriage, then expected to embark on the monotony of housekeeping, childrearing and self-sacrifice afterwards, often in the context of an unhappy relationship.[22] Or the urban working class women living a life of unrelenting drudgery, being paid at subsistence levels, with no support from family – two-thirds of the hysterics in the French asylum Salpêtrière were from this group.[35, p.34] (Salpêtrière is the Paris asylum where Charcot practised in the nineteenth century.) Developing symptoms that required complete bed-rest or hospitalisation could be seen a form of resistance – serving to force others to take on domestic drudgery, which gave the 'hysteric' some semblance of control.[22] In this vein, feminists have celebrated hysteria as 'a woman's response to a system in which she is expected to remain silent, a system in which her subjectivity is denied, kept invisible'.[67] Jane Gallop described the hysteric as a 'proto-feminist' because of her 'calling into question constraining sexual identities',[68, cited by 69, p.288] and Hélène Cixous argued that hysteria was the 'nuclear example of women's power to protest'.[70, p.154] Freud's (in)famous case study *Dora* (Ida Bauer) is thus recast as feminist heroine, rather than hysteric.[71] Dora was thwarted by her parents in her intellectual ambitions, and 'handed over' by her father to the husband of his mistress, Herr K., who attempted to seduce her when she was age 14. Dora terminated her 'talking cure' therapy after only eleven weeks, rejecting Freud's interpretation that her feelings were fantasies that reflected her desires for Herr K., her father, and Freud himself.[72] Cixous described Dora as 'the one who resists the system, the one who cannot stand that the family and society are founded on the body of women, on bodies despised, rejected, bodies that are humiliated once they have been used'.[70, p.154; see also 27; 69] The same has been said of the nineteenth century 'fasting girls', the foremothers of women diagnosed with anorexia today, who were seen as enacting a form of cultural protest, their starved minds symbolised by their starved bodies.[73]

The notion that modern manifestations of women's madness have an embodied aetiology is equally questionable. For many biomedical researchers today, the key to understanding women's depression lies in understanding adolescent onset – with Kessler and colleagues arguing that the higher prevalence of female depression observed in the US National Comorbidity Survey is 'largely due to women having a higher risk for first onset'.[12, p.85] This has led to investigation of the relationship between pubertal hormones and depressed mood, in the belief that the 'turning on' of the endocrine system in girls as they emerge from pre- to post-puberty might explain increases in depression at this age. However, there is little evidence to support this hypothesis. For example, while some evidence for a relationship between depressed mood and testosterone[74] or oestrogen levels[75] was reported in two studies, neither study found a relationship between hormones and depression in adolescent girls. Similarly, in a study of 103 girls aged 10 to 14, Brooks-Gunn and Warren[76] reported that only 4 per cent of the variance was accounted for by oestrogen levels, with life events, and the interaction of oestrogen levels and life events, accounting for 17 per cent. Similarly, in a study of 4,500 young women aged 9–13 conducted by Angold and colleagues, where it was reported that the onset of puberty predicted the emergence of the gender difference in depression more accurately than chronological age, an adrenarche explanation, tied to increased adrenal androgens, was ruled out, as 'those changes occur in later childhood'.[52, p.57]xi This should not be surprising, for a simple relationship between hormones and behaviour can be easily contested, and indeed is contested by many who work in this field. As Carol Worthman argues:

> hormones do not directly cause specific biological or behavioral effects. Rather, hormonal action is mediated through an array of other factors. These include: circulating binding proteins, metabolic enzymes, cellular receptors, nuclear binding sites, competing molecules, and presence of cofactors.[77, p.595, cited by 78, p.98]

Equally, there is evidence from the field of psychoneuroimmunology that a reciprocal relationship exists between psychosocial and physiological events, producing an interdependency between social processes and health,[79] rather than the body being the cause of problems.

The evidence for an association between hormones and distress experienced during adult stages of the reproductive life cycle – premenstrually, after childbirth, and during the menopause – is also equivocal. When 'premenstrual tension' (PMT) first appeared in the medical literature in 1931, it was attributed to the 'female sex hormone' oestrogen.[80] In the intervening years, many competing biomedical explanations have been put forward for premenstrual syndrome (PMS) and premenstrual dysphoric disorder (PMDD), the successors to PMT, including gonadal steroids and gonadoptrophins; neurovegetive signs (sleep, appetite changes); neuroendocrine factors; serotonin and other neurotransmitters; β-endorphin; and other potential substrates (including prostaglandins, vitamins, electrolytes, and carbon dioxide).[81] However, there is no evidence for a consistent association between women's hormones and mood,[82] and women report higher rates of depression than men regardless of whether they also report premenstrual distress, or PMS.[83] For example, in one study which reported premenstrual exacerbation of depressive symptoms in women who were diagnosed with PMS,[84] the blunting of the growth hormone response found across the cycle was not found in non-PMS sufferers, which was interpreted as suggesting that 'depression associated with premenstrual hormone changes is a consequence of a propensity to depression rather than offering an explanation of high rates of depression in women'.[4, p.315] Thus women who report depression may experience an exacerbation of symptoms premenstrually, but this does not mean that hormonal changes across the menstrual cycle cause the distress in the first place, or that hormones can explain women's higher overall reporting of depression.

Equally, while many women experience premenstrual *change*, the labelling of such change as a pathological condition PMS (or PMDD), and the experience of premenstrual *distress*, is not inevitable. The cultural context within which a woman lives,[85] and the ways in which she negotiates and copes with premenstrual change,[86] will influence whether this change is accepted as a normal part of her experience, or positioned as 'symptoms' that should be eradicated because they leave her feeling 'out of control' – issues that are explored in detail in Chapter 5. At the same time, there is strong evidence that premenstrual distress is more strongly associated with women's social and relationship context than with her hormonal status,[87] with over-responsibility, relationship dissatisfaction and communication problems exacerbating distress,[88–89] while social support and positive communication facilitate tolerance of premenstrual change outside of a pathological framework.[90–92]

A similar argument can be made for post-partum depression.[93] Current psychiatric orthodoxy tells us that the risk factors for prolonged misery in the post-partum period are the same as at any other time in life,[94] with the added strains of early motherhood serving as a stressor, activating a pre-existing risk for depression.[95] Indeed, the majority of psychiatrists now concur that hormonal or obstetric factors are not associated with non-psychotic post-natal depression,[96] and research suggests that there is no difference between women with and without children in the initial onset of depression.[97] Post-partum blues may be linked to hormonal changes, although the mechanisms of this are not clear, but there is no consistent relationship between the blues and ongoing diagnosis of depression.[4]

One of the most notable factors associated with reporting of post-partum depression is a previous history of depression;[98] women who have previously been depressed have also been found to be slower to recover post-partum, and more likely to relapse, than those who have not been depressed previously.[99] Other factors associated with prolonged misery at this time include stressful life events, maternity blues, infant temperament and unwanted pregnancy.[100] As is the case with PMS, the social and relational context of women's lives is also important, with reporting of post-partum depression associated with life stress,[101–102] and with the quality of the couple relationship.[103–104] Idealised cultural constructions of motherhood, internalised by women, are also influential. For example, in a study of 40 women interviewed about motherhood and post-partum depression, Natasha Mauthner found that the common denominator between the 18 women who reported depression was their high and unrealistic expectations of motherhood.[105] While women knew that there was no such thing as the perfect mother, they each had firm expectations of how they should 'cope', and found it difficult to accept any failure in meeting these impossibly high standards. As one interviewee commented, 'I'm my own worse enemy in a way because . . . I'm quite independent . . . and . . . I just like to think and show people that I can cope, and perhaps I couldn't at the time . . . But I didn't want to show it to anyone'.[106, p.153] These findings were confirmed by a study of 71 new mothers, where reporting of depressive symptoms was higher in women whose experiences of motherhood were more negative than their expectations.[107] At the same time, in countries that provide strong support for new mothers, lower rates of depression are reported post-natally,[108] whereas in countries where women have few reproductive rights, post-partum depression is higher.[109] When you look at the reality of women's experiences of early motherhood, this is not surprising. For example, Debbie described the relentless grind of her '24/7' experience as 'pretty horrendous':

I think I found that really overbearing, the fact that from the moment you wake up you are this mother feeding machine and cleaning and all that. See they're all the things I hate doing anyway so for me it was just horrific, there was nothing else to focus on but who needs feeding, who needs cleaning, cleaning the house, do the washing, do the dishes, do the floors, and to me it was just a total vicious circle of everything I didn't like. Not so much not liking the children, that didn't enter into it but despite whether you loved them or didn't, you really were locked in on a conveyor belt and pushing the pram to me was symbolic of handcuffs. . . . I had . . . probably eight years of just being totally locked in. Poor old Paul never knew quite what to say. . . . He'd be saying, look it's only about five years and I thought I can't visualise another five hours and he's saying it's only another five years. . . . I couldn't see myself living that long so that was all pretty horrendous.[87, p.106]

Indeed, as Wendy Hollway argues, 'is it any surprise that women's identities go through a life-changing transition or that so many new mothers become depressed',[110, p.68] when women are faced with the non-negotiation and incessant demands of this dependent life?

What of the 'psychological turmoil' experienced by the supposedly 'wretchedly depressed women' at midlife?[48, p.977] Researchers and clinicians confidently proclaim that these symptoms are caused by changing hormonal levels, which affect 'hypothalamic function', or 'neuropeptides and neurotransmitters', or cause 'neuroendocrine dysfunction of the limbic system', or affect the 'synchrony or coherence between components of the circadian system'.[111, p.19] However, as I have outlined above, research that has examined depression over the lifespan suggests that women are less likely to be diagnosed with depression at midlife and beyond than in their younger years. Equally, systematic reviews fail to find an association between major depression and menopause,[112] suggesting that the inevitability of menopausal (or perimenopausal) depression is a myth. For example, in a longitudinal study of 2,565 women aged 45–55 living in Massachusetts, the majority of women who entered menopause did not become depressed; the women who *did* report depression at midlife were more likely to have been depressed earlier in life.[113] Similarly, in a study of 2,000 Australian women aged 45–55, the majority reported that most of the time they felt clear headed (72 per cent), good natured (71 per cent), useful (68 per cent), satisfied (61 per cent), confident (58 per cent), loving (55 per cent) and optimistic (51 per cent).[114] This is illustrated by the findings of the Women at Midlife Study conducted by Janette Perz and myself (see Appendix).[115] All of the women we interviewed positioned midlife as a time of positivity, feeling comfortable with themselves and looking forward to the next phase of life, describing themselves as more confident in expressing their opinions and beliefs, regardless of the reactions of others.

As Helen said, 'I guess also you have got enough self-confidence . . . You don't worry so much about what other people think.' Implicit in these accounts was a sense of empowerment women felt as a result of valuing their own opinions, in contrast to the past when they would have attempted to please others. As Susan told us:

> I'll just do it, I don't really care what people say and if people have shots at me about it I'll just laugh it off and even though it might hurt me at the time and I'll take a little bit of it on board and think, maybe I'm overdoing it but the next week I find myself doing it again and thinking, I don't really care what they think.[115, p.295]

Women also expressed increased confidence in their ability to cope with life, as a result of being 'stronger' or 'wiser', through having experienced life. As Ruth said, 'That just comes with experience and age, maturity. You know what you can do and what you're capable of, you know you can do it. You don't worry about it, you just go and do it'. Midlife was also described as a point at which women experienced more freedom from caring responsibilities and from having to play particular roles in relation to others. Clare described it as 'freedom from school fees, freedom from being aligned to the house, having to look after them [children], having to take them places. . . . I've relinquished those responsibilities and I'm happy about that'. Similarly, Anjte said:

> There are no negatives. There's nothing to be negative about. That pressure and that responsibility that you've got in your thirties and twenties when you're trying to raise those kids and trying to make ends meet, that's gone. It's a nice time.

And while the majority of women gave accounts of still being closely involved in family life, this was no longer the centre of their existence. Indeed, there was a sense of pleasure and defiance in women valuing their own time; as Julie said, 'when my family come to visit it's like, it's lovely to see you but it's lovely to see you go'.

The majority of women also described themselves as having developed increased self-awareness and self-worth, being able to accept themselves for who they were, regardless of insecurities and past mistakes, through feeling more comfortable with themselves, and focusing on positive experiences and strengths. Rose told us that 'I think I'm actually a lot happier with myself, like I don't feel I give myself as much of a hard time', and Angela said:

> I would centre on the positives and the positives are you are more comfortable with yourself and more accepting of yourself and

knowing your strengths and your weaknesses and having many
years of established relationships and skills and abilities and things.

Central to this acceptance was a movement away from trying to be the
perfect woman, as Angela continued, 'in the past, you're just being hard on
yourself, like you just don't measure up to yourself . . . now I'm just a little
bit more reasonable in terms of not thinking I should be perfect or close to
it'. Thus, women were not idealising themselves at midlife, but were taking
up a less self-critical position than they had previously, emphasising self-
growth, rather than negative aspects of ageing.

Social and relational context, and women's negotiation of midlife change,
appear to be the factors associated with distress (or well-being) at midlife –
rather than hormonal changes in the menopausal body.[115–116] Thus, in a
study of 469 Manitoba women, family shifts and stresses were reported to
be the strongest predictor of depression at midlife.[117] Other studies have
found that married women report less depression than unmarried women at
midlife, although marital satisfaction was a greater predictor of emotional
well-being than marital status per se.[118–119] This suggests that relational
factors are associated with menopausal depression, as is the case with
depression at any stage in the life cycle (see Chapter 5), meaning that the
notion of the menopausal body *causing* turmoil and depression is nothing
more than a fiction. The cultural construction of women's ageing is also
important. For example, in a study which compared depression at midlife
in North American and Japanese women,[120] Avis reported that there were
much lower rates reported in the Japanese group, reflecting the different
cultural meaning of menopause and ageing in Japan. However, at the same
time, in a study of midlife women living in New York, the majority of
women said that they felt very happy,[116] with the factors which predicted
well-being including higher income, having a close group of friends, good
health, high self-esteem, goals for the future, and positive feelings about
appearance. Indeed recent Western cultural representations of feeling
'fabulous at 40', or 50,[121] challenge the age old negative stereotypes of the
decrepit menopausal woman in the West.[122]

The existence of this substantive body of research does not mean that
hopes of a hormonal explanation for gender differences in depression have
been expunged. In a review of women's health as a 'biomedical field',
Blehar[45, p.151] concluded that 'with the exception of post-partum onset
affective psychosis and bipolar disorder, there is relatively little evidence for
a causal role of sex steroids in clinical disorders'. However, Blehar[45, p.151]
goes on to say: 'A limiting factor in studies of hormones may be methodological. In the near future, sensitive technologies to image in vivo brain
function may allow researchers to test hormonal hypotheses more directly'.
Indeed, Blehar[45, p.140] confirms that the 'role of sex steroid in the etiology,

manifestation, and course of mental illness remains a important emphasis area' for the National Institute of Health (NIH), the primary funding agency for biomedical research in the USA. It seems that researchers will continue looking until they find this particular holy grail – an embodied cause of women's madness, tied to the reproductive body.

When the reproductive body is positioned as to blame for women's madness, this reinforces what I have previously described as 'the myth of the monstrous feminine',[87] wherein fecundity marks women as 'other' – as fickle, fearful and potentially dangerous. This pathologises woman for the very aspect of her being which most characterises her difference from man, at the same time as the complex roots of her despair are denied. However, the other strand of theorising that dominates expert accounts of women's madness is also beset with problems – psychological accounts of women's dysfunctional cognitions or insecure attachment style.

Psychological theories of women's depression: cognitive appraisal, rumination and attachment style

Cognitive appraisal and rumination

There are many psychological theories of depression, that attribute distress to factors such as cognitive style,[123] insecure early attachment experiences and childhood adversity,[124] or the intersubjective negotiation of experience in our adult lives,[125–126] particularly within families.[e.g. 127–129] One of the most influential psychological theories of gender differences in depression is that there are gender differences in cognitive appraisal and coping style.[130] For example, Susan Nolen-Hoeksema has argued that rumination, a pattern of thinking characterised by reflection and worrying about problems, in contrast to taking distracting action or changing the situation, is associated with depression in both men and women, with adolescent girls and adult women being more likely to show ruminative tendencies than adolescent boys or men.[131–132] She claims:

> women carry a triad of vulnerabilities to depressive symptoms compared to men: more chronic strain, a greater tendency to ruminate when distressed, and a lower sense of mastery over their own lives. In turn, these variables contribute to each other.[132, p.1065]

This gender difference in rumination has been reported to emerge by age 13,[133] which provides an alternative explanation to raging hormones for the apparent adolescent onset of depression in girls. Meta-analytic research has also been used to argue that in the face of stress, women are more likely to use coping strategies that involve verbal expression to others or the self –

including seeking emotional support, rumination, and positive self-talk – whereas men are said to engage in avoidance in the face of stressors that involve relationships or other people.[134] For example, in a large scale population study conducted in Australia, ruminative style and neuroticism were reported to be mediators of the significant gender differences found in depression and anxiety (along with physical activity, physical health and perceived interpersonal problems).[135]

In a similar vein, Hankin and Abramson[136] argue that adolescent girls' greater tendency for rumination is a key aspect of their 'depressogenic attributional style'.[136, p.785] Drawing on a general cognitive-vulnerability theory of depression,[123; 137] the emergence of gender differences in depression post-puberty is deemed to result from an interaction of pre-existing vulnerabilities, negative life events, and cognitive vulnerabilities. These are described as: genetic risk for depression, girls' greater tendency to report neuroticism,[138] and maltreatment (primarily sexual abuse), which is deemed to interact with negative body image and 'depressiogenic inferential style',[136, p.785] manifested by rumination. Within this model, the likelihood of depression is said to be increased by parental socialisation, involving high levels of control, which led to girls' negative self-evaluations and greater tendency to take responsibility for failure, compared to boys.[139] In apparent support for this view, beliefs about having no control of emotions, having responsibility for the tone of relationships, and feelings of lack of mastery over negative events, have been reported to mediate gender differences in rumination.[140] Awareness of the views of others has also been seen to be important, with women who have high levels of 'concern for disapproval' reported to be more likely to be depressed.[141]

Neuroticism is not the only so-called 'feminine' personality trait that has been associated with women's greater propensity to report depression. Interpersonal dependency and the tendency to have an affiliative orientation have also been considered to make women vulnerable,[142] with childhood experiences seen to encourage girls to develop what has been described as a 'dependent' or 'socio-tropic' personality type.[143] In this vein, a multifactorial model, with a psychobiological slant to it, has been presented by Jill Cyranowski and colleagues,[62] who explain adolescent onset of depression in terms of girls' heightened affiliative needs, interacting with adolescent transition difficulties and negative life events, particularly those with interpersonal consequences. They draw on meta-analytic research which claims that women are more concerned with affiliation, while men are more likely to be concerned with personal autonomy, instrumentality and agency,[144] to argue that heightened affiliative needs have an evolutionary basis. This is deemed to be located in 'women's historically greater investment in offspring care and their relatively greater use of long term sexual mate selection strategies', linked to the 'mammalian neuropeptide oxytocin'.[62, pp.22–23]

Attachment and self-silencing

Absence of a secure parental base, leading to an insecure attachment style has also been posited as a potential contributory factor in Cyranowski's model,[62] as insecure attachments are said to be linked to lower self-esteem, lower social support, and greater symptoms of psychological distress.[145] Similarly, in her work on self-silencing, a pattern of behaviour involving a focus on others at the expense of the self, accompanied by repression of a woman's own needs and concerns,[146] Dana Jack has integrated aspects of attachment theory, relational theories, and cognitive theories of depression,[147] to explain women's propensity to depression.[148] Self-silencing has been correlated with women's reporting of depression,[149–151] eating disorders,[152] and premenstrual distress,[153–154] as well as with women's risk of death from coronary heart disease.[155]

Self-silencing is characterised as the propensity to engage in compulsive caretaking, pleasing the other, and inhibition of self-expression in relationships, in an attempt to achieve intimacy and meet relational needs.[156] Jack argues that can lead to a self-division between an 'outwardly conforming and compliant self' and an 'inner self who is angry and resentful',[157, p.177] which she describes as 'the core dynamic of female depression'.[146, p.169] This is because women are taught to believe that they are not loved for who they are, but for how well they meet the needs of others, with the resultant silencing of desires and feelings, in particular anger,[158] as well as the use of external standards against which to judge the self, leading to feelings of worthlessness and hopelessness.[148] Jack associates self-silencing relational schemas with 'feminine attachment behaviours' which emphasise 'compliant connectedness',[146, p.40] and which are prescribed by cultural constructions of the 'good woman', who is 'pleasing, unselfish, [and] loving'.[147, p.7]

While attachment theory may have been taken up by many contemporary psychologists, the psychoanalytic underpinnings of John Bowlby's attachment theory[124] are invariably marginalised or ignored. This follows a long history of psychology as a mainstream discipline negating or decrying psychoanalysis, which has resulted in the absence of psychoanalytic insight in psychological research examining gender differences in depression. This is ironic, as the 'riddle of femininity',[159,p.113] or the 'woman question', has been central to psychoanalytic debate. However, psychoanalytic insight has been used to inform the body of work described as 'relational-cultural theory',[162]xii or feminist object relations theory,[163] which argues that from childhood, girls and women are taught to be attuned to the needs of others, to gain a sense of self through connection with others, and to participate in the development of others. As Alexandra Kaplan writes, 'while existing theories posit some form of autonomy or separation as the developmental path, women's core self-structure, or their primary motivational thrust, concerns growth within relationship – what we call the "self-in-relation".[164, p.235] Sometimes characterised as 'cultural feminism',[165] this body of thinking draws on the work of Jean Baker Miller,[160] Carol Gilligan,[166] Nancy Chodorow,[163]xiii and the Stone Center,[161] to posit that women develop a unique gendered subjectivity that results in qualities of empathy, intuition, and the capacity to care for others.

Within this framework, the relationship between mother and daughter is deemed to be central to women's connectedness with others, with girls learning to be attuned to their mothers feelings and 'be present with' her from an early age.[168, p.55] In contrast, it is argued that boys experience connection with the mother as 'invasive, engulfing, or threatening'.[168, p.55] At the same time, they are treated as gendered opposites by their mother and must relinquish their closeness to her in order to develop a separate masculine gender identity, which is not predicated on caring or nurturing.[163, p.207] However, girls continue with their identification with their mother, and thus experience themselves as 'less separate' than boys, resulting in girls being more likely to 'experience another's feelings as their own', in Nancy Chodorow's words.[163, p.167] Ideally this is a psychologically enhancing process, leading to expectations of mutual empathy being continued in adult life, particularly with a woman's partner and family. However, the loss of reciprocal connection with others, or the absence of intimacy, can be experienced by women as a 'failure of the self' which has been linked to reports of depression.[164, p.239] Similarly, women's propensity to self-silence, often resulting from the fear that anger will disrupt relationships and produce a loss of connection, is seen to lead to women feeling disempowered, constrictive and ineffective, as well as guilty for feeling angry.[160; 169] Gendered patterns of intersubjectivity are therefore deemed to be at the root of women's despair.

Body dissatisfaction

Reactions to morphological changes experienced at puberty have also been linked to adolescent onset of depression, with girls' dissatisfaction with breast and body fat development being seen as pivotal. Over 80 per cent of girls compared to 40 per cent of boys aged 12–18 report dissatisfaction with their body image,[170] leading Nolen-Hoeksema and Girgus,[131, p.435] in a review of the emergence of gender differences in depression at adolescence, to argue that body dissatisfaction 'may account for a substantial part of the gender difference in depressive symptoms in adolescence, but not all of it'. While there are suggestions that girls' body dissatisfaction is accentuated if puberty is experienced earlier than the rest of the peer group, as this can lead to unwanted attention from older males with 'conduct problems',[171] Angold and colleagues contest this claim,[52] reporting that depression was lower in girls with early onset of puberty.

Body dissatisfaction is not, however, confined to adolescence. A significant number of adult women see their bodies as deficient in some way,[172–173] with one study reporting that 90 per cent of women college students are dissatisfied with their weight.[174] Cross-cultural research reports that a thin or underweight body is now internationally accepted by women as the ideal,[175] suggesting that body dissatisfaction will continue to increase, with implications for women's mental health. There is also increasing evidence of women's dissatisfaction with genital appearance, which has been linked to lower sexual self-esteem and sexual well-being,[176] and has precipitated the popularity of the female genital surgery which aims to produce a 'designer vagina'.[177] This reflects what Leonore Tiefer describes as a social narrative of 'pudendal disgust',[178, p.475] part of the broader project of radical self-transformation promised by cosmetic surgery, which as a culture 'promotes the very anxieties it seeks to quell'.[179, p.90] As Anthony Elliot argues, these 'enhancement technologies' take advantage of women's views of themselves as deficient, encouraging adherence to a narrow and restricted cultural ideal.[180, p.13]xiv

Body dissatisfaction is not universal among women. An international study that included over 7,000 participants, reported that body dissatisfaction was associated with higher socio-economic class status and exposure to Western media (as well as higher body mass index).[175] Equally, morphological changes at puberty do not inevitably lead to body dissatisfaction. In a study of pubertal status and depression conducted with 3,216 adolescents in the USA,[182] Hayward and colleagues reported that while White adolescent girls reported higher rates of depression post-menarche than pre-menarche, this pattern was not found for African American girls and Hispanics. They explain this through the low rates of body dissatisfaction found in African American girls compared to White girls. White mothers have also been found to routinely engage in 'fat talk' about their own bodies, and those of their daughters, which leads to excessive concern about physical appearance and weight, in contrast to the experience of African American girls, who are more likely to receive positive feedback about their appearance from their parents.[183] Hayward and colleagues thus conclude that 'the association between puberty and depression in girls may be context-dependent'.[182,p.148] However, it is important to note that a more recent meta-analysis that examined body dissatisfaction in White and African American women reported a small effect size, suggesting that there is not a great difference.[184] The 'beauty myth' is clearly becoming more universal.

'Woman as problem': negating the political context of women's depression

While psychological explanations for women's higher rates of reported depression may appear more progressive than reductionist body blaming accounts, they do not deserve uncritical acceptance. The majority of the psychological accounts reviewed above provide us with at best partial, and at worst deeply flawed analyses, as they uncritically accept the existence of an internal pathology 'depression', and at the same time depoliticise the roots of women's distress, through positioning the causal pathways under scrutiny (as well as depression itself) as objective entities that can be simply measured or monitored. Thus constructs such as 'rumination', 'neuroticism', or 'depressogenic attributional style' are stripped of their gendered context,[185, p.81] and accepted as neutral causal mechanisms. As Janet Stoppard argues,[186] many of the 'cognitive tendencies' implicated in psychological models of depression, such as dysfunctional (or irrational) thinking, belief in personal helplessness, or perceived lack of control over events, are the obverse of masculine tendencies – rational thinking, a sense of personal mastery, and perceived control over events – that are valorised in our society. Equally, the conclusion that women are more affiliative than men, and thus more likely to engage in 'tend and befriend' than 'fight and flight' behaviours, is largely based on research conducted with rodents and primates.[e.g. 187] As Dana Becker argues, 'to generalize from the situation of a rat forced into a plastic tube from which it has no escape to the daily existence of a single parent with money worries . . . requires rather long inferential leaps'.[188, p.40]

There *are* examples of psychological researchers positioning the blame for misery outside of the women, and acknowledging the heteropatriarchal context of distress, even when psychological mechanisms, such as rumination or self-silencing, are the focus of attention. For example, in Susan Nolen-Hoeksema and colleagues' research, women's propensity to ruminate is deemed to be tied to the chronic strain they experience, 'the grinding annoyances and burdens that come with women's social power [including] . . . a greater load of the housework and child care and more of the strain of parenting than men' as well as absence of affirmation by their partners.[132, p.1068] Combined with women's lower social status, their unequal power and status in relationships, as well as greater lifetime prevalence of sexual and physical assault, this is seen to lead to feelings of chronic lack of control, low self-mastery and learned helplessness, and as a consequence, depression. The solution put forward by Nolen-Hoeksema and colleagues is to help women to gain more mastery over their lives, but also to change their social circumstances so they 'don't have so much to ruminate about'.[132, p.1068] Similarly, while Dana Jack's model of self-silencing draws on attachment theory – which has been criticised for placing too much emphasis on early development and the mother–child relationship, and neglecting the influence of environment and culture[189] – she also acknowledges the role of power imbalances in heterosexual relationships, and the cultural constructions of both gender and intimacy, in producing particular patterns of relating that can lead to women's depression.[146] She is also emphatic that self-silencing is not a 'stable personality trait', but rather, must be conceptualised in relation to a woman's social and relational context.[147, p.9] Carol Gilligan eloquently describes the social and gendered development of women's self-silencing thus:

> At adolescence, girls have the cognitive capacity to describe and reflect on their initiation into the codes and scripts of patriarchal womanhood. Thus, they signal the onset of dissociation: the splitting of mind from body, thought from emotion and self from relationships, leading to a loss of voice and signs of psychological distress. Listening to girls . . . sparked the realisation that the initiation into the gender codes and scripts of patriarchy bears some of the hallmarks of trauma: loss of voice, loss of memory, and consequently loss of the ability to tell one's story accurately. Once a woman has internalised the norms and values of a patriarchal order that requires her to care for others while silencing herself, she finds herself, in the words of Jean Baker Miller, 'doing good and feeling bad'.[190, p.xii]

A number of studies have reported that men self-silence as much as, or more than, women;[148–149; 151; 191] however, men's self-silencing appears to be motivated by intentions to prioritise their own needs and to maintain a feeling of self-sufficiency,[192] tied to cultural norms of masculinity, which does not result in depression, anger and a loss of self,[148; 193] further demonstrating that the experience of self-silencing is gendered.

Relational-cultural theorists also reject the criticism that they offer an essentialist perspective, conceptualising women as *naturally* more relational,[162] or the mother–daughter relationship as a universal constant, rather than as a 'contingent social arrangement' that is specific to 'Euro-American, postindustrial capitalism', in Jeanne Marecek's words.[165, p.299] The work of Jean Baker Miller,[160] from which relational-cultural theorising has developed, explicitly describes gender as a culturally constructed variable, framed in power dynamics between men and women. Equally, Nancy Chodorow, in her book *The reproduction of mothering*, argues that gender asymmetry in relational styles and needs are rooted in the structure of the hetero-patriarchal family:

> Women's mothering . . . produces the family as it is constituted in male dominant society. The sexual and familial division of labor in which women mother creates a sexual division of psychic organisation and orientation. It produces socially gendered women and men who enter into asymmetrical heterosexual relationships.[163, pp.208–209]

Nonetheless, awareness of the gendered nature of women's distress is the exception rather than the rule within psychology, where cognitions or personality are conceptualised in an abstract and gender neutral manner, dislocated from a woman's social and cultural context. This stands in contrast to social-cultural theories of women's depression, which focus on women's social environment as the cause of their despair.

Stress, social deprivation and gender roles: socio-cultural theories of women's depression

Inequality, discrimination and violence

In 1998, the WHO's *World Health Report* stated:

> Women's health is inextricably linked to their status in society. It benefits from equality, and suffers from discrimination. Today, the status and well-being of countless millions of women worldwide remains tragically low. As a result, human well-being suffers, and the prospects for future generations are dimmer.[194, p.6]

In 1997, the UN's *Human Development Report* stated:

> No society treats its women as well as its men.[195]

Gendered inequalities in society, leading to the discriminatory treatment of women, have been reported to be a significant factor in the development of women's depression. Women make up 70 per cent of the world's poor, and if they are in paid work, earn significantly less than their male counterparts,[196–197] and a strong inverse relationship exists between poverty and mental health. In a *World Mental Health Report*,[198] the social roots of women's mental health problems in low income countries were identified as low paid work, under-nourishment and domestic violence, leading to a plea for coordinated efforts to economically empower women and reduce violence in all of its forms. For example, research conducted in India, Zimbabwe, Chile and Brazil found that women with low education and who were living in poverty were more likely to report depression, anxiety and somatic symptoms,[199] and depression has been found to last longer when it occurs in situations of economic deprivation.[200] Additionally, women who live in US states which are high on the economic autonomy index, and where women have better reproductive rights, have been found to report significantly less depression.[201] Similarly, in European countries, women's reported life satisfaction increased after the introduction of abortion rights and birth control,[202] emphasising the importance of reproductive rights to women's mental health. Furthermore, political participation, as well as economic activity, has also been found to be significantly associated with women's physical health and mortality, in a study of 50 US states.[203] As physical health is associated with mental health,[196; 204] this is relevant to discussions of women's depression. These accumulated findings have led to the conclusion that depression can be reduced by increasing women's access to economic resources and employment, as well as facilitating autonomy over reproductive decisions.[196]

The experience of physical and sexual violence has also been linked to a range of women's mental health problems, including depression, anxiety, substance abuse and post-traumatic stress syndrome,[196; 205–207] as well as physical health problems,[208] as discussed in detail in Chapter 4. Indeed, women's higher rates of having experienced child sexual abuse,[205] or adult sexual violence,[209] have been described as going 'a considerable way to explaining the adult sex difference in depressive disorders'.[61, p.4] In one study, it was estimated that 35 per cent of the differences in rates of depression between women and men could be accounted for by sexual abuse occurring before the age of 18.[210] This is an issue for a significant proportion of women, as violence against women is so prevalent across cultures it is now recognised as a primary health and human rights issue by the World Health Organization.[196]

Discrimination on a broader level is also deemed to be an influential factor in women's depression. Researchers have reported that women who experience frequent sexism,[211] or who perceive themselves to be subjected to personal discrimination,[212] report higher levels of depression than those who experience little sexism or low levels of discrimination.[213] This could include name calling (e.g. bitch, cunt, chick), being treated unfairly at work because of being a woman,[214] being denied access to financial support, accommodation or education opportunities, or the daily experience of being positioned as second rate, the second sex. Some women are subjected to double discrimination. There is some evidence that lesbians are more likely to be diagnosed with psychological disorders than heterosexual women,[215–216] as well as higher rates of suicidal ideation and attempts.[217] In a meta-analysis, it was argued that this is the result of 'minority stress', the experience of stigma, prejudice and discrimination which creates a hostile and stressful social environment for lesbians.[215]xv Many women also experience a combination of sexist and racist discrimination. For example, in one study of African American women,[218] 98 per cent had experienced racial discrimination in the past year, with 64 per cent reporting discrimination by banks or universities, 54 per cent by health professionals, and 49 per cent having been called a racist name.[219] Internalised racism, combined with life stress and physical health problems, has been reported to be a significant predictor of reported depression in African American women.[220]

However, while gender differences in reported depression appear to remain constant across ethnicity/race and social class groupings,[221–222] lower rates of depression were reported by African American women, and higher rates reported by Latino women, in comparison to White women, in the first national study of psychiatric disorders conducted in the USA in 1994.[3] Socio-economic factors are considered to be a key contributor: two studies found no difference between levels of depression in Asian American, African American,[223] or Latino women,[224] when compared to White US women, when socio-economic differences were controlled. Indeed, research which examined levels of well-being and life satisfaction across the USA and Europe since the late 1970s has reported that while White women's levels of subjective well-being have fallen and their levels of mental strain have increased, both absolutely and relative to those of men, the well-being of Black women has risen – even more strongly than that of Black men – an outcome described as 'consistent with other indicators of economic and social progress' for Black women during this period.[225]

Acculturation has been put forward as explanations for higher rates of depression in particular cultural groups,[226] resulting from contradictions between the value systems of the country of origin and the host country.[227] For example, in one study of Chinese women living in the USA, those who were acculturated were twice as likely to report depression as those who were not acculturated, a difference that was not found for men.[228] A similar pattern has been reported with Latino women, who report higher rates of depression if they were born in the USA than if they are migrants.[224] Equally, in a national survey conducted in the UK, lower rates of depression were reported by migrant South Asian women (Indian, Pakistani and Bengali) in comparison to White women (2.5 per cent versus 4.8 per cent), whereas non-migrant South Asian women had the same rates as their White counterparts.[229] This does not mean that migrant women experience lower rates of distress: it may simply be the case that this distress is not conceptualised as 'depression' within the 'symptom pool'[230, p.x] that is drawn on by these women, as discussed on pp. 50–51. It has also been reported that Asian communities attach greater stigma to mental illness than White communities, and are therefore less likely to self-diagnose, or seek formal diagnosis.[231] Conversely, the high rate of self-harm and attempted suicide in young Asian women living in the UK has been attributed to 'culture clash', the disjuncture between the values of traditional Asian and Western/British culture.[232] The relationship between culture, discrimination and distress is clearly a complex one, which cannot be explained by minority stress alone. The recent move towards intersectionality acknowledges this complexity,[233–234] through examining the interrelationship of socially constructed categories of discrimination that lead to inequality, such as race, gender, social class and ethnicity.[xvi]

Gender roles and life events

In *A room of one's own* (1929), Virginia Woolf writes:

> Any woman born with a great gift in the sixteenth century would
> certainly have gone crazed, shot herself, or ended her days in some
> lonely cottage outside the village, half witch, half wizard, feared
> and mocked at. For it needs little skill in psychology to be sure that
> a highly gifted girl who had tried to use her gift for poetry would
> have been so thwarted and hindered by other people, so tortured
> and pulled asunder by her own contrary instincts, that she must
> have lost her health and sanity certainly.[235, p.47]

The construction and experience of gendered roles has been classified as a
significant factor in the development of women's depression. It has been
posited that 'gender intensification' occurs at puberty, characterised by
parental and peer expectation of girls' conformity to 'restrictive social
roles'.[131, p.436] Mothers have been reported to engage their daughters in
discussion of sadness and fear, while encouraging suppression of such
emotions in their sons, which has been linked to a greater focus on
depressive emotions in girls.[140]xvii Girls who resist feminine gender typed
activities, assert their intelligence, or pursue 'masculine type activities', have
been reported to risk rejection by boys, acting to 'contribute to their
propensity to depression'.[131, p.436]xviii This expectation of the suppression
of assertiveness or intelligence continues into adult life, when women
leaders, particularly if they behave in a manner deemed masculine, are rated
negatively and considered aberrant, when compared to assertive male
leaders.[243]

Gender roles have also been linked to the negotiation and experience of
life events and relationship difficulties. It is widely accepted that depression
is associated with both severe life events,[244–245] and cumulative adversity,[246] for women and men. Indeed, one explanation for higher rates of
depression reported by adolescent girls, when compared to boys, is the
higher levels of social and relational challenges,[131] life events,[247] or life
stress,[133] experienced by girls at this time. There are also reports that adult
women have a higher exposure to life events than adult men,[248–249] and are
more likely to report depression in response to life events than men.[250]
More specifically, certain groups of women, particularly those caring for
young children,[251] those experiencing poverty,[213] or without employment,[251] and those with problematic close relationships,[245] have been
reported to have a greater susceptibility to life events, and therefore to
experience depression. Experience of the loss of one's mother before the age
of 11 has also been identified as a factor that makes women vulnerable to

depression following life events.[251] At the same time, women have been reported to be more affected than men by life events involving their children, housing or reproduction,[97] as well as by interpersonal losses such as death of a close friend, relative or parent.[250] Described as 'network events', this is interpreted as being the result of women's greater involvement in the lives of those around them,[248, p.620; 252] with women's responsiveness representing a 'cost of caring',[253, p.492] which leads to elevated levels of depression, because of the salience of these events to women's role identity.[97] In this vein, women have been found to report more life events concerning crises or illnesses affecting significant others, or related to difficulties in getting along with others, compared to men.[252; 254] Indeed, while men and women have been observed to be equally likely to remember their own life events, men have been found to be less likely than women to remember life events affecting significant others, leading to the suggestion that men may avoid depression through 'blocking out', or not attending to, network events.[255]

Women have also been reported to experience more negative emotions in response to relationship difficulties and breakdown than men,[135] and to take longer to recover from partnership transitions.[256–257] At the same time, marriage has been found to act as a protective factor for men's mental health, with married men reporting significantly better mental health than single men, whereas the opposite is true for women,[256–257]xix as wives have been found to report over five times the rate of depression as husbands.[258] Conversely, a number of studies report that marriage is a protective factor for *both* men and women, as evidenced by research examining depression in menopausal women, discussed above,[118–119] as it acts to buffer psychological distress,[e.g. 256; 259] putting divorced or separated individuals at high risk of depression.[260] The apparent contradiction in these findings can be explained by looking at the nature of the couple relationship. A good relationship will act as a buffer against negative life events, offering social support, intimacy and companionship (as well as sexual fulfilment, an important aspect of quality of life).[261] In contrast, a difficult or destructive relationship can exacerbate distress, or act as the source of women's despair, particularly if it involves entrapment or humiliation.[262] Other factors in couple and family relationships that have been associated with reports of women's depression include the presence of dependent children (in particular three or more children under age 14),[104; 244; 263] relationship distress and dissatisfaction,[264] self-silencing,[151] humiliation,[262] partner violence towards the woman,[209] dissatisfaction with decision making, financial issues and childcare,[265] inequality in relation to domestic responsibilities,[266] absence of partner support,[267] the presence of demand-withdraw interactions,[268] communication problems,[265] and feelings of disempowerment.[269] This pattern is not particular or peculiar to depression:

relationships have also been implicated in the development of a range of diagnostic categories, including schizophrenia,[270–271] borderline personality disorder,[272–273] anxiety disorders,[274] and anorexia nervosa.[275–277]

The expectations of traditional gendered roles within heterosexual marriage underpin many of these negative relational experiences, and have been put forward as explanation for higher rates of depression found in married women compared to married men,[278] with young married women with small children deemed to be at particularly high risk.[251] Indeed, one study reported high levels of distress in middle class 'career' women who expected equal partner support with childcare and domestic duties but did not get it, in contrast to working class women who experienced distress if gender roles broke down and their husbands took on too much of the housework.[279] This suggests that cultural norms and women's expectations within a relationship are an important influence. It has also been reported that single mothers are at higher risk for depression than married mothers, due to the difficulties of childcare and multiple role responsibilities in what are often disadvantaged circumstances,[245; 259; 280] while women who have no children at home are less likely to report depression (with the presence of children having no impact on reporting of depression in men).[60] The cultural norms of a nation have also been linked to national depression levels. Indeed, it is interesting to note that in countries where a high value is placed on the homemaking role, married women report lower levels of depression.[61] Nations high on masculinity, where traditional gender role stereotypes are valued and adhered to – men as assertive, tough and materialist, women as modest, tender and concerned with quality of life – have also been found to have higher rates of reported depression than 'feminine' nations, where both men and women are expected to be modest, tender and concerned with quality of life.[281] What characterises the 'feminine' nations is that 'men and women are offered equal opportunities for the fulfilment of multiple social roles',[281, p.809] something which appears to be positive for the mental health of both genders.[259]

Acknowledging hetero-patriarchy and structural inequalities

These socio-cultural theories are a step forward from essentialist biomedical and psychological theorising. However, while we may correlate social inequalities, gender roles, or adult sexual violence with women's depression, the majority of socio-cultural accounts provide no analysis of the hetero-patriarchal political context and structural conditions which maintain deeply entrenched gender divisions in reproductive labour and economic activity, to the disadvantage of women. We need to question: 'Who benefits from the restriction of women's reproductive rights?' 'Why is it that domestic and sexual violence is so endemic, and that so few cases are prosecuted?'[see 282] 'Why are women still taking on the greater burden of childcare, resulting in their greater vulnerability to adverse life events?' 'Why do women earn less than men, even they are as well qualified?' and 'Why are women in a minority in positions of power in society?'

To take just one example, while women may suffer on an individual basis from the 'cost of caring', if they did eschew this traditional feminine role, the expenditure placed on the state would blow national budgets – estimated as £739 billion a year in the UK.[283] It would also mean greater demands would be made on men, who currently do far less unpaid caring, or housework, than women.[284–285] Men who *do* take on a share of household responsibilities are invariably described as *'helping* women cope with the burden of increased stress in their lives', in the words of John Gray,[286, p.4] creator of the *Men are from Mars/women are from Venus* distinction.[188, p.42] It is clear whose responsibility caring and housework is deemed to be – women's. Yet when women respond to this burden of responsibility with psychological 'symptoms', it is attributed to 'stress' which they are expected to 'manage' or 'cope with', serving to obscure the social origins of the tensions in their lives.[188, p.37] Stripping accounts of women's misery of any acknowledgement of historical or political context, while paying lip service to socio-cultural or psychological influences, thus serves to shore up the very structural factors that lead to distress in the first place, through making gender inequality an invisible issue.

A case in point is the argument that marriage is a risk factor for women's depression.[278; 287–288] In reporting the research findings above, I am not taking a naive hetero-normative position, for it is 'marriage' between a man and a woman which has been the focus of research in this area. Further, while the importance of gender roles within marriage is often implicitly acknowledged by researchers,[e.g. 289] there is rarely, if ever, any critique of the underlying tenets of hetero-patriarchy which may be instrumental in creating the particular conditions associated with 'marriage' or 'child-rearing' and women's depression. For example, George Brown and colleagues describe relational patterns as creating 'depressogenic effects',[262] describing one woman's account of being humiliated and 'put down' by her partner thus: 'He puts me down continually, shouting and swearing, walking out of the room if I try and discuss anything'.[262, p.17] As Pilgrim and Bentall argue, 'this could be reframed by simply stating that miserable women live with oppressive men'.[290, p.270] The very use of the medicalised term 'depression' thus acts to depoliticise women's distress.

These socio-cultural theories have also been incorporated unproblematically into bio-psycho-social[291] or diathesis-stressor[123] models within bio-psychiatry and psychology, which conceptualise the body as the starting point of analysis, but deem environmental and psychological factors to also be influential. Within this model, stable internal attributes, the 'diathesis', are assumed to interact with difficult life circumstance, the 'stressor', resulting in the outcome – depression.[292] As two reviewers (Paul Bebbington and Ronald Kessler respectively) conclude:

> There seems no doubt that biological factors are involved in the emergence of depressive disorder, it is just difficult to argue that they are responsible for the sex difference. This pushes towards a consideration of physical and social environment.[61, p.5]

> The key to understanding the higher rates of depression among women than men lies in an investigation of the joint effects of biological vulnerabilities and environmental provoking experiences.[293, p.5]

If we look to the accumulated body of research which underpins this integrative model, at face value it appears to be convincing, and a positive step away from unidimensional and reductionist biomedical or psychological theorising. Indeed, as epidemiological research has reported that the prevalence of women's depression has increased significantly over the last few decades,[13] this supports the notion that environment is an aetiological factor, as the increase cannot be explained by changes in either hormones or genes.[4] But it is not that simple. The bio-psycho-social model adopts the same epistemological standpoint as the biomedical and majority of psychological and socio-cultural theories – positivism/realism – which leads to hypothetico-deductive methods in research, linear models of cause and effect, and a negation of both the discursive construction and lived experience of women's distress. This implicitly precludes consideration of the political context of women's lives, the construction of gendered roles, or the meaning of 'depression' as a diagnostic category. Before exploring an alternative critical feminist perspective in Chapter 3, I examine the basic tenets of positivism, as well as the limitations it poses for understanding women's madness.

The problem with positivism

Lisa Cosgrove comments:

> The kinds of questions which structure our research on gender difference and psychopathology (for example, are the observed differences in depression/anorexia/agoraphobia due to environmental, biological or social role factors) support the reifications of

gender and disorder and continue to impose artificial dualisms between culture and biology.[294, p.248]

As the term 'positivism' has often been used in a loose and general manner, it may be helpful to outline a definition at this point. Keat has identified two major elements within the positivist position.[295] The first is methodological naturalism, the demand for equivalent methods across the social and natural sciences, with the latter providing the model for the former. This has resulted in the emphasis on hypothetico-deductive methodologies in research conducted by the psy-disciplines: experimental and quasi-experimental research designs, using standardised, validated measures of both dependent and independent variables (mental health problems and their causes), with an emphasis on objectivity, reliability, and replicability.[xx] The second element of positivism is that science is conceived within the following criteria: it is asserted that knowledge is possible only as the result of observation, and the only things that can be observed are those which are accessible to the senses; causality is understood in terms of antecedent conditions and general laws governing phenomenon, leading to linear models to explain gender differences in madness we have seen above; and facts and theories are clearly separated from values, leading to the absence of reflexivity on the part of researchers. The fundamental premise of a realist perspective is that objects have real existence independent of perception, or of any cultural knowledge or practice, so madness is conceptualised as a 'thing' that exists and can be objectively measured, leading to consensus definitions of diagnostic categories of madness, the DSM being the archetypal case.[1]

On the surface this positivist/realist framework may appear to be appropriate for research into women's madness. How can we know how many women are mad, if we don't have common agreement about what madness is? How can we compare the results of different research studies if we don't use standardised measurements? How *can* we examine aspects of madness not available to the senses? And what is wrong with objectivity on the part of researchers, or with linear theories of cause and effect? To the many critics who operate from what has been described as a 'new paradigm' approach,[e.g. 296; 297; 301] the answers to these questions and the problems with positivism are clear, as I outline below.

Critiquing categorialisation

I shall start at the beginning, with the categorisation of madness into discrete psychiatric syndromes, and the collection of epidemiological data, which have both been criticised from many different avenues. First, the focus on diagnostic categories reifies the construction of a particular set of experiences as pathological disorders that are perceived to have *caused* the distress that women report. Within a realist epistemological framework, disorders such as 'depression' are thus deemed to be discrete clinical entities that occur in a consistent and homogeneous way. Indeed, when women meet five out of nine, or two out of five, criteria for a diagnosis, they can be described as being 'A Depressive', or 'A Schizophrenic', respectively,[302] as if the woman *is* the disorder. This acts to deny the social and discursive context of women's lives, as well as the gendered nature of science, which defines how women's madness is defined and studied.[303] Equally, while epidemiological statistics may be positioned as unquestioned fact, uncovering the true rates of gender differences in depression in the community, as Dorothy Smith has argued, they can be seen as simply 'counting what psychiatric agencies do',[304, p.117] counting the practices of diagnosis and treatment enacted by the psy-professions. Similarly, Paula Gardner has argued that 'mental health statistics succeed in making depression epidemiology seem legitimate, sick "populations" factual, and pharmaceutical solutions appear the appropriate remedy'.[18, p. 109]

The practice of 'categorialisation' in positivist psychology has also been criticised[305, p.17] – the practice of dividing people into categories and searching for attributes that distinguish the categories, as if this reflects an essential difference. On the one hand, the belief that we can simply divide the population into two biological sexes is erroneous, as about 1.7 per 100 people fall into the category of intersex.[306] At the same time, as Lisa Cosgrove argues, the positioning of gender as a 'natural category of being' in examinations of women's madness is problematic,[294, p.249] because gender is something we 'do' rather than something we 'are'.[307] Rather than being a pre-given designation at birth, as is often assumed in positivist accounts, gender is something we *accomplish*,[294, p.249] something that is produced through a 'stylised repetition of acts', in Judith Butler's words,[307, p.140] and negotiated in an intersubjective context. Thus we learn how to 'do' femininity (or masculinity),[308] and if we fail in our performance, face the consequences of being positioned outside the boundaries of sanity, as is explored in the remainder of this book. Equally, distinguishing between Black and White women, or between heterosexuals and lesbians, is problematic, as the boundaries of such categories are not simple, or mutually exclusive.[309] As Nikolas Rose has argued, subjectivity is not unitary, but is 'fractured through sexual and racial identifications, and regulated by social norms'.[310, p.5] This raises questions about the assumptions behind the epidemiological research on which conclusions about gender or racial differences in depression are based, and the design of research studies which compare women and men in an unproblematic way, as if they are immutably separate categories. It also draws attention to the notion of madness as a social construction – rather than an objective entity that can be simply measured.

The social construction of madness

Bonfire Madigan Shive writes:

> The term 'mental illness' has been marketed as a sexy way to make money off people's distress, despair and disempowerment.[311, p.179]

Rather than being 'real' entities, many social constructionist critics have argued that all psychiatric diagnoses, including depression, can be conceptualised as discursive construction created by processes of expert definition[312–316] – fictions framed as facts, used to regulate and control those deemed deficient, dangerous, or merely different from the norm. In this view, madness is a socially constructed label, based on value-laden definitions of normality, with a diagnosis of madness determining how a person's future behaviour will be seen and addressed.[317–318] Analyses of the history of the psy-disciplines certainly provides ample evidence of the way in which diagnosis of madness is determined by social norms – what is odd or bizarre and deemed 'mad' in one context, may make perfect sense, or be unremarkable in another.[315] As societies change, so do definitions of disorders – even though there may be continuities in symptoms and professional treatment practice. Thus while 'neurasthenia' and 'hysteria' may have virtually disappeared as diagnostic categories today, we now have 'borderline personality disorder', 'post-traumatic stress disorder' or 'chronic fatigue syndrome', which share many common features with their nineteenth century predecessors.[see 35; 272; 319]

The vociferous 'anti-psychiatrist' critics of the 1960s and 1970s were most prominent in their condemnation of psychiatric labelling and treatment. They conceptualised madness as problems in living,[320] as the protest of the powerless,[321] or as misunderstood artistic genius.[29] Diagnosis of mental illness was seen to simply legitimise professional control, the latest phase in the enactment of disciplinary power in Western society that has been going on since the eighteenth century,[29] a process analogous to the sixteenth century witch trials, that were also premised on scape-goating and fictitious labelling as 'Other'.[313; 320] It is argued that the practice of regulation previously undertaken by the Church has simply been passed on to the experts whom Michel Foucault described as the 'psy-complex',[322] psychiatrists, psychologists, and psychotherapists who monitor and regulate psychological well-being and ensure individual functioning.[323]

This is not simply a matter of labelling, because these 'symptoms' or violations of social norms can lead to incarceration or other forms of psychiatric 'treatment',[317] which function, as Andrew Scull argues, to 'get rid of the troublesome people for the rest of us'.[324, p.260] At the same time, through defining a person as 'mad' or 'mentally ill', we determine what is 'normal' – producing the boundaries of desired behaviour, thoughts and feelings.[312] The fear of the stigma associated with madness thus serves to ensure self-policing:[322] self-surveillance and self-monitoring of our own behaviour, as we attempt to avoid being positioned as 'mad', with everything we say or do being judged within this medicalised mantle.[325] Foucault described self-policing as the modern replacement for external, authoritarian, methods of surveillance and social control, where discipline is instilled within, and punishment, if we waver from the norm, self-induced.[322] Colin Gordon writes:

> There is no need for arms, physical violence, material constraints. Just a gaze. An inspecting gaze, a gaze which each individual under its weight will end by interiorising to the point that he is his own overseer, each individual thus exercising this surveillance over, and against, himself.[326, p.155]

Indeed, it has been argued that self-policing practices are now so ingrained in the Western psyche that they are taken for granted, scarcely visible to conscious awareness, making them all the more effective as a means of social regulation.[322] Nikolas Rose thus argues that

> the history of the psy disciplines is much more than a history of a particular and often somewhat dubious group of sciences – it is part of the history of the ways in which human beings have regulated others and have regulated themselves in the light of certain games of truth.[310, p.11]

It is not coincidental that the anti-psychiatry critiques emerged in the 1960s and 1970s. This was a time of dissent in many areas of social life, and the need for overhaul of often archaic practices within psychiatry, such as mass institutionalisation of those deemed mad, and the compulsory imposition of barbaric 'treatments', was long overdue. However, these critiques are not historical anachronisms; they have continued in more recent decades. There is now a strong international movement of psychiatric survivors or consumers, collectively uniting within groups such as Mad Pride, Bonkerfest, On Our Own, or Mind Freedom, in order to 'celebrate mad culture' and to vociferously challenge psychiatric theory and practice. Thus Madigan Shive, a musician and member of The Icarus Project, a US based Mad Pride organisation that encourages the view that madness is brilliance, describes herself as having a 'mad gift . . . that creates this music and keeps me alive'.[327, p.1] Similarly, a fellow Icarus member, Will Hall, describes his madness (formally diagnosed as bipolar depression) as a 'dangerous gift' rather than an illness, saying that he does not want to be 'normal', at the same time as he rejects 'humiliating' psychiatric treatment, and the medication that made him feel as if he couldn't live his life.[327] A UK based 'Mad Pride Blog' summarises the aims of the movement:

What's Mad Pride about? It's about counteracting the incredible stigma and discrimination that mental health system survivors face both within the system and in general society. It's about reclaiming the word mad and other stigmatizing term of abuse – crazy, loony etc. It's about campaigning and lobbying – particularly against the drugs industry, the UK Government's mental health act and against society's indifference towards the large number of suicides.[328]

At the same time, women only groups, such as Women Against Psychiatric Assault, the Women Psychiatric Inmates Liberation Front, and Psycho Femmes function as places where, in Bonnie Burstow's words, 'both male chauvinism and sane chauvinism can be left behind and mad women's identities celebrated' as they act to 'help women reclaim and theorise those aspects of being a woman that the patriarchy labels "crazy"'.[329, p.250] Anti-psychiatry/survivor magazines such as the Canadian *Phoenix Rising* or the American *Madness Network News* and *Dendron*, serve as spaces for psychiatric survivors to publish accounts of their experiences, and to engage in debates about contemporary challenges to psychiatric authority. They contain moving (and sometimes chilling) accounts of psychiatric diagnosis and treatment, as well as stories of recovery, liberation, and fighting back. For example, in *Phoenix Rising*, Jean Skov described her experience of a course of tranquillisers (Thioridazane) prescribed for an undiagnosed trapped nerve, as feeling as if 'all the windows were closed. I couldn't see into the world anymore. I couldn't see any alternatives and became locked into my own little private, dark tunnel'.[330, p.5] She admitted herself for psychiatric treatment and was subjected to a naked strip search and rectal examination to check for drugs, followed by forced ECT and psychotropic medication, and threats that she would never be discharged because she was 'dangerous'. Describing herself as 'diagnosed with everything' – 'schizophrenia', 'depressed', 'manic depressive', 'mania', 'anxiety', 'psychosis' – Jean encapsulates her experience thus:

The first six months in hospital was just about the worst experience in my life. You have to have self-confidence to feel that you're a viable human being, but the whole thrust of a psychiatric institution is to make you feel like a nobody.[330, p.5]

This is a stark example of psychiatric regulation. Theoretical critique has also continued since the heyday of the anti-psychiatry movement, with Dave Pilgrim and Richard Bentall arguing that 'psychiatric diagnosis is a professional reification about human misery, not a fact'.[290, p.271] Indeed, the very existence and widespread acceptance of depression as a pathological condition is seen as part of a general medicalisation of everyday life,[36] where myriad experiences are defined as medical problems or illnesses, thus meriting medical scrutiny and 'treatment', which serves to legitimise the right of the medical profession and bio-psychiatry maintaining control.

Deconstructing depression

The framework of medical naturalism that led to the establishment of depression as a real entity which exists independent of perception, language or culture has its origins in psychiatric nosology first promoted by Emil Kraepelin in the late nineteenth century. Three now defunct separate diagnoses – melancholia, neurasthenia, and mopishness – stand as the precursors of 'mental depression', a diagnosis that first appeared in the mid 1900s,[290] characterised as 'the lowness of spirits of persons suffering under disease' or 'a reduction in general activity ranging from minor failures in concentration to total paralysis'.[331, p.386] 'Depression' became a widely used term only at the beginning of the twentieth century, translated into 'major depressive disorder', and reified as scientific truth in diagnostic manuals such as the DSM.[314] We are told that depression is the most prevalent mental health condition affecting individuals worldwide, estimated to become the second most significant cause of disease and disability by 2020.[332] However, the notion of a unitary category 'depression' is misleading, as is demonstrated by the findings of a longitudinal study of 4,856 individuals living in the USA, which reported that different 'symptom' profiles were associated with different life events.[333] For example, chronic stress and failure was associated with fatigue and hypersomnia; loss was associated with sadness, lack of pleasure and appetite loss; romantic breakups were associated with guilt. While the researchers Keller, Neale and Kendler concluded that depression was 'pathoplastic syndrome',[333] an alternative would be to question the very validity of the category of depression, which Pilgrim and Bentall dismiss as a 'disjunctive concept',[xxi] as it is given to individuals with no symptoms in common.[290, p.263]

The diagnostic category of 'depression' is very much a Western cultural concept. There is no word for 'depression' in many non-Western cultures,[334] and many so-called 'symptoms' of Western depression are not expressed, or positioned as signs of distress, in many non-Western contexts.[335] Rather, suffering is signified by bodily or psychological complaints as varied as a failed or painful heart (India),[336] snakes biting or crawling on the body,[337] chest pains (China), burning on the soles of the feet (Sri Lanka), semen loss (India), ants crawling inside the head (Nigeria), or soul-loss (Hmong).[165, p.289] Indeed, one of the explanations for the differences in reported rates of depression between White and South Asian or African American women is that distress is more likely to be somatised in the non-White groups,[338–339]xxii or presented as physical problems to general practitioners (GPs), as this is seen as having greater legitimacy.[342] 'Depression' is therefore less likely to be diagnosed. The very meaning and construction of emotional states has also been reported to vary across cultures, with many emotions commonly described by English speakers having no parallel in other cultural contexts.[343] For example, anger and sadness are not distinguished in many African languages,[344] and fear and shame are not differentiated by the Australian Gidjingali people.[290] If we can question the very existence of emotions outside of language and culture, we can certainly question the existence of a uniform pathology, such as 'depression'. And while many Western psychiatrists have dismissed arguments about cross-cultural variation in the existence of depression by claiming that such individuals are 'really' suffering from depression,[336] which they are misattributing to their feet, or chest, or heart, this is simply a manifestation of Western medical imperialism which is astounding in its arrogance.

Negating women's subjectivity and agency

Amedeo Giorgi writes:

> Psychology privileges quantification over description/qualitative methods and the psychologist is left 'dealing with *measured behaviour* as data rather than the *lived behaviour* of the subject'.[345, cited by 294, p.255]

If a phenomenon cannot be objectively observed and measured using reliable, standardised techniques, then it cannot be 'known' within a positivist paradigm. This has resulted in a methodology driven, rather than a theory driven, analysis of women's madness and its possible aetiology. For example, the role of unconscious factors cannot be easily assessed within a hypothetico-deductive frame, and so they are not included in the majority of mainstream accounts.[e.g. 4] Equally, as historical, political, and wider societal factors are not easily operationalised and assessed, they are only addressed within social constructionist or feminist critiques.[e.g. 78; 313; 316; 346–347] Within a positivist paradigm, madness is construed as an individual problem – a disorder affecting an individual woman, on whom biological, psychological or social factors impact in order to produce symptomatology.

The woman who presents with problems is implicitly positioned as passive and devoid of social context in positivist/realist analyses of madness, since agency is not easy (if at all possible) to observe. So it is inevitable that it is her body, or her symptoms, that are the entire focus of attention. Yet women are not passive objects in relation to either interpretation of physical or psychological symptoms, or in relation to the discursive construction of madness. Recognition of 'symptoms' or self-referral for treatment is a process of active negotiation of psychological and bodily experience, current life events and lifestyle, and cultural, medical or psychological discourse about madness. Many women make sense of their experiences through positioning themselves as suffering from depression, anxiety or problems such as PMS; others may experience change in state or level of distress but not make ascriptions of any of these diagnoses. To position these women as 'false negatives', as they are in the case of PMS research,[348] is to misinterpret the active negotiation and resistance of bio-psychiatric discourse associated with madness in which many women engage. It is to reinforce the notion of women as passive dupes, rather than active agents who continuously make sense of and interpret the social sphere, and their own psychological or bodily experiences.[86; 347]

As psychological symptoms are not visibly apparent, they have to be observed through the interface of subjective accounts. As these may easily fall outside the required positivist standards of objectivity and replicability, in empirical research they are often observed through the use of standardised instruments. This is why there has been an inordinate amount of attention given over to developing reliable and valid questionnaire measures for assessing the incidence of specific mental health problems, such as depression, anxiety or PMS. In mainstream research in this area there is almost total reliance on quantitative methods of data collection and statistical analysis of results, with all of the response restrictions inherent in such an approach.[296] The complexity and contradictions evident within women's subjective accounts is thus negated, and a potentially rich source of data is left uncollected and unexamined.[185]

Equally, within a positivist/realist frame, women are made to fit the researcher's model of each of these syndromes, in contrast to grounded methods of data collection and analysis, where the constraints of a priori assumptions are not imposed upon participants accounts, which are collected in a more open, qualitative manner.[185; 349] The use of questionnaires also assumes that 'symptoms' can be categorised and classified in a dichotomous manner as existing or not, with the only added complexity being the notion of a *degree* of symptomatology. That a woman might reply that she sometimes has a symptom and sometimes does not; that it depends on what is happening in her life, whether she has recently eaten, what she is thinking, or how recently she has had sex, among other factors, is not acknowledged at all; neither is her assessment of the meaning of her 'symptoms'.

Focusing within the person: biology or cognitions

The National Alliance on Mentally Illness (NAMI) claim:

> Mental illnesses are disorders of the brain that disrupt a person's thinking, feeling, moods, and ability to relate to others. Just as diabetes is a disorder of the pancreas, mental illnesses are brain disorders . . . [they] are not the result of personal weakness, lack of character, or poor upbringing.[cited in 350]

Within a positivist/realist paradigm, the body is implicitly considered to be more fundamental or 'real' than psychological or social variables, resulting in the emphasis within bio-psychiatry on measurable aspects of biology and on the efficacy of biomedical treatments. In this way, essentialist theories are positioned as unquestioned truth, as evidenced by the NAMI pamphlet cited above. This focus on the physical body is a direct result of the assumption that biological factors can be observed and measured in the most 'objective' manner, removing the potentially confounding interface of the woman's subjective interpretation, or reports of a symptom. In what is a totally reductionist viewpoint, the body or biology is conceptualised in terms of physical processes – the action of hormones, neurotransmitters, or ovarian function, considered separately from any meaning, or from social-cultural contexts. However, there have been many critiques of the notion of the body, or biology, as objective entities which can be understood as separate from socio-historical knowledge, experience or subjectivity.[298; 322; 351] As we have already seen, individuals do not experience symptoms in a socio-cultural vacuum and the bodily functions we understand as a sign of 'illness' or 'madness' vary across culture and across time.[312; 315; 352] Equally, women's recognition or interpretation of physical and psychological 'symptoms' cannot be understood outside of the social and historical context in which they live. Our interpretation of 'symptoms' will be influenced by the *meaning* ascribed to these experiences in a particular cultural context. For example, definitions of sexuality as a sign of madness differ greatly between the nineteenth century and today: in the nineteenth century it was the *sexual* woman who was at risk of being defined as mad; today it is the *asexual* woman who will be positioned as disordered, at risk of being diagnosed with a 'sexual dysfunction'.[353]

Expert knowledge and understanding of the influence of the body is also socially and historically situated. While the wandering womb was replaced by notions of women's weak nervous system, it was only in the context of the 'discovery' of sex hormones in 1905,[354] that hormonal theories of women's madness evolved. Rather than accepting the body as something which exists above and beyond the measurement tools and definitions of science, it can be argued that the aspects of biology and the body we are allowed to 'know' are those which meet the criteria of the measurement tools currently in use. The development of new technology for calibrating the body will undoubtedly lead to a new set of meta-theories for women's madness, as Mary C. Blehar prophesies in her hope that 'sensitive technologies to image in vivo brain function' will 'allow researchers to test hormonal hypotheses more directly',[45] discussed above (p. 30). In psychological models of madness, the emphasis on cognitions is arguably equally reductionist; it is still an essentialist view of madness, positioning the problem within the woman, as noted above. Socio-cultural theories may appear to offer a progressive alternative, however, still depoliticise the 'risk factors' that are associated with women's distress, which are framed within a 'discourse of stress', which 'locates the origins of many societal problems inside individuals rather than in the larger society', in the words of Dana Becker.[188, p.37] Equally, as is the case with biomedical and psychological research, socio-cultural factors are invariably conceptualised within a simple model of cause and effect.

Linear models of cause and effect

Within positivist/realist research on women's madness, each of the variables which appear in the biomedical, socio-cultural, or psychological models are clearly operationally defined, reinforcing the assumption that they are discreet antecedent 'risk factors' which exert independent causal influence in the aetiology of specific syndromes. Within this framework, both diagnostic categories and the symptoms women report are positioned as independent variables in research, invariably conceptualised in a dichotomous way as existing or not existing.[355] The need to test the influence of these antecedent variables within a hypothetico-deductive model has led to the almost universal adoption of linear models in both biomedical and psychosocial research, where the reporting of symptoms is correlated with individual predictive factors.

Given the predominance of these linear models of aetiology, it is not surprising to find that unidimensional approaches also dominate research on the effectiveness of both biomedical and psychological treatment. One worrying consequence of adopting a linear approach to treatment, is that causal assumptions are often made on the basis of treatment effectiveness. For example, in a study which reported the positive benefits of fluoxetine for treating premenstrual complaints, Menkes and colleagues concluded 'these findings thus support the proposed role of serotonergic hypoactivity in the aetiology of PMS'.[356, p.101] Similarly, in a study of oestradiol patches, Watson and colleagues argue that their findings support 'the earlier observation of a link between premenstrual syndrome and ovarian function'.[357, p.900] However, the finding that a particular treatment reduces premenstrual distress does not necessarily have implications for aetiology. Aspirin is an effective cure for headache, and inhalation of carbon dioxide an effective treatment for panic attacks, yet we would not propose that either aspirin or carbon dioxide are implicated in the aetiology of either disorder. There is also a substantial placebo effect with all 'treatments' for PMS,[358] which further undermines Watson's conclusions.

The very premise of a causal relationship is also flawed, as the discovery of a *correlation* between reported 'symptoms', and a particular biomedical or psychosocial substrate does not mean that the substrate *caused* the symptoms. Each may be related to a third variable, or not related at all. Indeed, indices such as 'neuroticism' or 'rumination' may simply be alternative measures or manifestations of 'depression',[135] with similar questions used to measure both,[4] rather than being distinct causal or mediating variables, as researchers have suggested. When women are distressed, there is a complex and fluid interaction between a number of different factors, which will be experienced differently by each individual woman, and cannot be encapsulated within a narrow positivist frame. Thus, the search for general laws underlying gender differences in madness potentially blinds us to the complexity of individual women's lived experience and negotiation of prolonged distress.

Multifactorial bio-psycho-social models of madness may appear to provide a lead in moving away from narrow linear thinking; however, they offer only a partial answer and arguably operate almost solely at the level of theory, having had little influence on research practice, which continues to be conducted in a one dimensional vein. For example, Paul Bebbington, in acknowledging the aetiological complexity of women's depressions, concludes:

> clinical experience suggests that depression arises because of a complex cascade, whereby for instance external circumstances interact with cognitive sets and induce physiological responses that in turn change the way circumstances are appraised. This may then change cognitions and physiological status, leading to a further spiral. . . . If this is actually how depression develops, *it becomes extremely hard to research*, and progress has to fall back on the integration of piecemeal approaches.[4, p.299, my emphasis]

It is only 'extremely hard to research' within the constraints of methodological naturalism, outlined above. It is only researchers who adopt this epistemological stance that feel constrained to remain within their own professional boundaries, only able to pay lip service to the notion of a multifactorial model at the conceptual level. There are a number of reasons why this is so. The practical difficulties of crossing professional boundaries, which include professional rivalries, differences in epistemological or methodological training, and the pressure to locate research funding in one institution as a result of research assessment exercises.[xxiii] At the same time, within a positivist paradigm, to measure the influence of myriad multi-layered factors simultaneously, could be seen as a sign of poor research design. It contravenes the notion of clear predictability, and introduces the likelihood of type 1 errors – where significant relationships between symptomatology and putative predictive variables are found by chance, due to the large number of variables being examined. The use of causal or structural equation modelling has been used to overcome this problem in other areas of psychology, but not, to date, in examining gender differences in 'depression'. At the same time, these multifactorial models are still framed within a positivist/realist epistemology, and so all of the criticisms which have been outlined thus far still apply.

Objectivity: the separation of facts from values

Underpinning the whole of the positivist/realist endeavour is the commitment to scientific objectivity. The goal of the scientific enterprise is to remove the possibility of bias or of values, and to examine research questions or test hypotheses in a precise manner that can be replicated by other researchers, in order to ascertain the reliability and generalisability of results. This emphasis on objectivity and neutrality leads to the elevation of the views of the scientific expert over the views of untrained observers, in this case, the women diagnosed as mad. Thus any information on symptomatology is collected in a systematic and objective manner, with any inconsistencies used as confirmatory evidence for the unreliability of women's subjective accounts.

The fact that women reporting mental health problems are considered to be biased or subjective, yet researchers are not, illustrates the absence of reflexivity in positivist/realist research – the refusal to acknowledge the influence of factors such as values, politics, and the constraints of disciplinary boundaries on the way research is conducted or interpreted. Yet as it has been argued elsewhere,[299; 359–360] the ideological stance of researchers affects the research questions they ask, the epistemological stance and methodologies they adopt, and their interpretations of the data they collect. Research or theory that is explicitly conducted within a feminist framework,[78; 313; 346] challenging the dominance of biomedical models of women's madness, and arguing instead for an attention to the social-political context in which diagnoses are made, is often dismissed or ignored by positivist/realist researchers, as not meeting the criteria for 'good science', because it is deemed biased or political.[xxiv] My own admission of a personal history and perspective may thus be viewed in this light, rather than as it is intended, a reflexive account which illuminates my own subjective experience, and my motivations for writing this book.

It is arguably political or ideological to conduct research within a narrow positivist model that ignores the subjective meaning of madness and of symptomatology for women, to negate the role discursive constructions of madness in the social construction of gender, and to conceptualise mental health problems within a narrow realist frame. It is political and ideological to elevate the researcher or the clinician to a position of power which implies that he or she is the only one qualified to 'know'.[362] It is equally ideological to reify the notion of madness as an illness, with biomedical treatments deemed to be the optimum solution,[297] as I demonstrate below, taking the role of Big Pharma as a case example.

Biases in bio-psychiatry: Big Pharma marketing depression

Janet Currie writes:

> The marketing of depression and the high incidence of SSRI prescribing means that more women experiencing minor symptoms of distress common to everyday living will be convinced that they have a mental disorder, and that the optimum treatment is medication, most frequently an SSRI.[363, p.19]

Ironically, the branch of the psy-professions that most closely adheres to positivism-realism, bio-psychiatry, can be demonstrated to be particularly biased. The influence of Western psychiatry in establishing and maintaining the legitimacy of the concept of depression, and at the same time reinforcing a bio-determinist perspective, cannot be underestimated.[364-365] Since the mid nineteenth century, psychiatry has claimed authority over the mad and melancholic, subjecting women 'patients' to myriad physical 'treatments', on the basis of the belief that madness had an embodied cause. Between the 1940s and mid 1960s, psychiatric theory was dominated by psychoanalysis, with 'neurotic disorders' being the diagnoses most commonly applied to women, and oedipal notions of gender development underlying explanations of distress. This was reflected in the classifications of madness outlined in the first version of the DSM, published in 1954, where mental disorders were considered to result from early experiences that become internalised through unconscious processes,[366, p.39] even if treatments such as electro-convulsive therapy were more common than the 'talking cure' at this same time.

However, in the early 1970s a backlash against psychoanalytic thinking occurred in psychiatry, with proponents of 'evidenced based treatment' and a biological model of madness taking control of the discipline, resulting in depression being firmly positioned as an illness occurring within the brain.[18] This heralded a new era of psychotropic drug management to replace psychotherapy, as the latter had been widely rejected by bio-psychiatry for lacking evidence of efficacy.[366]xxv Within bio-psychiatry, depression is considered to be a disorder of the brain, requiring 'anti-depressant' medication. 'Serotonergic abnormalities' are the most widely accepted explanation today,[368] which we are told can be 'corrected' by SSRIs,[369] the most common being *Prozac* – fluoxetine hydrochloride, or *Zoloft* – sertraline hydrochloride.xxvi

Marketing SSRIs – celebrating the 'Prozac nation'

While efficacy of treatment is deemed proof of a depletion of serotonin, there is no consistent evidence of specific imbalances in serotonin in individuals reporting depression,[370] and no evidence that making serotonin nerves more active, the aim of SSRIs, can help people overcome emotional problems.[371] Scientists themselves readily admit they are unsure how antidepressants work,[18] with even those who are advocates of SSRIs concluding that 'there are complex interactions between the various neuro-transmitters that are not yet fully understood'.[368, p.1737] Equally, the efficacy of placebos in comparison to SSRIs is so strong – the response to medication is duplicated in 80 per cent of placebo groups[372–373] – the pharmacological rationale for the treatment is undermined.[374] This was reinforced by the introduction of a new tri-cyclic antidepressant, Tianeptine, which does the exact opposite of SSRIs, enhancing serotonin reuptake rather than preventing it.[18] At the same time, the fact that the original US Food and Drug Administration (FDA) testing of SSRIs was conducted on small groups of individuals with diagnoses of major depression,[375] yet the major market for these drugs today are individuals with minor or 'shadow' depression,[18] is also problematic. While the majority of the clinical trials for the various brands of SSRIs lasted only six weeks,[376] many people are prescribed SSRIs on a long term basis, with disregard for the unknown consequences of blocking serotonin long term.[363]

SSRIs have also been associated with serious side effects, including suicide, aggression, harm to relationships, dystonia (muscle spasm), sexual dysfunction, akathisia (inner agitation), chronic dyskinesis (abnormal muscle movements), gastrointestinal and dermatological problems, and 'out of character' behaviour.[363; 377–378] The rates of side effects in populations taking SSRIs are startlingly high. For example, sexual dysfunction is estimated to affect 30–70 per cent of SSRI users,[379] agitation, dizziness, headaches or sleep problems affect 10–32 per cent,[380] and neurological problems affect 22 per cent.[381] The most serious side effect, suicide, denied for many years by the drug companies, is now accepted as double the risk of older antidepressants or non-treatment,[363] and three times the risk for low risk depression treated in primary care contexts[382] – the bulk of the prescription market. For example, of nine individuals who had taken SSRIs interviewed by Rachel Liebert and Nicola Gavey, eight reported suicide attempts after being prescribed the drug, something they had not experienced previously.[377] As women form the majority of those prescribed SSRIs,[363] and also experience a higher rate of the most serious side effects,[381] this is clearly a gendered issue.

There is also a very high rate of 'spontaneous remission' with depression (along with all so-called psychiatric disorders), meaning that the majority of people experience alleviation of 'symptoms' in a relatively short period without any outside intervention at all.[383–384]xxvii Diet and exercise can also be as effective as SSRIs in treating the 'symptoms' that are described as depression,[385] as can psychological therapy, including cognitive behaviour therapy or interpersonal therapy,[386–387] as well as narrative therapy,[388] or psychoanalytic psychotherapy.[389] These therapeutic approaches do have their own limitations, not least of which is the implicit acceptance of 'depression' as a disorder (in contrast to feminist therapy,[390–391] discussed in Chapter 6), but they do have the advantage of not being a pharmacological cure. However, those promoting non-invasive interventions (or the absence of intervention altogether) face the combined marketing might of Big Pharma – formidable competition. Pharmaceutical companies are among the most profitable in the world – with global sales topping US$400 billion in 2002[376] – driven by the economic imperative to keep profits high through retaining and continuously expanding their market.[363] Psychotropic medication plays a key role in these profits, with the top five SSRIs earning between $1 billion and $3 billion each,[372] despite the drugs being almost identical,[363] amounting to total profits of over $10 billion per year.[40] And it is not just Big Pharma marketers who promote a biomedical solution for misery and madness. In a study which examined the rhetorical strategies adopted by a range of professionals who worked in fields associated with depression, and who were supportive of SSRIs, Liebert and Gavey found that risk was minimised, or seen to be easily managed, benefits were believed to outweigh risks, and the existence of side effects was questioned.[392] For example, increased incidences of suicidal thoughts were dismissed by a registered pharmacist, because 'there wasn't increased risk of suicide'.[392, p.1884] A mental health pharmacist argued that 'there are always people who are going to have bad experiences with drugs . . . and there are others for whom it is life-changing. So I think you have to balance it'.[392, p.1885] A coroner commented:

> Somebody who's suffering from depression . . . [has] associated lethargy and inertia . . . the inability to actually do anything other than sit in their little black hole and feel sorry for themselves really. Where a drug can lift them out of that and enable them to do things it also of course enables them to do things like harming themselves. I don't think the drug's responsible for that, because that's a feeling they had in the first place. It's a bit like saying,

'Here's the keys to the car' and you don't expect the person to go out and deliberately crash it. But of course that's always a possibility isn't it.[392, p.1889]

As Liebert and Gavey conclude, these rhetorical strategies enable knowledge of adverse effects to be 'contained within discourses that did not interrupt participants' ongoing support for the drugs'.[392, p.1890] The use of these trivialising, justifying or pathologising discourses clearly functions to protect those who advocate SSRIs from having to take any responsibility for addressing the complex issue of serious side effects, while further obscuring discussion of these issues in public life. It also means that these drugs continue to be prescribed, as the problem is established as more problematic than the cure.

Marketing madness: pathologising everyday life

It is easy to see how this market for psychotropic medication is maintained. The pharmaceutical industry and its allies engage in what has been described as 'disease mongering' in their active encouragement of the pathologisation of 'ordinary ailments'.[393, p.888] In conjunction with much of psychiatry they act to legitimise medical intervention for 'common personal and social problems',[394, p.900] through direct-to-consumer advertising, promotion of self-diagnosis,[363] and the funding of national education campaigns on how to 'Beat Depression'.[395] The whole continuum of human misery from mild to severe depression is thus conceptualised as a unitary psychiatric disorder 'depression', which is deemed to *cause* the distress which individuals experience.[165; 316; 396–398] At what point does discontent about daily life become an illness? At what point does misery become 'abnormal', requiring psychiatric diagnosis and treatment? As psychiatrist Arthur Kleinman comments, 'severe depression is a clinical disease . . . but mild depression is a totally different kettle of fish. It allows us to re-label depression an enormous number of things'.[cited by 363, p.11] Similarly, Vivian Burr and Trevor Butt argue, 'the proliferation of names syndromes and pathologies . . . is part of the more general phenomenon of the *pathologization of everyday life*'.[323, pp.186–187]

If you open the DSM, it is not hard to find a diagnosis that fits – more than one, for most people. This does not mean that we are all 'mad', it means our behaviour or our emotions are just easily defined as such – with the boundaries expanding all the time. The extension of the DSM-III in 1980 to include 265 disorders was not prompted by the discovery of a new array of psychological problems. It was largely spurred on by the need for drug companies to establish diagnostic categories that they could gain approval to treat, as well as the insistence of US based insurance companies that they would pay out for psychological treatment only if a formal diagnosis was given.[365]xxviii The more diagnoses available, the more people can come under the mantle of medicalised treatment, which keeps Big Pharma happy. The attempt by a pharmaceutical giant to have 'compulsive shopping' recognised as a disorder is one of the latest examples.[399] The authors of DSM would not admit to this bias. They claim that their diagnoses are 'atheoretical',[400] not tied to any theory or treatment, and based solidly in empirical research.[401] This is patently incorrect, as many critics have demonstrated, with numerous DSM diagnostic categories lacking any empirical foundation.[402]

For while the expert panels who create the diagnostic categories laid out in the DSM may claim to be objective scientists, there is clear evidence that pecuniary interests may influence their deliberations. In a study of the 170 panel members who contributed to the diagnostic criteria produced for the DSM-IV and DSM-IV-TR, Lisa Cosgrove and colleagues reported that 56 per cent had one or more financial ties to drug companies, including research funding, consultancies and speaker fees.[403] Some panels appeared more closely linked to Big Pharma than others – notably the mood disorders and schizophrenia panels, where 100 per cent of experts had pharmaceutical connections; premenstrual dysphoric disorder with 83 per cent; eating disorders with 83 per cent; and anxiety disorders with 81 per cent. With the exception of schizophrenia, which is diagnosed equally in men and women, these are all disorders more commonly attributed to women. As women are also more likely than men to be prescribed psychotropic medication, it is hard not to be cynical about the connection of Big Pharma to the experts on these DSM panels.

When we look to the panel members convened for DSM-V, scheduled for publication in 2012, this interest and influence appears to have increased: 70 per cent of task force members reported an industry relationship – an increase of 14 per cent on DSM-IV.[404] When challenged about this conflict of interest by Lisa Cosgrove and Harold Bursztajn, in an opinion piece published in *Psychiatric Times*, the chair and vice-chair of the DSM-V task force offer a revealing defence. They (unsurprisingly) dismiss Cosgrove and Bursztajn as biased, refuting the claim that there is anything wrong with financial relationships between the American Psychiatric Association and the pharmaceutical industry, by claiming 'they [Cosgrove and Bursztajn] seem not to appreciate or understand how the collaborative relationships among government, academia, and industry are vital to the current and future development of pharmacological treatments for mental disorders'.[404, p.41] It is revealing that their focus here is on 'the development of pharmacological treatments', rather than on effective treatments, or on understanding of the phenomenology or causes of 'mental disorders' – issues one would hope to be at the forefront of the minds of those chairing the development of the world's most influential psychiatric diagnostic manual.

Their bias is evidenced by their defence, despite their best intentions to the contrary.

Drug company influence does not stop at the level of the diagnostic criteria. The former editor of the *New England Journal of Medicine* reported that it was difficult to find a research psychiatrist to write an unbiased editorial on the treatment of depression, because there were 'very few who did not have financial ties to drug companies that make anti-depressants'.[401, p.xxiv] There is also strong evidence that the majority of the authors of clinical practice guidelines (CPG), disseminated through the American Psychiatric Association, are supported by the pharmaceutical industry. In a study of twenty authors of the clinical practice guidelines for major depression, bipolar depression and schizophrenia, Cosgrove and colleagues reported that 90 per cent had at least one financial relationship to Big Pharma.[405] As these guidelines act as the primary means of communicating clinical aspects of emerging therapies and standards of care to physicians, through offering specific recommendations for treatment, this raises serious issues of concern in relation to bias and conflict of interest. Is the recommendation in the CPG, that psychopharmacology should be the standard care for both schizophrenia and mood disorders,[405, p.229] in the best interests of those who fall under these diagnostic umbrellas? Many would say not. As the combined revenue for antidepressants and anti-psychotics was over $25 billion in 2007,[405] it is clearly in the interest of the drug companies.

The influence of pharmaceutical companies in constructing and maintaining a medicalised market for madness is not confined to the USA. Take the case of Japan, where there was no term for mild depression before SSRIs were promoted by GlaxoSmithKline in 1999. Experiences such as melancholia, sensitivity and fragility were accepted as part of life, not deemed to be pathological conditions that needed to be alleviated. However, after vigorous 'public education campaigns' promoted by Glaxo-SmithKline, a new 'disease', *kokoro no kaze*, was established, with a message that it 'can be cured by medicine'. As a result, sales of SSRIs in Japan quintupled between 1998 and 2003,[363, p.11] through effectively recasting low mood as a medical problem.[398] This creation and expansion of a market for drugs through extending the boundaries of diagnosis to encapsulate all forms of sadness, misery or dysphoria is not unique to Japan. As Edward Shorter has argued,[406] the boundaries of depression have been extending relentlessly outward since the 1960s, now encompassing mild levels of mood change, as well as major intractable depression, which is why diagnoses of depression have increasing exponentially.[407] This 'diagnostic bracket creep' is applauded by proponents of SSRIs, such as Peter Kramer, who want the boundaries of mental illness to be continuously expanded to match the drugs that are developed to treat 'conditions'.[375] It is thus not surprising to find that prescriptions for psychotropic medication, primarily SSRIs, have dramatically increased in recent decades, because they are promoted as 'chemical cures',[370, p.301] that treat a supposed 'deficiency disease'.[363, p.4]

Many of these criticisms of positivism/realism could be levied at the diagnosis and treatment of madness in both women and men. However, these social constructionist arguments, and this critique of the psy-professions – psychology alongside bio-psychiatry – has been taken up and advanced further by feminists, who focus their gaze specifically on the madness of women. For feminist social constructionism provides us with an alternative explanation for higher rates of depression diagnosed in women, and for the apparent increases over time: that we are simply more likely to label women as mad, and regulate femininity through psychiatric 'treatment'. It is to these feminist arguments that I now turn in Chapter 3.

3

LABELLING WOMEN AS MAD
Regulating and oppressing women

Alexandra Kaplan writes:

> Depression may not be an 'illness' superimposed on an alien or
> indifferent personality structure, but rather may be a distortion –
> an exaggeration of the normative state of being female in Western
> society.[1, p.234]

A 47-year-old woman library assistant, interviewed by Elizabeth Ettore and
Elianne Riska reported:

> First I had this major depression. I took depression medication for
> several years. . . . These pills take away your memory . . . It is
> more acceptable for women to be ill because women, at least in a
> male society, are supposed to be weak. It is more understandable –
> a man is not allowed to be weak.[2, p.105]

Robert Menzies and Dorothy Chunn write:

> 'Ordinary' madwomen might be (re)constructed as the objects of
> pity, or dismissed as pathological monstrosities or nonentities, or
> incorporated into reigning narratives of feminine frailty and somatic
> inferiority, but those rare women who transgressed criminal as well
> as mental boundaries were in direct violation of gender identity
> standards of mind and action. As such, in the eyes of the authorities,
> they required extraordinary measures of conceptual and systematic
> domestication.[3, p.81]

Feminist critics have a long history of dismissing diagnoses of women's
madness, and of condemning psychiatry as a profession that acts to regulate and oppress women. As Phyllis Chesler commented in 1972, in her oft-
quoted book *Women and madness*: 'Most twentieth century women who
are psychiatrically labelled, privately treated and publicly hospitalised are

64

not mad ... they may be deeply unhappy, self-destructive, economically powerless, and sexually impotent – but as women they're supposed to be'.[4, p.25] Or as Naomi Weissten memorably argued in 1973, 'since clinical experience and tools can be shown to be worse than useless when tested for consistency, efficacy, agreement and reliability, we can safely conclude that theories of a clinical nature advanced about women are also worse than useless'.[5, p.402] In my own book *Women's madness: Misogyny or mental illness?*,[6] where I reviewed these critiques, I argued that 'madness acts as a signifier which positions women as ill, as outside, as pathological, as somehow second rate – the second sex'.[6, p.11] I would still agree, twenty years after writing these words.

First wave feminists living in the late nineteenth or early twentieth centuries made similar arguments, many drawing on their own experiences of psychiatric diagnosis and treatment.[see 7] After being released from asylums, many women dedicated their lives to informing the public of the outrages perpetrated under the guise of 'treatment', becoming advocates of all women deemed mad. Some, such as Louisa Lowe, who published *The lunacy laws at work* in 1883, conducted a sustained attack on the whole structure of Victorian psychiatry,[8, p.126] in particular the private profit making asylums that formed part of the 'trade in lunacy'.[9, p.95] Fast forward more than a century and many would argue things have not greatly changed. Those making profit from the diagnosis of women as mad may now be pharmaceutical companies and the psy-professions, rather than the lay asylum keepers who held the reins of power until the medics took control. However, the process is the same: women are at risk of being deemed mad for simply being 'woman' – for displaying archetypal feminine traits, or paradoxically, for rejecting their feminine role. It is a conundrum that places all women at risk, even if the risk today is a prescription for psychotropic medication, rather than incarceration in an asylum.

In this chapter I explore feminist social-constructionist critiques of women's madness. I examine gender biased diagnosis and the pathologisation of femininity, using hysterical and borderline personality disorders as case examples; explore the tyranny of treatment, whether it be hospitalisation, ECT, medication or psychotherapy; and examine of self-policing practices, wherein women take up the mantle of madness and self-diagnose through a process of subjectification. While I applaud the insights of this approach, which has been described by Ros Gill as a 'post feminist sensibility ... informed by post-modernist and constructionist perspectives',[10, p.64] I also explore some of its potential limitations, in particular, the negation of women's lived experience and negotiation of distress. I end the chapter by revisiting the critical realist material-discursive-intrapsychic model, outlined in Chapter 1, in order to acknowledge the reality of women's distress, while at the same time rejecting the medicalised positioning of this distress as sign of pathology within.

Controlling deviant or difficult women: treatment or torture?

I start with the past, the place where our current bio-psychiatric discourse originates. In the Middle Ages women who exhibited 'hysterical symptoms', such as falling into a trance, strange body pains or paralysis, or strange paroxysms, were deemed to be possessed by evil spirits or dark humours, and were liable to be burnt as witches.[11, p.107; 12] The *Malleus maleficarum*, the 1494 bible of witch-hunters, provided the justification for the inquisition that saw tens of thousands of women burnt at the stake. The 'treatments' implemented by the psychiatrists who took over from the lay asylum keepers in the mid nineteenth century may appear more benign, but many women were forcibly hospitalised, had their freedom curtailed, and were subjected to myriad 'treatments', because of being deemed mad. First hand accounts of those incarcerated, invariably against their will, tell of women brutally removed from normal life, and subjected to numerous deprivations and interventions which would drive anyone insane: being fed a diet of plain gruel, and forced to eat with no appetite; being kept in isolation for days at a time and assaulted by attendants, or strapped into manacles, a boxed crib, or a strait-jacket; being subjected to the cold pack or hydra water treatment, involving submersion in icy cold water, held down with straps and layers of wet blankets.[7] Here are two accounts of such 'treatment' – first Lydia A Smith writes in 1878:

> In a most inhumane way I was plunged into a bath, the water of which was not quite boiling hot, and held down by a strong grip on my throat, until I felt a strange sensation and everything began to turn black. . . . When I became conscious I found myself jerked from one side to the other, with my hands confined to the stocks, or 'muff,' as it is termed in the asylum, and a stout leather belt attached to an iron buckle, was around me . . . at this point I was . . . taken (or rather jerked) into a small division off from the main hall, and thrown into a 'crib.' This is a square box, on which is a cover, made to close and lock, and has huge posts, separated so as to leave a small space between for ventilation. The strap attached to the 'muff' was fastened to the 'crib' in such a manner as to tighten around my waist, and across the pit of my stomach, with such a pressure that it actually seemed to me that I could not breathe. My feet were fastened to the foot of the 'crib' so tight, and remained there so long, that when they did unfasten them they were so swollen that it was impossible for me to stand on them. . . . This was my first experience of an insane asylum.[7, pp.133–134]

Second, Margaret Isabel Wilson, who was hospitalised from 1931 to 1937, writes:

The cold pack treatment was considered one of the hardest ordeals for some. They dreaded it. Even a threat would pacify them and keep them quiet. First, there was a rubber blanket, then a dripping wet sheet placed over it. The attendants laid her down, held her, and tied her hands and feet as she lay on her back. If she were very troublesome, the nurse would get some of the older patients to hold her. Next, another wet sheet, then a wool blanket, two if it were bitterly cold; then they were tucked up neatly, a hot bag placed at the feet and an ice bag at the head, if the patient had a temperature.[13, p.279]

It is hard to see how these particular 'treatments' could be beneficial to distressed women; the aim appears to be to shock them into submission. Women also experienced drug treatment, electro-convulsive therapy (ECT), blistering, multiple operations, or amputations without giving consent.[14, p.201] Is this treatment, or torture? If it was carried out on terrorist suspects today, there would be no question, as is evidenced by Lydia A. Smith's description in 1878 of forced drug treatment:

I will give you some idea, my patient reader, a 'faint idea', how the drugs are forced down a patient. One attendant clinches the patient's hair, jerking her suddenly backward on the floor; another plants her knees directly on the pit of the patient's stomach, while another sits on their knees, holding them down; and the fourth one pries the mouth open with the wedge; and, with the assistance of the attendant who has hold of the patient's hair, succeeds in getting the contents of the cup down the patient's throat by pinching their nose and choking them, nearly strangling them.[7, p.135]

While all of the 'treatments' described above were also offered to men (or rather, men were also subjected to them), there was a range of invasive interventions practised solely on women, focusing on the sexual or reproductive body. These included injections of ice water into the rectum; placement of ice in the vagina; leeching of the labia and cervix;[8, p.75] removal of ovaries to calm raging hormones; enforced weight gain to keep the ovaries from slipping and causing discomfort; electrical charges applied to the uterus; hot water injections in the vagina; and clitoral cauterisation.[7, p.101] Following a diagnosis of puerperal mania, the treatment recommended was 'to shave and apply cold to the head, administer tartar-emetic, purge, and blister'.[15, p.175] Within the asylum, women patients who were 'violent, mischievous, dirty [and used] bad language' were put in solitary confinement,[8, p.81] a punishment not meted out to similarly behaved men. Noisy women were also kept silent through the use of a 'scold's bridle',[8] a metal helmet framing the head with a metal 'bit' placed in the mouth.

One feminised treatment, made infamous through its exposure in Charlotte Perkins Gilman's autobiographical novel *The yellow wallpaper*, was Silas Weir Mitchell's bed-rest cure. This involved a woman (and it was always a woman) being confined to her bed in a darkened room for between six weeks and two months, forbidden from any mental or physical activity, including talking, reading, sewing, writing or even sitting up, with a nurse undertaking feeding and bedpan cleaning. Some women were also given electrical massages, to stimulate their limbs.[16] Gilman wrote how this treatment drove her mad: 'I would crawl into remote closets and under beds – to hide from the grinding pressure of that profound distress'.[17] Weir Mitchell believed that women enjoyed being ill, and insisted that through making his rest cure so aversive, as well as by being fattened up – he boasted that one patient, Mrs G., had gained 40 pounds in two months[16] – his 'bitter medicine' would shock women into health and sanity.[8, p.139] He was not alone in exhibiting contempt for his patients. Henry Maudsley despaired about the 'moral perversion' and 'immoral vagaries' of young women who 'believing or pretending that they cannot stand or walk, lie in bed all day . . . objects of attentive sympathy on the part of their anxious relatives, when all the while their only paralysis is a paralysis of will'.[8, p.133]

Disobedient wives and daughters: regulating the Victorian madwoman

When we look to the 'symptoms' which provoked these pronouncements and treatments we can see how the very definition of madness functioned to control and arguably punish women for both enacting an exaggerated form of femininity, or for being 'unacceptable',[7, p.8] contravening the ideals of femininity circulating at that particular point in time. Take 'hysteria' as a diagnostic category. Elaine Showalter has argued that, it is in many ways synonymous with femininity, with 'its vast, unstable repertoire of emotional and physical symptoms – fits, fainting, vomiting, choking, sobbing, laughing, paralysis – and the rapid passage from one to another suggested the lability and capriciousness traditionally associated with the feminine nature'.[8, p.129] Paradoxically, if the hysteric was mad because she was ultra-feminine (or too feminine), many women were positioned as mad for not being feminine enough: for inappropriate self-expression, not being a 'paragon of domestic virtue', or for failing in their role as wife and mother.

Agnes E. was committed to the Auckland asylum in the late nineteenth century for having 'used horrible language, having been up to that time a decent and even religious woman, fully self-respecting', in the words of her case notes.[21, p.69] Phebe Davis spent three years in the New York asylum, from 1850 to 1853, diagnosed as 'insane' because she had the temerity to disagree with other people and make her views known. Elizabeth Stone was incarcerated in the McLean asylum, Charlestown, Massachusetts, between 1840 and 1842 because her family did not concur with her widely expressed religious beliefs. Elizabeth Packard was committed to the Illinois State Hospital for the Insane, for three years from 1860, for the same. Adriana P. Brinkle attempted to lead an independent life, describing herself as 'extravagant and too fond of dress'.[7, p.108] She was committed to the State Hospital for the Insane at Harrisburg, Pennsylvania in 1857, following the sale of furniture which she had previously bought on credit, as yet unpaid. Her family deemed a diagnosis of insanity preferable to a criminal court action, and she remained in the asylum for 28 years, long after those family members who had committed her (and could thus effect her release) had died. Conversely, in 1898 Alice Bingham-Russell wrote of a 'young woman . . . enticed into a madhouse' because she 'refuses to sell her property to suit the caprices of her husband':[i]

> He, acting on the advice of a lawyer, has her declared insane . . . with no friends at hand nor opportunity to notify them, while the judge, two doctors and her husband are under oath to faithfully perform their duty, this young and capable woman who has been doing, up to the very hour before, all her housework, including care of two children, leaves a good home and property worth $20,000, to become a public charity and mingle and associate continuously with maniacs.[19, cited by 7, p.195]

Charlotte Perkins Gilman underwent six weeks of the bed-rest cure – being confined to bed, in a darkened room, fed gruel, and denied all company or intellectual stimulation – in 1887.[ii] Her malady was exhaustion and apathy associated with mothering, housekeeping, and relations with her husband, 'symptoms' that were exacerbated by her desire for engagement in an intellectual life, according to her psychiatrist. Reflecting on her own 'malady', she writes:

> We had been married four years and more. This miserable state of mind, this darkness, feebleness and gloom, had begun in those difficult years of courtship, had grown rapidly worse after marriage, and was not threatening utter loss; whereas I had repeated proof that the moment I left home, I began to recover. It seemed right to give up a mistaken marriage.[20, pp.167–168]

Indeed, at the height of her illness, when she left home to visit friends, 'feeble and hopeless . . . armed with tonics and sedatives', she found that 'from the moment the wheels began to turn, the train to move, I felt better'.[20, p.165] When she eventually left her 'mistaken' marriage for good, and was able to engage fully in a life of thinking and writing, she made a full recovery.

THE MADNESS OF WOMEN

Other women were not so fortunate. Susannah E. was committed three times between 1869 and 1870 for attempting to leave her husband, and Helen C. was committed following a complaint of marital ill treatment, including being called a 'bloody whore' and being ordered out of her home, after asking her husband for a drink of water.[21, p.71] Wives were clearly expected to be compliant, respectful and satisfied – as were mothers. Mary O. was committed to the Auckland asylum for refusing 'to see her children in the room' and asking 'to take them away from her', and Jessie N. was hospitalised in the same place for 'being far more satisfied to be absent from [her children] than a sane mother would be'.[21, p.73] As Bronwyn Labrum writes in her analysis of the Auckland asylum cases, mothers were supposed to be 'self-less and giving, servers not takers, not self-absorbed as another "neglectful" mother was described'.[21, p.73] All of these women were incarcerated at the request of fathers or husbands. Once women were admitted to psychiatric 'care', they could remain hospitalised for many years, deprived of all contact with the outside world, particularly if their family wanted them to remain so. Many husbands and families wanted this for their own selfish reasons. Lydia A. Smith, who was committed to Kalamazoo Asylum, Michigan between 1867 and 1871,[iii] wrote:

It is a very fashionable and easy thing now to make a person out to be insane. If a man tires of his wife, and is befooled by some other woman, it is not a very difficult manner to get her in an institution of this kind. Belladonna and chloroform will give her the appearance of being crazy enough[7, pp.135–136]

The diagnosis of madness thus functioned very effectively to rid society – or husbands – of women who were 'difficult', or who were no longer wanted. This practice was immortalised in nineteenth century fiction, which reflected the increased interest in women's psychology (or insanity) within psychiatry.[22] Thus, Wilkie Collins wrote of The woman in white (1859), who was incarcerated in an asylum for knowing secrets about a powerful man, the same man who later incarcerated his wife in order to control her fortune. Bertha Mason, the mad wife in Charlotte Bronte's Jane Eyre (1847), was confined to the attic by her husband, Mr Rochester. Mad, sexually depraved Bertha, with her red staring eyes and wild hair, whose worst attacks came when the moon is 'blood red', or 'broad and red', reminds us of the link between madness and menstruation,[8, p.67] standing as the antithesis of governess Jane's chastity and sanity.[22] Bertha provides Jane with an example of how not to act and not to be,[23, p.361] and in marrying Jane, Rochester seeks to save himself from the clutches of his animalistic and degenerate first wife. However, Bertha has also been interpreted as Jane's doppelganger, standing as a distorted mirror image of Jane's own repressed 'hunger, rebellion and rage',[23, p.339] her dangerous propensities toward 'passion'.[24, p.16] This reminds us that the moniker of madness is a possibility for every woman. None of us is immune.

Bertha Mason exacts her revenge by burning down the house in which she is imprisoned, seriously wounding her jailor/husband and ending her own life in the process. Like all women who commit violent crimes,[18] she is seen as 'doubly deviant' because she has transgressed 'both law and reason'.[25, p.42] As Kathleen Kendall comments, femininity is deemed to be antithetical to violent criminality, which means that nineteenth century women who were deemed both mad and bad 'were even more alien to human civilisation than their male counterparts'.[25, p.51] In the Victorian court system, women positioned as 'criminal lunatics' were seen to be at the mercy of their reproductive bodies, which stripped them of any agency, and denied the social context of their lives (they were more likely to be poor, or from an ethnic minority).[26] If they were then sentenced to incarceration in an asylum there was no automatic release date, in contrast to those with a criminal conviction, resulting in women remaining in 'psychiatric purgatory',[3, p.95] until they were deemed 'sane' – which might be never. Adriana P. Brinkle escaped her 28-year sentence for selling furniture bought on credit only when a new lunacy law came into effect in Pennsylvania in 1883, which required a Committee on Lunacy to examine every claim made by an asylum inmate. Prior to that, all of her pleas for freedom were ignored, even though she had never been given a formal diagnosis. As Kate Millett has commented, when discussing her own contemporary diagnosis and treatment in *The loony-bin trip*,[27]

> madness is worse than a crime; crimes merit trials, counsel, stated sentences if convicted. If acquitted of crime, one is free to go. [With a diagnosis] you will never get acquitted and, as a matter of fact, you are not nearly as innocent as you claim'.[27, p.232]

Hospitalisation and ECT: constructing a 'good woman'

The forced incarceration of women and regulation through psychiatric labelling as 'mad' is not an anachronism peculiar to the nineteenth century. Frances Farmer was incarcerated at the Washington State Hospital for the Insane for six years between 1944 and 1950,[iv] for being 'out of control' – manifested by drinking, smoking, swearing and having sex with men. Farmer, a Hollywood film actress, was forcibly hospitalised by her mother, and subjected to psycho-surgery. Ironically, in this same era, Hollywood depicted fictional examples of women falsely accused of madness. The 1944 film *Gaslight*, directed by George Cukor and starring Ingrid Bergman, centred on a husband slowly sending his wife, Paula, mad. He did this by convincing her she had lost or stolen valuable objects, was hearing footsteps in the attic, and was imagining the gas-lights dimming in their home. He was responsible for all of this himself, in an attempt to have Paula admitted for psychiatric treatment, in order to free himself for more nefarious deeds (searching for hidden jewels in their attic).

However, while Hollywood stories may end well – Paula exposes her husband's plans and realises she is perfectly sane – in the real world, many women are not so fortunate. In the first half of the twentieth century, women were hospitalised for getting pregnant out of wedlock, after having been sexually abused, or for simply being too troublesome to have at home. If these women were distressed at their first admission it is not surprising, given the circumstances of their lives. Whether they were 'mad', however, is open to serious doubt. Take Olivia Brown,ᵛ who was hospitalised for 35 years between 1951 and 1986, at Shenley Hospital, North London, with a diagnosis of 'chronic anxiety', manifested by 'paranoia, sleepless nights, over-excitability and distractibility', following a sexual assault by a male colleague at work. Olivia was given 22 ECT treatments in 1951, which left her confused and suffering from memory impairments. While she was described as 'mildly elated, talkative and cheerful' in the intervening years, she did not leave the hospital until 1961, when she was abruptly returned to psychiatric care following an argument with her mother, with whom she was staying. Olivia's mother also complained of her daughter's 'severe dependency' and unwillingness to leave the house – unsurprising in a 39-year-old woman who had been institutionalised for 10 years. Her life sentence of incarceration – over twice the length of the average murder sentence – ended in 1986 only because the hospital was closing. Olivia was one of the first 'cases' I was given to work with when I was training as a clinical psychologist, and she was euphoric to be back in the world. I was helping her to develop road safety skills – there was certainly nothing 'disordered' about her mind.

Olivia's situation was similar to that of the many women committed to Glenside Psychiatric Hospital, South Australia, described by Jill Matthews in her book *Good and mad women*.[28] Irma Weiman was certified on the behest of her husband in 1960 because she would not speak to him, gave tinned food to their children, and then supposedly frightened them so that they avoided their father – accusations Irma vehemently denied.[28] Similarly, in 1970, Carmella Gniada was hospitalised because her husband said she was unbearable, could not cope with the family, was crying all the time, had affairs with two men, and did not like him. He also did not like her family, whom he found 'overpowering'.[28, p.145] Gwen Kirk was hospitalised in 1968, following depression associated with an 'illegal pregnancy' (she was not married), as well as a series of sexual relationships with men, conducted without any intention of commitment. Her psychiatrist described her as a 'femme fatale' and despaired of her 'illicit love activity', describing her behaviour as analogous to 'prostitution', even though Gwen had never asked men to pay for sex.[28, p.125]

Similarly, Susanna Kaysen was hospitalised in McLean Hospital, Massachusetts in 1968, at the age of 18, because of having 'an increasing patternless [sic] of life, promiscuous [sic], might kill self or get pregnant', as described in her case file.[29, p.11] She was diagnosed with borderline personality disorder. Kaysen documented her experience in the memoir *Girl, interrupted*, which was made into a Hollywood film. Katie Allen, who was admitted to Glenside Hospital in 1959 suffering from depression, was criticised in her case notes for being 'repelled' by her husband, leading to a diagnosis of 'latent homosexuality'.[28, p.116] A pejorative diagnosis of lesbianism can also be applied to single women. Eve Innes was admitted to Glenside in 1965, at the age of 24, and described as 'always schizoid; no boyfriends, no dancing, didn't want to go', with 'uncut and uncombed' hair, 'no makeup' and 'an unfeminine appearance', leading to suspicions about her attraction to one of the women nursing staff. Eve's later case notes express relief when she 'dressed in feminine clothes to attend ward social' demonstrating that she was a 'developing young lass with heterosexual feelings'.[28, p.122]

In all of these cases, women have contravened the ideals of femininity which were accepted as the norm at a particular point in time: espousing contrary religious beliefs or wanting an independent life in the nineteenth century; being sexual outside of heterosexual marriage in the first half of the twentieth century; being violent, or rejecting a narrowly prescribed role of wife and motherhood throughout. Thus, while the diagnosis of madness serves to define what is 'other', what is deserved of 'treatment' to engender conformity, it also maintains the boundaries of normative femininity. For by identifying what is deviant or disordered we shore up the very definition of what is 'sane', the very definition of the 'good woman'. At the same time, madness stands as a spectre for all women, a warning of their possible fate if they stray from their expected path. By positioning the mad woman as 'other', as one who needs treatment to modify her distress or disordered behaviour, we also serve to separate ourselves from this fearful creature, and pull back from having to stare into the abyss of our own demons or despair. As Sander Gilman argues,[30] it is our own fear of collapse that is played out, and assuaged, in Western images of illness, such as madness. For it is 'not we who totter on the brink of collapse, but rather the Other. And it is an-Other who has already shown his or her vulnerability by having collapsed'.[30, p.1]

Once women receive a psychiatric diagnosis everything they do can be potentially interpreted as a 'symptom'. And thus, Seymour Hallack argues in *The politics of therapy*,[31] we then stop listening to the individual, and do not look at the social environment that is causing them harm. The imposition of a diagnosis of manic depression resulted in Kate Millett feeling that she was dismissed. She believed that her partner Sophie saw her as 'no longer valid'. She was deemed to be 'incompetent, cancelled but what I have become to her, a crazy'.[27, p.64] Similarly, a woman diagnosed with borderline personality disorder remarked, 'having that diagnosis resulted in my getting treated exactly the way I was treated at home. The minute I got that diagnosis people stopped treating me as though what I was doing had a reason'.[32, p.128] Psychiatric diagnosis can also have material implications for women's lives, not only resulting in the forced hospitalisation and 'treatment' outlined above, but also creating problems with employers, health insurance, and child custody, as well as diminishing the right to make decisions about one's legal affairs.[33]

Yet diagnosis may also appear to have positive benefits. In discussing these complex issues, Emily Caplan presents the case of 'Tara', who had been able to get her specific educational needs met because of a diagnosis of 'attention deficit disorder', and avoided a jail sentence despite a conviction for petty larceny, because she was deemed to have 'diminished responsibility' due to 'post-traumatic stress disorder'.[33, p.52] In a similar vein, in an analysis of insanity pleas for violent crimes in England and Wales between 1832 and 1901, Jill Ainsley found that women were more successful in their pleas than men (at a rate of 87 per cent compared to 59 per cent), reflecting the tendency to attribute women's criminal actions to their reproductive biology, which then exonerated them from responsibility.[34] Yet this is at the cost of being positioned as mad, as outside of reason – which is not a positive place for a woman to inhabit, regardless of the short term benefits. Tara lost the custody of her child, and after her death had the bequests outlined in her will overturned, because of her psychiatric diagnoses. Equally, nineteenth century women incarcerated for criminal insanity were subjected to 'extraordinary measures of conceptual and systematic domestication' by the authorities, because they were 'in direct violation of gender identity standards of mind and action', in the words of Robert Menzies and Dorothy Chunn.[3, p.81] Little has changed. Women committed to secure hospitals nowadays are still infantilised, subjected to ECT at three times the rate of men, as well as being more likely to receive forced ECT and medication,[35] and report high rates of emotional and physical abuse by staff – punishment for not 'toeing the line'.[36, p.231] And this is a line that is very gender based, as idealised constructions of femininity still influence psychiatric diagnosis today.

Gender biased diagnosis

Phyllis Chesler writes:

> Women who act out the conditioned female role are clinically viewed as 'neurotic' or 'psychotic'. When and if they are hospitalized, it is for predominantly female behaviours such as 'depression', 'suicide attempts', 'anxiety neuroses', 'paranoia', eating disorders,

self-mutilation or 'promiscuity'. Women who reject or are ambi-
valent about the female role frighten both themselves and society
so much that their ostracism and self-destructiveness probably
begins very early. Such women are assured of a psychiatric label
and, if they are hospitalised, it is for less 'female' behaviours, such
as 'schizophrenia', 'lesbianism', or 'promiscuity'.[149, p.116]

These practices of pathologising femininity continue into the twenty-first
century – the difference today is that feminist researchers can provide
empirical evidence to support their claims, exposing the gender bias in
psychiatric diagnosis and treatment. For while in Chapter 2 I outlined the
argument that madness is a discursive construction, feminists have extended
this critique to demonstrate that it is a *gendered* construct. Much attention
has been given to research conducted by Broverman and colleagues in the
late 1960s,[vi] where it was argued that women who conform to the feminine
role, and paradoxically, also those who reject it, are likely to receive a
psychiatric diagnosis.[38] At the same time, definitions of mental health were
found to coincide with definitions of masculinity, whereas femininity was
seen as psychologically unhealthy. In the decade after this research was first
published, a flurry of studies attempted to replicate the findings, most using
analogue studies where psychiatrists were asked to make diagnoses on the
basis of anonymous case material described as male or female (or not given
a gender at all). While there has been some controversy over the initial
findings by Broverman and colleagues, focusing on the methodology and
type of statistical analysis used,[37; 39] most of the subsequent studies
confirmed their findings,[see 40] reporting that psychiatrists positioned
women who deviate from gender role stereotypes as the most disturbed.

For example, a study by Waisberg and Page found that women who
exhibited symptoms of the so-called 'masculine disorders' – alcohol abuse
and antisocial personality disorder – were seen as more severely disturbed
than their male counterparts.[41] In a similar vein, data on 666 emergency
psychiatric admissions analysed by Rosenfield revealed that women were
most likely to be hospitalised for 'masculine' symptoms of antisocial personality disorder, aggression or substance abuse.[42] This is reminiscent of
the Victorian asylums where women were incarcerated for speaking out
of turn, or for refusing to take up an acquiescent feminine role – being sent
to solitary confinement, or subjected to the scolds bridle, if they exhibited
'aggressive' behaviour within the asylum walls. However, it is important to
acknowledge that gender stereotypes are also used in the diagnosis of men.
In the Rosenfield study, men were most likely to be hospitalised for the
'feminine' symptoms of anxiety and depression,[42] and in the Waisberg
and Page study, depressed men were seen as much more disturbed than
depressed women.[41] As 'depression' is conceptualised as a 'woman's
problem', this is not surprising.

At the same time, it has been reported that medical practitioners over-diagnose depression in women, as a diagnosis is given even when women do not meet the standard criteria.[43] Conversely, when women and men *do* meet the criteria for depression, it has been reported that men are less likely than women to receive a diagnosis.[43] In one study, the over-diagnosis of women operated only with male psychiatrists,[44] suggesting that the gender (or perhaps the prejudices) of the physicians may influence their judgement – in line with previous reports that clinicans' personal identities and demographic characteristics influence how they relate to clients.[45] This suggests that gender role stereotypes used by clinicians lead to women being positioned as intrinsically more maladjusted; health professionals expect women to be mad (or 'depressed'), so are more likely to look for it, and to see it even if it is not there. It has also been claimed that gender bias exists in the standardised questionnaires which measure depression, as many categorise experiences that are normative for women, or part of the feminine role (such as crying, sadness or loss of interest in sex) as 'symptoms'.[46]vii Thus, instruments such as the Beck Depression Inventory (BDI), which are often used in large scale epidemiological surveys, may simply be overestimating depressive 'symptoms' in women,[46] and thus distorting conclusions about gender differences in psychopathology. Conversely, it has been suggested that standardised measures of depression may *under*-diagnose depression in particular cultural groups, such as South Asian women, as a result of being culturally or linguistically insensitive to the meanings of distress in a non-Western context.[48]

Women in specific demographic groups – in particular, working class women,[49] Black women,[44] older women,[50] and lesbians[51] – are at the highest risk of this (mis)diagnosis. For example, the landmark study conducted by Hollingshead and Redlich in 1958 reported that lower income clients were more likely to receive a diagnosis of severe mental illness, and were also more likely to receive ECT, drugs, lobotomies or custodial care, when compared to more wealthy clients.[52] Equally, therapists have been found to rate depressed African American clients more negatively than depressed Anglo-Americans,[53] with White therapists rating African American clients as more psychologically impaired than African American therapists.[54] In the UK, the lower rates of depression in South Asian women were explained by one group of health professionals through the adoption of a range of 'orientalist' stereotypes which acted to pathologise South Asian culture – positioning it as 'other', patriarchal and repressive – compared to an idealised liberated West.[55] This can result in South Asian women's distress and mental health needs going unrecognised and untreated,[56] as well as adding to the high level of stigma associated with discussing psychological distress that already exists in this cultural group.[57]

Older women are also vulnerable to both over- and under-diagnosis:[50] the tendency to pathologise everything about older people often leads to misery being seen as mental illness, when it is not,[31] while invisibility leads to lack of recognition of distress and the withholding of necessary services.[58] And while homosexuality has officially been removed from the DSM, many clinicians still view it as a pathology, and pathologise lesbians who are seeking help for problems with relationships or work, seeing their sexuality as an issue of concern.[51] From the perspective of intersectionality,[see 59] where it is recognised that we all have multiple cultural and social identities, being a member of multiple marginalised or minority groups can also exacerbate vulnerability to misdiagnosis. For example, differences in identity development have been reported between White and African American or Latina lesbians,[60] which has implications for mental health and well-being, and it has been reported that older women who are poor face the double discrimination of class and age.[50]

A further, related, explanation for women's higher rates of diagnosis as mad is that men and women differ in their presentation of distress, meaning that women are more likely to come under the scrutinising gaze of mental health professionals. This suggests that gender differences in depression are an artefact – the result of women being more likely than men to report either mild symptoms of depression,[61] or symptoms that last a few days.[62] Conversely, it has been suggested that men are more likely to forget their depressive symptoms than women,[63] or to underplay the severity of past episodes.[64] The fact that many health professionals believe this explanation is illustrated by the findings of the Gender and Therapy Referrals Study conducted by Janette Perz and myself (see Appendix),[65] where we asked general practitioners (GPs) and allied mental health practitioners (AMHPs) to explain why 70 per cent of the 746 referrals for psychological therapy within a twelve month period were women.[viii] The majority told us that women present more regularly at their general medical practice, often for the health care needs of their children or other dependent family members, allowing the woman, or the GP, to raise the issue of depression:

> Women participate in routine health checks so have a greater opportunity/comfort in raising psychological issues.

> More women attending GP's practice with family members, i.e. children, therefore they have a closer 'bond' with GP and GP may see family issues impacting on the female patient.

The second explanation they gave centred on the perception that due to perceived stigma, men are less likely than women to seek help because it may be seen as a weakness:

> Stigma about counselling that males find hard to accept.

> Women . . . don't view mental health as a weakness to the same extent as men.

Social stigma. Men being expected to be a stronger gender. Fear of inadequacy and failure.

Conversely, women were seen as more likely to ask for help and raise mental health issues with their GP:

Women are more vocal and 'expressive' in their demand. Women see themselves and health differently and therefore have different expectations.

Women are more likely to talk about psychological issues/raise psychological issues.

Generally women feel more comfortable seeking help for medical issues in general.

Finally, it was stated that women's and men's psychological symptoms present differently:

Women's symptoms of psychological distress are expressed externally and thus more evident to others compared to males who tend to internalise. Thus [women are] more likely to be advised/ encouraged by others to gain help.

Men are more likely to complain of headaches, dizziness. Women are more likely to identify that they are anxious, stressed or depressed.

There may be some basis in these beliefs, as there is evidence that men are less likely than women to self-diagnose with depression, seeing it as self-indulgent and unproductive.[66–67] Men who experience prolonged misery have been reported to be less likely than women to express their feelings openly, which can make it more difficult for clinicians to detect that there is a problem.[68–69] However, at the same time, belief in the veracity of these accounts can serve as a justification for gender bias in clinicians' judgements, and for the absence of self-reflection, as responsibility for over-diagnosis in women (as well as supposed under-diagnosis in men) is placed firmly at the feet of the 'patient'. It is interesting that none of these accounts contained descriptions of women as more maladjusted or mad than men, or of men as more psychologically healthy. Is this because GPs and allied mental health professionals have been schooled in a post-feminist discourse where they are aware of potential gender bias in diagnosis, and are determined not to fall into that trap themselves? As the study by Broverman and colleagues[38] which first explored this gender bias empirically, has been shown to be among the foremost cited articles in the field of psychology, and has 'impacted on the thinking of a generation of psychologists and mental health professionals',[37, p.126] it would not be surprising if this were the case. However, this does not mean that gender biased diagnosis is no longer taking place.

Hysterical and borderline personality disorders: pathologising exaggerated femininity

Janet Wirth-Cauchon writes:

> The symptoms of women diagnosed as borderline may be read as meaningful or intelligible responses to the double bind of feminine subjecthood. . . . the borderline patient's split self has its sources not in a flawed psyche, but in the overall context of the Western cultural split between a devalued realm of the feminine and the body, and the realm of the autonomous subject – the realm of reason and the mind. Women, on the borderline between these two realms, must negotiate both.[70, pp.157–158]

Depression is not the only diagnosis to be critically examined for being more readily applied to women. Similar arguments have been made about women's greater propensity to be diagnosed with hysterical personality disorder, the modern incarnation of hysteria. Hysterical personality disorder's depiction in the DSM-II, published in 1968, has been described as 'essentially a caricature of exaggerated femininity',[71, p.158] as the 'symptoms' included excitability, emotional instability, overreactivity and self-dramatisation. Indeed the description in DSM-II of hysterics, as 'attention seeking, seductive, immature, self-centred, vain . . . and dependent on others',[72, p.251] is almost identical to the nineteenth century description of hysterics, outlined in Chapter 1. It is also close to the archetypal version of femininity that women were expected to follow in the 1950s and 1960s, parodied (or perhaps celebrated) in the twenty-first century television series about Madison Avenue advertising executives, *Mad Men*. In DSM-III,[73] published in 1980, hysterical personality disorder was renamed 'histronic personality disorder', to avoid the negative connotations that were associated with 'hysteria'.[71] However, the descriptors of the typical patient outlined in DSM-III still depict an exaggerated femininity, someone who is 'typically attractive and seductive . . . overly concerned with physical attractiveness' as well as interested in 'control[ling] the opposite sex or enter[ing] into a dependent relationship [and continuously demanding] reassurance, approval or praise'.[73, p.348] Isn't this how we are taught to 'do girl' through teenage magazines, romantic fiction, and 'chick flicks'?[see 74]

But we should be careful. Enacting this particular version of 'seductive' femininity may attract more than a man: it can clearly attract a psychiatric diagnosis. This was evidenced in a study where psychiatrists were asked to judge a range of case descriptions, wherein a diagnosis of histronic personality disorder was given to women, even though the case studies gave little indication of the disorder.[44]

Changes in gender roles after the 1960s and 1970s, which saw Western women enter the workforce in unprecedented numbers, and reshaped sexual and family relations, resulted in the marginalisation of hysteria as a diagnostic category. However, as Mary Ann Jimenez has argued, this did not mean that exaggerated femininity was no longer pathologised, as borderline personality disorder simply took the place of hysteria, capturing 'contemporary values about the behaviour of women'.[71, p.161] Described as a 'feminised' psychiatric diagnosis,[75] because it is applied more often to women than men,[76] between three and seven times more frequently,[77-78] the criteria for borderline personality disorder consist of symptoms that characterise 'feminine qualities'.[71, p.163] These include depression and emotional lability, as well as 'impulsiveness in areas such as shoplifting, substance abuse, sex, reckless driving, and binge eating', and 'identity disturbance', evidenced by 'uncertainty about self-image, sexual orientation, long term goals or career choice'.[79, p.347] However, where borderline personality disorder differs from hysteria (or histronic personality disorder) is the inclusion of the more masculine characteristic of 'inappropriate intense anger' as a criterion for diagnosis.[71] So while both diagnostic categories adopt gender stereotypes in positioning particular women as 'mad', Jimenez comments, 'if the hysteric was a damaged woman, the borderline woman is a dangerous one'.[71, p.163] As almost half of the women who qualify for a histronic or borderline diagnosis meet the criteria for both disorders,[78] many women are clearly seen as both damaged and dangerous.

Mary Ann Jimenez has described the typical borderline patient as a 'demanding, angry, aggressive woman', who is labelled as 'mentally disordered' for behaving in a way that is perfectly acceptable in a man.[71, pp.162,163] Evidence that there is a clear gender difference in the pathologisation of emotions, in particular anger, is supported by research by Lisa Feldman Barrett and Eliza Bliss-Moreau, who examined judgements made about emotions expressed by men and women. They found that men's sadness and anger was considered to be related to situational factors – such as 'having a bad day' – whereas sad or angry women were judged as 'emotional'.[80] Thus women's emotions are deemed a sign of pathology, whereas men's are understandable. Two well known women posthumously 'diagnosed' with borderline personality disorder in the media were Diana, Princess of Wales,[81] and Marilyn Monroe,[82] whose 'symptoms' including anger, supposed sexual promiscuity, and discontent with their partner (or lover). Both experienced relationship conflict and breakdown; both had a troubled early life. Would men who behaved in a similar manner have been diagnosed as 'mad'? I suspect not.

While depression is deemed a 'symptom' of borderline personality disorder, the latter is a diagnostic category considered to be more a 'character pathology' than a disturbance of mood.[83] Janet Wirth-Cauchon has argued that the borderline diagnosis is typically applied to 'certain women patients' who are 'difficult, who resist the work of therapy, or who are socially marginal'.[84, p.87] Similarly, Dana Becker has described borderline personality disorder as 'the most pejorative of personality labels' which is 'little more than a short-hand for a difficult, angry, female client certain to give the therapist countertransferential headaches'.[78,p.423] As many women diagnosed as 'borderline' have been sexually abused in childhood,[85] their anger is understandable, as is their 'difficulty' with men in positions of power over them – the therapists who give out diagnoses. These women are pathologised, occupying the space of the abject, that which is 'other' to all that is desired in the feminine subject.[84] As the outspoken, difficult woman of the sixteenth century was castigated as a witch, and the same woman in the nineteenth century a hysteric, in the late twentieth and twenty-first centuries, she is described as 'borderline'. All are stigmatising labels. All are irrevocably tied to what it means to be 'woman' at a particular point in history. And while the nineteenth century hysteric was deemed labile and irresponsible, as a justification for subjecting her to the bed-rest cure or incarceration in an asylum, women diagnosed as borderline are often considered to be mentally disabled, and subjected to involuntary institutionalisation or medication, as well as being stripped of child custody or parental rights.[78, p.429] At the same time, a diagnosis of borderline can be used as a justification for denying women access to mental health care, because of supposed 'resistance' to treatment.[86] However, if we examine the negative consequences of contemporary bio-psychiatric 'treatment' for many women, this may not be such a bad thing.

Regulating women through bio-psychiatric 'treatment'

Oppression through incarceration and electric shock treatment

Kate Millett writes:

> The bin itself is insane, abnormal, a terrifying captivity, an irrational deprivation of every human need – or that maintaining reason within it is an overwhelming struggle. After a certain time many victims collapse and agree to be crazy; they surrender. And withdraw. And as time goes by, they cannot or finally will not return; it is too far, it is too unrewarding, it is too dubious – they have forgotten. And they live their lives in their own minds, the

diversions within them. The woes and gratifications of some care-
fully wrought fantast, built like a nest out of the tatters of what
was once a life but could be no longer.[27, p.67]

Critiques of the medicalisation of women's distress in the late twentieth and
twenty-first centuries do not stop at the point of diagnosis – they extend to
the 'treatments' offered to women by the psy-professions, in particular
those offered by bio-psychiatry. Forced psychiatric incarceration has been
the object of the most consistent condemnation, as is evidenced by Kate
Millett's autobiographical account in 1990.[27] For while the notion of
'asylum' suggests a peaceful and therapeutic environment, the reality for
many women is the opposite, with little access to any form of psychological
intervention, and the enforcement of a restrictive, demeaning culture of
containment. For example, Marina Morrow interviewed women residents
in Canadian mental health institutions and found that many were retrau-
matised by their experience of psychiatric care.[86] Similarly, Moira Potier, a
psychologist who worked from 1987 to 1993 at Ashworth secure psychiatric
hospital in the UK,[ix] argued that rather than being a therapeutic
environment, 'it's going to make things worse' for the women incarcerated
there.[36, p.228] The charity Women in Secure Hospitals (WISH) agreed,
commenting that women inmates 'feel unsafe', 'walk on eggshells all the
time', and live with 'a state of shock, a state of fear'; conclusions confirmed
by a committee of enquiry that examined the treatment of women at
Ashworth, which was described as 'infantilizing, demeaning and anti-
therapeutic'.[36, p.228] This is reminiscent of the descriptions of the Victorian
insane asylum as a 'place where insanity is made', where women were
'driven mad by the brutality of the asylum itself, and by their lack of legal
rights as women, and as prisoners'.[7, p.xxiii] The difference today is that the
physical restraints of the Victorian asylum have been replaced by drug
treatments, whose effects are eloquently described by Kate Millett:

> The drug as healer, as official method now – is insidious, the true
> evil. Generally the drug is advocated because it pacifies and makes
> work easy for the aids and nurses, the guards. Actually, it does a
> great deal more, all very contrary to sanity, it induces visions,
> hallucinations, paranoia, mental confusion. Nothing could be
> harder than to maintain mental sanity against the onslaught of a
> drug.[27, p.67]

Women who refuse to be pacified by drugs (as many do), or who are
deemed difficult or unresponsive patients, are subjected to particular
scrutiny and regulation, often finding themselves pathologised for their very
acts of resistance. This was illustrated by David Rosenhan in his ethno-
graphic study,[87] where the protestations of sanity expressed by the

researchers who had entered psychiatric wards as stooges were deemed evidence of their madness.[x] For women patients, their sexuality or femininity is central to this pathologisation. For example, Charlotte Ross, committed to Essondale secure psychiatric hospital in British Columbia in the early 1950s, was described as exhibiting 'arrest in psychosexual development', and suspected 'latent homosexuality' as a result of her resistance to medical authority.[3, p.92] In order to quash this resistance, and engender compliance and submission, women are often threatened with more aversive 'treatments', as is evidenced by Janet Frame's account in 1961 of the fear of falling outside the boundaries of acceptable patient behaviour in her autobiographic account of psychiatric hospitalisation:

> I dreaded that one day Matron Glass hearing that I had been 'difficult' or 'uncooperative' would address me sharply, 'Right. Single room for you, my lady.' Hearing other people threatened so often made me more afraid, and seeing that a patient, in the act of being taken to a single room, always struggled and screamed, made me morbidly curious about what the room contained that, overnight, could change people who screamed and disobeyed into people who sat, withdrawn, and obeyed listlessly when ordered Dayroom, Dining room, Bed. . . . And Ward Two was my fear. They sent you there if you were 'un-cooperative' or if persistent doses of E.S.T. [sic] did not produce in you an improvement that was judged largely by your submission and prompt obedience to orders . . . [So] you learned with earnest dedication to 'fit in'; you learned not to cry in company but to smile and pronounce yourself pleased, and to ask from time if you could go home, as proof that you were getting better and therefore in no need to be smuggled in the night to Ward Two. You learned the chores, to make your bed with the government motto facing the correct way and the corners of the counterpane neatly angled.[88, pp.82–83]

The ECT so feared by Janet Frame is one of the most common forms of treatment offered within psychiatric institutions (invariably offered alongside drug treatment). It was first used in Italy in the 1930s,[xi] following the observation that schizophrenia and epilepsy do not coincide, which led to the supposition that the inducement of grand mal seizures could cure schizophrenia.[89] The American Psychiatric Association recommends that ECT be used only as a last resort treatment, for cases of severe depression; however, there is evidence that it is used far more broadly, and instead of other treatments, rather than as the last resort.[89] Indeed, ECT has increased in popularity in recent years, following a drop in the 1980s. For example, in Australia in 2008 there were 20,121 treatments given nationally, an increase of 50 per cent on the figure recorded 10 years previously.[90] As was noted in the previous chapter, women make up the bulk of these cases. Thus in 2001–2002 in Ontario, Canada, ECT was administered to 889 women and 425 men, with 7,514 treatments given to women and 3,546 to men – women making up 68 per cent of the total in both counts.[91]

In contrast to the claim that patients experience ECT as a 'helpful treatment',[92] Bonnie Burstow has described it as 'state sponsored violence against women',[93, p.115] and Carol Warren as literally a 'shocking experience'.[89, p.287] Burstow goes on to argue that it is a 'frighteningly anti-woman' practice, as 'it is women's brains and lives that are being violated [and] overwhelmingly women's brains, memory and intellectual functioning that are seen as dispensable', with women 'being terrorized and controlled'.[93, p.116] The testimony of many women who have experienced ECT supports this viewpoint. For example, women interviewed by Lucy Johnstone described ECT as 'torture' or 'barbaric';[xii] 'like being hit over the head by a hammer'; 'going to your death, your doom'; feeling as if 'they were trying to kill me'; feeling 'bashed, abused . . . an assault'; feeling 'like a slave . . . no control, it was awful'.[94, pp.75–76, p.82] ECT has also been described by survivors as making them 'feel like an animal',[93, p.117] or as 'worthless', a 'non person and it didn't matter what happened to me',[94, p.76] as well as confirming that they were 'crazy' or 'mad'.[94, p.76] Fear of ECT is palpable in these accounts, partly resulting from seeing the effects on others. As one woman said:

> When you'd been on the ward there were other people who had had ECT and all the other people were scared by this . . . you would see them afterwards when they couldn't remember who they were and were very confused and had terrible headaches and weren't themselves at all.

Others were afraid because of their own experiences: 'I thought maybe the second time around it'll be much easier and I won't feel so scared and terrified, but it was just the same, if not a bit more'.[94, p.75] Mary Jane Ward, in her autobiographical novel *The snake pit* (1946), leaves little room for ambiguity in her account of her experience of ECT:

> They put a wedge under her back. It was most uncomfortable. It forced her back into an unnatural position. She looked at the dull glass eye on the wall and she knew that it would soon glow and that she would not see the glow. They were going to electrocute her, not operate upon her. Even now the woman was applying a sort of foul-smelling paste to your temples. What had you done? You wouldn't have killed anyone and what other crime is there that exacts such a severe penalty? . . . Now the woman is putting

clamps on your head, on the paste smeared temples and here came another one, another nurse garbed woman and she leaned on your feet as if in a minute you might rise up from the table and strike the ceiling. Your hands are tied down, your legs held down. Three against one and the one entangled in machinery. She opened her mouth to call for a lawyer and the silly woman thrust a gag into it and said, 'Thankyou, dear,' and the foreign devil with the angelic smile and the beautiful voice gave a conspiratorial nod. Soon it would be over. In a way you were glad.[95, pp.68–69]

While the World Health Organization recommends that ECT is offered only on a voluntary basis,[96] many women still endure forced ECT, as evidenced by the case of Simone D., whose lawyer unsuccessfully challenged the right of Creedmore psychiatric hospital in New York State to administer 30 'maintenance' shock treatments in 2007, to add to the 200 she had received previously.[97] Alternatively, women are threatened with continued psychiatric incarceration,[e.g. 98] with forced treatment, or with penalties such as losing custody of their children, if they do not agree to ECT. As one woman told Lucy Johnstone:

They asked me if I would agree to it, but they did say if I refused they'd go ahead with it anyway . . . being forced to stay there is bad enough but being forced to have something that you don't want is ten times worse, so I did agree yes.[94, p.74]

Another woman told the UK Advocacy Network: 'I was told my baby daughter would be put into foster care if I didn't have ECT (even though my husband could have looked after her)'.[99, p.37] For women who have experienced child sexual abuse – estimated to be over 50 per cent of psychiatric inpatients[100] – ECT can be experienced as a repetition of the abuse. As one woman interviewed by Johnstone commented: 'I did think about it a couple of times going through the ECT, that this was some form of abuse, being put on you when you don't want it, or being more or less said that you've got to have it'.[94, p.77]

As the benefits of ECT are highly questionable – there is evidence that it is no more effective than placebo in alleviating either depression,[101] or suicide risk;[102] there is little justification for forcibly subjecting women to this form of treatment. Citing experimental research, Bonnie Burstow argues that ECT causes brain damage, in particular, frontal lobe atrophy, which leads to memory loss and intellectual impairment.[93; 103] In Lucy Johnstone's interviews with ECT survivors, women's accounts of ECT confirm this picture,[94, pp.77–78] stories of forgetting people they know, their children's childhoods, or difficulties in comprehending books or television:

My memory is terrible, absolutely terrible. I can't remember Sarah's first steps, and that's really hurtful . . . losing the memory of the kids growing up was awful.

I can be reading a magazine and I get halfway through or nearly to the end and I can't remember what it's about, so I've got to read it all over again. Same with a film or program on the telly.

People would come up to me on the street that knew me and would tell me how they knew me and I had no recollection of them at all . . . very frightening.

It's a void, I can't describe it, and there's also a feeling of something fundamental that I don't even know what is missing . . . just like an intrinsic part of me that I feel isn't there and it was once. . . . Part of me feels like there was a real death of something, something died during that time.

My own recollections of my mother's ECT are of her complete loss of short term memory, as well as a drastic change in personality, accompanied by fear of future shocks which saw her desperately trying to pretend she was happy, when she clearly was not. These effects are acknowledged by psychiatrists such as Abraham Meyerson, who sees them as 'an important factor in the curative process'.[93, p.116] This is partly because ECT produces acquiescent patients, who are, in the words of Jonas Robitscher, 'easy to manage, sleep a great deal, [and] do not need much nursing care'.[89, p.298; 104] But it is also because ECT is deemed to restore women to 'normal' marital functioning, where previous resistance to the archetypal feminine role is literally forgotten. This is illustrated by the case of Wendy Funk, who was given ECT during her stay in a locked ward in 1989, under threat of being shipped away if she refused, with her 'problem' being identified by her psychiatrist as 'feminist-type thinking' and being resistant to control by her husband.[105] The profound amnesia that resulted from her treatment encouraged the prescription of a further course of ECT, with Wendy being told it was 'for the sake of your family', because 'making' her husband worry was 'not a good thing for a wife to do'.[93, p.119] Wendy's husband Dan was supportive of her treatment, as were many of the relatives of women ECT survivors interviewed by Carol Warren. For example, Mr Karr felt that it was 'for the good' that his wife 'couldn't remember anything' when she 'wasn't herself' prior to her hospital admission, being particularly pleased that the ECT had 'made his wife forget her hostile outbursts towards him'.[89, p.294] Other women are silenced by fear of further ECT: Mary Yale said that she had such a 'dread fear of shock' that she would not express her feelings to her husband any more, adding that 'shock treatment is a helluva way to treat marital problems – the problems involved both of us'.[89, p.298] Similarly, a woman (interviewed by Lucy Johnstone), who was feeling suicidal at the time, would not discuss her feelings with her community psychiatric nurse because she had previously had enforced ECT, and did not want this experience repeated. She commented: 'It was a useful lesson really. It's not sensible in this world to tell psychiatrists of your, what they call "delusional systems", and in fact I never told them another one'.[94, p.79]

Some women have embraced these side effects of ECT, citing forgetfulness, or feeling like a new person, as the benefits of the treatment. Thus Shirley Arlen (interviewed by Carol Warren) said:

I think the shock treatments are supposed to make you forget – when you do break down or whatever it is you do to get in here [psychiatric hospital] . . . I mean it succeeded with me – I can't remember a lot of things – but I'd rather not.[89, p.289]

Joan Baker described herself as a 'different person' because she could forget about her father not liking her as a child,[89, p.289] which was similar to the comment of one of Johnstone's interviewees, who said:

I felt as though I had become a completely different person . . . I felt as if I had totally gone off my head . . . I think ECT blasted me into this other reality . . . I felt I'd lost the person I used to be . . . before I had ECT, that all disappeared entirely.[94, p.78]

Conversely, Rachel Perkins described 'delight at being "me" again' after six sessions of ECT,[106, p.625] dealing with memory loss by writing things down. Some women wanted these effects and were regretful at not achieving them, such as Rita Vick, who told Carol Warren: 'I thought the shock treatments would help . . . they made me forget some things, but not enough. I haven't had enough I guess'.[89, p.290] These stand as examples of women erased or remade by ECT, with the aim of making them 'sane'. Reading these accounts, it is hard to disagree with Bonnie Burstow's conclusion that ECT functions as a 'formidable and comprehensive method of social control' of women.[93, p.118] However, the reality for most women who seek professional help for depression (or for a range of non-specific psychological 'symptoms') is a prescription for psychotropic medication. When we look at contemporary advertisements and media representations of psychotropic drugs, and the myths of madness they perpetuate, it is not difficult to see why.

Medicating women's madness

A Valium advertisement from 1970 in the *Archives of General Psychiatry* states:

> *Jan, 35, single and psychoneurotic* You probably see many such Jans in your practice. The unmarrieds with low self esteem. Jan never found a man to measure up to her father. Now she realises she's in a losing position – and that she may never marry. Valium (Diazepam) can be a useful adjunct in the therapy of the tense, over anxious patient who has a neurotic sense of failure, guilt or loss.[107, p.148]

Women have always predominated in advertisements for psychotropic medication, to a degree that far outweighs their representation in mental health statistics.[107] For example, in the 1970s, women were depicted as the dominant users of tranquillisers, whereas advertisements for other drugs depicted an equal number of men and women, or more men.[108] Similarly, in a study of antidepressant advertisements in the 1980s, women were found to outnumber men as examples of 'patients' by ten to one in *American Family Physician*, and by five to one in the *American Journal of Psychiatry*.[109] In all of these images, women are usually portrayed as having diffuse emotional symptoms and poor coping abilities, whereas the male patients who appear are seen to be suffering from temporary work related stress, with effective ways of coping at their disposal.[110] For example, in a study which tracked gender (im)balance in psychotropic advertising over three decades, reporting that the proportion of women in advertisements had increased between 1981 and 2001, Sarah Munce and colleagues found that women were depicted as well dressed and attractive, and located in the home, garden or a social setting,[111] while men were portrayed at work.[xiii] This places women in a traditional sexualised, domestic and dependent role, whereas men are depicted as productive, independent citizens who have a higher social status – reinforcing traditional gender stereotypes.

The ways in which women are depicted in pharmaceutical advertising has changed over recent decades, reflecting, to a degree, the changes in women's roles brought about by feminism. As Jonathan Metzl has argued in his book *Prozac on the couch*,[107] advertisements for tranquillisers in the 1960s depicted 'psychopharmacological momism' – a harried and anxious housewife, her wedding ring prominently on display, who cannot 'function' at 'home', seeking solace from a male doctor. In the 1970s, however, when the benzodiazepine Valium stood as the best selling drug in pharmaceutical history,[xiv] images of the drug itself had replaced the medicating man, and the woman 'patient' appeared alone. Thus one of the most widely circulating ads, quoted in the epigraph to this section, depicted 'Jan', who was

'35, single and psychoneurotic' because she had 'never found a man to measure up to her father'.[107, p.149] While apparently contradictory, both sets of images portray the potential threat to hetero-normativity by 'mad' women. The anxious housewife threatens the happiness and cohesion of the family, at the same time as she stands as an implicit criticism of her marital and family life – suggesting that this may be the cause of her pathology.[107, p.141] The 'single and psychoneurotic' Jan appears to be rejecting the family altogether, through being so picky that she cannot find a man to marry, which is not simply represented as the cause of the illness, 'but as the illness itself'.[107, p.145]

Both sets of advertisements promise chemical solutions for women's distress, restoring the rightful order of the 'male-female role system',[107, p.145] through relaxing women's discontent in order to enable them to be happy in marriage or motherhood. As the advertisements depicting the post-medicated woman declare, 'I got my marriage back', 'I got my playfulness back', 'I got my mommy back'.[107, p.155] Hetero-normativity restored. This depiction of women as mad because of being unhappy in love is not unique to psychotropic drug advertisements. Literary critics have dissected representations of mad women in nineteenth century literature and poetry, concluding that the most common motive for madness was desertion or disappointment in love.[22; 113] This narrative supports the perception of femininity as a labile, reactive, and characteristically unstable condition, with women's lives and minds irrevocably connected to those of men. It is the flipside of the happy ever after ending in fairy stories – the woman driven to despair because she *hasn't* found her man.

The advent in 1987 of the 'wonder drug' Prozac, the most widely known brand of SSRI marketed by the drug company Eli Lilly, changed the focus of psychotropic marketing from anxiety to depression, and depicted women in situations reflecting our changed position in society – less of the housewife or heartbroken singleton, and more of the career woman or 'working Mom'. There was also a shift to locating the problem within the woman's biology, mirroring developments in biological psychiatry at this time. For example, in a study which examined advertisements for SSRI antidepressants over the period 1985–2000, Jonathan Metzl and Joni Angel reported that there was a clear shift in later years towards positioning women's normative reactions to life events associated with marriage, motherhood, menstruation, or menopause as psychiatric illnesses which warrant SSRI medication, resulting in emotional experiences such as 'being overwhelmed with sadness', or 'never feeling happy' being positioned as depression.[114] This stands in contrast to the biomedical positioning of men's depression as 'an illness with bio-chemical roots',[114, p.580] suggesting that normal reactions to life's vicissitudes are less likely to be pathologised in men. A particular model of idealised femininity is being promulgated in these ads – a calm, coping, in control woman – with deviations from this script pathologised, and assumed to require drug treatment, as Prozac promised to restore a woman's 'Productive Days'.[114, p.578]

The representation of women's 'problems' associated with the reproductive body, or with their husbands, as indicators of the need for psychotropic drugs is not confined to advertisements in medical journals; it also occurs in the mass media, including newspapers, magazines and popular journals. *Cosmopolitan* celebrated the 'new nerve pills' of the late 1950s, telling us that after taking the relaxant drugs 'frigid women who abhorred marital relations reported they responded more readily to their husbands advances'.[115, cited by 107, p.105] Jonathan Metzl analysed popular articles on depression from 1985 to 2000;[116] he concluded that there was evidence of gendered diagnostic bracket creep, the widening of gender specific criteria for depression which legitimised the use of SSRIs for women. Thus stories in the popular press about SSRIs, in particular Prozac, portray it as a 'drug for our time' (*New Scientist*),[117,p.280] a miracle drug, which can help women to feel 'normal', 'grounded' and 'better than well' (*Prozac Nation*),[118, p.356] providing 'chemical help to be a supermom' (*Time*).[117, p.280] We are told that while '70 per cent of women suffer before their periods', Prozac can help to 'make their jobs and housework easier to manage' (*Health*).[117, p.280] The cause of these problems is firmly located in biology, with explanations including 'misfiring synapses', 'disregulated circuitary', and 'neuronal hardwiring'.[117, p.274] As women are described as experiencing 'lessened sensitivity' on Prozac (*Newsweek, American Health, Time, Psychology Today*),[117, p.280] is it that SSRIs make them more like Stepford Wives?

The woman represented in stories about Prozac is the antithesis of the cowed and dependent housewife who was encouraged to turn to 'mother's little help', Valium, in the 1960s and 1970s. Tapping into a post-feminist neoliberal discourse of equality, women are portrayed as being able to work productively alongside men, as long as they are liberated from hormonal or mood fluctuations. As Jonathan Metzl has argued, rather than being represented by 'strung out Neely in Valley of the Dolls', who could not cope with the pressures of working in a man's world, the 'Prozac hero(ine)' is more like 'Rebecca Buck, a.k.a. Tank girl, a fearless heroine with looks to match, who wears a necklace of silver-dipped Prozac'[118, p.356] Lauded as a 'feminist' drug by its (Eli Lilly funded) supporters, such as Peter Kramer,[119] we are told that Prozac allows women to be 'hyperthymic' – or more accurately, manically hyper-productive.[118, p.357] In their analysis of popular articles on Prozac from 1987–2000, Linda Blum and Nena Stracuzzi described the *Newsweek* story of Helen, a typical Prozac heroine,[117] who was a public relations executive previously 'paralysed' by 'looming deadlines', but who could now 'juggle competing priorities . . . gracefully . . . with a more buoyant personality'.[117, p.278] *New Scientist* is more explicit, describing Prozac as a drug that helps women to be 'ambitious, extrovert, go-getters' in order to achieve 'the success that society now expects of them'.[117, p.279] Prozac thus functions to 'normalise feminism as superwomanism'.[120, p.63] However, while the story might seem to be about success and accomplishment, the implicit message is that women need chemical help to be able to achieve this – like the men who were depicted as failing at work in the drug advertisements of the 1980s, needing antidepressants to keep them functioning.

The productive neoliberal feminine subject depicted in Prozac narratives (post-treatment at least) is not only disciplined in her work, but also disciplined in her body. Blum and Stacuzzi found that Prozac was often linked to losing weight, with reports that it is used by 'dieters' (*Business Week*), with a success rate that gives it 'cult status' (*New York Times*). In a similar vein, Prozac success stories describe women as 'hot young thing(s)', or as 'fit', 'taut' and 'lean'.[117, P.276] The ideals of body surveillance and management which constitute the ideal female subject are thus resurrected and reinforced,[121] and women encouraged to turn to SSRIs in their attempts to achieve these almost impossible ideals. This is again a hetero-normative version of womanhood; women thriving in the heterosexual marketplace post medication. One of the characters in Peter Kramer's best seller (and Eli Lilly funded) *Listening to Prozac*,[119] who is described in many magazine articles, is Tess, who was 'weary and lonely' before Prozac, but is now 'altogether more cool', and as a result is dating (men),[117, p.280] reminiscent of Jan in the 1970 Valium advertisement.

Similarly, in an analysis of Prozac heroines in popular novels and self-help books, Metzl concluded that Prozac is depicted as an 'agent restoring heterosexual normalization and stability'.[118, p.360] Thus one character, Julia, describes marital dissatisfaction that disappears after treatment; Anne got back together with her boyfriend and is now happily married; and Elizabeth Wurtzel writes in her autobiographical account *Prozac nation* of finding 'real love'. This is reminiscent of comments previously made about women 'hysterics': Plato's belief that heterosexual sex and pregnancy would cure a woman's symptoms; or comments made by Elizabeth Zetzel, treating women in Boston in the mid 1940s, that 'true good hysterics' had invariably 'failed to achieve a mature heterosexual relationship'.[122, p.327]

Medical practitioners take up this medicalised mantle and advocate psychotropic medication as the solution for women's misery, a recommendation which is often difficult to resist. As Daphne Gottlieb described in her autobiographical account *Lady Lazarus: Uncoupleting suicide and poetry*:

The doctor told me it was the best option: medication. There was a pill, she said, and the pill would help. I might not want to die every second. I would not feel boiled in my skin every moment . . . I would do anything not to hurt anymore. That's why I was in her office.[123, p.27]

However, psychotropic drugs are not universally embraced by women, despite the message promulgated in marketing campaigns or medical consultations. For women who initially accept a prescription, often because of feelings of desperation described by Gottlieb,[123] above, coming off the drugs is rarely easy, because of both physical and psychological dependency. Here are the comments of women interviewed by Elizabeth Ettore and Elianne Riska,[2, p.136] attesting to the double bind many women are in regarding such drug use:

I am afraid of the pills and would like to stop but cannot, so I am hooked in a way . . . I am . . . afraid of getting dependent (*57 year old teacher*).

I would be happy to quit because I am afraid of their effects (*59 year old dressmaker*).

It does feel terrible, but I am . . . you get addicted to them [these drugs] to some extent. My self-confidence gets really high if I can be without them for some time (*33 year old part time cleaner*).

The websites promoting antidepressants provide no information about overcoming psychological or physical withdrawal, means of safely stopping of treatment, or about the length of time such formulations should be taken. Why should they? Their aim is to increase market share for their particular product, not to help consumers to stop taking it. It is in this light that we should view all material promulgated by Big Pharma – profit is the bottom line, not patient care, which was never more transparent than in the discussion of another supposed wonder treatment, hormone replacement therapy.

Medicalising menopause: promoting hormone replacement therapy

In 1998, Jaquelyn Zita writes:

The nightmare is real. One can foresee a world where women are expected to discipline their bodies and modify their personalities into high premium 'first world babes', energetically self-injected into the capitalist-intensive corporate and increasingly hypersexualized capital markets of an expanding transnational and male supremacist economy.[120, p.70]

92

Psychotropic medications are not the only medicalised treatments recommended by Big Pharma and its allies as treatments for women's distress. As the reproductive body is deemed by many to be central to women's depression and dysfunction, it is not surprising to find that hormonal interventions are also strongly advocated as chemical cures. This is particularly the case with menopause, where hormone replacement therapy (HRT) is a multibillion dollar industry, despite recent evidence of the negative consequences of HRT for women's health. While the womb has been positioned as the centre of women's madness for centuries, with menopause in particular deemed to be the cause of 'almost all the ills the flesh is heir to', in the words of one nineteenth century physician,[14, p.191] the gynaecologist Robert Wilson was the first to normalise the practice of a medically managed midlife for all women. His highly influential book *Feminine forever* (1966) described menopause as a deficiency disease which could be ameliorated by hormone replacement, resulting in a quadrupling of HRT sales in the years after its publication. It is no coincidence that Wilson's book and lecture tours were paid for by the drug company Wyeth Ayerst, which manufactures HRT.[124] Wilson described menopause as a 'living decay', manifested by 'thinning of bones, dowager's hump, ugly body contours, flaccidity of the breast, and atrophy of the genitals',[125, p.192] accompanied by 'low spirits, sadness or despondency'.[126, p.36] This view is perpetuated today, as is evidenced in this quote from a self-help booklet aimed at women *You and your menopause* (published in 2002):

> For one in four women the menopause is simply a ripple on the surface of their lives. The symptoms don't bother them and it doesn't cause any heart-searching. But a similar proportion of women can suffer physical and *psychological turmoil* which makes this time a stormy passage.[127, p.443, my emphasis]

Where HRT differs from psychotropic medication is that it is often offered as a prophylactic – creating a potential mass market of all menopausal women. Robert Wilson was the first to advocate HRT as 'menopause prevention',[126, p.19] telling women that 'instead of being condemned to witness the death of their own womanhood', they can 'remain fully feminine – physically and mentally – as long as they live'.[126, pp.16, 19] Women who resist this medicalisation have been warned of the dangers they are courting if they position menopause as 'just another physiologic event in the course of female reproduction, and do not seek medical help' for 'even "asymptomatic menopause"' may initiate silent, progressive, and ultimately lethal sequelae'.[128, p.2] HRT was thus advocated as a universal treatment for women at midlife, with experts proclaiming: 'It now seems reasonable to recommend that all post-menopausal women – regardless of age or menopausal symptoms – seriously be considered for hormone replacement therapy'.[129, p.67] And if women were not experiencing 'physical or psychological turmoil', they could still be persuaded to take HRT by its depiction as an anti-ageing elixir or beauty treatment, as evidenced by Lauren Hutton, the supermodel featured in Wyeth HRT ads, telling *Parade* magazine that oestrogen is 'good for your moods, it's good for your skin'.[130] It is also purported to be good for your sex life. The British politician Teresa Gorman has long been an outspoken advocate of HRT, claiming:

> My husband thinks it's terrific. Until you get to 50 he chases you around the bedroom but after HRT you are chasing him. HRT keeps you out of hospital, out of an old folk's home and out of the divorce courts.[131]

The multibillion dollar HRT industry admonishes women to do everything within their power to resist hormonal decline and atrophy – and the 'moodiness' of menopause. As one health guide sponsored by drug company Hoechst Roussel warns: 'Mood changes . . . respond well to hormonal replacement therapy and you should talk to your doctor about the range of treatments available'.[127, p.427] Advertisements for HRT published in medical journals continue to reinforce the view of the unwholesome or deficient menopausal body, with women at midlife depicted as 'out of control', 'grotesque', or stressed and confused.[132] For example, an advertisement for Premarin in the *Australian Medical Journal* warns in large bold print: 'This year nearly 80,000 Women will be introduced to Depression, Anxiety, Hot Flushes, Night Sweats, and Vaginal Problems'. In small print, the text continues: 'Not to mention an increased risk of osteoporosis and cardiovascular disease, among other things. The condition, of course, is the menopause'.[133, p.131]

Wilson's principal research, on which he based his book *Feminine forever* (1966), was an uncontrolled study of 304 women, aged 40 to 70, taking HRT, published in the *Journal of the American Medical Association* in 1962. It was on the basis of similar nonrandomised observational studies that HRT was promoted as a drug to reduce the risk of heart disease and osteoporosis. Indeed, the US Food and Drug Administration (FDA) was so confident that an advisory committee recommended that randomised controlled trials were not necessary.[134] When the FDA overruled its advisors, following pressure from the National Women's Health Network, the results were sobering. Large scale randomised controlled trials of HRT conducted in the UK,[135] and in the USA,[136] found that while HRT may reduce bone fractures and colorectal cancer, as well as hot flushes in the 25 per cent of women who suffer most severely,[137] it also significantly increases women's risk of breast cancer (by 26 per cent), heart disease (by 29 per cent) and strokes (by 41 per cent). Further UK research demonstrated a link between

HRT and ovarian cancer.[138] The findings of the Women's Health Initiative (WHI) trial, conducted with 160,000 US women, were so striking that trial was stopped three years early, in order to prevent further negative health consequences (including death) in the HRT group.

Unsurprisingly, the drug companies, and many in the medical profession, did not accept these findings without question. The *New York Times* reported that immediately after the release of the WHI findings,[139] Wyeth, the pharmaceutical company that supplied the drugs used in the trial, sent 500,000 'Dear Doctor' letters stressing the symptomatic benefits of HRT.[140] Subsequent publications in medical journals focused on critiquing minor points of the methodology of the HRT trials, in the attempt to promote the benefits of HRT,[e.g. 141, 142] and medical spokes-people have continued to recommend HRT as a widespread treatment for women.[e.g. 143, 144] David Sackett has sardonically commented that we should not blame the drug companies for their unscrupulous behaviour in promoting HRT,[140] as they were simply behaving as a model industry should in attempting to increase market share and profit for their share-holders.[xv] It will be interesting to see if this continues following the 2009 Philadelphia court judgment that ordered Pfizer (which bought Wyeth in 2003) to pay US$113 million as punitive damages to two women who contracted breast cancer following HRT.[145] As the market for HRT was over US$1.4 billion in 2008,[145] the profits still vastly outweigh financial damages, and so this court case may have little impact, unless it is opening the floodgates for future widespread litigation. The fact that drug com-panies, and their allies, continue to promote HRT when the damages to women's health are incontrovertible is inexcusable. Is there any drug that would be promoted to men, if it had the same health consequences? It is hard not to conclude that a deep seated misogyny underpins both Big Pharma and much of bio-psychiatry. What other explanation can we put forward to explain this dreadful state of affairs?

Therapy as tyranny

Vivien Burr and Trevor Butt write:

> The 'discovery' and isolating of syndromes and pathologies – and the provision of therapy and counselling as a response – is the latest phase in a long process of the development of disciplinary power in Western societies that has been going on since the eighteenth century. The practice of confession has been passed down to those experts and professionals – psychiatrists, psychol-ogists, psychotherapists, counsellors, among others – who are thought to be the appropriate monitors of our psychological well-being.[146, p.192]

Psychological and psychotherapeutic interventions may appear to be a positive alternative to biomedical and psychiatric modes of conceptualising and treating women's madness. Indeed, therapy is embraced by many women (including many feminists), as is outlined in Chapter 6. However, therapy has not escaped feminist scrutiny. Mary Daly described therapy as 'mind rape',[147, p.287] and compared it to Chinese footbinding, witch-hunting, suttee,[xvi] and sexual slavery. Lenora Fulani argued that 'traditional mental health treatment has done little but provide a label for emotionally disturbed women, often adding to their hardships with no plan for empowerment'.[148, p.xiii] Phyllis Chesler argued that 'the institution of private therapy is a patriarchal one'.[149, p.166] She compared therapy to marriage in that it involves an unequal relationship, serves to isolate women from each other, emphasises women's dependence on a stronger male authority figure, and enables women to diffuse anger by expressing it as emotional symptoms, which are then labelled as 'neurotic'. Both marriage and therapy are condemned for encouraging women to talk, rather than to act, and for serving to suppress women's righteous rage. Chesler also documented the widespread sexual abuse of women patients by their (primarily male) therapists, as well as the devastating consequences for these women, who have been violated when they are at their most vulnerable. More recent research has reported that between 4 and 12 per cent of male therapists admit to having sex with at least one client, demonstrating that this is still a significant problem.[150]

At the same time, psychological theories which underpin therapy have been dismissed by feminists for being overgeneralised and oversimplified,[151, p.298] or for being based on a positivist epistemology which positions women's distress as symptoms of an underlying disorder.[152, p.83] Indeed, feminist critics have argued that both biomedical and psychological theories of depression decontextualise what is often a social problem, simply acting to legitimise expert intervention, while negating the political, economic and discursive aspects of women's experience.[6; 153–154] And while cognitive behaviour therapy (CBT) is now recommended by many governments (including Australia and the UK) as a first line treatment for depression,[155] feminist critics have argued that there is little evidence of gender differences in the majority of cognitive 'deficits' deemed to underlie depression from a cognitive-behavioural perspective, which undermines the utility of such theories for explaining women's higher rate of reported depression.[156–157]

One of the primary feminist criticisms of psychological therapy is that the problem, as well as the solution to distress, is located solely within the woman. As Rachel Perkins, criticising therapy for lesbians, argued:

> Understandable unhappiness is rendered personal, private and pathological. The individual lesbian is rendered isolated and alone

in her distress. Something has gone wrong with her and there is nowhere to turn for help and support other than her therapist. Unhappiness becomes an individual problem that the individual must resolve rather than a shared event that our communities must address, accept and accommodate.[158, p.327]

As well as ignoring social context, psychological therapy is criticised for encouraging women to engage in self-management strategies which function as self-policing,[159] serving to maintain the status quo and produce more productive citizens.[160] The latter is evidenced by the 2006 Layard report,[161] published in the UK, which recommended setting up therapy centres across the nation, offering CBT in order to ensure that distressed people remain in the workforce, or return to work, with the justification that 'depression and anxiety make it difficult or impossible to work, and drive people onto Incapacity Benefits'.[161, p.1] Neoliberal concerns were clearly a primary motivator in the report – rather than the well-being of individuals who experience distress, or their families.

Psychiatrics and other health practitioners who make diagnoses, and offer psychological therapy, are not operating in a cultural vacuum. The discursive construction of women's unhappiness as the diagnostic category 'depression' in health policy,[159] medical journals,[162] self-help books,[163–164] drug company literature,[111; 114] women's magazines,[159] and other mass circulated literature,[117] has also been criticised for playing a significant role in women's distress being labelled as a pathological illness, with women being positioned as mad as a result. In each of these contexts, the 'truth' of women's greater propensity to depression is repeated as un-questioned fact, as is illustrated by a NIMH self-help pamphlet,[165] entitled *Women and depression: Discovering hope* (2008): 'Depression affects both men and women, but more women than men are likely to be diagnosed with depression in any given year'.[165, p.2] Women are encouraged to adopt a biomedical discourse as explanation for their 'down' times, as is illustrated by the earlier NIMH self-help pamphlet, *Depression: What every woman should know* (2000), quoted below:

> Life is full of emotional ups and downs. But when the 'down' times are long lasting or interfere with your ability to function, you may be suffering from a common, serious illness – depression. Yet, because it often goes unrecognized, depression continues to cause unnecessary suffering.[166]

In this pamphlet, women are depicted as emotional by nature, resulting in their diagnosis as depressed being harder to recognise. Indeed, we are told it 'seems almost a natural outgrowth of their personalities'.[166, p.113] Women are thus encouraged to be vigilant for signs of this insidious illness – to engage in self-surveillance, and subsequently, in self-policing, by presenting to a doctor for a 'complete diagnostic evaluation', or to engage in self-management, where they are expected to 'pull themselves out of' depression.[167]

Self-management of madness: promoting self-policing

Nikolas Rose writes:

> In the nineteenth century psychology invented the normal individual . . . It has invented what one might term the therapies of normality or the psychologies of everyday life, the pedagogies of self-fulfilment disseminated through the mass media, which translate the enigmatic desires and dissatisfactions of the individual into precise ways of inspecting oneself and working upon oneself in or to realize one's potential, gain happiness, and exercise one's autonomy.[168, p.17]

Biomedical models do not stand alone in popular representations of women's madness. There is an alternative discourse of 'self-management', which locates the solution to problems such as 'depression' within the woman. In a study of representations of depression in popular Australian women's magazines, from 1998 to 2002, Susan Gattuso and colleagues found that the most common representations of depression was of a reaction to life events or relationship issues, with self-management strategies, followed by support from family and friends, being the most commonly advocated solutions.[159] The strategies suggested included reading self-help books, meditation, self-sufficiency, seeking support from friends and family, as well as leisure and lifestyle remedies. Even though depression was predominantly positioned as an 'illness', drug treatments were mainly suggested as an adjunct to other coping strategies, such as 'a form of counselling called cognitive behaviour therapy, which teaches you to have a more realist attitude to yourself and life-events' (*Australian Women's Weekly*).[159, p.1645] In a similar vein, the UK *Daily Mail* newspaper encouraged women 'with hectic jobs . . . [who] are often most in denial about the stress in their lives' to engage in 'simple talking therapies . . . designed to give women a better sense of perspective and improved self-worth to help cut stress levels'.[169, p.41]

On the surface, this may seem positive: women are not being encouraged to medicate themselves into oblivion, and are given a sense of agency about their 'nameless misery'. However, in common with the majority of consumer literature on depression,[164] these accounts completely ignore socio-cultural explanations for women's distress, locating the problem solely within. The 'self-management' strategies women are encouraged to embrace are also implicitly about self-policing and self-regulation. Women are told to engage in self-surveillance, and diagnose 'depression', even when they thought they were merely 'sad'. As the following extract from the widely circulated, and authoritative, *Australian Women's Weekly* (November 2001) states:

Are You Secretly Sad? If you can't remember the last time you felt anything but the blues, you could be suffering from one of the least diagnosed forms of depression in which chronic sadness feels 'normal' . . . For a growing number of Australians the blues are a way of life rather than an occasional hiccup.[159, p.1642]

As surveys tell us that increasing numbers of Australian women feel 'stressed out', 'time poor', with negative consequences for relationships and feelings of well-being,[170] there is every reason to think that significant numbers of women reading this magazine would pause for thought and decide they merited a diagnosis of depression. Given the implicit message of 'get over it' (or rather, 'get yourself over it') that accompanies the exhortation to self-diagnose, these same women are likely to feel responsible for their 'blues', for they are firmly told that they have the means for happiness at their own disposal, if they could only manage their moods (or life) more effectively. As Dana Becker has argued, 'the 19th century rest cure has been supplanted by scented candles and pastel yoga mats'.[169, p.39] When women *cannot* simply reduce their 'stress' or 'depression', this can result in feelings of inadequacy, shame and self-blame, which can send women running to the biomedical experts, who promise a simple drug induced miracle cure, as this locates any control for emotional distress outside of the woman.[159]

Similarly, 'self-help' books reinforce the message of menopause as a deficiency disease, with women's midlife experiences positioned as 'symptoms', and women positioned as 'patients'.[171] The menopause may be described as a 'natural process' in these contexts, with 'alternative' remedies suggested, and women encouraged to take control of their bodies,[see 172] but the menopause is still framed as a 'battle to be won', or an 'imbalance', leading to problematic bodily and psychological experiences.[127] Menopause is also positioned as 'confusing', or as a 'complicated' time in a woman's life,[171] reinforcing the notion of the reproductive body as a mysterious force which merits surveillance to ensure 'management'. Ironically, the feminist notion of 'menopause as natural', which set out to challenge the dominance of the medical model of menopause as an illness, has also now been harnessed by the drug companies as a rhetorical strategy to construct HRT as a 'natural' replacement for menopausal hormonal deficiency, in an attempt to counter many women's reluctance to take HRT in the face of claims of the increased risks of endometrial and breast cancer.[173]

A process of subjectification: women taking up the mantle of madness

In 1987, Michel Foucault commented:

> Nothing could be more false than the myth of madness as an illness that is unaware of itself as such . . . The way in which a subject accepts or rejects his illness, the way he interprets it and gives signification to its absurd forms, constitutes one of the essential dilemmas of the illness.[174, pp.46–47]

This is not simply about fictions framed as facts, frozen in the sphere of representation. Contemporary constructions of women's madness, and of the marvels of psychotropic drugs and hormones, or the importance of self-management to treat disorders such as depression, function as regimes of truth which facilitate the diagnosis of women as 'mad' – by health professionals, or by women themselves. Within medicalised discourse, women's negative emotions and reasonable responses to daily living, or to family life, are positioned as 'symptoms' worthy of psychiatric diagnosis. Symptom checklists in women's magazines or on websites (the latter often funded by Big Pharma) facilitate the process of self-diagnosis, at the same time as they deny the complexities of women's experiences.[175] This acts to position all women as potential patients, if they ever feel sad or 'blue', have 'low self-esteem', lack desire for sex (with a man), feel overwhelmed by responsibilities at work or at home, or feel regretful about their current relationship status. How many women can say that they have never felt any of the above?

The direct influence of SSRI advertising in the positioning of women as mad was illustrated in a study of medical records of patients diagnosed with 'depressive disorder' across a 15 year time period (1985–2000) – the post-Prozac generation.[xvii] Jonathan Metzl reported that descriptions of women's depression as being related to marriage, relationships, motherhood or menstruation increased from 50 per cent in 1985 to 97 per cent in 1995 and 2000,[116] mirroring the pattern of SSRI advertising prevalent during that same period reported above.[114] The depiction of women in pharmaceutical advertising has also been implicated in the greater likelihood of physicians diagnosing women with anxiety, psychoneurosis or depression,[111; 176] and then treating them with psychotropic medication, as advertising is known to play a major role in guiding physicians' drug prescription.[177]

Regimes of knowledge about women's madness are also implicated in self-diagnosis, or acceptance of professional diagnosis, a process that has been described as subjectification[168] – women taking up the subject position of the psychiatric other, accepting diagnosis of 'mental illness', as madness is medically defined. There is evidence that many women only label their unhappiness as 'depression', and as a result take up a biomedical model to explain their 'symptoms', seeing themselves as 'depressed', after receiving medical diagnosis and treatment.[160; 178] For example, in a series of interviews with women who had received a formal diagnosis from a physician, Deanna Gammell and Janet Stoppard found that prior to diagnosis, all but one of the women attributed their experiences to their everyday lives.[178] They described feeling 'messed up' or burnt out, being unable to function at work, having problems with concentration, and 'feeling kind of down',[178, p.116] but did not see this as an illness, depression. As Sarah commented, before her diagnosis:

> I just thought it was more like a burn out, like I thought maybe it was just my job . . . I thought maybe it had partly to do with that . . . thinking oh, I can't handle it any more . . . I kind of blamed it on that initially, thinking, ok, it's maybe I'm not handling my job in perspective.[178, p.116]

After formal diagnosis, the women reinterpreted their experiences as 'symptoms' which were primarily seen to be caused by chemical imbalances in the brain, with medicalised terms such as 'illness', 'disease', 'sick', and 'cure' being used. This functioned to absolve women from blame for their symptoms, as Kelly commented 'I'm not crazy, I'm not just a spoiled brat . . . I'm not being selfish'.[178, p.117] It also neutralised the stigma associated with madness, as Gloria commented 'it isn't anything to be ashamed of, I mean, it's the same as any other illness. You're depressed, well you've got a bad heart, so what's the difference?'.[178, p.117]xviii At the same time, the women made a distinction between their 'real' (non-depressed) self and the depressed self, suggesting that they were now disowning the sick self, over which they believed they had no control. This obviously has implications in terms of women's coping, as the women are accepting the medicalised positioning of passive patient, subject to the drug 'treatment' provided by the all powerful medical physician.xix

In this vein, Tess, the case study 'patient' in Peter Kramer's *Listening to Prozac*, is described as feeling truly herself after taking SSRIs,[179] saying 'as if I had been in a drugged state all these years and now I am clear-headed'.[119, p.8] Julia, another case, says, 'I don't feel myself' after coming off the medication, having turned into 'a witch again',[119, p.29] a 'pessimistic angry demanding' wife. Following the use of Prozac, Tracy Thompson said she noticed a 'moment of silence' in her brain: 'I was a body floating to the surface of the water, and then my face felt the air and I breathed, for the first time in a long time, a long cool draft of oxygen'.[180, p.249] If women who are diagnosed with depression identify with these messages of splitting, and are receptive to the messages promulgated about such drugs as solutions, it is not surprising that so many accept the prescriptions passed over by physicians and psychiatrists who offer a chemical cure (see Chapter 5 for a discussion of this in relation to PMS).

Acknowledging the construction and lived experience of women's distress

All of these arguments support a social constructionist analysis of women's madness, wherein psychiatric diagnosis is seen as a historically and culturally specific process which functions to position those deemed to have 'disorders' such as depression, PMDD or BPD as outsiders, as mad, serving to legitimise medical intervention and control.[xx] The very legitimacy of individual diagnostic categories is questioned, as is the objectivity and neutrality of those making diagnoses and offering treatment – in particular the bio-psychiatrists with their pecuniary connections to Big Pharma, the industry that most profits from women's madness, as outlined in Chapter 2.

Despite the welcome addition of these critiques, there are limitations in taking a solely social constructionist analysis of women's madness. First, the focus on language and discourse can appear to negate women's lived experience and negotiation of distress,[xxi] women's agency, and women's subjectivity, 'ending up with a socially determined subject', in Wendy Hollway's words.[196, p.5] Social constructionism has also been criticised for negating the 'real',[see 197; 198] and in its denial of realism, leading to an 'abyss of relativism . . . in a world where "truth" is all but abandoned'.[199, p.50]xxii We have to acknowledge that many women *do* undoubtedly experience extreme and debilitating despair, which comes to be categorised as 'depression'. This was described by one sufferer as a 'psychic freight train of roaring despair', which felt as if 'the waters were going to suck me down into some huge waterfall that somehow existed below the surface, a silent, downward rush of current'.[180, pp.4,43] Emily, interviewed by Michelle LaFrance about her diagnosis of depression, described her experiences thus:

> I couldn't think straight. I just sat there and spun my wheels and . . . it got to the point I didn't even want to come home . . . wouldn't answer the phone . . . wouldn't do anything with anybody . . . wouldn't even shower . . . I just felt so rock bottom. That I was just nothing, I was no good for anything, I was a failure.[154, p.14]

In her memoir *Prozac nation* (1995), Elizabeth Wurtzel described her depression thus:

> That's the thing about depression: A human being can survive almost anything, as long as she sees the end in sight. But depression

is so insidious, and it compounds daily, that it's impossible to ever see the end. The fog is like a cage without a key.[203, p.24]

Similarly, Daphne Gottlieb described her depression as 'real, pervasive, unshakable. It was eating me from the inside and wouldn't stop . . . It felt like a dark wave, its shadow looming from miles above. Sooner or later, the crest would curl like a fist, crushing me below'.[123, pp.30–31] Many of the women we interviewed about PMS gave accounts of debilitating anger, anxiety or depression premenstrually:

Emotionally I get angry, really angry about nothing. I'm talking really angry and anxious, I start . . . sometimes I start shaking or you know sort of you know, sort of, you know, I have high anxiety and angry and I tend to blow things out of proportion . . . I can get teary too but mainly just I feel agro more than anything . . . Oh, it's horrible and scary, I just want to explode, I feel like I want to arrgh, explode (*Rachel*).

I know that I'm sort of pre-menstrual because I'm very irritable. Um . . . hypersensitive. Ready for an argument with anyone. Um . . . and where . . . overly emotional, as well, you know, like, I sort of cry at the drop of a hat, you know . . . everything seems so much worse during that time (*Fiona*).

I stayed in bed all day crying, um I just spent days just um crying, and wouldn't come out of my room and that's when my mum, had to get back involved and helped, took the kids for a couple of days, demanded that if I don't go an get some help, she's gonna take them permanently (*Sandra*).

Penny, who was interviewed by Helen Malson about her experiences of anorexia, said the 'anger and the fear were kind of just . . . being Penny I think, of being me . . . I think it was a fear of being me . . . I just wanted to fade away'.[204, p.142] Kate Bornstein described her own experiences of self-injury and starvation thus:

I hated my body so I spent as little time as I could connected to it. I cut on my body so I could return to it. I cut I could feel *something*, better than nothing. It was temporary relief. Then I taught myself how to stop eating.[205, p.217]

Ginny Elkin, who was diagnosed with borderline personality disorder, wrote an account of her therapy in conjunction with her therapist, Irvin Yalom, describing herself as living 'in a confusing and unsystematic fashion', accompanied by a 'litany of self-hatred'.[84, p.129] This is her summary of her experiences, presented in the third person:

> She is masochistic in all things. All her life she has neglected her own needs and pleasures. She has no respect for herself. She feels she is a disembodied spirit – a chirping canary hopping back and forth from shoulder to shoulder, as she and her friends walk down the street. She imagines that only as an ethereal wisp is she of any interest to others . . . She is consumed with self-contempt. A small voice inside endlessly taunts her. Should she forget herself for a moment and engage life spontaneously, the pleasure stripping voice brings her back sharply to her casket of self-consciousness.[206, p.xii]

We cannot deny these vivid accounts of distress. Equally, we need to understand why women experience such extreme distress and debilitation, even if we are critical of diagnostic categories such as depression, PMDD, or borderline personality disorder. Feminists who dismiss medicalisation are also left with the dilemma that at an individual level, diagnoses such as depression can serve to validate to women that there is a 'real' problem, isolating prolonged misery from 'the character of the sufferer'.[160, p.130] For some women, adopting a biomedical model to explain their experiences as 'depression' means that they aren't simply 'crazy' or 'malingering', as depression is positioned as something they cannot avoid, rather than it being a personal failing. For example, Kate, who was interviewed by Michele LaFrance, commented:

> It was a validation that I had never had before and I had a name. It was like, you know, it's a bad attitude, it's not. I'm not . . . you know maladjusted, I'm not ill socially or whatever. It's just that I'm depressed. And that's cool. Like it was really neat to have a name for that.[160, p.130]

In the same way, many women embrace a diagnosis of PMS,[207–208] or post-partum depression,[209] in order to assure themselves (and others) that they are not 'going mad'. As Jill, who took part in the PMS and Relationships Study, said, 'There is a real problem. There is, I'm going through it, I know that it's real'. Adopting metaphors of illness can serve to legitimise the woman as really sick, as well as legitimise the illness itself.[210] Thus, experiences such as depression are not 'all in the mind', a concept that to many women means 'not real', which can lead to the woman herself feeling dismissed.

In focusing attention on 'madness' as a discursive construction, we may also implicitly deny the influence of biology or genetics, or appear to relegate the body to a passive subsidiary role, which has meaning or interpretation imposed upon it,[211] or something that is separate from the psychological or social domain.[212] We cannot deny the somatic and intra-psychic concomitants of the experiences that are constructed as disorders such as 'depression': the exhaustion, insomnia, problems in concentration, appetite disturbance, or the feelings of heaviness, agitation, despair and desperation. Equally, while the emphasis on social and discursive phe-nomena is understandable as a reaction to biological reductionism, posi-tioning the body as irrelevant or marginal in the aetiology, interpretation, or meaning of madness is clearly inappropriate. To take one example, research from the field of neuroscience has provided convincing evidence that the nature and quality of our intimate relationships has a direct impact on neural pathways, and that these pathways in turn influence our ability to cope with frustration and life stress,[213–214] and therefore our lived experi-ence of distress. It is also important to acknowledge the existence of the neuro-biological changes that are associated with severe distress, which can be conceptualised as an embodied response, rather than a root cause (as the drug companies would have us believe), as there is convincing evidence that social exclusion or relationship breakdown causes neurological changes that are experienced as 'real pain'.[215, p.103] Other material aspects of women's lives may also be negated in a discursive analysis: the influence of age, social class, power, economic factors, ethnicity, sexual identity, personal rela-tionships and social support, or a prior history of sexual abuse, among other factors. At the same time, the dismissal of positivist research, and the focus on a qualitative approach,[e.g. see 152] could also function to negate substantial bodies of research that may be useful in understanding women's experiences that comes to be categorised as 'depression'. For while we may be critical of both the epistemological assumptions and methods of existing 'mainstream' research,[xxiii] as outlined in Chapter 2, we cannot afford to completely reject this research out of hand, if it provides some insight into women's experiences.

It is also not clear how a social constructionist critique which 'normal-ises' madness, and denies its status as pathology, would impact upon clinical intervention. While social constructionist and feminist therapy *has* been developed in a number of areas, it is notably absent at the level of official discourse – training on mainstream clinical courses, as well as articles in refereed academic journals. If we are to deconstruct the very notion of madness, how can we offer women support at times of severe distress without being accused of reifying its status as pathology? If we are focusing on the social or discursive construction of madness, is the woman an appropriate focus of attention? Does this not reinforce the notion of madness as an individual problem, to be solved by the woman herself?

A material-discursive-intrapsychic analysis of women's madness

Reconciling competing theories and research findings on the subject of women's madness has previously been described as 'impossible', because 'the premises behind the stories and the disciplinary commitments they entail are incommensurate'.[151, p.304] However, the adoption of a critical realist standpoint allows for acknowledgement of social constructionist critiques of the medicalisation of women's misery, as well as acknowledgement of the reality of women's distress. It also allows us to acknowledge the findings of a range of research studies which examine the roots of this distress, without having to resolve competing disciplinary commitments.

Critical realism is an epistemological standpoint which lies between the two apparently oppositional positions of positivism/realism and constructionism.[see 216] As was outlined in Chapter 1, critical realism recognises the materiality of somatic, psychological, and social experience, but conceptualises this materiality as mediated by culture, language and politics.[217] The legitimacy of subjective experience is acknowledged, yet the constructionist focus on theoretical debate at the expense of empirical research,[198] or the focus on discursive practices alone ,[218] is rejected. The utilisation of a variety of methodologies is also accepted, both qualitative and quantitative, without one being privileged above the other.[219] This allows us to incorporate the findings of research conducted from a range of theoretical perspectives (biomedical, psychological, socio-cultural, or discursive) into one framework, without having to reconcile competing epistemological assumptions,[199] or the truth claims present in positivist research. Thus a broad body of research, ranging from large scale epidemiological studies to single case designs, can be used to provide insight into women's experiences of distress or diagnosis as 'mad', whether the diagnosis be depression, PMDD, borderline personality disorder or any of the other myriad 'disorders' in the DSM.

This approach moves beyond the mind–body divide or realism–constructionism divide, and avoids the unnecessary distinction between the subjective and objective, or mental and physical aspects of experience.[220] This is because materiality is not deemed reducible to discourse, or without meaning unless discursively interpreted, rather, 'material practices are given an ontological status that is independent of, but in relation with, discursive practices'.[202, p.102] Materiality and discourse are thus deemed of equal importance, and inseparable, leading to the description of research as material-discursive.[185–186; 211] 'Material-discursive' approaches have

106

recently been developed in a number of areas of psychology, such as sexuality, reproduction, and mental or physical health,[153; 185–186; 221] in parallel with the move within post-structuralism towards acknowledgement of the 'extra-discursive', the material aspects of experience.[222] This integrationist material-discursive approach is to be welcomed, yet arguably does not always go far enough, as the intrapsychic – and intersubjective – is often still left out,[xxiv] because of being seen as individualistic or reductionist by constructivists[190] – assuming a 'pre-given, unitary and rational (masculine) subject', in Wendy Hollway's words.[196,p.5] Equally, when intrapsychic or intersubjective factors are considered (for example in both psychoanalytic and cognitive theorising) they are invariably conceptualised separately from either material or discursive factors.[xxv]

The developing body of psychosocial theory currently flourishing in British academia goes some way towards bridging this divide, acknowledging both the materiality of our lives, and our intrapsychic experience, by 'conceptualizing and researching a type of subject that is both social and psychological, which is constituted in and through its social formations, yet is still granted agency and internality', in the words of Stephen Frosh and Lisa Baraitser.[223, p.349] Wendy Hollway describes how this (hyphenated) psycho-social approach differs from positivist notions of the (non-hyphenated) psychosocial:

> In this perspective, we are *psycho*-social because we are products of a unique life history of anxiety- and desire-provoking life events and the manner in which they have been transformed in internal reality. We are psycho-*social* because such defensive activities affect and are affected by material conditions and discourses (systems of meaning which pre-exist any given individual), because unconscious defences are intersubjective processes (i.e. they affect and are affected by others with whom we are in communication), and because of the real events in the external, social world which are discursively, desirously and defensively appropriated.[224, pp.467–468]xxvi

This is an important body of work that is extending our understanding of the complex relationship between subjectivity and the social world. However, it marginalises embodied aspects of experience, as well as the gendered context of women's lives – with former staunch feminist critics appearing to occupy an apolitical domain.[e.g. 196; 226] It also draws heavily on psychoanalysis, which has been much criticised for displaying arrogant certainty about the 'true' nature of human subjectivity, seeming to know subjects better than they know themselves,[227] as well as for being focused on early development, rather than adult agency and intersubjectivity.[xxvii] Psychoanalysis has also been described by Louise Gyler as having a 'gendered unconscious' which serves to reproduce explicit and implicit gendered power relations, leading to socially normative gendered assumptions going unchallenged.[230]

What we need is not only an approach that can address 'how what is social is also psychic and also somatic, or bodily',[212, p.273] but also an approach that acknowledges the gendered context of women's lives and of psychiatric diagnosis. A material-discursive-intrapsychic (MDI) approach can do this, providing a multidimensional analysis of the irrevocable interconnections between the material context of women's lives, madness and gender as discursive categories, and the distress or misery many women experience. It allows us to question the increasing medicalisation of misery in the West, in particular the way in which women who experience mild distress or understandable problems with everyday life are defined as having a mental disorder such as 'depression', then told that the optimum treatment is medication, most frequently an SSRI. It also allows us to acknowledge the 'real' of women's psychological and somatic distress, whether this distress is mild or severe, conceptualising it as a complex phenomenon which is discursively constructed as madness within a specific historical and cultural context. We can acknowledge that an individual woman, living in the West in the twenty-first century, with a particular set of relational and other life circumstances, and a particular set of beliefs and coping strategies, may come to experience psychological and somatic distress, and label it as 'depression', 'PMDD', 'BPD' or 'PTSD', because this is the diagnostic category available to make sense of her experience. Indeed, she will experience and express a particular set of 'symptoms' that concur with the categories of madness available in a particular place at a particular point in time – the 'symptom pool',[231] which communicates distress. If that same woman lived in the nineteenth century, she might construct her experience as hysteria, or neurasthenia (or have it categorised in such a way by others), and experience fainting, palsies or paralysis, rather than sleep disturbance, hopelessness, or irritability – key symptoms of disorders such as depression today.

However, this does not mean that I would dismiss the materiality of women's embodied or psychological distress, or the biological and sociocultural concomitants of the phenomenon positioned as psychiatric illness, such as 'depression' – reducing disorders to social constructs. The woman experiencing the reality of a depressive (or hysterical) state incorporates the social (the 'discursive') fully within the very possibility of her existence, and so the cause of women's madness is not deemed to be inside the woman, or outside the woman, but rather reflects a mediated 'both'.[see 212] For within a critical realist framework, none of the material, discursive or intrapsychic levels of analysis is privileged above the other. This stands in contrast to the diathesis-stressor or bio-psycho-social approaches that dominate social psychiatry,[232] which are at essence medical models which privilege biology, positioning the body as a mechanistic vehicle and culture as a 'surface coating on the universal human'.[154, p.184] They also negate the discursive construction of both madness and gender, thus providing a partial analysis of the construction and lived experience of women's distress.

In the following two chapters I use this framework to examine the ways in which the materiality of a woman's embodiment and life context, the discursive construction of madness and of gendered roles, and the intra-psychic negotiation that women, and their families, engage in, contributes to the lived experience of distress, or a woman being positioned as mad. I take two specific areas of women's lives as case examples, examining the objectification and violation of women in the context of sexual violence, focusing on a case study of women who have been sexually abused in childhood in Chapter 4, and examine the construction and lived experience of premenstrual distress, categorised as premenstrual syndrome (PMS) or premenstrual dysphoric disorder (PMDD), in Chapter 5.

4

WOMAN AS OBJECT, NOT SUBJECT

Madness as response to objectification and sexual violence

The apologists

Richard Gardner writes:

> Men are looking for girls, and girls are looking for husbands. Men are on the prowl. They are not only out hunting for prey to kill and eat, but hunting for female prey to serve as sexual companions . . . sexual thoughts (are) associated with a large percentage of the man's encounters with females from the teen period and upward. . . . Secretaries, stewardesses, nurses, receptionists, waitresses, and the wide variety of other women that men inevitably encounter in the course of their day become stimuli for such sexual fantasies.[1, p.297]

The statistics

Patricia Tjaden and Nancy Thoennes write:

> Almost 18 million women and almost 3 million men in the United States have been raped. One of every six women has been raped at some time. In a single year, more than 300,000 women and almost 93,000 men are estimated to have been raped.[2, p.iii]

The consequences

Sam Warner writes:

> Women who have been sexually abused represent a significant proportion of the users of psychiatric services. For example, studies suggest that over 50 per cent of American female psychiatric patients in state facilities . . . and as many as 70 per cent of

110

involuntarily detained female psychiatric patients in the UK have been abused in childhood.[3, p.19]

Simone de Beauvoir memorably described women as the 'second sex',[4] a moniker that is still relevant more than sixty years after she first made this claim in 1949. In 2006 the World Bank concluded that 'unequal treatment of women – by the state, in the market and by their community and family – puts them at a disadvantage throughout their lives and stifles the development of their societies'.[5, p.20] That is, if they are allowed to live in the first place. In China, 39,000 baby girls die each year because their parents do not give them the same medical care and attention offered to boys. Combined with high rates of female infanticide, and selective abortion of girl foetuses, this contributes to China having 107 men for every 100 women in its overall population. China is not alone – India has 108 and Pakistan 111.[6, p.xiv] These statistics led Amartya Sen to argue that 'more than 100 million women are missing' because of inequalities in health, medicine and nutrition – 100 million women dead when they could, and should, be alive.[7] At the same time, across the world millions of women are systematically denied reproductive rights, through forced sterilisation, denial of access to safe and effective methods of fertility control, denial of privacy during intimate gynaecological examinations, safe care in pregnancy and childbirth, and affordable, effective methods of treatment for sexually transmitted diseases, all of which can have consequences for their mental health.[8] Women also significantly outnumber men among the world's poor and dispossessed,[9–10] and if they are in paid work, earn significantly less than their male counterparts.[9–10] Indeed, one of the impacts of globalisation has been an increase in poor quality, insecure and poorly paid jobs for women, as well as weakened social support systems.[11–12] The decline in real wages has resulted in an increased time burden on women, which has resulted in reduced utilisation of health services,[9] with negative consequences for women's health and well-being.[i]

Within social theories of depression, these factors are seen as *causes* of women's distress, as outlined in Chapter 2. However, an alternative standpoint would be to conceptualise these systemic inequalities as a reflection of women's objectification in a patriarchal culture, a reflection of the disregard for women's rights that stems from deep seated misogyny and disrespect. As Jill Astbury has argued, 'previously identified social risk factors for depression in women might more accurately be conceptualised as proxy variables for a range of rights violations'.[5, p.23]

Objectification and disregard for women's rights is most blatant in the context of sexual violence and abuse. This will be the focus of this chapter – an exploration of the construction and lived experience of women's madness in the context of sexual violence and abuse. I begin by examining the scope of the problem – the nature and extent of sexual violence against

111

women, then look to the reported effects, and the construction of women survivor's responses as 'madness', drawing on a study I conducted in the UK with women who had been sexually abused as children, the Long Term Effects of Sexual Abuse Study (see Appendix).

The sexual objectification of women occurs on a continuum – ranging from the depiction of girls and women as sexualised objects in the media or in pornography, to the enactment of sexual violence and abuse.[14–15] Apologists would have us believe that the widespread proliferation of images of naked or semi-naked women is a benign, if somewhat titillating practice, which simply reflects male fantasy and desire, and has no proven negative effects on women.[16–17] It has also been claimed that sexual relationships between adults and children should be considered normal and healthy expressions of sexuality, which can affirm a child's sense of personal worth, sexual power and independence,[18–20] and that children can benefit from a sexual relationship with an adult.[see 15, p.279; 21] Indeed, paedophilia has been positioned as serving evolutionary 'procreative purposes' as a sexually 'charged up child' is more likely to become sexually active before puberty, and more likely, therefore, to transmit his or her genes to his or her progeny at a young age'.[1, p.302, cited by 22, p.43] At the same time, learned medical men have claimed that a woman 'should not be able to have her legs separated by one man against her will',[23, p.33] or that 'no man can effect a felonious purpose on a woman in possession of her senses without her consent',[24, p.65, cited by 15, p.371] thus negating the reality of rape. Allegations of rape have also been dismissed as the product of female fantasy, made for 'psychological reasons', in the words of one defence lawyer.[25, p.74]

Nothing could be further from the truth. Indeed, there is incontrovertible evidence that the objectification of women is a problem of epidemic proportions, which significantly contributes to distress and the diagnosis of psychiatric disorders on the part of women and girls. Sexualised and objectifying media imagery depicting men does exist, and men and boys do experience rape and sexual abuse. However, objectifying depictions of women by far outweigh those of men,[14] and sexual violence occurs much more frequently in women and girls, at a rate of between 2:1 and 10:1. Indeed, it is seen by many commentators to provide explanation for gender disparities in psychiatric diagnosis, as discussed in Chapter 2.[26–30] However, this does not mean that these women who are distressed or disturbed following sexual assault are 'mad'. For as I argue in this chapter, their symptoms can be reframed as a 'reasonable response', the only means available to cope in the face of violation and abuse.

The continuum of abuse against women: from representation to rape

In 2006, the APA Task Force on the Sexualization of Girls reported:

> We view the sexualization of girls as occurring along a continuum, with sexualized evaluation (e.g. looking at someone in a sexual way) at the less extreme end, and sexual exploitation, such as trafficking or abuse, at the more extreme end.[14]

The continuum of objectification and abuse against women and girls starts with the sexualised imagery that is endemic in Western culture. The 2006 report published by the American Psychological Association, which examined the sexualisation of girls and women,[14] documented the extent of the problem. For example, in one study of primetime television, 84 per cent of programmes were found to contain incidents of sexual harassment, including sexist and sexual comments about women, sexualised body language, and depictions of men or boys leering at women.[31] Analyses of music videos indicate that between 44 and 84 per cent contain sexualised imagery,[14, p.6] with the majority being depictions of semi-naked or provocative women,[32] and sex is used to signify success in women music artists,[33] with being a sexual object depicted as the way to make it in the music industry.[14] Similarly, women outnumber men at a ratio of 4:1 in scenes of nudity in R-rated movies (i.e. restricted movies, where those under age 17 need to be accompanied by an adult),[34] yet are in the minority in non-sexualised roles in mainstream film – with one analysis of successful films in the period 1990–2004 reporting that 75 per cent of characters were male.[35] This glaring absence of alternative roles for women reinforces the discursive positioning of 'woman' as sexual object, to be desired and derided in equal proportions.

Sexualised representations of women and girls in magazines have also been much discussed in recent decades, ranging from the sexualised instructions on how to 'do girl' in teenage magazines,[15; 36] to the 'costuming for seduction' that women are taught to practise,[37] in order to shape themselves into objects of male desire. Advertising depicts women as sexual objects much more frequently than it depicts men in such a way, at a rate of between 2:1 and 3:1,[38–39] with women represented as attractive, and men as authoritative.[40] One study of adverts in *Time* and *Vogue* reported that 40 per cent featured women as decorative objects,[41] and a study of fashion and fitness magazine adverts found that 80 per cent contained images of women in sexually exploitive poses.[42] Men are used in 80–90 per cent of voice-overs in television advertising, and when women are used, they are likely to be addressing 'dogs, babies, cats and female dieters'.[40, p.78] Indeed, despite the advent of so-called post-feminism, the sexualised depiction of women in advertising has increased dramatically since the early 1970s.[43–44] The incorporation of feminist critiques into advertising might have resulted in a repositioning of women as desiring sexual subject, rather than simply sexual object, epitomised by the 1994 Wonderbra advert featuring Eva Herzigova stating, 'Or are you just pleased to see me?' However, as Ros

Gill argues, this depicts women gaining control through the commodification of their appearance, which 'represents a shift from an external judging male-gaze to a self-policing narcissistic gaze. It is a move to a new "higher" form of exploitation: the objectifying male gaze is internalized to form a new disciplinary regime'.[40, p.89] At the same time, there has been a proliferation of sexually explicit representations of women in men's magazines such as *Zoo*, *FHM*, or *Loaded*,[45–46] which mirror and mimic soft core pornography, a medium that has graduated from an illicit item sold in a brown paper bag, to a ubiquitous pastime available at the click of a mouse – making up a significant proportion of daily traffic on the internet,[15] as does pornography featuring children.[47–48] Woman as object, not subject, discursively legitimising sexual violence and abuse.

Child sexual abuse: modern day slavery

Catherine Itzen writes:

> Child sexual abuse . . . is what men do, because they want to; because they can; and because, largely, they can get away with it.[49, p.5]

These representations are not simply the stuff of fantasy. The objectification of girls and women is enacted on a daily basis through sexual violence and abuse, and while there is some disagreement about exact prevalence rates, it is undeniable that it is a problem of epidemic proportions,[50] with various studies suggesting that between 12 and 46 per cent of girls have been sexually abused.[ii] In an attempt to reconcile inconsistent research findings, prevalence rates across studies have been calculated, adjusting for variances in response rates and definitions of abuse. In one such study that examined sixteen cross-sectional community studies,[56] Gorey and Leslie concluded that 16.8 per cent of women and 7.9 per cent of men had experienced child sexual abuse. This is close to the figure of 20 per cent of women and 5–10 per cent of men put forward in a similar analysis by Finkelhor.[57] However, these figures are seen as serious underestimates by many experts in the field,[49] and indeed are invariably recognised as such by the researchers who report the data. For example, Beth Molnar and colleagues, in describing the population who took part in the US National Comorbidity Survey, acknowledge that they did not include people in treatment programmes or prisons, or homeless people – populations who have shown higher rates of child sexual abuse than the general population – which means that their calculation that 9.6 million women and 1.8 million men aged 15–54 living in the USA had experienced abuse before the age of 18 'was likely to be [an] underestimate of the total number of girls and boys at risk for CSA in the USA'.[30, p.757]iii

Equally, many women are not willing to disclose sexual abuse to inter-viewers and some women do not remember being sexually abused as children, due to defensive dissociation. Bolen and colleagues thus conclude that 'female child sexual abuse is of epidemic proportions in the United States'.[60, p.184] International rates of child sexual abuse paint a similar picture, ranging from 7 to 36 per cent for girls, and from 3 to 29 per cent for boys.[61] There are, however, some things on which all of the research studies agree: men are the perpetrators in the majority of cases of sexual abuse, with girls more likely to be abused within the family, whereas boys are more likely to be abused by a stranger.[62]

In many instances, particularly in the case of incest, sexual abuse is not a single incident; rather, it is a repeated violation of the child. For example, in a community based survey of 775 women who had been sexually abused as children (which I conducted in the UK with Chris Dewberry), the abuse continued for over five years on average, with 80 per cent of the women reporting that the abuse had gone on for over two years.[63] Only 6 per cent of women in this study had been abused outside the family, with father (28.4 per cent), stepfather (12.6 per cent), uncle (12.1 per cent), family friend (11 per cent) and brother (10.5 per cent) being the most common perpetrators. Similarly, in a further in-depth community based study that I conducted with 608 UK women, 369 of whom had been sexually abused as children – the Long Term Effects of Child Sexual Abuse Study that acts as a case study in this chapter – only 9 per cent of women had been sexually abused by a stranger, with father (17 per cent) and uncle (12.5 per cent) being the most common perpetrators and the abuse continuing for four years, on average. These statistics give lie to mainstream cultural represen-tations of sexual abusers as 'sex beasts', a monstrous minority of strange and disordered men who prey on vulnerable children because they suffer from the 'disease' of paedophilia,[3, p.39] or are priests reacting to celibacy enforced by the Catholic Church,[64] men who are deemed to be 'out of control' at the moment of abuse.[65] Perpetrators who are close relatives or family friends of the child they repeatedly abuse cannot claim to be 'out of control' for a period of four or five years, or longer.

Equally, these were not consenting 'sexual relationships' between an adult and a seductive child, as apologists for child–adult sexual contact would have us believe.[18–20] In both of the studies I conducted on child sexual abuse, the average age the abuse started was 8 years old, with 44 per cent of cases involving sexual intercourse in the first study,[63] and 53 per cent involving attempted or successful intercourse in the second. In both studies the abuse involved threats or force in the majority of cases. The perpetrator attempted to maintain the child's silence and prevent disclosure, through using threats or violence (29 per cent and 25 per cent of cases, respectively),[iv] saying that nothing was wrong (31 per cent and 53 per cent of cases), saying it was the child's fault (21 per cent of cases in both studies), or saying it would split up the family (25 per cent and 18 per cent of cases).[v] For example, one of the women we interviewed in the Long Term Effects of Child Sexual Abuse Study, Gina, described how her uncle maintained her silence by threatening to harm her sister:

> G: Yeah, he masturbated me.
>
> I: Right. Was there anything else involved?
>
> G: Um, performing oral sex on him and if I didn't do what he wanted, he would, um, touch my baby sister.
>
> I: So that was his threat?
>
> G: Yes, yes. Or he'd touch my next sister, so that I'd do, I didn't realise until my sister told me, I thought I'd taken the brunt of the abuse, but I thought I'd protected both of them, but she told me afterwards that he was abusing her as well.

Melanie, who had been raped three or four times a week by her brother for four years, starting at the age of 12, told us that he put a pornographic picture with a knife through it in her pillow and saying 'This is what's gonna happen to you' if she told anyone about the abuse.

These threats, or the discursive positioning of the abuse as 'normal' or as 'love', were effective. In both of these studies, nearly 50 per cent of women had never disclosed the abuse, either at the time or later in adulthood. Of those who did disclose the abuse, the person did nothing in 72.5 per cent and 46 per cent of cases; the perpetrator was confronted in only 27 per cent and 18 per cent of cases, and the authorities informed in a smaller proportion (18 per cent and 15 per cent). These are not unusual statistics. The majority of children who are subjected to child sexual abuse never report it, and of those cases that are reported, only a small proportion of perpetrators are prosecuted, with an even smaller proportion of prosecutions resulting in convictions.[57] Official statistics on convicted child sexual abuse are thus the tip of a particularly nasty iceberg. In decrying the absence of legal sanctions directed against child sexual abuse perpetrators, Louise Armstrong has argued that it is a problem that has become normalised, because so many men do it (it is acknowledged that women commit sexual abuse, but the majority of perpetrators are men).[22] The result is that child sexual abuse and incest has become medicalised and professionalised, with the focus on 'incest families', and 'paedophilia' as a pathological condition covering up the reality of the child rape, and drawing attention away from the social and political structures that condone violence against women.[3] As Catherine Itzen argues in the epigraph to this section: 'Child sexual abuse . . . is what men do, because they want to; because they can; and because, largely, they can get away with it'.[49, p.5]

In a number of cultural contexts, the sexual abuse of girls is not simply medicalised; it is legalised, through the institution of child marriage, described by the World Health Organization as 'a form of sexual violence, since the children involved are unable to give or withhold their consent'.[66, p.156] The WHO reports that early marriage is most common in Africa and South Asia, with marriage at the age of 7 or 8 being common in both Ethiopia and parts of West Africa, at age 11 in parts of northern Nigeria, and before the age of 10 for a percentage of girls living in Nepal, where 40 per cent of girls are married by the age of 15.[67] Child marriage is also common in the Democratic Republic of the Congo, Mali, Niger and Uganda, and in a number of states within India.[67] In one recent case, a 13-year-old Yemeni girl, Ilham al-Ashi, died after being sexually violated by her husband, Abed al-Hekmi, in his attempt to consummate the marriage, resulting in the girl receiving a deep rupture to her genitals. Hekmi had brought his young wife to a gynaecologist to 'tear her hymen' two days after the marriage, and when this request was refused, attempted to obtain sleeping pills to drug her. He admitted sexually forcing himself onto his young wife when she resisted his attempts to deflower her.[68] In the previous year, a 12-year-old Yemeni girl, sold as a child bride (the parents receive a 'bride price'), died in childbirth.[69] These cases may seem extreme, however they are simply one end of a continuum of violation of pre-pubescent child brides, described by one survivor as 'modern day slavery'.[70]

The practice of forced sexual initiation of girls is another form of sexual violence common in many countries, in particular sub-Saharan Africa. The WHO has reported that the percentage of girls experiencing forced sexual initiation ranges from 7 and 9 per cent of New Zealand and US girls respectively, to 18 per cent of girls in Mozambique, 21 per cent in Ghana, 28 per cent in South Africa, 29 per cent in Tanzania, 37 per cent in Cameroon, and 47 per cent in the Caribbean.[66, p.153] Cultural mores can result in boys also experiencing forced sexual initiation: in studies conducted in the Caribbean and Peru, 30 per cent and 11 per cent of adolescent men reported coerced sexual initiation, respectively. However, these rates were substantially lower than those reported by women in the same context – 48 per cent in the Caribbean and 40 per cent in Peru.[71–72] Adolescent girls who attempt to resist may also be subjected to violence. In one study of teenage girls attending an antenatal clinic, where 32 per cent reported forced sexual initiation, 78 per cent said that they feared being beaten if they refused to have sex.[73]

Rape and sexual assault of adult women

Nicola Gavey writes:

> The divide between rape and what was once 'just sex' has well and truly begun to crumble. Rape is no longer rare. It is almost

ordinary. The implications of this simultaneous remaking of sex and rethinking of rape are profound ... everyday taken-for-granted normative forms of heterosexuality work as cultural scaffolding for rape.[74, pp.1-2]

Sexual abuse and violence is not confined to childhood. A longitudinal National Women's Study estimated that 13 per cent of US women had experienced lifetime rape (with 61 per cent of rapes taking place before the age of 18), with an additional 14.3 per cent of women having experienced molestation or attempted sexual assault.[75-76] In a similar vein, a National Violence Against Women survey conducted with 8,000 women in the USA estimated lifetime completed rape of women at 14.8 per cent, with an additional 2.8 per cent having experienced attempted rape (compared to a total of 3 per cent of men in both categories).[77] The USA is not unusual. In a survey of women conducted in the Czech Republic,[78] 11.6 per cent reported forced sexual assault at least once in their lifetime, in the majority of cases involving rape, with 3.4 per cent reporting that this had occurred on more than one occasion. If we include *attempted* forced sex into the equation, the figures are much higher. For example, a survey of US women reported that 44 per cent had experienced rape or attempted rape[79] and a WHO report published in 2002 found reported rates of attempted or completed forced sex by an intimate partner in 15.3 per cent (Canada), 21.7 per cent (Nicaragua), 23 per cent (Mexico; London, UK), 25 per cent (Zimbabwe), 29.9 per cent (Thailand), 46.7 per cent (Peru), and 51.9 per cent (Turkey) of women.[66, p.152] Research has also shown that asking women specific questions such as 'Have you ever been forced to have sexual intercourse against your will?' produces higher rates of positive response than questions asking women whether they have been 'abused' or 'raped'.[80] This is not surprising, as rape in marriage is often constructed as 'just sex',[74] a man exercising his rights to his wife's body. As Adamo, a Catholic priest, wrote in a newspaper column in 1984:

> Rape in marriage! When I first heard the phrase some years ago I laughed – not because it was funny, because it struck me as being goofy. How could a husband rape his wife? Did he not have a right to sexual intercourse with her as a result of the marriage bond? ... Wasn't he merely helping her to perform her wifely duties? I remember being taught ... that when two people got married they surrendered themselves to each other. It was a mutual giving and taking so that a wife's body (sexually speaking) was no longer her own to do with as she pleased, nor was the husband's body his own. Because it was mutual it always struck me as fair.[cited by 74, pp.39-40]

118

The majority of rape perpetrators are known to their victims,[81] (in the US National Violence Against Women Survey, only 16.7 per cent of women were raped by a stranger),[2] and thus it is not surprising to find the high percentage of women reporting sexual assault being committed by their partner in the WHO study outlined above. Indeed, the image of the typical rapist being a stranger who attacks in the street in the dark, described by Wood and Rennie as 'Hollywood rape',[82] is the stuff of fiction, as the danger for most women lies within their own home. For example, in the US National Violence Against Women Survey, 43 per cent of women who had been raped reported that the perpetrator was a current or former partner,[2] and sexual violence was often accompanied by physical violence or verbal abuse. Indeed, 38 per cent of women who had been raped reported being hit with an object, choked, kicked, slapped, or 'beat up' as part of the rape.[2] At the same time, in research conducted in both Mexico and the USA, it has been reported that 40–52 per cent of women who had experienced physical violence in an intimate relationship also experienced sexual coercion from their partner.[83–84] Equally, in a study of 613 women in Japan who had been abused by their partner, the majority had experienced a combination of physical, psychological and sexual violence within the relationship.[85] The WHO estimates that between 10 and 69 per cent of women are physically assaulted by an intimate male partner at some point in their lives, basing their conclusions on the findings of 48 population-based surveys from around the world.[66] This suggests that a lot of women are living in an atmosphere of physical violence and sexual coercion. For many women this is ongoing, as violence within intimate relationships is rarely an isolated incident. In one study conducted in the UK, women reporting partner violence had experienced seven incidents in the last year,[86] while in a national study conducted in the USA, it was three.[87] However, dominant narratives about rape still adhere to the myth that 'Hollywood rape' characterises the typical assault, serving to silence and dismiss women's pain.[88]

Nevertheless, sexual violence is not confined to the home. National data on rape and sexual assault in the USA reveals that 15 per cent of assaults against women occur in a public place and 16.7 per cent of women are raped by strangers.[2] About 10 per cent of assaults involve multiple perpetrators, usually strangers,[89] colloquially described as 'gang rape'. There is also a long history of rape being used as a strategy of war – from the mythical rape of Troy, to more recent conflicts in Rwanda,[90] East Timor,[91] or the former Yugoslavia,[92] a practice recognised by the WHO as a deliberate strategy to subvert community bonds.[66] Women refugees are also at high risk of rape, both in transit from their country of origin,[93] and in refugee camps.[94] At the same time, sexual trafficking of girls and women is occurring at epidemic proportions – a new slave trade predicated on objectification and exploitation, which results in hundreds of thousands of women and girls being sold into prostitution or sexual slavery every year. For example, it has been estimated that more than 200,000 Bangladeshi women were trafficked between 1990 and 1997, and approximately 7,000 Nepali women and girls are trafficked to India each year.[95] Europe and North America are also significant destinations for sexual trafficking. It is estimated that between 45,000 and 50,000 women and children are trafficked annually to the USA,[96] and 10–15 per cent of foreign prostitutes in Belgium and Italy, many of whom are between 15 and 18 years old, have been forcibly sold from abroad.[97–98]

Sexual harassment in a public setting is another common form of sexual violence towards women. For example, in a study conducted in Canada, 23 per cent of girls reported having experienced sexual harassment at school,[99] while in a study conducted in the USA, the rate was 63 per cent, including being the object of sexual jokes, comments, gestures or looks, and being touched, grabbed or pinched in a sexual way.[100] In surveys conducted in Belarus and the Rostov area of Russia, 12.6 per cent and 60 per cent of women, respectively, reported that they had been subjected to sexual harassment in the workplace.[101] Similarly, 25 per cent of women in Poland and in the Czech Republic reported sexual harassment at work, as did 22 per cent of women in Australia,[102] 50 per cent of women in the UK,[103] and 25–58 per cent of women in the USA.[104] In a Swedish study of 6,926 women, 69 per cent reported that they had been harassed by strangers,[105] and it is estimated that 1.2 million women in the UK were subjected to stalking in 2003.[106]

In citing these statistics it is easy to get caught up in a somewhat abstract debate about the validity of one set of figures, or one study, versus another, and to lose sight of the reality of the experience of sexual violence for women and girls. This reality is stark and discomforting. Young girls, sometimes as young as infants, subjected to repeated oral, anal and vaginal sex by a father, brother or uncle. Women raped by a bottle or broom (31 per cent of women who reported rape in the US National Violence Against Women Survey had been raped by objects or fingers).[2] Nightly violence and forced sex by a husband asserting his marital rights. Continuous comments in the workplace about tits and bums, or groping and pressure to have sex. To bring the reality of sexual violence to the fore, before looking to its purported effects, I now turn to the accounts of women and girls who have survived such violations of their bodies, and of their very sense of self.

It was only when he got into the back of the car, pulling at the same time at his trouser belt to unbuckle it, that I realised in an instant of the purest quality what was going to happen. I opened my mouth to scream as I edged away but no sound came. I couldn't believe it. Surely I could *scream* at least. Then it was too late. His hand was on my mouth and I was being forced down on the floor of the car. All I could register as the belt was pulled around my head like a noose, was that the name of the car was 'Avenger'. I shall spare you the details of what followed, suffice to say I was raped orally and anally as well as vaginally and under the continuous threat of the noose being pulled tighter I submitted, if submit is the word, because I realised I would rather be alive than dead. (*Woman who was raped by a taxi driver*)[107, p.41]

At first the women and girls were beaten black and blue, especially on the lower body region. Later on we didn't find any kind of injury on them any more. The first ones probably told the others the best way to survive. A nineteen year old girl told me she closed up tight inside. She lay down, tried to think of something else, and wasn't there; she blocked it out mentally. She said that all she felt was a foreign object penetrating her, something cold and hard that caused a ripping feeling. (*Rape in the Bosnia Herzgovina war*)[92, p.90]

I can remember um being very young, very little and I remember actually sucking on something which I presume to be a penis now, I remember that sensation of sucking . . . My other memory is that of being 2 or 3ish and my feet being too little to reach the floor and this person being on top of me and holding my hands down on the bed and trying to kiss me and I remember that quite a lot. I remember the kissing, I remember the person on top of me, I don't remember penetration even though when I think about it logically I imagine that was what was happening, but I don't remember that, I remember the kissing and this horrible wetness around my face and my hands being pinned down and my legs being opened and not being able to touch the floor and I think that's one of the earliest memories I've had. (*Valerie, sexually abused by her uncle from the age of 3*)

I had to participate in their sex, I was invaded with fingers, he made mum abuse me herself, he touched me, squeezed me, fondled me, photographed and invaded me.

I: What did he make your mum do?
D: Um, while he was, I'm not going to say making love, I mean it was beyond it [laughs], *fucking* her she had to put her fingers up me and try and rub my clitoris and that

sort of thing. It hurt because she'd got finger nails, long finger nails, [crying] it hurt and it was, it was *awful*, awful. Yet mother said, 'don't think about it, ignore it' . . . It was almost that we were sisters in a way . . . we were both victims. (*Elizabeth, sexually abused by her mother's boyfriend, from the age of 8*)[vi]

A common thread runs through all of these accounts – girls and women objectified, their bodies used for both the sexual gratification and enactment of power by men. Subjecting a child or a woman to non-consensual sex is to treat them as an object, to deny their subjectivity and human rights, and in many instances, to engender both physical and psychological pain. It is to this I now turn: the impact of objectification and sexual violence on women and girls, in order to critically evaluate the view that this is what – literally – drives many women mad.

The consequences of objectification and sexual violence for women and girls

UN Secretary-General Ban Ki-Moon stated, on 8 March 2008:

Violence against women and girls continues unabated in every continent, country and culture. It takes a devastating toll on women's lives, on their families, and on society as a whole. Most societies prohibit such violence – yet the reality is that too often, it is covered up or tacitly condoned.[cited by 108]

Debates surrounding the impact of sexualised imagery, in particular pornography, have tended to focus on men – on the question of whether the proliferation of such imagery can explain why rape and child sexual abuse is primarily committed by men.[see 2] Those who would argue for a direct causal relationship between sexualised representations and the act of rape,[109] or child sexual abuse,[110] stand in opposition to those who argue that pornography simply reflects men's fantasies,[111] or indeed, that pornography can reduce rape,[112] because men are watching women being violated, rather than actually violating them. These debates are not my focus here. Rather, I am interested in the impact of sexualised imagery and sexual violence on women and girls.

The evidence is unequivocal. Girls and women who are surrounded by objectifying imagery internalise these sexualised messages and engage in a process of self-objectification, which means that they are more likely to see themselves as an object who is judged in relation to societal norms of sexual attractiveness and hetero-femininity.[113] Self-objectification has been found to be associated with reports of low self-esteem,[114] impairments in

122

cognitive functioning,[115] feelings of shame about the body,[115] and anxiety about appearance.[116] It has also been linked to the relatively high rates of cosmetic surgery in girls living in the USA,[14] and to eating disorders, such as excessive dieting and exercising, anorexia nervosa or bulimia nervosa.[117–118] Self-objectification is also significantly associated with diagnosis of depression;[119] the more girls objectify their bodies, the more likely they are to report depression.[114]

If these consequences are associated with one end of the continuum, images of objectification, what are the effects of sexual abuse and violence? Until the 1970s child sexual abuse was an invisible crime, with little recognition of its magnitude, or potential for long term negative effects on mental health. It was in the late 1970s, at the same time as feminist scholars were identifying incest, in particular, as a major social problem,[49] that high proportions of childhood sexual abuse cases began to be recognised in psychiatric populations, with rates ranging from 30 to 64 per cent.[120–122] Equally, comparisons of adult women who have experienced child sexual abuse (CSA) with those who have not suggest significantly higher rates of psychological and sexual problems for those who have experienced abuse. The most commonly reported long term effects include depression, anxiety, low self-esteem, difficulties in interpersonal relationships, sexual or reproductive problems, self-destructive behaviour, alcohol and drug substance abuse, post-traumatic stress disorder, borderline personality disorder, eating disorders and a tendency towards later victimisation.[for reviews see 123–126] Beitchman and colleagues summarise the findings of the extensive research literature thus: in comparison with women not reporting a history of CSA, women who do report a history of CSA more commonly

- show evidence of sexual disturbance or dysfunction
- report homosexual experiences in adolescence or adulthood
- show evidence of anxiety and fear, which may be related to force or threat of force during the abuse
- show evidence of depression and depressive symptomatology
- show evidence of revictimisation experiences
- show evidence of suicidal ideas and behavior, particularly when they have been exposed to force or violence.[126, p.115]

In the Long Term Effects of Child Sexual Abuse Study survey, 369 women who had been sexually abused in childhood did report significantly more anxiety and depression, lower quality of life, as well as more somatic symptoms and sexual problems than 239 women who had not been abused. Being abused at a younger age, and not having experienced therapy, were associated with the highest levels of reported distress. Similarly, in the National Comorbidity Survey conducted with 5,877 US citizens,[30] higher rates of fourteen mood, anxiety and substance abuse disorders were reported by women who had experienced child sexual abuse, with rape, knowing the perpetrator, and ongoing abuse associated with the higher levels of distress.[vii] In a study of 1,411 adult twins living in the USA conducted by Kendler and colleagues, sexual abuse was associated with higher rates of depression, anxiety disorders, bulimia, alcohol dependence, and drug dependence, with genital sexual abuse, especially intercourse, associated with the highest rates.[52] This was also the case in the UK study I conducted with 775 women sexually abused in childhood, where women who reported intercourse and genital sexual contact were more likely to report negative effects, which included anger (68 per cent), anxiety (50 per cent), shame (66 per cent), guilt (59 per cent), fear of sex (31 per cent), and fear of men (24 per cent).[63]

The rate of lifetime post-traumatic stress disorder is reported to be 32 per cent for women who have experienced child sexual abuse, compared to 10 per cent of women who have not been abused.[127] Indeed, the higher rates of child sexual abuse experienced by women is seen to provide at least partial explanation for gender differences in diagnoses of PTSD, with the US National Comorbidity Survey reporting that 10.4 per cent of women and 5 per cent of men meeting the criteria for diagnosis.[128] Women who experience sexual abuse in childhood have also been reported to be more likely to attempt or commit suicide than non-abused women,[129–130] an association which exists even when factors such as age, education, symptoms of PTSD and presence of psychiatric diagnosis are controlled.[viii] It is also increasingly recognised that a significant proportion of women diagnosed with borderline personality disorder (BPD) have experienced childhood sexual abuse, with one study reporting that 86 per cent of women with a BPD diagnosis had been sexually abused.[132] This has led commentators to argue that a diagnosis of BPD should be replaced with PTSD, in order to acknowledge the impact of the trauma.[see 133]

Rape or sexual assault in adulthood is also associated with reporting of psychological distress, that can persist for a number of years following the incident,[134] and will remain long term for approximately 50 per cent of women, even in the presence of counselling or therapy.[75; 135] Depression or PTSD are the most common diagnoses given to women who have experienced adult sexual violence,[136–137] with women who have been raped being found to be three times more likely than those not raped to meet the diagnostic criteria for major depression,[138] and six times more likely to suffer from PTSD.[75] Rape is also more likely to be associated with PTSD than other traumas, with one study reporting that 65 per cent of women who have been raped report PTSD,[139] compared to 24 per cent of women exposed to other forms of trauma.[140] In a 1997 review it has also been reported that between 51 per cent and 97 per cent of women diagnosed with 'serious mental illness', such as schizophrenia, have experienced lifetime sexual abuse.[141] For example, in one New Zealand community study, the prevalence of symptoms or signs which could lead to diagnoses such as schizophrenia was 33 per cent in women with a history of sexual abuse as adults, 15 per cent in women with a history of physical violence by an intimate partner and 6 per cent in non-abused women.[142]

Sexual violence by an intimate partner has been reported to aggravate the effects of physical violence on mental health, suggesting a cumulative effect of assault.[66] And the negative effects of physical partner violence on women's mental health are well documented,[143] with rates of depression ranging from 39 to 83 per cent and rates of PTSD ranging from 31 to 84 per cent.[29] One study reported that 44–65 per cent of women who had separated from their violent partner still experienced post-traumatic stress symptoms nine years later,[144] with the primary stressor of male violence being exacerbated by secondary stressors, such as emotional and financial losses, or family life changes.[145] There is also increasing evidence that sexual violence in childhood or adulthood is associated with a range of physical illnesses, including chronic pain syndrome, cardiovascular disease, diabetes, and metabolic syndrome, the precursor to type 2 diabetes.[146–147] Experiences of sexual harassment have also been reported to result in psychological distress,[148] and in suicidal behaviour, as evidenced by a study of adolescent girls in Canada where 15 per cent of those experiencing frequent, unwanted sexual harassment had exhibited suicidal behaviour in the previous six months, compared with 2 per cent of those who had not had such harassment.[99]

One conclusion to be drawn from this considerable body of research is that sexual abuse and violence drives women mad – literally – leading to major depression, PTSD, BPD, or schizophrenia. However, this is a problematic conclusion, as it medicalises women's misery and again positions the problem within the women, whose 'reasonable responses to trauma', in the words of Sam Warner, are decontextualised as psychiatric 'symptoms'.[3, p.17] Diagnoses are assumed to reflect an underlying pathology, or women's greater vulnerability in the face of stress, rather than simply being descriptors applied to women's lived experience of violence, their coping strategies in the face of an untenable situation, or the adoption of a culturally constructed script for 'sexual violence survivor' that women are taught to follow.

The link between sexual violence and madness: women's vulnerability or a reasonable response to trauma?

Louise Armstrong writes:

> We seem to be witnessing the birth of an incest industry involving a staggering array of clinicians and counsellors and therapists and researchers and authorities and experts all with their careers sighted on one aspect or another of incest and its aftermath. Incest, medicalized, was neutralized, stripped of its character as a

deliberate act of male aggression, a violence based on the belief in male right.[22, p.36]

There have been many explanations for the association between psychological distress and sexual violence against girls and women. The cluster of behavioural 'problems' associated with child sexual abuse, summarised by one reviewer as difficulties in 'affect regulation, impulse control, somatization, sense of self, cognitive distortions, and problems with socialization',[149] have been attributed to 'developmentally sensitive neuronal and behavioral periods related to brain maturation and early caretaker interactions'.[149, p.273] Thus attachment theory and neuro-biological theories of development are combined, in a reductionist nature-nurture model that leaves little hope for recovery, beyond drug treatment that helps women 'feel less',[150, p.186] ECT and hospitalisation,[151] or in a minority of cases, long term psychotherapy.[152] This reductionist thinking is reinforced by the claim the abused children and adults experience 'deleterious effects on the hypothalamic-pituitary-adrenal axis (HPA), the sympathetic nervous system, and possibly the immune system'.[153] The view that women are inherently more vulnerable to posttraumatic stress,[154]ix because of hormonal differences,[156] HPA responses and oxytocin levels, or cognitions,[for a review see 157] put forward for the higher rates of depression reported by women sexually abused in childhood,[158–159] also acts to individualise the effects of sexual abuse, attributing it to female biology or psychology.

Finklehor and Browne's influential 'traumagenic dynamics' model of child sexual abuse,[160] which posits that child sexual abuse negatively affects a child's cognitive and affective orientations to the world, resulting in disturbances in four domains: betrayal, powerlessness, stigmatisation, and traumatic sexualisation, is also a reductionist model. The same could be said of Marsha Linehan's conceptualisation of borderline personality disorder as a response to childhood trauma.[161] The attention here is on the dynamics (or deficits) within the child, rather than on the social and familial context where ongoing abuse takes place, gendered power relations between women and men, or the 'regimes of truth' that define the expected response of sexual violence survivors. Along with other deterministic medicalising models, this assumes that sexual violence and abuse inevitably leads to harm, and frames women's experiences within a medical discourse of recovery and healing from trauma.[88] The assumption that damage has been done can be devastating to survivors of abuse, as Fiona told us: 'You get into conversation and folks say "people that have been abused can never be normal again". And it's like "thanks very much"'. This positioning of abused women as 'damaged goods' also serves to discredit girl's and women's coping, as well as their future sexual and other life choices,[162] which can play an important role in their negotiation of misery, or conversely, of health and happiness.

126

A similar criticism could be made about one of the most widely accepted theories of the long term effects of abuse and violence, the stress model, where women and girls' distress is assumed to be a direct response to environmental stressors, particularly those of 'considerable magnitude'.[163] The ubiquity of this model explains why the PTSD paradigm has been in the ascendant, driving research and clinical responses to violence against women[29] – memorably described by Judith Herman as giving 'a new diagnostic name to the psychological disorder found in survivors of pro-longed, repeated abuse'.[164, p.3] Indeed, the definition of trauma used in diagnoses of PTSD was widened from an event 'outside the range of usual human experience', as described in DSM-III,[165, p.236] to include 'an event or events that involved actual or threatened death or serious injury, or a threat to the physical integrity of self and others' in DSM-IV,[166, p.427] opening the floodgates to women being diagnosed with PTSD as a result of sexual or physical violence.[133; 167] Many feminists have viewed this posi-tively, as PTSD can be conceptualised as a 'normal response to trauma', in the words of one feminist therapist interviewed by Jeanne Marecek.[168] As many women experience multiple episodes of sexual or physical violence across the lifespan, with childhood sexual abuse, in particular, increasing the likelihood of adolescent or adult sexual violence,[169] this PTSD model also allows for acknowledgement of cumulative effect of trauma, which is widely recognised to have negative psychological consequences.[170]

While this may appear to be a progressive step, allowing acknowledge-ment of the negative effects of sexual violence and abuse on women, this apparent normalisation of women's distress is at odds with the definition of PTSD as a psychiatric disorder, which acts to pathologise and stigmatise women subjected to sexual and physical violence, medicalising women's reasonable response, where 'misery is transformed into madness through diagnostic specification'.[3, p.17] The same can be said of the diagnosis put forward by John Briere, 'postsexual abuse syndrome', characterised by symptoms of fear, periods of dissociation and withdrawal, problems with anger, chronic muscle tension, and self-injurious feelings.[171] As PTSD (and other psychiatric diagnoses applied to abused women) is conceptualised as individual pathology, this minimises the responsibility of the abuser and detracts energy from looking at the wider social and political factors that surround the objectification and sexual abuse of women.[29] At the same time, psychiatric diagnosis can serve to undermine the veracity of women's accounts of abuse, which are dismissed as 'just their symptoms talking',[172] and behaviours that are not pathologised in non-abused women – such as 'promiscuity' or lesbianism – are problematised and deemed to be *caused* by the abuse,[3] as we see in the review of 'effects of CSA' conducted by Beitchman and colleagues,[126] cited above.[x]

We also need to acknowledge the cultural and historical location of women's responses to objectification, sexual abuse and violence. Today in the West negative psychological responses to sexual violence are expected, and a whole industry has evolved to diagnose and treat madness in girls and women who have been abused, described as an 'incest industry' by one critic.[22, p.36] In medicalising sexual violence and its consequences, women are encouraged to position themselves as 'child-sexual abuse survivors', and embrace a psychiatric diagnosis to explain their distress, with drug treatment or therapy being the sole solutions. As Paula Reavey and Brendon Gough argue, 'sexual survival is culturally and socially produced and the positions of guilt, shame and victimisation reinforced thereof'.[173, p.327] This serves to direct attention and energy away from other forms of action, such as political lobbying, or a focus on the social conditions that normalise the actions of abusive men. Feminists, particularly those who lobby for specific trauma diagnoses to be applied to women who have been sexually abused,[164] or those advocating therapy as the solution,[152] thus leave themselves open to the criticism that they are colluding with the psy-professions in the medicalisation and pathologisation of women. As Louise Armstrong argues, 'rather than feminism politicising the issue of incest, incest as illness had overwhelmed and swallowed feminism. The result was the mass infantalisation of women'.[22, p.43]

Assuming that sexual violence has universal effects has the function of disassociating women's distress from the socio-political context of women's lives,[133] as well as the social construction of gender, madness and sexual violence, while denying women's individual subjectivity at the same time. It also has the potential to revictimise women through positioning sexual violence survivors as inevitably disordered, with madness as the unavoidable outcome. This does not mean that we deny the reality of women's distress, or dismiss the many epidemiological studies which draw attention to the association between sexual violence and women's suffering. We simply need to avoid conceptualising this suffering as an illness that is located solely within the woman, the focus of our attention being on the development, or treatment, of this supposed pathology. Instead, we need to acknowledge the complexity of women's responses to sexual abuse and violence – the ways in which the consequences of abuse can be highly individualised, located in a woman's socio-historical context, her negotiation of distress, and the availability of options open to her to cope. Equally, while a response may be 'maladaptive' in that it causes more pain – self-harm, avoidance of intimacy, or alcohol and drug abuse can cause problems in and of themselves[see 174, p.46] – it does not mean that the woman responding in this way is mad, and is thus worthy of psychiatric diagnosis. Understanding the meaning of her response, and the way in which it evolved in reaction to an untenable situation, can be the first step in developing more 'adaptive' ways of making sense of experience and surviving.

Thus while I am not alone in arguing that the behaviour and emotions of women who have been sexually abused as children can be seen as a response to intolerable conditions, as others have already made this claim,[160–161; 164; 175] I reject the pathologisation of this response, concurring with Sam Warner[3] that it can be seen as a reasonable, understandable, and sometimes adaptive, reaction. In order to explore women's 'reasonable responses' to sexual violence as both a lived and constructed experience, and question the psychiatric diagnosis of their misery and distress, I now turn to the case example of women sexually abused as children who took part in the Long Term Effects of Child Sexual Abuse Study, and who completed surveys (369 women), or were interviewed (25 women), about their experience. I will begin each section by outlining the DSM-IV diagnostic criteria for PTSD, borderline personality disorder (BPD), or major depression, the most common psychiatric diagnoses levelled at women who have experienced childhood sexual abuse, and then examine women's accounts of experiences deemed to be 'symptoms' of these disorders. For while we now acknowledge the link between distress and childhood sexual abuse – unlike Freud, who denied its existence when he retracted his seduction theory in 1897 – the pathologisation and subjugation of women who have been sexually abused in childhood is the same as it was for women diagnosed as hysterics or neurasthenics in the nineteenth century. Women who have been objectified and sexually violated being positioned as 'mad'.

The constructed lived experience of child sexual abuse: long term consequences for adult women

Powerlessness and forgetting: suppressing memories of being sexually abused as a child

---

Persistent avoidance of stimuli associated with the trauma and numbing of general responsiveness (not present before the trauma), as indicated by three (or more) of the following:

(1) efforts to avoid thoughts, feelings, or conversations associated with the trauma

(2) efforts to avoid activities, places, or people that arouse recollections of the trauma

(3) inability to recall an important aspect of the trauma

(4) markedly diminished interest or participation in significant activities

(5) feeling of detachment or estrangement from others

(6) restricted range of affect (e.g., unable to have loving feelings)

(7) sense of a foreshortened future (e.g., does not expect to have a career, marriage, children, or a normal life span)

309.81 DSM-IV Criteria for Posttraumatic Stress Disorder (PTSD)

We have abolished slavery in the Western world, yet we still condone the rights of adults to have absolute power over children. A child who is sexually abused by an adult is not simply subjected to sexual invasion (if such violation can ever be described as 'simple'), but is also subjugated to the will of an adult, who is exerting their societal right to exercise power and control. This places the child in a position of unquestioned power-lessness that allows the sexual abuse to continue unreported, and in some instances, unremembered, dissociation or 'forgetting' being the only means by which the child, or adult woman, can cope.

Take the case of Susan, who grew up in a fundamentalist household. She attended church every Sunday and there were family prayers before dinner. Her father's role in the household was to bathe Susan, read her a bedtime story and hear her night-time prayers. Part of their routine was the 'tickling' game which gradually became an excuse for sexual touching. Susan's father never physically hurt her. At the age of 8 the bedtime stories became pornography and the touching became mutual. This happened nightly. After each incident her father would hear her prayers and tuck her in. At age 12 when Susan began to menstruate, the games and bedtime stories stopped. Shortly after this Susan began attending classes at the church and the minister kept her back for special instruction. She remembers not questioning his right to touch her in any way and said, 'After I would put my pants back on and go home.' She told no one. This went on until the classes ended after about six months. At 15 she was hospitalised for anorexia and was discovered to have been cutting herself severely for several years. Her parents were both involved in her counselling and worked with her to overcome the eating disorder. The abuse was never disclosed, even when a psychologist asked Susan directly if she had ever had an abusive experience. She recovered enough to attend university, get a degree and marry. She maintained a warm relation-ship with her parents and credited them with her surviving her illness. It was only when her daughter was born and she found she could not bear to see her father touch his granddaughter, and the memories of the abuse resurfaced, that she spoke about it for the first time.

Jenny described waiting in her room for her father at the age of 8, not knowing whether she would receive a beating or a rape. She remem-bers the sounds of her mother cooking in the kitchen and the smell of dinner. She would wait and try to 'go out' of her body, picking some-thing in her room to focus on and go into while the abuse happened.

The 'punishments' were never mentioned outside the bedroom by either her mother or her father. After dinner the father would take the children for ice cream and play with them in the park. Jenny was expected to participate in games even when her body was sore and she had difficulty moving following the rape. She learnt to ignore the pain. Jenny remained at home until she was 17 and the 'punishments' continued throughout this time. Her father had told her he would kill her if she ever told anyone what was happening and she had no reason to believe he would not. When her 7-year-old daughter disclosed sexual abuse by her grandfather, Jenny spoke for the first time of her own abuse. She had been effectively silenced for twenty years.

These case examples are not unusual; they illustrate the complete lack of power a child has in the hands of an abusive adult, particularly when that adult is a parent or caregiver. These women rapidly 'forgot' the abuse, or aspects of the abuse, as they were expected to do – indeed, they needed to do so to survive. In no way was the reality of their experience affirmed by the adults around them and in no way did they see themselves as having any agency to stop what was happening to them. Like Jenny, many children who are abused 'forget' during the act of sexual assault, when dissociation from the experience occurs. Lesley, who was abused by her uncle for six years from the age of 11, described her experience thus:

> While he was actually doing it, I don't, I just don't think I felt anything, um. I just completely cut off. I didn't think anything. I used to think other things apart from what he was doing um, like, oh what shall I do when I go home and um, I'll have to go and do my homework and I wonder if I can go out and play on my bicycle tonight and things like that.

Similarly, Gina, who was repeatedly abused by her uncle from the age of 8, said:

> It was removed. It was sort of, you know, I can see myself as a child being abused and, it was quite distressing to watch, but after a while you got used to that sort of [intake of breath], it was just there, you know. It's always there.

Anne, who was abused by her father for ten years from the age of 4, recalled that she used to 'space out'. 'You know, just kind of go somewhere else in my head 'till it was over. And particularly when I was smaller with my Dad, 'cos it was painful if I stayed there.'

This 'forgetting' can be pathologised as part of a diagnosis of 'severe dissociative symptoms' (BPD) or 'efforts to avoid thoughts, feelings, or conversations associated with the trauma' (PTSD) in DSM-IV,[166] as outlined in the text box at the start of this section. However, it is not a sign of mental illness, it is an adaptive response for the child that allows her to survive the horrors of physical and psychological invasion, as well as cope with living on a day-to-day basis with the perpetrator of the abuse. As Judith Herman commented, 'the ordinary response to atrocities is to banish them from consciousness'.[164, p.1] How else would a child make sense of moving from rape to eating sausages within a 20-minute period, as Cerena, who was raped by her stepfather from the age of 8, described:

> You know, they, I mean I can't, it's difficult to remember a transition between sitting eating sausages and being raped. . . . You know, we could be going [laughs] you know, 20 minutes after being raped we could be doing quite sort of normal, friendly things. It's that bizarre really.

Forgetting is rarely complete – all of the women who took part in the Long Term Effects of Child Sexual Abuse Study now remembered the abuse, to some degree, by the very fact of their volunteering to take part in such a study. Many women reported flashbacks and memories being triggered by something in their adult life, which took them back to the abusive experience. This too can be deemed a 'symptom' of psychiatric disorder.

Flashbacks and memories: the return of the suppressed

The traumatic event is persistently reexperienced in one (or more) of the following ways:

(1) recurrent and intrusive distressing recollections of the event, including images, thoughts, or perceptions.
(2) recurrent distressing dreams of the event.
(3) acting or feeling as if the traumatic event were recurring (includes a sense of reliving the experience, illusions, hallucinations, and dissociative flashback episodes, including those that occur upon awakening or when intoxicated).
(4) intense psychological distress at exposure to internal or external cues that symbolize or resemble an aspect of the traumatic event.
(5) physiological reactivity on exposure to internal or external cues that symbolize or resemble an aspect of the traumatic event.

309.81 DSM-IV Criteria for Posttraumatic Stress Disorder (PTSD)

The experience of dreams, intrusive memories, flashbacks or intense physiological reactions in response to cues that resemble the abusive event, were reported by many of the women we interviewed.

> Valentina, who was abused by her uncle from the age of 3, told us she experienced flashbacks while she was having therapy, where she regressed to her childhood so that she perceived her stature as that of a child. She said that she remembered and re-experienced the physical sensations of being forced to provide oral sex.

> > I went into the room and I remember feeling anybody's going to come in any minute now and catch us doing this, I remember feeling fear, I remember him, I remember oral sex, him putting me on the bed and spitting in this bucket after oral sex. But I also remember the oral sex being very comfortable, comfortable and soothing, I think that's because it came after intercourse . . . which was very sore.

> Ellen, who was abused by her father three times when she was 8, talked about an experience when she 'hallucinated' a figure at the end of her bed when she was 18 years old:

> > And it frightened the life out of me. It wasn't anyone real because after focusing on this figure, um, it just disappeared, but it, looking back, it was probably my Dad and definitely the eyes were the same.

> She later said that this experience made her feel unsafe again and contributed toward bouts of depression. She said that at these times, she would

> > look under the bed and keep waking up in the night, checking cupboards and, I moved my bed nearer to the door so that I could get out, whereas previously it had been over in, in the far corner. Um, also waking up in the night, panic attacks, sitting up in bed, couldn't breathe.

> This flashback had been triggered off by the recent awareness that her father was ill.

Anna, who was repeatedly abused by her father from the age of 4, talked about having flashbacks since she was about 16, when feelings came back into her consciousness:

> I'll just be standing in a shop, maybe I'd see something, or hear something, but I'd just get this [exaggerated intake of breath] this rush! . . . It's like a really overwhelming feeling, but it's only for a couple of seconds, of the most despicable feeling. It's like, shame, it's feeling dirty. And it would just come and then it would just go.

Olga, who was abused for four years by her stepfather from the age of 9, described the emergence of memories of sexual abuse during sex with her partner:

> I'm there thinking, kissing is fine, cause I really like him and every now and then thoughts creep into my head this is horrible, this is disgusting and then I tell myself no it's not horrible, it's not disgusting, it's someone you like. The sex is really, really quite frightening in some ways because the same thing happens, I get to that stage just before entering, I remember the abuser.

Olga could distinguish between memories of the abuser, and memories of her childhood fear, in contrast to previous relationships where she used to relive 'the squashed feelings'. She said that now she 'just remember[s] the abuser which feels better because I can tell myself it's not the abuser, I literally think of the abuser more than the abuse which I think is a step forward for me'. Olga achieved this by 'making love with the light on because then I can see who this person really is'.

For many women, when memories do return, they can often be partial. For example, Val, who was abused by her father on thirty-two occasions, starting when she was 8 years old, told us that she could not remember everything that she felt she needed to remember about the experience:

> He used to masturbate. He used to sort of rub himself off against my body and you know, press me tight so that, as I say, I felt I couldn't breathe or whatever. Whether there was

> any more to it I wouldn't be surprised you know, um, as I say, these flashbacks imply there was a lot more there.

> Similarly, Anna told us that while she now remembered being abused, she was concerned that she might never come to recall everything about this experience, because she does not have a 'real sense of exactly what did happen'.

All of these accounts of memories, flashbacks and physical reactions meet the diagnostic criteria for PTSD, but they are not a pathology: they are the corollary of the 'forgetting' many children engage in in the face of trauma, particularly repeated sexual abuse,[176] where suppressed memories are triggered by experiences or situations in adult life. The very existence of 'recovered memory' has provoked much controversy in recent decades, described by some as the 'memory wars'.[177] On the one hand, cognitive psychologists have argued that repressed memory is a myth,[e.g. 178] leading to the widespread discussion of 'false memory syndrome'. On the other hand, feminists have decried false memory syndrome as yet another example of the negation of the experiences of women and girls, part of the general denial of abuse that allows sexual violation to continue to occur.[e.g. 22] Detailing the extensive experimental research which has been conducted to prove (or disprove) the false memory hypothesis would take a book in and of itself, one that has already been written.[e.g. 179] It is sufficient to state that there is strong evidence, even from the most sceptical of cognitive psychologists,[e.g. 180–182] that suppression of memories of childhood sexual abuse commonly occurs, often as a result of deliberate avoidance on the part of the child, and that these memories can return in adulthood.[xi]

However, while the 'memory wars' can rage in the pages of academic research journals, with experts pitted against each other, and reputations made, or lost, in the ensuing debate, we should not lose sight of the effect the resulting publicity can have on those who have been abused, who are positioned as liars or fantasists,[e.g. 183] rather than being believed.

> Jenny recalled the effect of media coverage about the issue of False Memory Syndrome, and said that it made her doubt her beliefs about her abuse:

> No way, no way was this False Memory Syndrome. But I did have to really sit down and think about whether it could be or not, whether somebody put that into my head and um, and I went through a real crisis stage about it, and I went to see my counsellor and I said, you know, 'Fuck, do you think I've made this whole thing up?'

When pathologisation and disbelief is added to the violation of sexual abuse, is it surprising that so many women are angry?

Anger and betrayal

Inappropriate, intense anger or difficulty controlling anger (e.g., frequent displays of temper, constant anger, recurrent physical fights)

301.83 DSM-IV Criteria Borderline Personality Disorder (BPD)

For many women, the experience of child sexual abuse is not a distant or suppressed memory, but is an event that remains clearly in their minds as adults, resulting in feelings of intense anger and betrayal. This can be experienced as 'rage', which Janet Wirth-Cauchon described as

> the eruption of emotion that has been held back behind a barrier and has been allowed to grow in intensity and force. It is anger that has crossed the threshold of normality or reason, and is therefore out of control. Rage is therefore a word that connotes the fury of madness; its latin route is *rabies* or madness.[184, p.169]

Rage, as thus defined, stands as a symptom of BPD. A number of women we interviewed gave accounts of feeling angry with their abuser.

Shona remembered wanting to kill her abusive father before she left home when she was 17:

> I was about 17. I just snapped. I remember something inside me, and I remember just turning around and I was just all fists and feet. And I just remember punching him, kicking him, lashing out. Kicking him in the groin as hard as I could and him just collapsing to the floor.

Trying to explain her actions she said:

> Because there was this conflict going on inside about thinking that he loved me but what he was doing to me and then suddenly rejecting me and, then accusing me of being a whore and accusing me of doing this and of doing that and

136

beating me and, there was just such conflict, you know, I couldn't put all this together.

Jessica, who was sexually abused by her father on countless occasions between the ages of 13 and 16 had feelings of great anger and rage towards him, saying, 'This rage was unmanageable for me'. Other women expressed rage towards family members who did not protect them, in particular their mothers. For example, Maggie, who had been repeatedly sexually abused by her grandfather, starting at the age of 4, told us of how as an adult she expressed anger to her parents about their lack of support and inaction, saying:

> 'Didn't you know something was going on? I was raped when I was six, I wouldn't have been able to walk properly, didn't you know? I used to plead not to go down to my grand-parents, why didn't you do something about it?' And their excuse was that thirty years ago sexual abuse wasn't talked about, wasn't known about . . . [so] I wouldn't have been believed anyway.

Carrie, who was abused more than thirty times by her father, starting at the age of 4, then by her brother, felt angry that her mother had known that she was being abused, but chose to ignore it:

> But I know she knew, she, she could never admit it now. But I know she knew, cos each time it happened she just, she, she conveniently wasn't there. Or she was there, she was downstairs, or she was in the kitchen, or she was some-where else, she was always occupied. I don't think she couldn't have known.

Rose, abused on countless occasions by her father starting at the age of 4, also felt angry that her mother did not want to acknowledge the abuse:

> She was actually out of the house in hospital when this happened. And was kept in the dark, because for one thing she always wanted to be kept in the dark, she wanted to be protected, so it's a circle, isn't it?

Alice, interviewed by Catherine Itzen, described her mother standing in the doorway and watching Alice being sexually abused by her grandfather thus: 'It was probably worse than the abuse itself, watching while my mother turned away'.[185, p.125]

These feelings can last for a long time. Ellen told us that she continued to feel anger and hatred toward her parents even though they recently died:

> I can still get angry with my parents and I can still as I said, feel hatred for them. But it's usually something's triggered off like reading about child abuse or lack of awareness about child abuse.

Ellen also spoke about her rage at the 'seductress' label that had been imposed on her by her father. She said that she felt 'very angry, isolated, and I just feel it's unjust . . . the putting on to me of the role of seductress, but not a willingness to discuss i . . . there was a label on me and, and the label was there'.

Are these expressions of 'intense anger' symptoms of a disorder, such as BPD, as many women are told? Or rather, are they another aspect of women's 'reasonable response' to childhood sexual abuse? Anger towards the perpetrator is understandable, and can be positive, as it directs the feelings outwards at the source of the woman's violation and distress. Anger towards adults who turned a blind eye to the abuse, and thus who implicitly support it, is equally understandable. In our interviews anger towards unsupportive mothers was as strong as that towards perpetrators, with women giving accounts of feeling doubly betrayed.[xii] Who wouldn't be angry in such circumstances? Janet Wirth-Cauchon quotes from Toni Morrison's novel *The Bluest Eye* (1970): 'Anger is better – there is presence in anger'.[184, p.195] As bell hooks says: 'it's important to maintain the kind of rage that allows you to resist'.[186, cited by 184, p.195]

One of the explanations for women's depression is the tendency for women to internalise distress, and self-silence, as we have previously seen.[187] Is it thus not ironic that women's anger is pathologised in the context of child sexual abuse? The diagnostic definition for BPD specifies that this is 'inappropriate, intense anger', but who defines 'appropriate'? Not the women who receive this damning diagnosis. Equally, the ascription of 'difficulty controlling anger' as a symptom of BPD levels a gender biased evaluation on women who may be remembering their abuse for the first time, or are reliving it in a current abusive relationship. The notion that women *should* control anger, and that women who do not are mad (or bad) is based on culturally constructed ideals of femininity which regulate all women. Women who have been sexually abused in childhood find themselves experiencing and expressing emotions they were not able to express as a child, when they were silenced and disempowered, at the same time as being physically and psychologically violated. Anger is more than a 'reasonable response' – it is arguably a healthy expression of feelings that would otherwise be turned inward. However, for many women these feelings *are* directed inwards, with guilt and self-blame being associated with reports of self-injury – deemed to be further 'symptoms' of psychiatric disorder.

Guilt and self-blame

Feelings of worthlessness or excessive or inappropriate guilt (which may be delusional) nearly every day (not merely self-reproach or guilt about being sick)

296.2 DSM-IV Criteria Major Depressive Disorder

Identity disturbance: markedly and persistently unstable self-image or sense of self.
Recurrent suicidal behaviour, gestures, or threats, or self-mutilating behaviour

301.83 DSM-IV Criteria Borderline Personality Disorder

Child sexual abuse perpetrators often ensure silence on the part of their victims by telling them that they wanted and enjoyed the abuse – that they asked for it, or were too attractive or seductive, as we have already seen.[63] It is thus not surprising to find that many survivors internalise these pernicious narratives, and blame themselves, because they feel that they could and should have stopped the abuse. When we asked women in the Long Term Effects of Child Sexual Abuse Study survey why they did not disclose the abuse, the reasons they gave included: 'I thought it was my fault, (40 per cent); 'I thought I would be blamed' (40 per cent); and 'I felt guilty' (41 per cent).

Helen told us that she felt that she had 'allowed' the abuse to happen, and said, 'I still feel ashamed about it', even though she 'didn't want it to happen' at the time. Rose described herself as having been frightened when the abuse happened, and said, 'It's when you think back you think you could have done something [crying], but the damage has already been done, hasn't it?' Naomi, who was abused by her uncle for eleven years, starting at the age of 11, talked of only recently accepting that it wasn't her fault when she recognised her daughter's inherent innocence:

> My daughter's 12 now and I think that when I had my daughter was when I really started to come to terms with what had happened to me. Because I *had* internalised it. Somewhere along the line, it was my fault. I had brought this about. I had been too pretty, or I'd given out the wrong signals, or I'd not observed the signals, so somewhere it was *my* fault. And I think it's only since I had my daughter that I think 'Nothing could be her fault'.

Other women never rid themselves of the self-blame. Gina told us how she engaged in self-harm to punish herself for not stopping the abuse. She said:

> [I feel] anger, that I didn't, you know, that somehow I didn't stop it. I still keep thinking that I'm responsible. You know logically that you're not but it's still this feeling that you should have stopped it, that you know, you should have gone to so-and-so.

The complexities of wanting to be close and connected to the abuser, particularly in an incestuous context, yet wanting the abuse to stop, can function to increase feelings of guilt and self-blame.

> In describing abuse by her brother, Carrie said that: 'I was getting the attention I wasn't getting anywhere else, and although it was the wrong sort of attention, at least I was getting some attention, so he must have made me feel worthwhile'.

These feelings can also play out in an adult incestuous relationship.

> When she was 21, Jean's biological father, whom she had recently met following a childhood adoption, tried to force himself on to her and she did not stop him, because she had a fear of losing 'everything'. She was frightened that she would lose him as a father, frightened that she was just overreacting, frightened that she was

enjoying the sexual experience. She also had nowhere else to live at that time. She said:

> I didn't know how to say 'No', I didn't know how to assert myself at all and, I felt somehow to blame even though I didn't do anything. But, because he was pretending that he just wanted to be friendly with me, it was all like a game you know. And at the same time I know he just wanted one thing, but even though I knew that, I was going along with what he was saying. Not that I was doing anything but, or lying but, I don't know I, it, I felt I should of stopped what he was doing at one point you know.

Guilt and self-blame can also be associated with physical responses that take place during the abuse – the response of the body to sexual stimulation. Indeed, while the majority of women in the survey reported that their initial reactions to the abuse were negative, including fear (41 per cent), shock (22 per cent), unhappiness (23 per cent), or anxiety (28 per cent), a number also reported interest (15 per cent), pleasure (9 per cent), or excitement (4 per cent). These reactions were more likely to occur when the child initially thought that the sexual abuse was 'normal', as was the case with 31 per cent of survey participants. Later realisation that it was *not* normal, exacerbation of the abuse, or the presence of threats and violence, led to a re-evaluation in all cases. Remnants of these initial reactions could sometimes remain, however, adding to feelings of guilt and self-blame.

> Jenny experienced 'horrendous guilt' when she recalled having a dream about her father having sex with her, where she had felt quite 'turned on'. Jenny described how she generally enjoyed sex as an adult, in particular foreplay, but she did not feel good after orgasm, which she explained thus: 'Maybe when I was being abused my body responded in the natural way that it should and maybe that, I felt bad about that'.
>
> Sharon, who was abused by her father on countless occasions for ten years from the age of 4, expressed similar feelings saying, 'I actually felt torn at that time because I began to feel the stirrings of, of sexuality and I, I, um, I partly wanted to have sexual contact with my father. That was very, very confusing'.
>
> Positive feelings associated with the abuse were not always sexual. Fiona, who had been repeatedly abused by her stepfather from the age of 3, described how being sexually abused was

associated with comfort, as well as fear and punishment. Her step-father would say she'd 'been cheeky' and 'he would have to hit me or something. I was to go into the bedroom and take my pants off and come back 'cos he was gonna hit me'. After being hit with a brush, when Fiona was 'in tears', her stepfather 'comforted' by fondling her and 'using his fingers' in her vagina. At the time Fiona was taught to feel that 'that was all right, sort of thing, we accepted that easier than getting a good smacking'.

Jean said that when she looked back on the sexual assault now, her reaction was about 'wanting to be loved and not knowing what was right and what was the wrong sort of love anymore, because I'd never really know the right sort of love'.

Many women experience guilt about the abuse every day of their lives, as Shona told us: 'I have carried dreadful guilt all my life. I couldn't go into public places. Even now I find it difficult. I felt guilty for what he had done to me, and for what others have done to me'.

A corollary of this guilt can be negative feelings about the self. Many of the women we interviewed described themselves in very negative terms, ranging from feeling 'different', 'not worthwhile/worthless', 'completely inferior' and stupid, to feelings of 'total and utter self-loathing and shame'.

Sharon referred to herself as a 'monster' and said she thought she was 'completely bad'. Lesley described herself as 'a weak character'. Fiona said that she 'still thinks she is bad in the back of her mind'. Sarah said that she always dreaded that she was (underneath) a 'naughty, nasty person'. Carrie talked about not liking her own moods, her aggressiveness, and anger, saying she also did not like the fact that she was very critical of people in her mind: 'I sometimes feel that I'm a failure because I'm not sort of getting on with it, not dealing with this thing better'.

Ellen felt that 'deep down she didn't like herself . . . I just hated, you know, loathed myself, but I'd kid myself that I looked good. Um, I never thought I was ugly, just felt completely inferior really'. Ellen was in a car crash when she was pregnant and said that she used to feel that it happened because she deserved it: 'I just felt I was the most wicked and awful person on earth, and the car crash had been to pay me back'.

The belief that others would think badly of the child, or blame her, can act to maintain a child's silence and add to feelings of guilt and shame: 51 per cent of women who completed the survey said that they did not disclose the abuse because of feeling ashamed, and 46 per cent said it was because they felt embarrassed.

> Diana, who was abused around fifty times by her brother and his friends, between the age of 7 and 11, said that she knew 'somehow that it was all really bad' and she thought that 'if the parents ever found out about it, you know, they would just think I was, you know, really dirty and everything'.
>
> Jenny remembered an incident that occurred when she was 13, when she was followed by a man who touched her breast in the street. She did not tell her mother about this incident for months because

>> I was too scared. I felt in some way that I might be to blame and for a really a long time afterwards, more than a year, I found it impossible to touch myself where he had touched me. Um, and it was this deep, deep feeling of shame.

As accounts of sexual assault in the media, as well as defence barristers in the courts, often position the woman as to blame,[15] it is not surprising that Diana and Jenny held such fears. Indeed it has also been reported that adults expect children who have been abused to react in a negative way, and to avoid any future contact with the abuser,[188] thus undermining accusations of abuse when this is not the case,[189] as well as serving to blame the child for precipitating or enjoying the abuse.

It has been reported that feelings of stigma and self-blame mediate levels of psychological distress in women who have been sexually abused as children, with higher levels of self-blame being associated with greater distress.[190] However, the feelings of worthlessness, guilt and negative or unstable self-image (to draw directly on the language of DSM) reported in this study are not the sign of pathology. They are an understandable response to the child being told by the perpetrator that she wants or deserves the abuse, reinforced by a cultural context where women who are subjected to sexual violence are blamed,[108; 191–192] or considered to be despoiled. From Thomas Hardy's heartbreaking heroine in *Tess of the D'Urbervilles*, whose husband rejects her when he discovers she was raped as a girl, to contemporary cases where abducted girls are forced by their families to marry their kidnapper, because no one else would now have them,[193] we are reminded of the consequences of women being 'damaged goods'.[xiii] It is thus not surprising to find that guilt and self-loathing are often directed at the body, the focus of the sexual abuse.

Blaming the body

> Recurrent thoughts of death (not just fear of dying), recurrent suicidal ideation without a specific plan, or a suicide attempt or a specific plan for committing suicide
>
> *296.3 DSM-IV Criteria Major Depressive Episode*
>
> Impulsivity in at least two areas that are potentially self-damaging (e.g., spending, sex, substance abuse, reckless driving, binge eating). Recurrent suicidal behaviour, gestures, or threats, or self-mutilating behaviour
>
> *301.83 DSM-IV Criteria Borderline Personality Disorder*

Many of the women we interviewed reported directing self-hatred against the body – with 29 per cent of the women surveyed also saying that a long term consequence of the abuse was body hatred.

Mary, who had been abused by her stepfather over a period of three years, starting when she was 11, said that she did not like looking at herself. Sarah said that as a teenager she loathed her body, which was 'all just part of a terrible feeling that there was something awfully wrong with me'. These feelings of self-loathing were often accompanied by a sense of being dirty and filthy. For example, Janice said, 'it makes you feel dirty and filthy right through. And that's all you know, and that's your self image'. Olivia referred to 'not being clean' because of the loss of her virginity. Carrie said she continues to feel 'dirty' when she feels depressed and low.

In a similar vein, Sharon said, 'this body has been sexually abused and it feels dirty'. She maintained that her experience of abuse had marked her body in some way and was visible to others. She said:

> Um, since I've become aware of my body I've, I've never liked it. I've always felt that it's a product of the abuse. Um, and that I would be a different shape and that I would look different if I hadn't been sexually abused. Um, I don't know if other people can see that in me, I mean I think people can tell, see the signs of depression in my face.

Given these narratives, it's not surprising to find that the body can also be the focus of women's attempts to cope with the abuse, or attempts to block out the memories, or current pain.

Rose talked about overeating, even though she said, 'I don't like my body when it's big'. She described 'being out of control and eating like mad and I can't seem to stop myself', even though she knew 'I shouldn't be doing it'. Other women talked about self-harm as a way of expressing anger and hatred towards the body. Jean, who was abused daily by a teacher for twelve months, when she was 9 years old, said, 'I was very keyed up and the only way I could really let it out was to harm myself, it was the only way I could do anything'. Diana said that harming herself always calmed her down, because 'physical pain is so much easier to handle than mental pain'.

Gina was conscious of 'this part of you that wants to destroy yourself'. She said that she was numb to the pain she inflicted on herself at the same time as she hurt herself in order to feel pain, 'just to feel something you know, it feels like you're real then'. She had strong fantasies about giving herself a mastectomy and wanted to throw herself off a bridge. She said, 'You know, you think if you just cut, you feel something you know, it feel like you're real then'. She added, 'I used to joke that going under a train would be the ultimate cutting experience, it's almost like some kind of thrill, the thought of actually being physically cut up [laughs]'. She referred to this as being both 'a wonderful feeling' at the same time as being 'horrific'. When asked why she hurt herself she responded that she did so because she was punishing herself for not having stopped the abuse.

Lesley described how she used to scratch and dig herself, associating these actions with 'total, utter self-loathing', 'self-blame and shame'. Lesley told us that she wanted to punish herself for not being a 'good and worthy' person, and so she 'went back to cutting':

> My initial intention was actually to, to try and excise the whole breast and get that off. Didn't actually like having . . . I didn't actually get that far which is just as well. Um. All the same I made quite a nasty mess actually.

However, she said that it felt 'relief' to be in pain, as she was in her 'comfort zone' at these times.

Inga Musico has described her experience of cutting in similar terms: 'The sting of pain felt good. It was such a luxury to identify and know a pain'.[194, p.88] This is echoed in the following anonymous account:

how much I know about cutting, about the way the skin breaks apart and shows the mess inside us, about the grey fog of panic that evaporates like steam as the marks were made . . . what is so hard about not cutting is that cutting worked. It made the invisible story exist on the outside.[195, pp.200, 202]

A number of women we interviewed also talked about contemplating suicide.

Janice imagined cutting her wrists in order to 'destroy myself because it's, I'm, so awful'. She told us that 'the reason is, because the blood will let all the filth and all the nastiness out, so I can be clean because the blood's going to take it away and its worth dying for to get rid of it'.

Ellen talked about a number of times when she had become depressed during her life, focusing on a suicidal episode after the birth of her daughter. She mentioned post-natal depression but did not link the suicide attempt directly to it. When asked to describe her feelings at the time she said:

Complete and absolute des . . ., despair, just unbelievable. I mean in, before I'd experienced that and I'd only ever experienced that once, I've, I've never before that or never since then felt so desperate again and it was, it was like, um, there must have been a chemical change because I felt as if I'd been transported onto another sort of planet or some- thing, I wasn't part of this life anymore . . . um, and I just, as I say, the only feelings were this overwhelming guilt, shame and um, despair. There, and that didn't let up. I had that 24 hours a day, seven days a week, for I think three weeks.

Self-harm and attempted suicide are clearly designated as pathology in the DSM, as symptoms of either major depression or borderline personality disorder. However, if we examine the accounts of women who have been sexually abused as children, we can reframe these experiences as coping responses to physical violation.[3] When the body has been violated so many times – being urinated on and penetrated by a group of boys (Diana), objects inserted into the vagina by a teacher (Jean), or raped then forced to perform oral sex on your father (Sharon) – is it surprising that the body is constructed and experienced as 'dirty and filthy'? This is what the girls were often told, and so how can it be a sign of mental illness if this is what they come to believe? Is it surprising that physical pain, or death, can seem

146

preferable to reliving the pain of past – or present – abuse? This is not an 'adaptive' response, but it may feel like the only option to a woman who has been made to feel powerless and worthless, and who has been told that sexual violation is what she deserves. Why is it that self-mutilation of the female body is deemed pathology (or perversion) when similar behaviours in a non-abused context (such as piercing or other forms of body modification) are not derided? Is it that self-mutilation is the opposite of what the idealised woman is expected to do, even if the very essence of such transgression adds to its attraction, standing as an act of anger and defiance?[see 196]

In her reading of 'feminine disorders' such as hysteria or anorexia, Susan Bordo has argued that the somatic 'symptoms' of these disorders are 'literalizations' of women's social situation, with symbolic and political meaning 'within the varying rules governing the historical construction of gender'.[197, p.168] Bordo believes that women can be conceptualised as unconsciously protesting the constraints of their gendered experiences through their bodies, with the body acting as 'a surface on which the conventional constructions of femininity are exposed starkly to view'.[197, p.175] This is reminiscent of Helene Cixous's argument that hysteria was the 'nuclear example of women's power to protest',[198, p.154] discussed in Chapter 2. The same could be said of self-mutilation following child sexual abuse – that it is protest and resistance, rather than 'psychiatric symptoms'. As Nicole Blackman has argued, 'starvation and self-abuse often become[s] a twisted kind of secret respite, a determined flag planted in the psyche that says "*I run this body, mother-fucker*"'.[199, p.100]

Reliving sexual abuse in adulthood: the paradox of 'revictimisation'

> Frantic efforts to avoid real or imagined abandonment.
>
> A pattern of unstable and intense interpersonal relationships characterized by alternating between extremes of idealization and devaluation.
>
> Impulsivity in at least two areas that are potentially self-damaging (e.g., spending, sex, substance abuse, reckless driving, binge eating).
>
> *301.83 DSM-IV Criteria Borderline Personality Disorder*

One of the most widely reported consequences of child sexual abuse is difficulties with adult sexual relationships, which includes avoiding all intimate relationships,[200–202] difficulty forming lasting and satisfying relationships,[203] or avoidance of sexual relationships with men (lesbianism pathologised).[126] Conversely, it has also been reported that women who have experienced childhood sexual abuse are more likely to become involved with men who misuse women,[204] a tendency termed 'revictim-isation'.[205–206]xiv

There have also been numerous reports that women who have been sexually abused are more likely to engage in 'high sexual risk' behaviours, such as prostitution, 'alcohol and substance abuse', 'indiscriminate sexual behaviour', and 'hyper-sexuality',[213] which can be positioned as 'symptoms' of borderline personality disorder, as is illustrated in the text box at the start of this section. Dysfunctional sexual tendencies of CSA survivors frequently reported in the literature include: 'engaging in compulsive or inappropriate sexual behaviours',[214] 'continuously searching for relationships designed to make up for what is lacking in childhood',[200] and 'engaging in relationship with the "wrong" and "inappropriate" male partners'.[204] These so-called symptoms have been blamed for women's revictimisation,[215] as Van Bruggen and colleagues argue:

> There is increasing evidence that women with a history of child sexual abuse are more likely to engage in risky of dysfunctional sexual behaviours in comparison to women without a history of child sexual abuse and that these behaviours might contribute to a vulnerability to further victimisation.[215, p.133]

This is a view widely propagated by self-help and clinical texts which focus on understanding and treating the long term effects of child sexual abuse,[e.g. 216] and which can be summarised as 'the experience of being unable to protect oneself from pain'.[217, p.19]

Many of the women we interviewed described themselves in such a manner, giving accounts of abusive sexual relationships in adulthood for which they blamed themselves.

Fiona told us:

> It was like there's a big neon sign above my head, yeah, it was it was almost acceptable because it had happened before so you can't say it's a one off, and you've gotta look at yourself and think, 'It's gotta be you'.

Shona explained this through her visibility as a victim, as 'the wrong kind of people latch onto you and they then abuse you because they know you are gullible'. Shona said that she felt she was 'going into a vortex, and everything seems to get worse and worse' as she 'just went from one relationship to another that was bad', ending in a relationship with a married man from whom she 'suffered six years of verbal, physical and sexual abuse'. She said: 'I was beaten dreadfully. Some of the things he did to me sexually were abominable'.

Carrie told us that a previous partner who raped her knew about her father, so it was 'well, you've been treated like this so what difference does it make if I treat you this way as well'.

> He was mentally abusive, like my father. Just the way he'd speak to me and put me down constantly. Just the way he used to frighten me, he'd threaten to hit me and then when I got frightened, he'd laugh at me. Say, 'Oh, look at you, look at the state of you'. He knew about my father, so it was 'Well you have been treated like that, so what difference does it make if I treat you like that as well'. For a long while I thought, 'this is my life, this is going to be it forever now'.

Olivia, who was abused as a 10-year-old child by her stepfather, described being unable to protest when she was subjected to a sexual advance made by her second stepfather when she was 38 years old, which triggered memories about how she had responded as a girl when she had been abused:

> Now, I was 38, 39, and I froze just like I'd frozen with [name of her first stepfather] and I just ran out of the flat and spend the whole afternoon crying and shaking and I was so angry with myself because I was no more capable of dealing with that than I had been in dealing with [second stepfather], and I'd spent all my life saying 'if it ever happened again I'd shout, I'd do this, that and the other'. And yet, when it happened with [name] I turned back into a ten year old and I found that very frightening, you know, the same button had been pressed.

When women apparently repeat this pattern of abusive relationship in adulthood, it is often positioned as resulting from their poor judgement of sexual partner,[160] with researchers commenting on women's 'abused tendencies' and 'inappropriate sexual repertoire' as precursors to revictimisation.[212] Thus Messman-Moore and Long have argued that a woman who has been abused in childhood is more likely to be sexually assaulted in adulthood because she is 'less skilled at self-protection, less sure of her own worth and more apt to accept re-victimisation as part of being a woman',[218] which means that 'abuse is not seen as unusual, but expected and acceptable'.[212] Equally, Finkelhor and Browne, in their model of 'traumatic sexualisation',[160] propose that children are sexually groomed through affection to accept inappropriate sexual activity, which then comes to be associated with negative emotions and memories, causing confusion in later sexual relationships and uncertainty about sexual norms. At the same time, perpetrators of abuse are considered to be skilled in identifying, tracking and targeting women who 'show signs of vulnerability'.[218]

The flaw in this analysis is that it pathologises the woman, and positions the blame for any relationship difficulties within her – a pernicious discourse which many women sexually abused in childhood come to accept as the truth of their condition.[173] The inevitability of this outcome is encouraged by authoritative statements that pervade self-help books. As one such text claims: 'some women do not go quite as far as selling their bodies but, instead *find a string of men* who dominate and hurt them, mentally . . . who remind them of their abusers'.[219, p.39, cited by 173, p.337] It is clearly women who are considered to be doing the *finding* here – seeking out abuse. These same descriptions do not circulate about men who have been abused in childhood: we do not see comments in self-help texts, or the research literature, about men's revictimisation, or about men being 'either promiscuous or sexually avoidant';[220] rather, they are positioned as potential future perpetrators.[221] 'Promiscuity' (or conversely, frigidity) is problematic for women – as it is at odds with idealised constructions of femininity, as outlined in Chapter 3. It is not problematic for men, so is not categorised as a 'symptom'. At the same time, the research literature tells us that women who have been sexually abused as children report a 'higher level on a variety of symptoms',[222, p.223] and are more likely to be depressed, than men who have experienced childhood sexual abuse.[158–159] A number of researchers have suggested that this is due to women's greater response to trauma.[157] However, there is another explanation for this, and for men's avoidance of so-called revictimisation, located in the social construction and lived experience of gendered roles within a heterosexual matrix, and the pathologisation of *women's* 'reasonable' responses.

What we see played out in sexually abusive relationships is the extreme end of a continuum of the subjectification and objectification of girls and women which is not merely condoned, but celebrated in popular culture, as discussed at the beginning of this chapter. At the same time, the male brute is idealised, from Heathcliff, to Mark Darcy, to the heroes of Mills and Boon romantic fiction.[15] The sexual abuse of girls within family relationships is the extreme end of a continuum of sexualisation and mistreatment of women, which is endemic across the world. The men who perpetrate abuse are not monsters, they are just ordinary men, enacting a role that is so common that it is rarely prosecuted, and until recent years, has been openly accepted as 'normal'.xv At the same time, while women are blamed for rape and domestic violence, or conversely are disbelieved,[see 108; 191] how can we expect anything other than silence, self-blame, and a feeling of inevitability when this abuse is repeated in relationship after relationship? This is not a sign of madness. If a woman is told that sexual abuse is normal when she is a child, it is hard for her to challenge this view, particularly when she encounters it again and again. As Carrie told us of the series of men who abused her, 'each one would tell me I was nothing and worth nothing'. This is as much about the gendered construction of heterosexual men, as it is about the desires or supposed pathology of abused women. So why is the focus on the madness of women, rather than the violence of men?

We also need to pay attention to the acceptance of gendered power relations within families, where the needs of the father are positioned as pre-eminent, and notions of 'family responsibility' maintain girls' silence.

> Take the case of Cara, who was the oldest of a family of three girls. Her mother suffered depression and was emotionally unavailable, and so Cara took responsibility for the house and her younger sisters from about the age of 9. Her father began to sexually abuse her when she was 8, claiming that he was lonely and desperate for sex. If she did what he wanted he was in a 'good mood' and would provide money for food and clothing. On the few occasions she refused him or hid from him he became depressed, cried and would withdraw for days to his room. Her mother frequently told Cara to 'try and keep your father happy' by allowing him to have sex with her. When Cara at age 13 asked her father to stop abusing her, he told her that he 'had to have it' and would use one of her younger sisters if she would not cooperate. When Cara tried to leave home at 16, her mother threatened suicide and her father told her she would be responsible if this happened. Cara remained at home until her mother's death two years later. When she discovered, after her mother's death, that her father had also abused her younger sisters, she felt an immense sense of failure. Her primary memories of her childhood are of being exhausted, being afraid and desperately trying to create 'a happy family'. This dynamic was re-created within her adult relationships.

Cara was not unusual. Many children love or like their abuser, particularly in the case of interfamilial abuse, and do not disclose to protect them, or to protect the family unit.[225] In the same way, many adult women protect violent male partners, refusing to prosecute them, or leave them, following domestic violence, particularly when men express sorrow and vulnerability, or claim that they cannot survive without the woman.[226] This is not a reflection of individual pathology on the part of the woman or girl who is being abused, as 'victimology' would suggest. Rather, it reflects the power imbalance between men and women within heterosexual family relationships, and the discursive constructions of femininity and masculinity, where women are taught that they need a man, whatever the cost or consequences; where girls are taught to be 'good' and please their fathers (or other trusted men); and sex (or domestic violence) are subjects that are not discussed outside the home. This may be changing, with many women now living alone,[227–228] their subjectivity, success and happiness not dependent on a man, and child sexual abuse now a subject that is spoken of, which makes it harder for perpetrators to prevent disclosure. However, this does not mean that sexual violence and abuse no longer occurs, and that children are not silenced, in the way that they have always been, through disavowal and disbelief.

This chapter has examined the objectification of women, with a specific focus on the context of sexual violence and abuse, arguing that objectification is an endemic practice that functions to maintain women's position as the 'second sex'. The lived experience of objectification and sexual violence is distressing for many girls and women – at the time it is occurring, and when it is relived in memory. This cannot be denied. However, this is not about weakness, inherent vulnerability, or pathology in women. It is a 'reasonable response' to the materiality of abuse, within the gendered construction of heterosexual relationships, where sexual violence against women and girls continues to be enacted. By exploring and exposing the regimes of knowledge that position women survivor's distress as psychiatric disorder, our attention is re-focused on the abuser, and the cultural conditions that condone or deny sexual violence and abuse, rather than on the supposedly 'disordered' woman. We need to understand the material conditions of women and girls' lives that facilitate such abuse – powerlessness, patriarchy, and absence of voice (or refusal of others to hear).[xvi] We need to deconstruct discursive constructions of rape as 'just sex',[15; 74] and of child sexual abuse as innocuous, or good for the child,[18–20] and acknowledge the impact of these constructions on women and girls who are subjected to sexual violation: they can significantly add to women's pain. And finally, we need to acknowledge the lived experience of intrapsychic and embodied distress, as well as women's means of coping and resistance. A similar pattern of women's reasonable responses being pathologised, and of gendered inequality being associated with distress, is also evident in the case example I turn to in Chapter 5: the construction and lived experience of premenstrual distress.

5

THE CONSTRUCTION AND LIVED EXPERIENCE OF WOMEN'S DISTRESS

Positioning premenstrual change as psychiatric illness

As I wrote in *Managing the monstrous feminine*:

> The female reproductive body is positioned as abject, as other, as site of deficiency and disease . . . We are told that menstruation is sign of pollution, source of debilitation and danger, leading to psychiatric illness, criminality and violence . . . Premenstrual change is positioned as sign of the monstrous feminine within, necessitating restraint and control on the part of the women – breakdown in this control diagnosed as PMS, a pathology deserving of treatment . . . The post-natal period is a time when raging hormones are seen to be at their peak, leaving women fragile, anxious, angry . . . [and] menopause brings . . . a disease of deficiency and decay, from which no woman can escape . . . This is a dismal litany.[1, pp.161–162]

Anne E. Figert writes:

> What is really needed is the return to a menstrual hut . . . and its monthly release from traditional women's roles of cooking, cleaning and family duties. This thought is echoed in a cartoon I saw that portrayed an obviously worn out woman holding a screaming child and telling her husband (sitting in the lounge chair and reading the paper) that 'this is stress, not PMS'.[2, p.110]

Premenstrual dysphoric disorder (PMDD) or premenstrual syndrome (PMS) are clear examples of normal female behaviour being discursively constructed as mad, resulting in women taking up (or being given) a psychiatric diagnosis, with consequences for how their behaviour is subsequently judged. In this chapter I examine how this pathologisation legitimises the biomedical management of 'symptoms', and encourages women to position premenstrual change as sign of disease or dysfunction. My argument centres on a contestation of this process of medicalisation, drawing on extensive interview material to demonstrate that PMDD and PMS are constructed and negotiated in a relational context, wherein a woman's partner influences levels of distress and ability to cope. In particular, I focus on the *gendered* construction and lived experience of premenstrual distress, through a comparison of lesbian and heterosexual women, arguing that the context of a lesbian relationship is more conducive to women's ability to cope with premenstrual change, and resist the mantle of madness associated with the reproductive body: the myth of the monstrous feminine.

Deconstructing PMDD as a bio-psychiatric disorder

As I have described elsewhere,[1] premenstrual change was first categorised as a 'disorder' in 1931, described as 'premenstrual tension' (PMT).[3] It was renamed 'premenstrual syndrome' in 1956,[4] and now sits in the DSM-IV as PMDD,[5] officially categorising premenstrual mood or behaviour change as a psychiatric disorder.[see 1; 6]i At the time of writing, a 'mood disorders work group' is 'accumulating evidence' as to whether PMDD should be included in DSM-V.[7] Women who report a range of psychological and physical symptoms premenstrually, including anxiety, tearfulness, irritability, anger, depression, aches and pains, or bloating, can be diagnosed as having PMDD. It is estimated that around 8–13 per cent of women meet a PMDD diagnosis each month, with around 75 per cent meeting the lesser diagnosis of premenstrual syndrome (PMS) – the same conglomeration of symptoms, just experienced to a lesser degree.[8] It also means that the majority of the female population of reproductive age could be deemed 'mad' once a month, as PMS and PMDD are both widely accepted as a pathological condition.ii

However, PMDD was included in the DSM-IV in the face of widespread feminist opposition, on the basis that there is no validity to PMDD as a distinct 'mental illness'.[6] Feminist critics have dismissed this process of pathologisation, arguing that premenstrual change is a normal part of women's experience, which is only positioned as 'PMDD' or 'PMS' because of Western cultural constructions of the premenstrual phase of the cycle as a time of psychological disturbance and debilitation.[e.g. 9–11] In cultures such as Hong Kong or China, where change is accepted as a normal part of daily existence,[12] women report premenstrual water retention, pain, fatigue, and increased sensitivity to cold, but rarely report negative premenstrual moods.[13–14] This has led to the conclusion that PMS is a culture bound syndrome,[15] which follows unprecedented changes in the status and roles of women in the West,[16–17] with the belief that women are erratic and unreliable premenstrually serving to restrict women's access to equal opportunities.[18] Indeed, belief in the negative influence of premenstrual 'raging hormones' has been used to prevent women being employed as pilots,[19] physicians and presidents,[2] which by extension casts doubt on the reliability of *all* women occupying positions of responsibility.

It is the regimes of truth within Western medicine, which position pre-menstrual change as pathology, that provide the discursive context wherein women learn to define themselves as a 'PMS sufferer'.[20] Medical textbooks and academic journals convey the message that raging hormones are the cause of women's higher rates of reported depression, as we saw in Chapter 3. At the same time 'Dr Google' ensures that this message is taken up by the masses, warning of the danger and difficulty of a woman who is 'pmsing'. Try it for yourself. Google 'PMS' and this is among the first pieces of advice you will be given:

> **Premenstrual Syndrome:** PMS is a disorder characterized by a set of hormonal changes that trigger disruptive symptoms in a significant number of women for up to two weeks prior to menstruation. Of the estimated 40 million sufferers, more than 5 million require medical treatment for marked mood and behavioral changes.[21]

Current medical advice is that PMDD and PMS should be treated with hormones or SSRIs, as Steiner and Born concluded in their review of treatments for the 'disorder', PMDD:

> The serotonergic system is in close reciprocal relationship with the gonadal hormones and has been identified as the most plausible target for interventions. Thus, beyond the conservative treatment options such as lifestyle and stress management, and the more extreme interventions that eliminate ovulation altogether, *the selective serotonin (5-hydroxytryptamine; 5-HT) reuptake inhibitors (SSRIs) are emerging as the most effective treatment options for this population.*[8, p.288, my emphasis]

Medical marketers are quick to take up the baton, persuading us to use their particular products. In 2001 Eli Lilly repatented the SSRI Prozac as Sarafem, repackaging it in pink and lavender capsules,[iii] accompanied by an aggressive marketing campaign which told women 'PMDD affects millions of women . . . but the good news is that your doctor can treat PMDD symptoms with a new treatment called *Sarafem*'.[22, p.39] Similarly, the website for Zoloft, which tells us that the drug has been approved for the treatment of PMDD, addresses the question 'What causes PMDD?' We are told:

> No one knows for sure. But there is a natural substance in the body called serotonin (sair-uh-toe-nin). The symptoms of PMDD may

occur when serotonin is out of balance. In PMDD, this imbalance may be related to your monthly changes in hormones.[23]

We are then reassured that 'Zoloft may help to balance serotonin in the body. And that may help you find relief from PMDD'. The success of such marketing is reflected in reports that in the first six months after the US Food and Drugs Administration (FDA) approved SSRIs for PMDD, 2.5 million prescriptions were written.[24]

If women, or their doctors, want to adopt a hormonal approach to treatment, the website for contraceptive pill Yaz tell us confidently:

> YAZ® (drospirenone & ethinyl estradiol) is the ONLY birth control pill proven to treat the emotional and physical symptoms of pre-menstrual dysphoric disorder (PMDD) in women who choose the Pill for birth control.[25]

However, in 2008, Bayer, the maker of Yaz, was sanctioned by the FDA for misleading television commercials which did not distinguish between PMDD and PMS,[26] and asked to broadcast a corrective commercial which rectified the situation.[27] The Yaz website now distinguishes between PMS and PMDD, telling us that 'YAZ is not for the treatment of premenstrual syndrome (PMS)'. Bayer is not alone in this misrepresentation of women's premenstrual experiences. The marketers of Sarafem provoked a similar letter of objection from the FDA on the basis that their advertising was 'misleading and lacking in fair balance',[22, p.39] because they did not distinguish between PMDD and PMS, and did not define PMDD. As I write, the Zoloft website continues to make no distinction between PMS and PMDD, suggesting that any woman who identifies with the list of symptoms laid out below will consider herself eligible for SSRIs:

> The symptoms of PMDD start a week or two before a woman gets her period, and may last up to a few days after her period starts.
> If you have PMDD, you may:
> Feel angry, tense, or tired
> Cry easily, or feel sad or hopeless
> Argue with friends or family for no reason
> Have trouble sleeping or paying attention
> Feel 'out of control' or unable to cope
> Have cramping, bloating, food cravings, or breast tenderness[28]

This list has the potential to include the significant proportion of women of reproductive age who experience premenstrual mood or behavioural change – categorising these changes as 'symptoms' of a 'disorder' that need to be medically managed. A similar process is being enacted with another 'disorder' that has the potential to be diagnosed in a significant proportion of adult women, 'female sexual dysfunction' (FSD), with drug companies avidly vying to develop a pill to increase women's sexual arousal and desire.[29] So far the search has proved elusive. With PMDD the drug companies have clearly been more successful, positioning the message that SSRIs reduce premenstrual distress as unquestioned truth. However, as was noted previously, the placebo response for SSRIs is very high,[30–31] as is the case for all medication given for PMS and PMDD.[32] Indeed, there is a significant 'revolving door' problem with treatments for PMS, particularly those of a biomedical nature, with many women trying treatment after treatment and finding that while they may 'work' for a short time, over a longer period the 'symptoms' return.[32] Equally, the prescription of SSRIs for PMDD is not without material consequences, as is evidenced by the acknowledged side effects. On the Zoloft website we are told:

> The most common side effects of taking *Zoloft* in studies for PMDD were dry mouth, sweating, diarrhea [sic], upset stomach, nausea, less interest in sex, feeling tired, and having sleep problems. In these studies for PMDD, most women did not have to stop taking *Zoloft* because of side effects.[23]

Women have also reported problems with vision,[33] bleeding to the fingertips, and substantial weight gain after taking SSRIs for PMDD.[1] The fact that many women continue to take psychotropic drugs to alleviate 'PMDD' despite these side effects is testimony to the level of distress associated with premenstrual change, and to the influence of the medicalised message that the problem is solely within, and that it must be eradicated.

Women's subjectification: taking up the subject position of premenstrual madness

This is the message that many women in the West have taken up, accepting a diagnosis of PMS or PMDD, and positioning themselves as mad – even if only temporarily – as a result of premenstrual change. We can see clear evidence of this in the findings of the PMS and Relationships Study that I conducted with Janette Perz, where we interviewed 60 Australian women who described themselves as PMS sufferers (see Appendix). Given the prevalence of biomedical discourse on PMS, it was not surprising to find that many of the women blamed their bodies for premenstrual change, with the focus being on 'hormones'; the absence of direct consumer advertising in Australia limited the likelihood of messages promoted by SSRI marketers permeating women's consciousness.

Gillian said, 'your hormones can be off, and not where they should be', Judith described her PMS as 'hormonal rushes', and Joan described 'hormonal imbalances' over which she had no control. Ruth described this hormonal change as 'pretty horrible':

> I presume it's a chemical something or other is happening inside me, but I've tried various lotions and potions. It's not always exactly the same every month. But it's generally pretty horrible. And as I say I just, I think it's got to be chemical.

This attribution of PMS to the body was not a neutral judgement. Many women gave accounts of hating their bodies premenstrually – adopting the mantle of the 'monstrous feminine', where the reproductive body is positioned as abject.[1] In the interviews, dislike of the premenstrual body was focused on women's feelings of bloatedness, such as when Jacinta told us, 'Oh, I look at myself and I go, "You big fat pig!"', or when Mary said she wore baggy clothes at this time of the month, because of 'my swollen breasts and my tummy gets swollen'. Many women also reported feeling self-conscious and insecure as a result of embodied changes premenstrually. Janice said that she felt 'uncomfortable in my own skin'. Lorna told us that 'you feel bloated so you feel unattractive and you feel down, then you feel that people are viewing you differently'. Nancy said, 'I feel fat. I feel ugly. I feel unattractive, unwanted. My face will just break out, so that'll make it even worse so you know I'll feel really paranoid'.

As bloating signifies 'fat' for many women, an abhorrent state in a cultural context where women are expected to regulate the boundaries of corporeality,[34] it is not surprising to find that perceptions of premenstrual weight gain are experienced in such a negative manner.

The premise behind PMS and PMDD, that subjectivity, mood, and bodily experience *should* be consistent and constant reflect a modernist Western view which conceptualises identity as rational and unitary, with deviation from the norm as sign of illness.[35] Hegemonic constructions of idealised femininity in Western culture place particular emphasis on women being calm and in control (as well as slim), with deviations from this norm being positioned as pathology. When combined with negative constructions of menstruation,[1] this leads to women engaging in practices of self-surveillance, monitoring moods, behaviour and bodily sensation in relation to unrealistic ideals,[36] then blaming themselves, or their bodies, for transgressions.[37] Women come to anticipate negative premenstrual change,[38] and thus take up the subject position 'PMS sufferer', through a process of subjectification.[20; 35] Feeling 'out of control' is a primary 'symptom', reflecting the Western cultural construction of 'control' as a signifier of sanity and well-being.[39–40]

PMS as a constructed and lived experience

This emphasis on the constructed nature of PMS and PMDD within feminist social constructionism could, however, be read as negating agency, the existence of premenstrual distress (both psychological and somatic), as well as other material aspects of women's lives that may be associated with self-diagnosis as a PMS sufferer. This is problematic, as premenstrual change is not simply a discursive construction. There is convincing evidence that many women experience embodied and psychological change, accompanied by an increased sensitivity to emotions, or to external stress, during the premenstrual phase of the cycle.[41–44] Many women report that their perception is more acute premenstrually – with noises seeming louder, and their sense of smell more acute,[45, pp.94–97] which can result in stress being potentially experienced as more problematic at this time.[46] The multiple tasking which is a normal part of most women's lives can also be more difficult,[47] leading to distress when the responsibilities of home, work and study cannot be accommodated at the same time.[43] And emotions such as anger, sadness or irritability – as well as creativity or sexual desire – can be experienced as more powerful than usual premenstrually.[36; 48]

There is also a growing body of research reporting an association between relationship strain and premenstrual symptomatology, suggesting that problems in relationships may underlie many women's premenstrual distress,[43; 49–51] with relationship satisfaction deteriorating premenstrually for some women.[52–56] The responsibilities of childrearing and domestic responsibilities, in particular, have been found to be associated with reports of premenstrual distress,[36; 40; 43; 57] and many women worry that 'PMS' has an impact on their partners and their children.[58–59] Direct expression of emotion has also been found to be lower in relationships where women report PMS,[50] which increases the likelihood of premenstrual change being experienced or viewed as problematic, while conversely, effective communication between couples has been linked to lower levels of premenstrual distress.[60–62] At the same time, the use of belittling or demeaning constructions of PMS on the part of men has also been reported to be common,[63–64] reinforcing a gendered power imbalance where menstruating women are positioned as dangerous or dysfunctional.[1] In this vein, the responses of male partners to premenstrual change has been found to be particularly influential, with partner support being associated with lower levels of premenstrual distress in women, and lack of support with higher levels of distress.[65–66] In couples where men demonstrated empathy, understanding and awareness, marital satisfaction was also higher, and women's coping with premenstrual distress more effective,[53] which has led to the conclusion that partners may act as 'moderators' of symptoms.[67–68]

These findings are not at odds with a constructivist analysis if we acknowledge that PMS is both a constructed and a lived experience,[see 69] with premenstrual change constructed as 'PMS' in particular socio-cultural contexts, and premenstrual distress developing and being negotiated in the context of women's lives, in particular, within the context of their intimate relationships. However, the majority of research conducted to date on the construction and experience of premenstrual distress in the context of relationships has focused on heterosexual women and couples. This has either been by explicit intention, or by omission, as women who take part in research on PMS are generally not asked about their sexual orientation, or the gender of their intimate partner. This means that it is not possible to disentangle the gendered nature of relational dynamics, or the influence of men's constructions of PMS, from the negotiation and experience of premenstrual change that would take place in a relational context. This raises the question: if PMS is a gendered experience, as many feminists have argued, is premenstrual change constructed and experienced differently in heterosexual and lesbian relationships? To answer this question, as well as to explore the construction and lived experience of PMS in the context of relationships more broadly, we included both lesbian and heterosexual women in the PMS and Relationships Study, where of the 60 interviewed women who defined themselves as suffering from PMS, 45 were hetero-sexual, and 15 lesbian. We also interviewed 25 partners – 10 women and 15 men (see Appendix). The findings of this research are presented below.

The relational construction and lived experience of PMS

'All the relational pinches come up at that time': premenstrual irritation with partners

When we asked women in the PMS and Relationships Study to describe their 'PMS', we found that premenstrual vulnerability, or changes in mood, were primarily defined as 'symptoms' within an intersubjective context – as a reaction or response to others.[57] All of the women described 'PMS' as being characterised by heightened premenstrual irritability, intolerance of others and oversensitivity, using terms such as 'irritable', 'cranky', 'short-tempered', 'snappy', 'confrontational', having a 'short fuse', 'bitey', 'impatient', 'grumpy', 'stroppy', 'frustrated', 'stressed', 'annoyed' or 'teary' to describe themselves premenstrually.

As Gillian told us, 'People around me just cheese me off more [laugh] so whatever I've felt about them, if they do something that I don't like, I'll react more'.

Women's partners were positioned as the major focus of irritation, across both heterosexual and lesbian relationships. Mistakes that would normally be tolerated by the woman were described as a source of conflict.

Fiona reacted with anger when her husband 'destroyed' her clothes when doing the washing: 'You know, your husband put some washing through and, you know, destroyed your clothes . . . so even when people are doing the right thing, it's still the wrong thing at that time of the month'.

Similarly, Janna said that 'things that probably wouldn't bother me otherwise tend to bother me a whole lot more, not with other people, probably more towards Christy' (Janna's female partner).

Other women talked of being less intolerant of their partners' foibles premenstrually, such as when Elaine described her husband as 'a bit of a hoarder and a collector, and three weeks of the month that does not bother me'. However, when premenstrual, Elaine said, 'it bothers me a lot and I want to throw everything out, to put everything into plastic bags and dump it on his desk [laughs]'.

Irritation at 'little things, sort of akin to leaving the lid off the toothpaste' was also commonly expressed, as Katie told us:

We've got a tea-towel at home on our stove, on our oven and hand-towel for your hands, and he's always screwing up the tea-towel instead of using the hand-towel, wipes his forehead with it and things like that, just little things, you know, he always leaves the toilet seat up.

Similarly, Jacinta described being angry premenstrually because her partner 'didn't wring the washer out before she picked the washer up . . . it was full of water and she picked it up and went, "Oh"', describing her reaction as 'the silliest one I can think of at the moment where my fuse is short'.

Descriptions of irritation triggered by apparently minor incidents could also be interpreted as masking deeper feelings of hurt or frustration.

Melanie told us that when she was tired, and her husband had 'the TV up too loud' she'd 'ask him to turn it down and he won't listen', which would result in Melanie becoming 'really angry and I'll sort of almost go overboard and I'll say "You don't care about me!" And "If you cared about me you'd know!"'

Bella said of her husband 'The guy can't do or say anything right' when she is premenstrual. She described herself as 'just highly sensitive' and 'picky on him', giving as examples, 'I don't like the shirt you're wearing' or 'Gee, you know, aren't we ever going to have the money to do up this bloody house'.

Premenstrual ruptures in self-silencing

The above accounts of feeling uncared for, or feeling angry because planned renovations were not underway, were substantive issues not raised during the three weeks of the month when Melanie and Bella were not premenstrual. This was not unusual in heterosexual relationships.

As Joyce said, 'Everything comes up at that time, yeah. Everything that might just be a slight pinch normally comes up at the PMT time and it's intensified'.

Approximately half of the women in heterosexual relationships (but none of the lesbians) gave accounts of self-sacrifice and self-silencing in relation to their partner for three weeks of the month, and reported finding this more difficult, or speaking out, when they 'have PMS'.

Caitlin described herself as 'facilitating and accommodating' for most of the month and then being a 'little bit more assertive . . . touchy . . . saying what I think, instead of being so nice' when she was premenstrual.

Nadia wondered whether it was her 'true feelings that are coming out more at a time like that'. She continued:

I find it harder to hide, perhaps, negative feelings that I am feeling at other times as well, that I manage to hide, and maybe at that time the defences are a bit down and I can't hide them as much.

Katie said that 'all these things that you sort of kept inside before, because things were OK, and you don't want to upset the applecart, when you're feeling emotional you start complaining about things they've done that you haven't said before'.

162

These accounts of 'PMS' could be characterised as a rupture in women's self-silencing, where the hetero-feminine ideal of caring compliance is replaced by anger and assertiveness.[36; 40; 70]iv As discussed in Chapter 2, Dana Jack has argued that women repress their anger and self-silence in an attempt to maintain connection with others, under the belief that anger is inevitably destructive to relationships.[74] However, this is an erroneous belief as there is consistent evidence that the open expression of anger and disagreement within intimate couple relationships leads to greater relationship satisfaction in the long run, whereas couples who avoid conflict are the least satisfied.[73] Indeed John Gottman and Lowell Krokoff, in a detailed analysis of the role of communication and relationship satisfaction in heterosexual relationships, conclude that 'wives should confront disagreement and not be overly compliant, fearful and sad but should express anger', because it is women who generally raise and 'manage' marital disagreements.[75, p.51] Premenstrual self-silencing has been found to be associated with reports of higher depression and anxiety,[40; 70] confirming reports of a relationship between self-silencing and women's depression more generally.[71; 73; 76] In a survey completed by 257 women who took part in the PMS and Relationships Study, we found that women reported high levels of self-silencing, as assessed by Dana Jack's self-silencing scale, the STSS,[77] in particular the inhibition of thoughts and feelings to avoid relationship conflict and loss (which Jack calls 'Silencing the Self'),[73] and behaving in a compliant manner while feeling angry inside (the 'Divided Self').[40] However, as is evidenced by the accounts presented above, premenstrually a 'rupture' in women's self-silencing occurs, with suppressed emotions being expressed.

In an attempt to explain premenstrual ruptures in self-silencing within relationships, it has been argued this is the only time that some women 'allow' themselves to be angry, as they can attribute anger to their hormones,[68] described as a 'redeployment' of the reproductive body to meet women's emotional needs.[78] This implicitly suggests a calculated decision on the part of women to express anger and use PMS as an 'excuse'.[79] Some of the young women interviewed by Marlee King in the Positive Premenstrual Experiences Study (see Appendix), were overt in their talk of enjoying 'venting' feelings premenstrually.

Sally told us, 'I like it that I do get angry because I let it out for something that I haven't let out before'. Or as Joanne told us:

I'll tell my boyfriend exactly what I think and it can relate to something that he did at the start of the month and that's the way I bring it up at the end of the month, which I kind of like.

> Being premenstrual, according to Lillie, 'just allows us to express ourselves – just to be how we want to be at times . . . If there's something negative, you're just like "I'm getting my period, so just leave me alone". You're allowed to be a bitch'.

A post on the website PMSBuddy, by 'MsQ', entitled *Can't help it!*, tells a similar story.[v]

> I don't know if I can say I mind all that much when my cycle comes and I experience PMS. Despite the series of thoughts and emotions – I'm more forward, saying how I feel – normally I put up with a lot but when I start to experience PMS I care more about how people treat me and I quickly speak up when perhaps before, I didn't/ wouldn't have the balls to do or say anything. Maybe its just that my life kinda sucks and I just see it more when I'm on my period/ experiencing PMS because my emotions are stronger. I can't say I enjoy crying for no reason, loosing [sic] the desire to do things, or eating everything. . . . But, the forwardness is GREAT![80]

In the PMS and Relationships Study, a number of women described the premenstrual release of emotion as cathartic in the short term, allowing them to 'get things off my chest'.

> As Joyce said, allowing 'the annoyances or the things that might be needing work in the relationship actually get dealt with'. Similarly, Olivia decided, after much reflection on her cyclical changes, that they must 'mean something':

> > I've been repressing things for years, and dismissing things for years, just saying, 'Oh, it's just PMS.' That's bullshit. You need to look at it and say, 'Well, if I keep feeling this way, about this particular issue, at this time of the month . . . then, it's got to mean something'. You know. Yeah. [laugh]

Rather than being 'PMS', a problem tied to the body, Olivia's 'symptoms' could be reframed as an emergence of emotions that are repressed during the rest of the month, either because the feelings are too difficult to face, or because she doesn't want to rock the boat in her relationship by being angry. However, cathartic expression of these feelings was invariably followed by guilt and self-criticism, suggesting that PMS is not simply an excuse, allowing women to get away with 'bad' behaviour.

Rachel told us, 'you feel horrible about it the next week . . . it makes you feel sick'. Susannah describes her premenstrual experiences as 'embarrassing'. Stephanie said she feels 'really upset' and 'angry' with herself afterwards. Jacinta said she hates herself when she thinks about this time of the month. Linda said, 'I feel terrible about it'. This criticism extends beyond premenstrual behaviour to women's view of themselves. Joyce said, 'My perception of me [premenstrually] is lousy because I feel pretty lousy about myself, why would anybody want to be on side with me?' Similarly, Penny said, 'I don't like myself very much, in lots of ways, at that time and it doesn't help'.

Each of these women was exhibiting what Casey described as her 'inner critic', the surveillant, judging, self which is most vigilant when women express anger or discontent within intimate relationships. These are clear examples of the 'failure of the self' which relational-cultural theorists attribute to women's loss of reciprocal connection with others.[81] This is because the expectation of care for others, and the emphasis on 'emotional maintenance', is invariably translated into an 'ethic of responsibility', where women are positioned (and position themselves) as bearing full liability for relationships.[73; 82] This can result in women experiencing guilt and over-concern for maintaining relationships, in particular those with partner and children, which leads to the feeling, in Jean Grimshaw's words, that 'not upsetting people must always be given priority'.[83, p.196] Indeed, for the majority of the women we interviewed, both lesbian and heterosexual, it is the impact of their premenstrual moods on others that stands at the centre of this self-castigation, as Leah commented:

> I just feel guilt and it's, or just, like, knowledge from my inner self goes 'That's not like you, you know, this is not what you want in so far as who you are, there's no reason to bite that person's head off, like that was nothing,' you know, so it's like . . . and I feel remorse, because it's like, 'Oh, I'm really sorry,' because I've visibly hurt somebody's feelings and I don't like to do that, that's not who I am as a mature loving person.

As was evident in Leah's comments above, many of the interviewees positioned PMS as something separate from themselves, as 'not me', or as the 'PMS self', as has also been reported in previous research.[6; 36; 84]

> Tracy said, 'It wasn't me, the person's, fault, it was the hormonal stuff'. Kylie said, 'I'm another personality'. Susannah said, 'I want to pretend to myself that I'm an intelligent person who knows what's

happening in today's world and be well presented in everything. Then
I have this thing for a few days when I'm not necessarily that person'.

In each of these instances women are escaping self-blame for expressing
anger by disavowing or 'masking' it,[74] through positioning anger as an
out-of-control pathology, PMS, rather than accepted as a legitimate
reaction or response. At the same time, they are adopting the cultural
construction of the reproductive body as sign of the 'monstrous feminine',[1]
in this instance as cause of premenstrual irrationality or anger. Eli Lilly's
advertising for the PMDD medication Sarafem draws on and reinforces
this same cultural discourse, positioning premenstrual behaviour as sign of
a deviant 'other' self, while at the same time promising a chemical cure:
'*Sarafem* helps you be more like the woman you are, everyday of the
month, even during your most difficult days'.[22, p.50]

The contrast between levels of self-castigation reported in the PMS and
Relationships Study and the Positive Premenstrual Experiences Study is
interesting. One simple explanation was that we recruited the women
differently – asking for women who had moderate to severe PMS in the
first study, and positive experiences premenstrually in the second. Another
difference was that the women in the Positive Premenstrual Experiences
Study were younger, having an average age of 21, in comparison with the
women in the PMS and Relationships Study, whose average age was 37.
Many of the cultural constructions of PMS directed at younger women
(and men) parody the 'PMS bitch',[vi] which may allow young women to
embrace a hitherto stigmatising moniker, in the same way that gay men and
lesbians often embrace the label 'queer'. The other explanation is that the
younger women were generally not in long term cohabiting relationships,
which meant that they were less reliant on their partners' responses to
changes in their premenstrual mood or behaviour, and were less likely to
have to negotiate the material consequences of gendered power relations.
They could literally escape to a room of their own, rather than having to do
housework and look after children, a major source of distress premenstrually for other women, as is outlined below.

'I just want you all to stop putting demands on me': burden of care and responsibility

In a letter from Anne Sexton to her psychiatrist, Dr Martin Orne (6
February 1957) she writes:

My heart pounds and it's all I can hear – my feeling for my
children does not surpass my desire to be free of their demands on

my emotions . . . What have I got? Who would want to live feeling that way?[85, p.120]

The responsibilities of being a parent and managing a home at the same time, often on top of paid work, were positioned as a source of premenstrual distress by women who had dependent children.

Merrin told us, 'The major thing that I probably notice is that I get most irritated about the burden of care type activities, which tend to weigh most heavily on me'. She described this as 'the coming home and the doing the dinner, particularly after a day of paid work, and the home work, the cleaning up, the school notes, whatever else needs to be done'.

Similarly, Eleanor said, 'I guess that's the time where I feel, Hey, I'm just not feeling 100 per cent and I just want you all to stop putting demands on me, you know? The son, the dog, the work, everybody'.

As is evidenced by Merrin and Eleanor's comments, the burden of childcare was often a focus of women's premenstrual irritation.

Sophie described being angry because she wished her children would 'clean the room' and 'take the rotten sandwiches from under the bed', rather than expecting her to do both.

Maggie described mornings as the hardest time: 'when you are getting up and getting the kids ready and if they not like doing the right things, it's the worst thing that could happen in the day, and you get really, really angry, over silly little things'.

Monica described herself in a similar way, saying, 'I have to watch my anger and [being] snappy at the kids, unnecessarily so. Little things will really bother me much more'.

Kylie described her anger being triggered by an argument between her younger children: 'they were fighting over my son's Bob the Builder spoon and I just said "right" and I snapped it in half and said "no one's having it" and that was it. I regretted it later on, of course'.

Other women described the premenstrual phase of the cycle as a time when they weren't able to give emotionally to their children. As Elaine told us:

With the kids, you know sometimes, maybe they want me to sit there and chat with them at night, and I feel like, for me, at that point [premenstrually], you know, I'll give them a kiss

and cuddle goodnight and have a quick chat but I don't want
to sit there and chat to them. It's almost fake. I'm not there.
I'm not there so it's better if I, I feel remove myself from it
than not giving the hundred per cent.

The majority of interviewees reported guilt and self-remorse for
expressing anger or irritation with their children. Thus Katie told us
that she 'felt so bad'. Rachel that she 'felt really horrible', about being
irritated with her children premenstrually. Elaine 'felt terrible' for not
being 'calm and nurturing'. Kylie told us: 'I actually started seeing a
psychologist because I was really concerned the effect it [PMS]
would have on my children because they're so young and I think it
has settled down since I've been seeing her'.

However, rather than questioning why women become irritable with their
children once a month, perhaps we should acknowledge the fact that these
same women repress their reactions to arguments, noise, mess, disobedi-
ence, lack of help in the home, whinging, tardiness in getting ready for
school or doing homework – some of the triggers reported in our interviews
– for the remaining three weeks. Indeed, when we look to the materiality of
the mothering role, combined with the predominant cultural representation
of the mother as 'ever-bountiful, ever-giving, (and) self-sacrificing',[86, p.2]
women's irritation is not surprising. Unrealistic expectations are placed
upon mothers, that require the 'patience of a saint', in the words of one of
our interviewees – yet premenstrual changes in vulnerability or tolerance
make it nigh on impossible to retain a saintly demeanour.

The contrast between the reality of the demands of the mothering role,
and idealised cultural constructions of motherhood, has been recognised by
many feminists to be a cause of depression for women.[87–88] Natasha
Mauthner argues that post-partum depression 'arises out of the discrepancy
(women) experience between the mother they want to be and the mother
they feel they are'.[88, p.470] Adrienne Rich has eloquently described the self-
castigation that invariably follows maternal anger, drawing on her own
experiences.[89] The same could be said of women who report PMS.
Women's premenstrual inability to enact an ideal of perfect motherhood
can a source of premenstrual distress, with irritation or anger towards
children being positioned as a pathology, 'PMS'.

Bill, who was Olivia's partner, identified this as a clear pattern in her
distress: 'She has this ideal version of what she, as a mother, should
be. And she can't adhere to it. She can't live up to it. And so that
depresses her, at times. Mainly at this time of the month'.

The structure of the family within hetero-patriarchy is also centrally implicated in many of these accounts. In heterosexual relationships, women are expected to take the major responsibility for domestic tasks, and invariably do so,[90–91] particularly in the presence of children, where women do 70 per cent of the unpaid caring and housework, even if they are working full time.[92] It has been argued that parenthood 'crystallizes gendered divisions of labour',[90, p.413] with the fact that the mother is described as the 'fundamental organizational feature of the sex-gender system'.[81, p.41] Nancy Chodorow argued that 'it is basic to the sexual division of labor and generates a psychology and ideology of male dominance as well as an ideology about women's capacities and nature'.[81, p.41] Indeed, in a study of 150 US women, Patricia Coughlin reported that women with a career and childrearing responsibilities reported the highest levels of premenstrual distress.[43] These are women who typically have little time for themselves, undertaking a 'double-day' of home responsibilities following a day of paid work, and who find themselves irritated or angry premenstrually. This is not pathology – it is an understandable response. Many of our interviewees explicitly acknowledged these pressures.

> Maggie said, 'When I go on holidays and I have PMS, I actually feel a little bit better than when I'm working all the time'. This was because she had respite from her normal routine, where 'I've got to come home and I've got to take kids to sport, then I've got to cook dinner, and stuff'. Being on holiday didn't mean that Maggie didn't experience premenstrual changes, but she had more space to cope 'because you're a bit more relaxed . . . a bit more aware'.

Neglecting time out and self-care: differences between lesbian and heterosexual women

It was thus unsurprising to find that the most common means of coping with premenstrual change reported by the majority of women we interviewed was the desire to take time out from responsibilities, or from being with others.

> Jill said, 'solitude is wonderful, being by yourself, doing your own thing', which allowed her to avoid all the demands being made of her, 'be it sort of work related, personal related, family, relations, whatever'.
> Jackie said, 'I can't give anything to anybody. I just want to be by myself'. Helena told us, 'I'm more likely to want to be on my own . . . because I don't feel like having people in my face'.

169

Danni described a fantasy that many women shared, of being alone and being totally free of responsibilities when she was pre-menstrual:

> It just feels too hard and that . . . it's all burden . . . and I sometimes just think, 'God, if I was by myself, I would just do nothing for that two weeks!' [laugh] I wouldn't have to worry about anyone and I would just come home, sit on the sofa and not move for a fortnight [laugh].

This is reminiscent of the 'room of one's own' that Virginia Woolf identified as so important to women's creativity – as well as their sanity,[93] described more recently as an essential 'health promoting resource for women'.[94] All the lesbian women we interviewed described taking time out for themselves premenstrually as an unquestioned right that they exercised without difficulty.

> Nancy commented, 'I can just say "I actually don't give a fuck about anyone else but myself right now" and I'll be self-indulgent and precious and that's all right'.
> Simone described 'having a bath' in order to 'just have the time on my own', to 'remind me that everything's not going to fall apart, everything's okay' and to allow her self 'down time'.
> Kathryn described feeling that she was 'on an uneven keel' at work, 'so I just diverted my phone, and let people know that I wasn't taking calls, so then I can manage quite effectively'.

In contrast, half of heterosexual women interviewed described the desire for time out or solitude at home remaining as such, a desire.

> Anna is a typical example, 42 years old, married for twelve years, and with three children, aged 4, 8 and 10. She told us: 'It's very hard to say, "I'm just taking time out for myself," or "I need a slower pace," or, you know, "I don't care if it's your soccer presentation, I'm not coming" [laugh]'. This inability to take time for herself was partly a result of Anna positioning 'anything that's based around you personally' as 'self-indulgent'. As she told us, 'When you work full-time, and you've got three kids, you literally have to pretend you're going to the toilet to have some time to yourself'. While the materiality of family responsibilities were partly the issue here, as was the case

170

with most of the heterosexual women we interviewed, Anna's own self-policing of how she 'should' behave was also a factor:

> You feel guilty just saying, 'I'm taking the afternoon off'. In fact, I can't remember the last time I did that. Because there's always a million things that you've got to do. And there's always things that you feel you should do, you know, rightly or wrongly.

In a similar vein, many heterosexual women who did manage to take time out experienced guilt. As Lillian commented:

> My husband will just say to me 'go off and do something for yourself' but when I go and do that . . . I'll be sitting there thinking oh I've got this to do at home I've that to do at home and this to do at home and like you just never relax and that's really bad.

Anna and Lillian are engaging in self-surveillance,[95] judging their own needs in relation to the discursive constructions of woman as responsible, self-renunciating, and always able to offer unlimited care and attention to others,[36] the 'best mother' or 'best worker', in Anna's words. When women are in the premenstrual phase of the cycle, living up to these ideals can feel more difficult, as the woman feels vulnerable, or finds juggling multiple responsibilities more taxing, which can cause distress, and which then gets attributed to PMS. As Lillian told us

> You try to live up to this expectation that the world gives you that you're supposed to be supermum and superwoman and if you don't live up to that expectation life's very tough . . . I expect perfection and when I don't get it I get cranky. Maybe that's a contributing factor.

While mothering was central to many women's feelings of over-responsibility and self-judgement, it is not mothering per se that is the issue here: women in lesbian relationships did not report the same difficulties in negotiating sharing the burden of care with their partner.

> Sophia described how she could defer parental responsibilities premenstrually: 'I can say [to the children], "Look, I'm not dealing with that right now. You can go and talk to [partner] about it"'.

171

The key variable here is the response of Sophia's partner, who was willing to take responsibility for the children. This is where the difference between lesbian and heterosexual women's accounts was most evident – in the response of partners to a woman's premenstrual change or distress.

'He says it's all in my head': accounts of rejection and lack of support from male partners

Cultural expectations of 'appropriate' gendered behaviour are policed through the privacy of intimate relationships, and the reactions of partners and family to a woman's expression of her needs, or her discontent, can significantly influence her negotiation of premenstrual change, with supportive partners alleviating distress and unsupportive partners exacerbating it. Concurring with Jessica Benjamin's concept of 'recognition', the need to be seen by the other in order to experience subjectivity in the other's presence,[96, p.186] many women in the PMS and Relationships Study wanted their partners to recognise that PMS was 'real', to empathise, understand, and not to judge.

> Jackie said she wanted 'a bit more of an understanding that it's real . . . acceptance that it's not just laziness' from her husband. Half of the heterosexual women told us that their male partners did not accept the legitimacy of premenstrual change. As Jill commented, 'He just can't get his head around what PMS is . . . he says it's all in my head which irritates me more than anything else'. Melanie said, 'I think they think it's just all in your head. They don't realise what it's actually like for me'.

The majority of women we interviewed wanted their partner to recognise the embodied root of their distress, as they saw it, in order to understand premenstrual changes, and absolve the woman of responsibility for her behaviour.

> Joanne felt that her husband had little understanding of her pre-menstrual mood swings, believing that 'it was me the person's fault, not me the hormonal woman's fault'.
> Nadia expressed a desire for her husband to 'realise that it had something to do with my hormones and that I wasn't trying to be mean to him, or I wasn't just being a bitch'.

Communication about premenstrual change can facilitate partner understanding and empathy.[67; 97] However, approximately one-third of the heterosexual women we interviewed reported that there was no discussion with their partner of premenstrual change, or PMS, or of the ways in which the woman would like to be supported at this time.

> While Nadia told us that she would like her partner to be 'like my mum, gave me a bit more leeway and didn't take things personally', she conceded that he couldn't do this, because 'he's not a mind reader, so how would he know if I didn't tell him, and I didn't tell him. I'd like him to know, but I wouldn't tell him'.
> Celia never named herself as 'having PMS' to her male partner because 'I don't want to trivialise some of the issues that come up during this time by saying, "Oh, it's just that I had PMT"'.
> Jill was pessimistic about men's ability to understand, because 'they need to experience it and they're not going to do it unless they have a sex change operation or a curse and come back as a woman'.

Even if women *do* attempt to explain premenstrual change or distress, many are pessimistic about men's ability to understand.

> Judith commented, 'I have tried to explain it over the last couple of years . . . since we've had children [laugh] but it's like talking to a brick wall. So I don't think many men really comprehend what happens'.
> Katie gave a similar account, equating her husband's inability to understand with lack of emotional support:
>
> > We've talked about when I'm cranky or depressed and I feel like I've told him a million times that all I need you to do is just hug me, but he just doesn't seem to understand and he still doesn't do it. He's very defensive and he thinks it's all about him and when most of the time I'm angry at myself more than anyone else.

However, recognition of premenstrual change by their partner is a double-edged sword for heterosexual women, as men can carry out the rhetorical accomplishment of splitting the PMS and non-PMS self – the good and bad woman – through adopting negative constructions of PMS.

> Approximately one-third of the heterosexual women we interviewed described their male partners as behaving in a rejecting manner

premenstrually – not only of the woman's moods, but also her very self, as Gillian told us:

> I had a particularly bad PMT experience, and my husband, like, he wasn't my husband then, he actually got a bit frightened, he thought, 'Oh gosh, I don't want to marry that person,' and he called our relationship off. And it's funny that that happened because the PMS has been an issue throughout the whole marriage.

Joanne told us:

> I would often be teary and stuff and rather than him come forward, he would withdraw, too, at the same time, because he was like, 'Well, you're not, um . . . reliable' . . . And it's like, 'But I want to spend time with you,' and he was like, 'Well I don't know who I'm talking to, so I don't want to . . .'.

Susannah described her partner as 'losing his temper' with her: 'He might call me names, or he might say "Oh get away from me", or something like that, and yeah, I think if he would be able to comfort me I might calm down'.

Joan said that her partner had got to the stage where 'he really wanted me to go live in another house for two weeks of the month, which is a bit detrimental to a marriage'. She said that she felt so bad about this that it was 'slit your wrists time'.

Attributing a woman's emotional reactions to 'PMS' could also mean that a woman is dismissed by her male partner premenstrually.

Katie told us, 'Men, you know they think "oh, she's got her periods, so it doesn't mean anything what she says"'.

Merrin said that 'if I'm making a complaint or I'm asking for something, he hears that as irritation, rather than a legitimate request'. Thus rather than 'attending to what I'm saying' her partner would say '"Oh it must be that time of the month" or "you're coming into your period" and so, he would be more dismissive' of what Merrin was 'asking for at that particular time'.

Angela described her partner as saying 'Now, how long till your periods?' if she was ever angry. She continued:

and it'd be two weeks away. And he'd pick up on it like that. And everything would be blamed on that. So, in other words, he was saying to me, 'Well, I'm not going to take you seriously, because you're premenstrual'.

The labelling of women's emotions, requests or criticisms as 'PMS' can serve to negate her needs or concerns, which has implications for power (im)balances in the relationship, and can exacerbate premenstrual distress.[57]

Other heterosexual women gave accounts of their male partners overtly positioning them as mad premenstrually.

Elaine said, 'One day, probably three months ago or so he came in and said "Who am I talking to today? Is it schizo Elaine, nice Elaine, sexy Elaine, or cranky Elaine?"' The impact of this was to increase Elaine's premenstrual distress. 'I was so premenstrual that day, and I thought, "that's so unnecessary. I'm not that bad"'.

In a similar vein, Joanne told us that her partner saying 'I don't know who I'm talking to' when she was premenstrual made her feel like a 'paranoid schizophrenic'.

Anna's partner was overt in his view that she needed psychiatric help premenstrually, saying: 'It's your shit, you go deal with it on your own, 'cause I have fucking had enough and I can't deal with this shit . . . get a therapist to sort it fucking out, I don't care what it is'.

On the website PMSBuddy, where men share 'stories' about their partner's PMS (as well as being warned by a monthly email of when menstrual madness will occur), we see similar examples of women being positioned as mad or bad premenstrually. Take 'Yosho', who had asked for advice from other men with the following post 'My girl goes NUTS when she's about to have her period . . . nothing I do is right and everything I do sets her off. Any suggestions??? Please help!'.[98] The reponses were:

A fucking pussy. tell her to stop being a bitch. you don't like it. go sleep at a friends house for the week. guarantee you'll only have to do this once.

Dump her for the uglyist chick you can find, and let everyone know that you would rather hump a cow, than live with her one more second.

Or take the following comment by 'Rui', which also appeared on the PMSBuddy website: 'My best friend always said that PMS is bad but the most truthful thing he has ever stated is: "you should never trust an animal that bleeds for 5 days and does not die"'.[99] Or the post entitled 'PMS is the harbinger of worse to come':

> Dr. Spiff: OK, let's take a look at this PMS thing . . . Assume that her periods are regular and for 4 days out of every 28, she morphs into a Charles Manson/Attila The Hun clone. So 14 per cent of the time you have together is spent with a person you don't know and really don't like.

These men are not aberrations. They are reproducing negative cultural discourses about the 'monstrous feminine' – the premenstrual mad/bad woman who must be contained, controlled or rejected. These discursive representations are not simply misogynistic fantasy. They are part of the intersubjective context wherein women construct and experience premenstrual change. It has been argued that 'the intersubjective context' plays 'a constitutive role in *all* forms of psychopathology',[100, p.3] because, in the words of Steven Mitchell, the 'mind is composed of relational configurations . . . [and] experience is understood as constructed through interaction'.[101, pp.3-4] While we may question the status of PMS as 'psychopathology', it is clear that women who are told by their partners that they are mad or bad premenstrually are more likely to adopt this subject position, and see themselves and their emotions in such a manner.

> The heterosexual women we interviewed who described their male partners as critical, lacking understanding, or being unsupportive, were more likely to position themselves as mad premenstrually, describing themselves as 'crazy' (Susannah, Joan and Stephanie); 'out of control' (Melanie); a 'nut case', 'absolute psycho' or 'schizo' (Sandra); 'mad' (Stephanie); 'out of my mind', 'I've lost the plot', or 'a complete loony' (Joanne); 'off my tree' (Caroline), or 'having a nervous breakdown' (Bec). As Susannah said, 'I thought I was losing my mind or something', describing herself as 'manic' and 'not-me' when she was premenstrual. Some women also overtly positioned the premenstrual self as monstrous, describing themselves as 'scary' (Susannah), 'a bitch' (Nadia), 'a demon' (Bella), or like 'Jekyll and Hyde' (Jackie).

Women interviewed in the UK[84] and the USA[22] adopt a similar language in describing their premenstrual changes, with 'devil mummy', 'something out of the exorcist',[1, pp.52–53] or 'a totally insane person',[22, p.49] being pejorative labels commonly used. For a number of the heterosexual interviewees, this was also associated with feeling unequal or inadequate in the relationship.

> Susannah told us that her partner would say, 'Most of the time I really, really love you but when you have these days you're a very difficult girl', which made her 'feel like a bit of a child' and 'kind of patronised'.
>   Joanna said:

>> I felt horrible, and I felt angry because I was apologising for something that I really couldn't do that much about that wasn't as a result of me being, um . . . choosing to be that way or being inadequate in some way and it made me feel inadequate, it made me feel really, my self-esteem just was . . . pathetic. It was, you know, I felt like a really bad person, like I'd committed a crime [laugh] that I needed to say sorry for.

Jessica Benjamin argued that the absence of recognition can lead to distress and the experience of the self as not existing, as is evidenced by women's responses to their partner's withdrawal or rejection premenstrually. Benjamin argues that 'when the other does not survive and aggression is not dissipated it becomes almost exclusively intrapsychic'.[96, p.192] This provides further explanation for self-pathologisation of women whose partners do not recognise their premenstrual vulnerability or distress, and who can not 'hold' this distress through offering support. The woman turns inward for an explanation of her experience of negative premenstrual mood, be it anger or anxiety, and blames her body for her premenstrual state, rather than looking to her social or relational context. This can serve to protect her view of her relationship as 'good', in the same way that a biomedical model which positions PMS as embodied illness allows women to position premenstrual negative affect as 'not me', and thus avoid an assault on the self.[35] However, it also ensures that relational issues, and other discursive, intrapsychic, or material factors which may precipitate women's distress, are not addressed.

Partner support alleviates premenstrual distress

Dana Jack described similar patterns of relating in couples where the woman was diagnosed with depression, where the husband would describe the woman as a 'bother', and reject her need for physical or emotional support. She described this as 'the essence of inequality: one person governs the relationship and the other person's feelings are ignored'.[73, p.47] In the case of many heterosexual women reporting PMS, approximately two-thirds of the sample, inequality was also marked by the absence of practical support, particularly for those with dependent children, where receiving help in the home premenstrually could alleviate their caregiving burden and allow them to take time out to engage in self-care.

> Jill told us, 'even if he said "Is there anything I can do?" as simple as that, which to me is not much to ask . . . "do you want me to cook dinner?"', she would be happy.
>
> Olivia said that what she wanted was 'help with the housework somehow manoeuvring life around so that I don't have to do a thing, or that at least I feel like he's contributing, and the kids are contributing'.
>
> Carmen said she would like her husband to 'take control of more things, even little things, if he'd cook dinner, realise that washing needed doing and [if] he did a load of washing and put it out'.
>
> Maggie said she wished her partner would 'maybe take the kids a bit more, just you know, for me to have a bit more time out'.
>
> Anna said she'd like her husband to 'sort of make things easier for me. Help out with the kids, or if he can hear I'm having a hard time with the kids, maybe step in, or take them out . . . just generally make it a bit easier'.

While many heterosexual women, particularly those with children, positioned anger or irritation about burden of care as a premenstrual 'symptom', we could reframe it as a legitimate response to lack of partner support in the home. This is reminiscent of the cartoon described by Anne Figert at the beginning of this chapter, of 'an obviously worn out woman holding a screaming child and telling her husband (sitting in the lounge chair and reading the paper) that "this is stress, not PMS"'.[2, p.110] Figert concludes that we need a 'return to a menstrual hut . . . and its monthly release from traditional women's roles of cooking, cleaning and family duties' – a release from responsibility that remains an impossible fantasy for the majority of heterosexual women.

A small proportion of the heterosexual women who asked for practical support in the home did receive it.

> Janice told us, 'on my anxious day . . . he is really supportive, like, he'll do the housework, or dinner, and all kinds of stuff'. However, many women reported that this support was often given reluctantly, as Jackie told us:

He's accepting. Like, he doesn't say 'Oh, the house is a mess' . . . If he's upset about it, he'll help clean it up. He won't be happy about it. But it won't be a big issue . . . When I haven't cooked the dinner, I haven't washed up . . . he helps out as well. It's something we do together.

Merrin described

a couple of occasions where I've felt so unwell, when I was so exhausted that I've just said that I can't cook dinner tonight, and I just sort of left him to it, with very little notice and he mobilised take-away [because] he's not a good cook.

Merrin implicitly suggests that this might be an unreasonable demand on her part with her final comment: 'there wasn't any sort of [fuss], he was fine around that'.

Only one of the men we interviewed, Gary, Bella's partner, talked of 'helping around the house' because 'the demands seem to build up, [so] that she probably can't cope as much, and puts more onto me'.

Others showed an awareness of the premenstrual woman's desire for practical support, but did not offer support without being asked, as is evidenced by the comment made by Sean, Merrin's husband: 'I think probably I should work a bit harder perhaps when I think about it really, when I know that she's like that . . . [giggles] perhaps do something like "cook the dinner"'.

In contrast, all of the lesbian women interviewed described being able to absolve themselves of responsibility for household tasks premenstrually, if they needed to, with the support of their partner.

Jocelyn said that her partner was 'very understanding', and that she'd do the 'housework on those days [and] doesn't expect too much from me'.

Bec described worrying about household finances when she was premenstrual, and her female partner saying, 'Don't worry about it, I'll fix it up and we'll work it out later'.

Casey described how her partner would 'take some of the responsibility', cook dinner, and run her a bath when she was premenstrual, allowing Casey to 'just be'.

> It's about . . . someone just . . . recognising that you're actually feeling really out of sorts and taking some of the responsibility off you to actually manage it: 'Well, now you're feeling crap. And I know there's nothing that much that can fix that, and you don't have to worry about, where the food's coming from', or, I mightn't even think about a bath, and then she'll say, 'How about you go and have a bath? And I'll run it for you,' and I'll be like, 'Oh, that would be really nice!' It's about just being able to just *be*.

So how do these heterosexual women tolerate the disparity between the reality of their relational context and their premenstrual needs and desires? In her book *Our treacherous hearts: Why women let men get their way*,[102] Ros Coward argues that women have a tendency to idealise their male partners, denying the reality of failures within the relationship, as a way of defending themselves against disappointment and potential relationship breakdown.

> This was evident in accounts in the PMS and Relationships Study where many heterosexual women juxtaposed accounts of their male partner's lack of support with idealising statements such as: 'He's a lovely guy, don't get me wrong' (Jill); 'He is good to me, I would be hard pressed to find another man like him' (Lillian); 'He's actually quite a good husband' (Katie); 'He loves me a lot really and tries to make me feel good when we have time to ourselves' (Susannah); 'He's fantastic, he's a wonderful husband and I love him to death' (Elaine); 'He is good, you know, and caring, up to a point' (Celia).

These rhetorical strategies serve to further reinforce the positioning of the premenstrual woman as problematic and her emotions as unreasonable, as her partner is entirely exonerated for playing any part in her distress. It is a vicious cycle that acts to pathologise women. However, when they were premenstrual, these same women expressed frustration, anger or irritation, suggesting that this idealising rhetoric no longer had currency, or perhaps it was simply the case that their defences were down.

Impact of premenstrual change on women's partners

At the same time, premenstrual change was not without consequences for women's partners. Many of the men we interviewed gave accounts of experiencing distress themselves.

Kylie's partner Craig told us, 'sometimes I do think "Geez I hate this life"'. Chris said that Lillian's mood swings 'just puts the whole family on edge'. Sarah's partner Amir commented that 'sometimes it's hard for me because if it's directed at me, I'm not really sure why she has to be quite angry'.

Men who post their feelings on the PMSBuddy site are more frank in their views:

She is such A bitch
All I have is my hand: I've been married for 25 year's just found this site. PMS means to me. Please Men Suck. At that time of the month. Nothing I can do is good enough for her. I'm sick of having to take care of my own need's. If she doesn't come around soon I will be leaving.

I JUST DON'T GIVE A CRAP
Just busted my hump all week: I just worked all week. She stay's home and take's care of the house. She want's to go to some crappy home show on Sunday. I need A day off and said I don't want to go. She just went fuckin nut's. I can't believe you don't want to spend time with me. She keep's blaming me for this I think I may get a hotel once a month. HELP WITH PMS !!!!!! HELP can't come soon enough.

Lesbian partners also gave accounts of premenstrual mood or behaviour change exacting consequences on the relationship, or on themselves.

Helen told us, when talking of her partner Pip, 'If she gets cranky about something and at me, it's not pleasant'. Or as Casey said about her partner:

I find it very hard to be around her when she's in that zone. And I have to work very hard at not reacting to it. So actually having a bit of separateness is actually a healthy thing for both of us.

Having to figure out how to support their premenstrual partner each month could also be exhausting.

Denise said, 'I think part of my problem is . . . I don't want to have to find the solution every month'. There was also acknowledgement that having two women with PMS could be difficult. As Ellen said:

being with a woman during the time just makes it entirely exhausting and difficult um and far more complex than I ever thought it would be . . . when one is withdrawing, the other one's wanting more of an outward impact or something . . . so it's two opposites coming together which causes a lot of discomfort.

At the same time, a number of women partners also gave accounts of maintaining boundaries around what was acceptable premenstrually, and would indicate that things had gone too far if these boundaries were crossed.

Sophia commented:

People are accountable for what they do, and, um, if I felt like Tina was really out of control and saying and behaving in a way that I really felt strongly was not okay under any circumstance, premenstrual or otherwise, I would certainly say it at that time . . . so I might say, 'Your behaviour right now is really shit and makes me feel like you don't care about me right now. And if you did care about me, you wouldn't be raising your voice'.

Sophia described herself as not having become a 'passive person', concluding 'I think you still engage, and you still, you know, respond. But you have a framework for it'.

The need for boundaries reflects the 'emotion work' in managing their own feeling states,[103] and those of their partner, being conducted by partners of women who experience premenstrual distress, demonstrating that communication and responsiveness requires effort within the relationship.

The gendered negotiation of PMS within relationships

This analysis clearly documents the complexity of the construction and lived experience of 'PMS' – a 'disorder' that is said to affect 75 per cent of women, as noted above. Rather than being a pathology that occurs within the woman which merits psychiatric diagnosis and biomedical management, PMS can be conceptualised as a gendered experience located in medical and cultural discourse about premenstrual change and (hetero)femininity, the social and relational context of women's lives, and women's intrapsychic negotiation of somatic and psychological change as 'symptoms' of a disorder:[48] a material-discursive-intrapsychic phenomenon. These inter-view accounts also support the view that partners play an important role in the construction and lived experience of premenstrual distress. Negative constructions of PMS on the part of a woman's partner can exacerbate distress, and result in the women being positioned as mad premenstru-ally.[see also 63; 66; 104–105] The materiality of lack of support, legitimised by cultural constructions of caring femininity, can make it difficult for women to absolve themselves of responsibilities, and can increase anger and irritation at inequalities in the relationship. Women's premenstrual anger, as well as their partner's inability (or unwillingness) to discuss and under-stand premenstrual change, can also impact on the relationship itself, which can increase women's distress (as well as that of her partner).

This particular pattern of premenstrual relationship conflict was more commonly reported by heterosexual women, in comparison to lesbians. In the lesbian couples interviewed, there were no accounts of relationship conflict or tension escalating premenstrually because of a woman's partner rejecting or dismissing her, or her partner actively engaging in conflict, a theme found in previous research on heterosexual women's experiences of PMS.[57] This is not to suggest that lesbian partners are passive in the face of premenstrual irritation or intemperance, but rather, that they are more likely to adopt a positive and conciliatory mode of communication which serves to diffuse conflict and offer support. The evidence that a number of women partners had boundaries associated with unacceptable behaviour also suggested that dealing with premenstrual distress is the subject of a complex negotiation between two women, which requires 'emotion work' from both parties, in managing their own feeling states and those of their partner. In all of the women we interviewed this emotion work was not described as a burden, but as part of being in a committed relationship, in contrast to many heterosexual women's accounts, as well as PMSBuddy posts, where premenstrual emotions are described as 'too much' work by their male partners.[66] However, this is not simply an issue of relationship cohesion and satisfaction; the gender of a woman's intimate partner can have significant implications for her psychological well-being. In our research, women in lesbian relationships reported lower levels of depression and anxiety and higher levels of premenstrual coping than women in heterosexual relationships.[106] These findings are not unique to PMS. In other areas of women's reproductive health, such as perinatal depres-sion[107] and menopause,[108] women in lesbian relationships also report lower levels of distress.

The fact that lesbians are less likely to conform to the traditional feminine gender role is also of relevance.[see 109] This was evidenced by absence of ideals of (hetero)femininity being used in a self-policing manner, and the egalitarian relationship structure described in the lesbian interviews, which meant that there were few accounts of lesbians feeling overburdened by emotional or practical responsibilities in the home premenstrually, and becoming angry or irritable as a result. This gendered non-adherence has been linked to the greater instrumentality and masculinity, combined with expressiveness, that has been found in lesbians, in comparison to hetero-sexual women.[110] Green and colleagues emphasise that this is not about lesbians being like men, but about their being more androgynous when compared to heterosexual women.[111] It is further demonstration that gender is not something that we *are*, but something that we *do*, a perform-ance that is invariably negotiated differently outside of the constraints of the heterosexual matrix, as different role expectations, opportunities and constraints apply.

The absence of children in the majority of lesbian relationships could be put forward as an explanation for relationship differences between hetero-sexual and lesbian couples, because the burden of family responsibility falls disproportionately on heterosexual women after having children.[112] However, in our research, accounts of unsupportive relationships, over-responsibility and self-silencing were reported by heterosexual women with and without children.[36] Equally, lesbian couples have been found to be less likely to adopt the divisions of labour commonly found in heterosexual couples (the biological mother taking on the greatest burden of childcare) even if they do have children, and have been reported to rate relationship satisfaction very highly compared to child-free lesbian couples.[113] In our study, there was no evidence of difference between lesbian couples with and without children – possibly because lesbians were able to take 'time out' from children when they were premenstrual, supported by their partner, and were less likely to attempt to adhere to cultural ideals of the perfect, self-sacrificing 'wife and mother'. This suggests that it is not simply the materiality of the burden of childcare that produces distress for women, but the intrapsychic and intersubjective negotiation of maternal discourses,[vii] and the discursive construction of mothering that is negotiated differently in same-gender relationships.

However, this is not to suggest that heterosexual couples cannot experi-ence awareness, recognition, understanding, communication and responsi-bility sharing in relation to PMS. Many heterosexual women do have partners who provide a supportive context for their experience of premen-strual change, which acts to facilitate self-care and reduce distress.[66] Indeed, support and understanding offered by partners can reduce guilt and self-blame in women who experience premenstrual change, allowing them to engage in coping strategies premenstrually, such as taking time out to be alone, or engage self-care,[66; 70] as is explored in Chapter 6, when I examine women's strategies of recovery and resistance.

6

WOMEN'S MADNESS

Resistance and survival

Reflecting upon the Vermeer painting *Girl, interrupted at her music*, Susanna Kaysen writes:

> Interrupted at her music: as my life had been; interrupted in the music of being seventeen, as her life had been, snatched and fixed on canvas: one moment made to stand still and to stand for all moments, whatever they would be or might have been. What life can recover from that?[1, p.167]

Janet Wirth-Cauchon writes:

> What feminist analyses offer . . . is a way to understand women's madness as an intelligible response to unliveable conditions in which other modes of response are blocked off.[2, p.201]

Marina Morrow writes:

> Any reconstructive project must balance women's individual experience of distress with the social and political origins of this distress.[3, 159]

Madness may stand as the spectre that haunts all women, but it is not our inevitable fate. As I have argued throughout this book, we can challenge the myths of madness that mark women as 'other' and resist the biomedical monikers reified as truth within the DSM – diagnoses such as 'depression', 'premenstrual dysphoric disorder', or 'borderline personality disorder'. These diagnostic classifications do not reflect an underlying disease state that *causes* the problems women experience; they are merely labels imposed by a clinician (or researcher) that reflect the construction of madness (or illness) that circulate in a particular culture at a particular point in time. You can no more *have* depression than you can *have* Catholicism; both are socially constructed categories that describe a particular set of behaviours (or beliefs) – or the prejudices of those in power who want to exercise their 'divine' right to regulate our bodies and minds.

This does not mean that women's misery is a fiction – a discursive act conjured up to justify the actions of those who would confine us in chains – literally in the case of nineteenth century asylums, or metaphorically, in the case of psychotropic medication and ECT today. Many women *are* distressed, many to such a degree that they harm themselves, live life on a knife edge of agony and despair, or attempt to take their own lives. Some succeed, as death can seem like the only conceivable way to end unendurable pain. Acknowledging the reality of this psychic pain is central to women's recovery and survival. Acknowledgement legitimises suffering, as well as the need for support, and for many women is the beginning of their road to happiness and healing – as well as resistance of the conditions that drove them to despair. Acknowledging misery does not mean that we accept that it is madness, or 'mental illness', however; we can reframe women's distress as a reasonable response to the material circumstances of their lives, to gendered roles and their discursive or intrapsychic concomitants, and to the intersubjective context within which women negotiate suffering.

Acknowledgement is only the first step. We also need to develop solutions to prevent or ameliorate women's misery. To do this, we should look to women who have faced the abyss and survived. Therefore, in this final chapter I examine women's accounts of resistance and survival, exploring how women *can* move from misery to 'living well',[4] through rejecting idealised femininity, self-care, asking for support and engagement in creativity. In some instances, women feel stronger as a result, as Emily and Kirsten said:

> I can certainly see the difference [after being depressed] and it's made me a much stronger person (Emily).[5, p.101]

> So, in a way, having been depressed was a good thing for me. I think I'm much hardier than I was before, in some ways, stronger (Kirsten).[6, p.487]

This reminds us of R.D. Laing's comment, cited in Chapter 1, that 'madness need not be all breakdown. It may also be break through. It is potentially liberation and renewal as well as enslavement and existential death'.[7, p.47] This is not to suggest that survival or living well is the sole responsibility of women themselves, who are expected to pull themselves up by their own boot straps and recover from the deep hole of despair.[4] I also reflect on the need for changes in the material conditions of women's lives in order to prevent and ameliorate women's distress, and explore strategies of individual support.

A reasonable response: acknowledging the reality of women's distress

One of the most pernicious consequences of the medicalisation of women's misery is the pathologisation of reasonable responses to everyday life (or to everyday violence and abuse). If all we do is label women's responses as a psychiatric illness, and then prescribe drugs (or ECT) to dull the pain (or the memory), we are limiting women's capacity to explore the source of their distress, and to understand what this distress means to them, as well as their ability to find lasting solutions. This can mean facing pain, rather than simply making it go away in a haze of numbness, which is always a sorry substitute for 'normality', anyway.

> Carrie (one of the women we interviewed as part of the Long Term Effects of Child Sexual Abuse Study) told us that 'I'm at a point where I really feel the effect of the abuse, more so than I ever have, because I really, understand it all a lot, lot more'. This recognition was experienced by Carrie as a positive thing, even though it caused her distress, because it marked the beginning of 'dealing with' the abuse and its consequences, allowing her to leave it behind:

>> I've accepted that it's happened, and I think I've just got to deal with any sort of effect it's having on me now. Which otherwise, I'd just go on living, living in it you know, an' letting it take over everything, and it would ruin my life. I don't think I could afford to do that after it taking up, you know, I feel like I've lost a childhood, I feel like I've lost a chapter of it, [of a] normal teenager's [life].

Acceptance of the materiality of abuse and its effects was the first step made towards Carrie living well – but also the first step in her resistance to being defined by the abuse, not allowing it to 'ruin' her life. Similarly, in her research with women who reported depression in the post-partum period, Natasaha Mauthner found that recovery was marked by women's ability to accept themselves and their children for who they are. She described this as 'being able to let go of their standards, come to terms with what they saw as their "imperfections", abandon their condemnatory attitude toward themselves, and acknowledge their strengths and positive characteristics'.[8, pp.474–475] As Dona said:

> I think probably for me the biggest thing I've changed was just that it's okay to feel certain things. And I think, again, a lot of this was just the way I was brought up and the way that I've learned to cope is that everything that ever concerned me or that I was scared,

frightened, or whatever about, stayed inside, so that now what I'm able to do is kind of say, 'Okay, this is bothering me'.[8, p.475]

This can mean acceptance that unhappiness or misery is something that women cannot escape. However, this acceptance often comes with a greater confidence in ability to cope. Thus Theresa, interviewed by Rita Schreiber, said, 'don't ever think that . . . you'll never feel bad again, because you will . . . but I'm learning . . . that the next time it doesn't last quite so long or isn't quite so deep or whatever'.[6, p.487] Similarly, Gail said that 'maybe three or four times when I've felt myself sliding back down to the valley . . . I have the skills now to get out of it. I don't go there any more'.[6, p.487] Awareness of premenstrual changes was also the first step in effective coping for the women we interviewed in the PMS and Relationships Study.

Eleanor said, 'I think once you're aware of your reactions then it's easier to control if you like . . . or manage is a better word'. Similarly, Joan told us:

I find that it's being more aware that's most helpful because I know what's happening in my world then and I know what's happening within myself and I can give myself space and others space and I know it's not just me being completely irrational . . . and feeling like I should be locked up.

Awareness allowed Joan to resist the mantle of madness, rejecting the notion that she was someone who 'should be locked up'.

Bec gave a similar account, telling us that she had 'become aware, I'm like "hang on a minute I'm PMTing. I'm not losing the plot, I'm not having a nervous breakdown"'. This allowed Bec to experience her premenstrual changes without undue distress, saying to herself, 'It will pass, I'll get my period and it will pass', whereas previously she would think, 'God, what's wrong with me? I need to go to Rozelle [local psychiatric hospital], they need to book me in [laugh]'. Catherine, who was interviewed as a part of an earlier study I conducted with Janette Perz on self-help treatments for PMS, also told us that she now accepts premenstrual changes in emotions as part of herself. Rather than seeing her PMS-self as dangerous and beyond her control, she is now able to express her feelings to those around her, and to engage in coping strategies to reduce distress:

I never realised what was happen[ing] to me in my head or even in my body . . . now it never creeps up on me. If I feel

188

weepy I can now say to my husband, 'I've got PMT, get away from me'.[9, p.357]

As a result, Catherine no longer feels that she is behaving like a 'monster' premenstrually, and is more comfortable about addressing relationship issues that concern her when they arise, rather than erupting in an explosive and aggressive way during her premenstrual phase: 'I used to think I was really neurotic because of my PMT, but I think I've realised myself that it was all right for me to say, right, hang on a minute . . . I'm not bloody putting up with this'.

Awareness can also involve attending to the times when distress is absent, and valuing those times. Lauren Slater has written of her diagnosis with obsessive compulsive disorder in her memoir *Black swans*, and her realisation that part of her was 'still free, a private space not absolutely permeated by pain'.[10, p.150] She writes:

I noticed that even in the thickest of obsessions my mind some-times struggles into the world, if only for brief forays. There, while I struggled to take a step, was the sun on a green plate. *Remember that* I said to myself. And here, while I stood fixated in a doorway, was a beetle with a purplish shell like eggplants growing in wet soil. *Appreciate this* I told myself, and I can say I did, those slogers of seconds when I returned to the world. I loved the beetle, ached for the eggplant, paddled in a lake with black swans.[10, p.150]

Women living in the USA previously diagnosed with depression, who were interviewed by Rita Schreiber,[6] described 'seeing the abyss' of their despair and feeling 'being lost at sea', 'beyond sadness', as well as scared that they would 'always feel this bad'.[6, p.478] This abyss was associated with fear – of what the woman might do to herself, and of being out of control – however, it was also a turning point which led women to tell their stories, to seek understanding, and to develop a consciousness about themselves and their world, a process which Schreiber called 'Cluing In'. As Linda said, 'All of a sudden, I knew "what was wrong with this picture". And every-thing was changed after that'.[6, p.484] This 'Cluing In' led women to weigh the evidence about what did and what did not make sense in their world, what felt right and what did not feel right, often leading to immediate change as a woman began to conceptualise her world differently. For many women, nothing is the same again after this experience of sudden clarity, as Kirsten said:

Well, it's kind of like an orgasm. If you've never done it, you wouldn't know what I'm talking about, but if you have . . . well then that's different . . . I just KNEW that things were different inside me. I knew.[6, p.486]

After this revelatory awareness, Schreiber described women as '(Re)Inventing' themselves, changing how they saw themselves and their relation to others, and accepting parts of themselves that they had rejected or disowned. This is analogous to the narratives of personal transformation Michelle LaFrance found in her interviews with Canadian women who had survived depression, exemplified by Amanda's account: 'there was a shell underneath [and] . . . I felt that I had broken free . . . and then *I* stepped out'.[5, p.85]

> In a similar vein, Jenny, who took part in the Long Term Effects of Child Sexual Abuse Study, spoke about rediscovering aspects of herself 'which have lain dormant for such a long time', and recreating herself through this rediscovery:
>
> > In order just to kind of survive through all that experience, lots of sides of me have had to be repressed. [Now] a whole kind of creative side is kind of coming out of me which I never knew, well, I did know but it was just wasn't allowed to come out. And what I'm doing now is kind of trying to find that *me* that is buried and that has been repressed.

This (re)invention can also move women to take action to try to change the conditions of their suffering. Elizabeth, interviewed by Damien Ridge and Sue Ziebland, said

> I get to a point, when the depression is not so severe . . . and I know it in my bones, when I can choose either to change certain ways I live, attitudes I have, or go back to the old ways which will probably result in another depression.[11, p.1046]

> Rose, who took part in the Long Term Effects of Child Sexual Abuse Study, described how she took up yoga and learnt that she could talk herself out of despair: 'If you can change your thought patterns, you can change the way you are'.

These changes can also involve letting go of pain. bell hooks has written that

> recovery for me has meant letting go of sorrow that overwhelms. I no longer need to daily release toxic pain by crying . . . strategic mourning not only helped me to resist it helped me to heal. In recovery sadness takes its place within a pantheon of many

emotions the most powerful of which is the experience of sustained and ecstatic joy.[12, pp.191–192]

This does not mean that these women are accepting responsibility for their pain or distress, or locating the problem within. Many women engage in what Suzanne McKenzie-Mohr and Michelle LaFrance describe as 'tight-rope talk' where they can make sense of their experiences through both honouring agency and rejecting blame, by rejecting dominant narratives that rely on either/or binaries (such as 'strong or vulnerable', 'agent or victim').[4]

These accounts stand in stark contrast to the instantaneous 'cure' promised by psychotropic medication. As Inga Musico describes her own process of survival: 'healing is not a destination or an objective. Healing is a daily thought process, a series of infinite questions and choices, a skill that is not taught, much less revered, in our culture'.[13, p.79] And for some women, these choices and changes centre on resisting the very scripts that define them as 'woman'.

'They get dust on them, screw it': resisting idealised femininity

In the nineteenth century, Charlotte Perkins Gilman recovered from the misery that resulted in her subjection to Silas Weir Mitchell's bed-rest cure by resisting and rejecting the constraints of the role of wife and mother, as outlined in Chapter 3. It is unsurprising to find that the (re)invention that is part of contemporary women's survival can involve changes in relationships with others. For example, while many of the women we interviewed as part of the Long Term Effects of Child Sexual Abuse Study gave accounts of abusive relationships in adulthood, particularly when they were younger, the majority talked of this in the past, following a realisation that this was 'abuse' and not 'love' or a 'normal relationship'.

Carrie told us:

> I started to realise, you know, what was normal, what wasn't normal and eventually I had the strength to end it with him and it sort of made me realise that there was more to life than what there'd been in that relationship. So I got out and moved on. I started living for a bit.

Similarly, Jenny said:

> I've reached a place in my life now where I'm really starting to like myself, really starting to get my life together . . . and

now I'm telling myself that I deserve to be loved, and I deserve to be taken care of in a very healthy way.

Loretta, who also took part in the Long Term Effects of Child Sexual Abuse Study, spoke about taking more control and responsibility for herself, and not being so 'passive' in relation to others:

> I'm first of all prepared to take more control and more responsibility. I think I've been very passive in the past and just allowed other people to make decisions for me or to look after me or, um, sort things out. And I'm now prepared to do that myself, because I can more identify what it is I need to look after myself.

Diana, who took part in the same study, spoke about how she no longer had the need to be constantly reassured by others, saying 'I don't feel that I need to have someone who makes me the centre of their world . . . and spends the whole time building up my esteem'. She said that in the past she had felt that she 'needed somebody to be constantly reassuring me that I was the best thing for them'; however, 'now, I don't feel that I need that any more so I'm really pleased'.

Resisting previous patterns of relational inequality, particularly the notion that they should attend to the needs of others regardless of the cost to themselves, is also central to many women's accounts of recovery and resistance. In a UK based study I conducted, recovery from moderate to severe premenstrual distress was marked by women putting boundaries around the caring role, and rejecting relational subservience.[14] Thus Jane talked of learning to be clear about where her responsibilities to other people start and finish, describing an incident where her son tried to talk her into giving him extra money for petrol and she refused to because 'I'm more decisive . . . I will not be swayed by people making me feel guilty if I don't do something they want [now]'. In realising that she was 'entitled to a life as well', Jane also now refuses to do her two sons' ironing, having bought them their own ironing board. She accepts that they won't tidy their rooms, but doesn't do it herself, and no longer picks up their washing: she does it only if they put it in the laundry.[15, p.79] She told us: 'I'm no longer upset and angry when I'm premenstrual, because I've changed the goal-posts, as well as my expectations. It feels very liberating'.

In her study of Canadian women, Michelle LaFrance also found that women described 'letting go and saying no' to undesired demands and requests, in particular the responsibilities of cooking, cleaning and caring, as central to their recovery from depression. Barb explained this process thus:

> How am I different? Well I dropped some of the things that I thought were required of me. I don't have that feeling about them any more . . . my husband makes his own breakfast. I cut his grapefruit up at night because he's absolutely helpless that way and they would drop otherwise [laughs] . . . But if I don't get up for breakfast with him, I don't feel guilty about it.[5, pp.100–101]

Barb went on to say that her 'house is not always the cleanest', but she now doesn't 'feel guilty about it'. Emily, interviewed as part of the same study, gave a similar account:

> I can certainly see the difference in me . . . I'm still a nice caring person . . . but I learned to say no . . . I'm not Susie homemaker, your socks are probably going to be real dirty when you leave here. But things that I felt were important things are no longer as important.[5, pp.101–102]

Rejecting the mantle of the 'good woman', the fantasy of idealised femininity, which is internalised from childhood, is thus central to women's recovery and resistance. Rita Schreiber described this as women giving up the 'good girl', allowing themselves to be vulnerable and have needs of their own. Rose told her, 'I learned I didn't have to do it alone. He said "listen, I've given you a cross to bear and you have people to help you carry that cross"'.[6, p.485] Sandra told Natasha Mauthner that she now realised that she'd set herself 'goals that were impossible',[8, p.472] goals that contributed to the depression she experienced four months after her child's birth, when economic pressures sent her back to full-time work. Sandra said that she 'couldn't work out how you were supposed to deal with the baby and do everything else as well', which she now realised 'you can't'. She had previously compared herself to an idealised fantasy of a 'stay at home mum' at the same time as juggling full-time work, which had made her life impossible, and her emotions raw:

> It tends to be the mothers who are at home that seem to go everywhere with the kids, go swimming, go to ballet classes, do this, do that . . . and that's what I feel I should be doing. I should be sewing and baking and cooking and going swimming with her and I mean . . . that's cloud cuckoo land.

> I'm not very good at sewing anyway. I don't particularly like baking.[8, p.472]

Michelle LaFrance found similar narratives of the perfect woman in her study of women's recovery from depression. For example, Heather said, 'My make-up was good, my hair was good, my house was tidy . . . I used to wash my baseboards . . . and then the process in getting better . . . was realizing that you don't need to have clean baseboards'.[5, p.90] In letting go of the unrealistic expectations that had contributed to her distress, Heather said she came to the realisation that her baseboards 'get dust on them, screw it'.[5, p.90] Similarly, Joanne realised that trying to be a 'very good girl' had contributed to her depression, a re-evaluation that helped her to move away from this way of being:

> I was always expected . . . to have really good marks . . . be a very good girl . . . do everything you're told . . . I did all the cooking, all the cleaning, bought all the groceries, paid all the bills . . . I suppose that might have had a fair bit to do with getting depressed later on.[5, p.86]

These accounts are reminiscent of women's experiences at midlife, discussed in Chapter 2 – where reports of increased confidence, ability to say no, and attention to self-care made midlife as a positive life transition, rather than a time of atrophy and decay. As Toni, who took part in our Women at Midlife Study, told us:

> You seem to spend that first half of your life trying to be fairly perfect, you try to fit that mould and what you may see as the right sort of thing by doing all the right things and keeping everyone happy because that's a big thing and always trying to keep things in balance. Maybe you get to 50 and you think, well bugger it, you've done all that work and all that effort and you think, gee have I ever really given myself enough pleasure and consideration.[16, p.295]

Or as the feminist author Kate Millett said in an interview in 2010, 'Of course I'm older, of course my body is not like it was . . . But in my mind and my heart I feel much better. That's the benefit of age; I'm freer'.[17]

Perhaps *this* is why women at midlife (and beyond) report lower rates of depression than younger women;[see 18] they are resisting discursively constructed ideals of femininity, and finding time for themselves, often for the first time. Women's accounts of recovery from misery are associated with rejection of these same gendered discourses and roles.

'A room of one's own': women's engagement in self-care

Resistance and survival is also associated with women reporting greater engagement in self-care.

> Linda, who took part in the UK PMS and Relationships Study, told us that when she was premenstrual, 'I try to do things that I enjoy doing, not putting so much pressure on myself . . . work pressure, even things like exercise pressure'. She said, 'I'm kinder to myself' at this time of the month, which functioned to reduce her premenstrual distress.[15, p.62]
>
> Carmen, interviewed in the Australian PMS and Relationships Study, told us that she coped with premenstrual distress by 'trying to keep the door closed and have a long hot bath, and read a book, and try to be a little bit spoilt and do things that I know I'll enjoy'.
>
> Danni said, 'I'll maybe sometimes be a bit nicer to myself . . . try to take some time out to relax, and treat myself to a massage for sore shoulders, which also helps me to relax'.
>
> Likewise, Merrin said, 'I'll actually give myself permission to actually go and lie down for half an hour, even half an hour will make a substantial amount of difference'.
>
> Susannah said, 'the biggest help for me was to realise which days they are [difficult days] and take the time for myself and listen to myself'.
>
> Monica used this realisation to reorganise pressures at work:

> > I won't book out my days so much. So I will manage my work load in a very different way [premenstrually], whereas before people would prevail on me to do things and I would keep doing more and more, and there'll be a whole full 8 til 6 every day, plus every night.

In studies of women recovering from depression, analogous patterns of self-care have been reported. Ridge and Ziebland found that women re-evaluated their priorities and took more time for themselves as part of the recovery process. As one woman said, 'if I want to go and walk in the hills

195

on the weekend and when I'm off, I will go and do it, whereas before there were always other people I had to consider'.[11,p.1047] Evelyn, interviewed by Michelle LaFrance, gave a similar account, saying that she now tries to:

> have a bath at night to soak. Not just the quick bath jump in and clea- you know get out, like you would. Like I always thought I didn't have time to take that time to sit. Me is is number – should be with all of us looking after ourself as we say in nursing, who takes care of the caregiver? But I haven't quite got that good yet.[5, p.105]

Evelyn is not alone in struggling with her desire for self-care, and her desire to be 'good' and look after the needs of others. Many women find self-care difficult, positioning it as 'selfish',[19] as outlined in accounts of PMS in Chapter 5. One way that women enable themselves to take time for self-care is to position it as essential at a point of crisis. Thus Joan, interviewed by Michelle LaFrance, said that 'it takes a melt down to make you stop'.[5, p.131] Pat said, 'I'd been so ill, that there was no question' of giving up household responsibilities and going 'off to bed'.[5, p.130] Similarly, Caroline said that taking time for exercise 'was my only sanity. That was my only one hour to myself'.[5, p.131] Another strategy was to position self-care as a necessary part of women caring for others – a discourse often repeated in women's magazine, where women are told 'you can't be there for your family, your employees, or your friends if you're not there for yourself' (*Homemakers Magazine*).[5, 145] Jaqueline drew on this 'oxygen mask device' in saying 'It's ok to look after you, cause how can you look after someone else if you don't care for you first'.[5, p.146] Charlotte argued that she can't give 'mommy time' to her daughter if she doesn't have 'time for me . . . strictly selfish time'.[5, p.147]

There is a danger that exhortations to women to engage in self-care can be construed as an additional pressure in already frenzied lives,[20] acting as a further measure of their performance of idealised femininity, and thus as a regulatory strategy of self-management.[5] As Michelle LaFrance points out, the use of the 'oxygen mask' rhetoric to justify women taking time for self-care colludes with discourses of femininity, reinforcing the belief that women *should* be caring for others, by implying that this is the only way women can justify attending to their own needs. However, for many women recovering from distress, making time for themselves, or engaging in self-care, also stands as resistance to archetypal discourses of femininity, as women are learning to stand up for themselves, finding out 'who me is',[5, p.162] and moving from self-sacrifice to a position of independence, self-nurturance and assertiveness. Indeed, women's descriptions of self-care as part of recovery are reminiscent of Virginia Woolf's comment that 'a woman must have money and a room of her own if she is to write fiction'.[21] We are not talking here about fiction, but rather about rewriting the self – having time to think, to reflect, or just 'be'; time to escape from the everyday demands of life, particularly from the responsibilities of being in relation – of looking after others, of having to be always attentive and caring. Indeed, Annika Forssen and Gunilla Carlstedt demonstrated the health giving properties of 'a room of one's own' in their study of Swedish women,[22] where they found that the need for privacy from others was imperative to mental health; as Linnea said, 'it's heavenly to be alone without anyone needing consideration or attention'.[22, p.177]

Few women have a 'room of one's own', almost a century after Woolf made her impassioned plea, but they find ways of resisting the demands of others in order to maintain their own sanity. Some do this by cutting themselves off from their surroundings, as Greta said, 'I really need to concentrate on something else, so I would choose a knitting pattern with a very difficult design'.[22, p.177] Other women physically escape the home. Sara described how she would 'take the train and sit down at a café. Nobody knew where I was. It felt such a luxury to be alone!'[22, p.177] Being alone, paradoxically, can also be achieved through being at work. Malin, interviewed by Forssen and Carlstedt, said, 'I really appreciated being able to leave home in the mornings'. Elina said, 'it was fun being alone in the evening, cleaning the offices',[23, p.918] even though she did not particularly like the cleaning work. The first part of Virginia Woolf's aphorism, cited above, is also pertinent here: 'a woman must have money'. For while the dual pressures of work and family can be a cause of distress for many women, work can also provide a sense of identity, social support and financial security that protects women from poverty and powerlessness. My own mother's journey from distress to happiness was marked by taking up employment outside the home. This gave her a network of friends, a modicum of financial independence, and an identity other than wife and mother, for the first time in decades. Feminist therapist Laura Brown has described her own mother's survival of depression similarly.[24] In this vein, Linnea, interviewed by Forssen and Carlstedt, described how she had been depressed but 'it became much better when I decided to go back to work . . . I was so happy to be able to work. I found that fantastic!'[23, p.920] Similarly, Gertrud, interviewed in the same study, said, 'I have felt satisfaction in my job; that's one of the things that have made me feel well, and given me happiness in life'.[23, p.916] Vera, who suffered periodically from anxiety, said that being extremely busy at work was good for her mental health: 'I think it's a happy thing to have too much to do, without much time for brooding about yourself and how you're feeling'.[23, p.920]

The discursive construction of the 'working woman', as professional, calm and in control, can also serve to provide boundaries for the experience and expression of distress.

Bella, who took part in the PMS and Relationships Study, said, 'I'm not picky at work, because once I'm at work . . . you have to just be very controlled'. Similarly, Pip described the importance of being able to 'maintain my work persona'.

Many women described these work boundaries as a relief, as it protected themselves (and others) from what they saw as the 'PMS-self'. As Mary told us,

> I don't think it affects anyone else 'cos I feel different at work. I mean I probably go to work to escape myself. I don't feel as though I take it out on my colleagues or anything like that. I just feel quite relieved to be at work really.

Similarly, Rachel said:

> I can sometimes say to myself, 'Well it's probably a good idea I go to work,' because I might get cranky or something like that . . . for some reason when I'm at work I'm all right, I can handle things all right . . . I'm pretty busy and I just get on with it.

We could interpret this as women policing themselves at work, in order to maintain a position of equality and avoid being positioned as the epitome of the 'monstrous feminine', the abject reproductive body which is out of control.[15] Alternatively, we could say that work is a context where many women can escape the constraints and conflicts of gendered roles as they are played out in heterosexual families, where family members make incessant demands on a woman, precipitating distress, and making it impossible for her to take time for herself. As Anna describes below:

> Look, I definitely get more irritated [premenstrually, at work]. But if that's the case, I just get up and walk out for 10 minutes. I go for a walk. And it's easy to do at work, because you don't have kids trailing after you or . . . 'Where are you going? When are you coming back?' You know, 'Can I have the . . .' [laugh] as you're trying to shut the door in their face. So, in that respect, it's much easier. People are more professional. They have to be. So you just go, 'I'm taking a break'. And 'I'll be back'. And I have the sort of job where I can do that, you know, pretty easily, so I do.

198

As Anna's comments illustrate, work colleagues observe professional boundaries, while children are often incessant in their demands, making a woman's irritation and anger an understandable response, in a context where she literally cannot take a moment for herself. This is why work can be analogous to a 'room of one's own',[23] a route to resistance and survival.

'I now realise I'm not alone': women asking for support

For many women, the realisation of the extent of their misery, and acknowledgement that it is legitimate, is also the first step in asking for help. Janet, interviewed by Rita Schreiber, said that 'my needs weren't being met, but I wasn't asking so why would they be. So I started asking for what I needed'.[6, p.486]

> Lesley, who took part in the Long Term Effects of Child Sexual Abuse Study, told us that she used to self-harm, but could now recognise when the desire to do so was about to come upon her, which she described as 'tunnel vision'. This realisation allowed her to ask for help or to make a 'positive effort' to so something else to 'keep it out of the way':

> > So that's an episode that's over, but that's what I thought the first time and so it's something that's always at the back of my mind that it's something I have to be careful of. And when I do start beginning to feel tunnel vision, I'm sort of learning to go looking for ways out. Either to find somebody sufficiently trustworthy and to say, 'Look, I've got a problem, I need some support'. That's probably the best way out of it. And also sort of trying to face it head on and say, 'Look you know this is something that comes from somewhere that I don't want', and so making almost a positive effort to be involved in something else and try and keep it out of the way.

> Lesley faced her difficult feelings head on, used distraction rather than self-harm as a coping strategy, and sought support. For some women, support from others in the same situation can be most beneficial. Gina said that most of her friends are child sexual abuse survivors and she finds it easier to be with them than others: 'You speak your own language, you know, you have your own lingo, and people understand if you, you know, if you're through a bad space or whatever you don't have to explain at all or whatever'.

Melanie found it particularly helpful to be part of an incest survivors group, because 'there were other people who had other stories . . . so I could see that I really wasn't the only one'. She said that previously, 'I couldn't get past this idea that it was something sort of branded on me, that I should be abused', but now she saw herself very differently, which had been important in teaching her that she was not a 'natural victim'.

Conversely, Naomi described how she was able to gain the support of a prominent figure in the community to support her in her actions against the perpetrator of her abuse. This reinforced her sense of self-worth: 'I'd been quiet too long, I mean I've been letting everybody walk all over me'. With hindsight, she was aware of how distressed she had been in the past, but recognised that 'it's been really hard with not that much support. And I think that's, that's what I'm looking now, to get some support'. But this was not an easy process. Naomi said that she had 'only just realised . . . how hard it is for me to let people take care of me':

> And I think that's something to do with having to cope and having to be strong all the time. I'm a single parent, and coping as a child and coping, coping, coping all the time, it's hard for you to let people in. But I'm now starting to realise that it's okay for people to take care of me, and when I can afford it I have a little bit of counselling, you know, just to sort of back up the support and stuff.

Naomi was not alone in finding counselling or therapy helpful.

Valentina described her experience of intensive therapy soon after her experience of adult rape as 'excellent'. She said she found the therapy a painful process because of memories that came back to her about the abuse she had experienced as a child, but that it gave her the strength to move forward positively in her life:

> So the therapy was hard and um, painful, and I stuck with it because the therapist was really very good and she gave me hope. And I was just about embarking on my social work training and um, she was very clear that we were going to get through this and 'You were going to be qualified', and, and I believed her and she was like somebody on my corner, and I went back cause it was good to have this person saying 'You can do this'. She was brilliant.

Melanie, who took part in the same study, talked about recovery not being linear.

> It's not a straight line, it's like good periods, bad periods, and there may be years or months or weeks or days, but there's periods where it comes back, and it comes back with a vengeance. And then usually I see a therapist and then I'm better for a few more years.

Janice told us that she had found art therapy to be very useful in dealing with the effects of childhood sexual abuse:

> It's like going to playgroup; it's a safe place to be in. I can take risks there, I can explore my feelings and find out where these feelings come from. I can understand it's exhausting and that's ok. What I am, what I am is ok.

Through this therapy Janice learned about anger, its ability to harm her, and the difficulties in trying to express it. She also learnt to stop hating herself and blaming herself for the abuse.

A number of women who took part in the PMS and Relationships Study also described therapy as beneficial. Susannah said she saw a 'lady psychologist' who 'advised me . . . don't put anything on that [premenstrual] day, after work don't plan anything just have time for yourself. And she was very right because it really helps so you don't get the stress'.

Similarly, Jacinta told us:

> my shrink would say 'What's the evidence for that? You're having this reaction and you're having this feeling, well why don't you process this by showing me what's the evidence for it' . . . which allows you to dissipate the feelings that aren't fact.

For some women, accounts of recovery are associated with medical intervention. Rachel Perkins has written about 'choosing E.C.T' to alleviate her depression,[25, p.623] and says she would choose it again if she became depressed.[i] Other women associate recovery with taking psychotropic medication. As Sarah told Deanna Gammell and Janet Stoppard 'I know I do need medication . . . we've tried three, well four different drugs now and this is the one that seems to be working . . . the best'.[27, p.122] Sarah said that she felt she needed her medication to 'alter the thought process'. The UK PMS Study, which I conducted with Myra Hunter, compared SSRIs and a woman centred psychological intervention, and found that both were effective in reducing premenstrual distress.[28] However, the effectiveness of the SSRIs was not simply pharmacological, changing women's patterns of serotonin uptake, as advocates of such treatments would have us believe.[e.g. 29] A number of women in the SSRI group reported that they did not notice a significant reduction in premenstrual symptoms, but that their premenstrual distress was relieved because they were completing daily diaries which increased awareness of their symptoms. They also had the opportunity to talk to the prescribing physician, Rosanne Jelley, who was asked to mirror normal clinical practice by conducting a brief assessment of the woman, and to see them for follow-up appointments, which served to increase women's awareness and provide support, as Tracy explains:

> I'm pretty much the same as I always have really, although over all a bit more positive. I don't think the Prozac itself was as much help but actually it made me a lot more aware of what I was going through the whole treatment, the keeping the diaries and the making notes, um so generally I feel a bit more positive and I can't actually stop the symptoms, and I know that my behaviour will change and that I will react differently to things but that's, you know, I just accept it; that's the way I'm going to be.

Equally, many women reported that the most significant part of the SSRI treatment was being taken seriously, and their experiences being validated, through being offered a 'cure' for PMS.

> Angela said, 'The most important thing was realising that what I had wasn't imaginary and I actually, there is a cure for it, or there is help for PMS, for women who suffer with PMS'.

In a similar vein, a number of women talked about using their participation in the study as a means of communicating with others about their pre-menstrual experiences, allowing them to ask for support, which reduced feelings of isolation, and meant that significant others were less likely to overburden the woman at this time.

> Leoni told us: 'being part of this study has helped me to actually talk about it and to get more information so that as well the feeling of not being so isolated with it has been a help'.

'A dance of moving in and out': partner support alleviating distress

Being in a supportive intimate relationship is also central to many women's accounts of moving away from misery, as well as resistance of the mantle of madness. For example, in the PMS and Relationships Study, a number of the participants (the majority of lesbians and one-third of the heterosexual women) gave accounts of supportive partners, and emphasised the positive influence that this had on their premenstrual distress. Understanding and acceptance of premenstrual change was a key feature of this support.

> Shea commented: 'In terms of her response . . . it's just really understanding and I guess supportive . . . Like, it's not that big an issue that it becomes an issue . . . it's just like, "This is how I'm feeling. That's okay"'. Similarly, Linda told us, 'I'm extremely lucky that Helen [her partner] is an extremely understanding person and so I get what I need at that time'.

In this vein, making an attribution of mood or behaviour change to 'PMS' was experienced as a positive thing, as Pip commented, 'It's almost as though it's a relief [she knows] there's a reason for it'. Similarly, Casey told us:

> [I know] how important it is, to have someone kind of go, 'Yep, you really do . . .' and it's not being silly and it's not, um, dismissed as being, you know, um . . . Like, it's actually real. 'I get that. I believe you.' That sort of stuff. It's not just an excuse for having an off day, sort of thing.

Sarah described how her partner's recognition of 'PMS' also made him feel 'more relieved, because he thinks that maybe it wasn't that bad, or that there was something else on top'. She said that 'he worries quite a lot about . . . you know, like how happy I am or how unhappy I am' and is 'glad to know I'm not there forever, I guess, I'm not in that stage of unhappiness forever'.

Penny described her female partner as recognising 'that I had PMS before I knew I had it', which Penny 'felt was good on her part' because it allowed her to think 'okay, maybe it is', which then diffused the situation. In these instances 'PMS' was invariably named, but in a non-judgemental manner.

Sheridan said:

> we talk about the fact that I'm probably premenstrual . . . so what would normally would have, I guess in past

> relationships, become an argument, these days would
> probably just mean that she would make me a cup of tea
> and a hot water bottle and I'd lie down and um get a bit
> pampered.

This recognition functioned to protect the relationship, because irritability and moodiness could be positioned as 'not something personal', or something which would have a major impact upon the relationship. It also meant that women did not enter into a spiral of increasing distress in response to partner rejection or pathologisation, and were more likely to engage in effective coping, such as taking time for self-care or avoidance of conflict.

At the same time, in order to avoid issues or feelings which are raised premenstrually being ignored by a woman's partner, or dismissed as 'just PMS',[30–31] the majority of women in supportive relationship contexts gave accounts of open discussion of premenstrual feelings, leading to communication about concerns and needs within the relationship. This allowed issues to be resolved more effectively, even if it involved some negotiation and effort on the part of the couple.

> Casey told us that she and her partner had very different sexual
> needs premenstrually, with her own libido disappearing, while her
> partner's 'went through the roof when she's got PMT'. How-
> ever, because they could 'talk about it, there's a respect', Casey's
> apparent sexual rejection of her partner was not positioned as 'a
> personal thing':

> > It's really one of those hard things to talk about initially, but
> > then it was like, well, you know, we have to. And just that
> > understanding of it's not about personal rejection . . . It's
> > bigger than that. So . . . we kind of worked it out. Worked the
> > zones out. Almost like there's a map on the wall.

Participants who portrayed their relationship context as supportive also described their partner reacting to premenstrual expressions of anger or irritation with a calm, non-reactive response, so that discussions would not escalate into an argument.

> Joyce described herself as 'very fortunate to have a husband who's
> prepared to deal with it and has learnt the subtleties'. She described
> their interactions premenstrually as 'almost like a dance of moving in
> and out' where her husband would think, 'okay, give her some space

now, be tender now, and we'll talk at a better time on this issue'. This meant that Joyce could express issues of concern, and they would 'work on it in a calmer time'.

Similarly, Bec described her female partner as a 'very laid back' person who reacted to Bec's premenstrual anger by saying, 'Why are you bringing this up like this' and then saying 'You're PMT-ing aren't you? . . . Maybe we should talk about this later'.

Many supportive partners also gave accounts of learning to give the woman space through removing themselves when she was premenstrual, in order to avoid conflict.

Bill, Olivia's partner, said, 'There's a time of the month where we're not going to get along. And it's best for me to just hide in the garage or the shed'. Likewise, Gary, Bella's partner, described himself as trying to 'tiptoe around her a bit . . . give her a bit of space', saying, 'It's a good time to be out doing a bit of gardening'.

While this could be experienced by a woman as withdrawal, and could thus be detrimental to the relationship,[32] many partners were motivated by awareness of the woman's need for time for herself premenstrually, and actively facilitated this, as is evidenced by Lucian's account of his partner Carmen:

She likes comfort food, chocolates, yes, so um, cherry ripe, she'll sit down have a coffee, or I'll take Elizabeth [their daughter] out for a while. But I go to bed early and she has time after I go to bed, to herself, she likes to do her craft and she'll get very adamant and say, 'I don't care about the dishes tonight, I'm going to do craft', you say 'okay' [laughs] it isn't hard for me.

Denise described her partner Stephanie as saying, 'I just want to be on my own', when she was premenstrual which Denise thought was 'fine', encouraging her to 'go to her own room' or 'potter in the garden' or do 'anything that helps her resolve it, that's my preference'.

Similarly, Jocelyn described her partner Deborah's support:

I've got a really big garden that I maintain and I like to take myself out there . . . I do like to be a little more alone around that time . . . she's very understanding, maybe does a little

205

bit of housework on those days, ah, doesn't expect too much from me at those times.

Other partners provided physical comfort, exemplified by Maggie, who said that when she cried premenstrually her husband 'usually comes and gives me a cuddle, and says, 'Oh, don't worry about it, it's that time of the month'. Her partner Dave told us:

> I just try and be as nice as possible. You know, try and offer a bit of physical comfort by trying to give her a hug or a cuddle and just to tell her that I love her and 'Look, it's not the be-all and end-all. No point ruining everything over one comment I've made'.

Eleanor also told us that her partner offered both reassurance and physical support, 'He would ask how I am, and he would always say, "Geez, that's unfair". So sweet. "Oh, that's really no good, can I get you a hot water bottle"'. Sheridan said her female partner would 'go off and make me a tea, or remember little things that are going to comfort me, practical things'.

Casey was typical of the lesbian interviewees, in describing mutual support and reassurance being offered premenstrually:

> When I'm in those zones, if it's the weekend, I'm more than happy to stay at home and just with the DVD and put music on and just kind of be in my own bubble. And be in the zone. I can't affect anyone. [Partner] can be very, um, accom-modating around, you know, baths and you know, going out and getting good food, and putting DVDs on, and just kind of really . . . that real pampering stuff which, um, makes a huge difference. And I can do the same for her.

Confirming previous research on premenstrual change in women with positive attitudes to menstruation,[33] none of the women who reported having supportive partners adopted a stance of self-pathologisation, or used derogatory terms to describe themselves premenstrually, such as 'mad', 'loony-tune', 'bitch', 'monstrous-mummy' or 'Jekyll and Hyde', terms which are commonly found in heterosexual women's accounts of PMS, as outlined in Chapter 5.[34–35] There was also less evidence of guilt and self-blame in these accounts, and very few accounts of feeling 'out of control' premen-strually, as premenstrual change was more likely to be accepted as a normal part of a woman's experience, even if it wasn't necessarily pleasant for a woman or her partner. This allowed women to avoid the concomitant distress associated with feeling 'out of control'.[36, p.285]

> Helena told us, 'I would just go with it and go, "Oh look, in two days [laugh] this will be fine [laugh]"'. Similarly, Amy said, 'I just keep plodding along'. Janice said, 'You just hang on for a couple of days'. Jacinta told herself, 'Oh well, that's life', and Nina said, 'You just forget about it'.

This does not mean that premenstrual mood change is necessarily embraced, but it is not positioned as an illness or sign of madness, rather, as something that a woman accepts as part of being a woman. Having a supportive partner was not a necessary requisite for women adopting this position in relation to premenstrual change, however all those who reported a supportive relationship context did so, with some women embracing premenstrual change, experiencing it as a positive thing. For example, Sophia told us,

> I might use it, in a way, because I do a lot of creative work, as a playwright. So sometimes I go, 'Good, I might lock myself away now, and just get a lot of work done'. And sometimes you can really connect with some deeper ener-gies that are going on, . . . I feel like something in me, creatively, is willing to go further in that time . . . which can be really exciting and invigorating. Mm. So sometimes you can really channel it.

Equally, in the Positive Premenstrual Experiences Study,[37] we found that over 80 per cent positioned at least one premenstrual change as positive.

> Many women reported feeling good, including being 'high and happy' (Hannah); wanting to 'jump around' (Kate); having 'more self-confidence and being more affectionate' (Jillian); being 'more moti-vated to do things' (Bianca); and feeling 'more patient' (Lacey). Feeling more orderly or tidy was also commonly reported, with Clare telling us that 'just before I go to sleep I have to tidy my room up', and Sabrina saying that she cleaned her boyfriend's flat when she was premenstrual, 'which he appreciates and I feel really good'. Increased sexual arousal or desire was also commonly reported, as exemplified by Madison's comment that 'I'm more interested, and I initiate sexual relations more than I would [normally], which is nice'. Mary described

herself as 'more raunchy' premenstrually and Rachel described the 'actual sexual act' as 'more heated, because I'm more aroused than I normally would be, so it's more intense'. Sex can also function as a release of tension premenstrually, with Hanna telling us she felt 'more relaxed' afterwards, 'you feel much better when you do it at this stage'.

Positive experiences are rarely associated with descriptions of 'PMS' because researchers and clinicians seldom ask women about positive pre-menstrual changes, as they are not positioned as 'symptoms',[35] reinforcing the positioning of premenstrual change as sign of pathology. However, if women *are* asked, the majority, like the women in our study, report at least one positive experience premenstrually, including feelings of well-being, sexual arousal, increased tidiness, increased energy, more attractive breasts and increased creativity.[33; 38–40] Premenstrual change is thus not inevitably constructed or experienced as a negative, pathological disorder; it can be normalised, or even embraced, transforming 'unwantedness into wanted-ness',[33, p.30] with relational support facilitating this process.

Resistance and survival through creativity

> I am changing my name
> I am burning my past
> I'm laying yesterday to rest at last
> I am owning these actions
> then setting them all aflame
> I'm not sorry for who I am
> or who you wanted me to be
> Bonfire Madigan Shive, *Mad Skywriting*[41, p.184]

From the women who escaped from incarceration in asylums in the nine-teenth century, to present day feminist artists, writers and poets, women have also resisted the mantle of madness through creative expression. It has long been said that madness is a manifestation of creativity, with many male artists and writers – Nietzsche, Van Gogh, Goya, Artaud, de Sade – cele-brated for their disordered minds; indeed, madness deemed to be the source of their genius. As the anti-psychiatrist David Cooper has declared 'the mad*man*, like the poet, would refuse Wittgenstein's proposition that "that which one cannot speak one should be silent". It is precisely the unsayable that must be expressed in mad and poetic discourse'.[42, p.28, my emphasis] Mad*men* is the apposite term – for it is *men*'s madness that is invariably celebrated, while women's madness is deemed confirmation of frailty or foolhardiness, and 'mad' women artists derided or dismissed – as women artists have often been, whatever their state of mind.[43–44] Yet despite this exclusion, many women have given voice to their distress and misery through art, poetry, film or writing, as we have seen in the many auto-biographical accounts that appear throughout this book. These accounts provide insight into the complexity of women's pain, situate 'madness' firmly within the context of women's lives, and lay bare the realities and regulatory constraints of psychiatric 'treatment'.

Thus Elizabeth Stone, who was labelled mad and incarcerated for two years in 1840 because of her religious beliefs, wrote of how

> that countenance that once was lit up with happiness is now marked with sorrow; those eyes that once sparkled with joy are now dead sunken with grief, and the language, and the voice are so different that some form of destruction has come upon [me].[45, p.40]

Elizabeth Ware Packard, incarcerated for three years from 1860, described how 'once I was in the asylum I was beyond reach of all human aid, except what could come through my husband . . . and my husband determined never to take me out'.[45, p.61] Dorothy Dix wrote of the barbaric treatment of the mad she had witnessed in her book *On behalf of the insane poor*, published in 1843:

> Some say these things cannot be remedied; these furious maniacs are not to be raised from their base conditions. I *know* they are; could give *many* examples; let *one* suffice. A young woman, a pauper, in a distant town, *Stanisfield*, was for years a raging maniac. A cage, chains, and *the whip*, were the agents for con-trolling her, united with harsh tones and profane language. Annually, with others (the town's poor) she was put up at auction, and bid off at the lowest price which was declared for her. One year, not long past, an old man came forward in the number of applications for the poor wretch; he was taunted and ridiculed; 'what would he and his old wife do with such a mere beast?' 'My wife says yes,' replied he 'and I shall take her.' She was given to his charge; he conveyed her home; she was washed, neatly dressed, and placed in a decent bed-room, furnished for comfort and opening into the kitchen. . . . 'After a fortnight' said the old man 'I knocked off the chains and made her a free woman.' . . . Go there now and you will find her 'clothed', and although not per-fectly in her 'right mind,' so far restored as to be a safe and comfortable inmate.[46, pp.11–12]

Other women have turned to fiction to describe their own misery and its consequences. Charlotte Perkins Gilman described her disintegration into madness, and her subjection to the bed-rest cure in *The yellow wallpaper*. Sylvia Plath wrote of her experiences of adolescent breakdown and psychiatric treatment in her fictionalised memoir *The bell jar*. Mary Jane Ward described isolation and despair in her description of the vagaries of asylum life in *The snake pit*.[47] Many memoirs of madness have also been written, including Kate Millett's *The loony-bin trip*,[48] Janet Frame's *Faces in the water*,[49] Susanna Kaysen's *Girl, interrupted*,[1] Lauren Slater's *Black swans*,[10] and Elizabeth Wurtzl's *Prozac nation*,[50] and the anthologies *Live through this: On creativity and self-destruction*,[51] *Hysteria: An anthology of poetry, prose, and visual art on the subject of women's mental health*,[52] and *Out of her mind: Women writing on madness*[53] edited by Sabrina Chapadjiev, Jennifer Savran, and Rebecca Shannonhouse respectively – all of which have been cited throughout this book. Women have also written about the madness of their mothers, and how this has marked their own lives. I began my own book *Women's madness: Misogyny or mental illness?*[54, p.3] with the statement

> when I was an adolescent my mother was mad. Because it was the 1970s she was deemed to be afflicted by her nerves. Had it been 100 years ago, she would probably have been called 'hysterical' or 'neuresthenic'.

The desire to reveal the misogyny behind women's diagnosis and treatment led me to research and write that particular book, a motivation that still drives me today. It is a motivation that is embedded in the fear of a child watching her mother suffer at the hands of those who purported to make her well, as I wrote:

> They gave her ECT which left her shaking and crying, and gave her a cocktail of drugs so that she forgot everything. She forgot her pain, her misery, her loneliness, the fear which kept her awake at night and which I can even now only imagine. But she forgot everything else. Sometimes she forgot our names, confusing us, calling us each name in turn before reaching the right one. So she must have been mad. My father told me she was. Her nerves had given in. She was ill. And it was a secret. We weren't allowed to tell our friends, or our relatives and we didn't talk about it ourselves. I learnt the lesson of the stigma of madness early in life: shame, fear, guilt, perhaps for many people more debilitating than the symptoms called madness.[54, p.4]

Linda Gray Sexton, in her memoir *Searching for Mercy Street*, described the madness of her mother, the poet Anne Sexton, the fear that infused their relationship, and how she felt that she was somehow to blame:

Small and blond, with a shy smile and blue eyes that held a tentative expression, I had been, Mother said later, an impossible three year old. 'You cried all the time,' she explained. 'You whined. You were a difficult and annoying child.' . . . I averted my eyes with shame when she told me how hard I was to care for: perhaps my ugly nature was to blame for my mother's difficulties with being a mother. What I remembered from those early years was my own fear, the anxiety that lived inside me like a boa constrictor and made it hard to breathe. My mother had been hospitalised in a terrible place, my mother had left me, my mother – the centre of my small universe – was as fragile and precarious as the translucent Limoges my nana kept on high shelves at her house. Who knew when she would next break? The years would bring suicide attempts, trances, fugue states, fits of rage – and depression so intense that she sat for hours staring into space or paced restlessly like an animal in a cage, or spoke to the voices inside her head. Fear was the four letter word with which I lived, locked inside me like a dirty secret.[55, p.122]

These accounts are far removed from medical or psychological descriptions of 'symptoms', 'diagnostic categories', or 'interventions'. They bring women's distress and despair to life; the messy, murky, painful feelings and complex web of relationships that extend out from the woman who is invariably the sole object of the psychiatric gaze. For many women, the very act of writing is a catharsis that makes sense of experience, and keeps madness at bay. Daphne Gottlieb says:

writing is useful, good important – it gives us insight into ourselves and our world and sometimes helps us to find our way to a better place. We can make better worlds, word by word. I have written from the depths of depressions, long signal flares I throw up in the air, hoping they will light the terrain around me, show me the way out. When it's working wonderfully, I get some insight or create the beginnings of something that's beautiful.[56, p.33]

In a similar vein, Bonfire Madigan Shive uses music to explore her experiences of distress:

These so-called symptoms are just part of us, instead of just cutting them off, exploring where they come from allows us to understand ourselves and our untapped capacities. In fact, each time I sit down with my cello, I learn something about myself. Sometimes when I start to make sound, I'm like 'what do you want to tell me today,

Cellina, what are we feeling, where are we at?' And I let the sounds inform me.[57, p.185]

Thus creativity can be a means of escape, of making sense of the world, and of reframing madness outside of the boundaries of pathology. At the same time, for many women, it is out of pain that creativity grows, turning misery into richness and strength, a source of light rather than darkness and pain.

Changing the conditions that precipitate women's distress

In examining women's strategies of survival and resistance I could be accused of placing the onus on women to change – to sort themselves out, or pull themselves together, as women who express misery are often told.[see 4] This is *not* what I am saying. It is important to recognise women's ability to face the abyss of despair, and to come out the other side. It is also important to recognise that for some women this can be a process of break through, rather than breakdown; that recovery and resistance can be a process of personal transformation. However, for many women resistance is not possible. The material conditions of their lives, the constructions of femininity that prescribes their gendered roles, and the intrapsychic and intersubjective context within which difficulty and distress is negotiated, may make misery the unavoidable outcome. This is why solutions to women's misery need to operate at each of the interconnected levels – material, discursive, intrapsychic and intersubjective. So how do we address this misery, without pathologising women, and reinforcing myths of madness?

First, we need to question the increasing medicalisation of misery in the West, in particular the way in which women who experience mild distress or understandable problems with everyday life are defined as having mental disorders such as 'depression', 'borderline personality disorder', or 'PMDD', and then told that the optimum treatment is medication, most frequently an SSRI. Indeed, we need to be wary of reinforcing medical naturalism through our very critiques of madness, or our research into women's experiences of distress, by using diagnostic categories such as 'depression', 'BPD' or 'PMDD' – or any of the other so-called 'disorders'. In the same way that feminist psychologists have used the term 'pre-menstrual change' or 'premenstrual distress' in order to avoid the medical-ised connotations of the diagnostic categories of PMS or PMDD,[15] we may need to deliberately subvert taken-for-granted assumptions by using terms such as 'severe distress', 'prolonged misery' or 'continuum of depres-sive experiences', to make the point that experiences such as 'depression' are not unitary, global, transhistorical pathologies.

Diagnostic labels such as the term 'depression' may function to com-municate the extent of a woman's distress, and validate her subjective experience; however, they can also serve to obscure the conditions that lead to distress in the first place, and simply dismiss a woman as 'mad'. Some would argue that diagnosis can be used in a non-pathologising, non-pejorative way,[e.g. 58–59] and that it is a useful, indeed, necessary part of delivering appropriate services and support. However, diagnosis is useful for a woman only if it is part of creating meaning about her experience, rather than being used to establish diagnostic classification. One solution is for a formulation approach to be used in clinical settings,[60] wherein explanations for problems and appropriate solutions are co-constructed with the woman, acting as a 'process of ongoing collaborative sense-making',[61, p.8] without the need for a specific diagnostic label – similar to the approach Richard Bentall advocates for individuals diagnosed with schizophrenia.[62] This allows us to focus on the individual woman and her relation to her world, not just on an abstract 'mental disorder', in order to understand why distress occurs, and determine how we can help to ameliorate it. We can thus examine in an individual woman's social and relational context, the fantasies, desires and constructions that frame her interpretation of her lived experience, as well as her history of distress – or abuse – which will influence her current level of well-being.

This does not mean that we should conceptualise women's suffering as a individual pathology – we need to understand it within the social-political context where it occurs, and work towards changing that context. We need social and political change so that women are not living in a context of inequality, violence and abuse; if we engender this change we can modify the conditions that precipitate so much of women's despair. This is no mean feat. We need an end to violence against women – both sexual violence and intimate partner violence – which includes prevention strategies to reduce offending, education of girls and women to encourage disclosure, and public rejection of the notion that domestic or sexual violence is in any way normal or acceptable.[63] This will include critical examination of our very notions of hetero-sex as it currently stands, as Nicola Gavey has undertaken in her book *Just sex? The cultural scaffolding of rape*,[64] so that male dominance, and the 'male sex drive discourse',[65] are not reified as truth. We also need an end to sexual trafficking, and forced marriages, as well as forced sexual initiation of young girls. Women need to have ownership of their own reproductive bodies, including access to contraception and legal abortion. There also needs to be an end to women's poverty and inequality – including inequality in the workplace, in politics and in the home. Outside of the privileged context of the industrialised West, this means access to education, a basic minimum wage, and in many contexts, the freedom to take up paid employment. In the West, it means women genuinely being paid equal wages for work of equal value, being represented on boards, in management hierarchies and on governments, and not being taken for granted as unpaid unrecognised skivvies in the home. As long as women are positioned as second rate – the 'second sex' – our subjugation will continue, which creates conditions for the development of despair.

We also need to critically examine the gendered socialisation of girls and women, which increases their likelihood of rumination, self-silencing, self-objectification and the internal attribution of problems. All of these supposedly psychological traits are in reality reflections of women's performance of femininity, embodied constructions of the 'good woman', which leave little room for speaking out, or for feeling positive about the self or the body. We also need to challenge the taken-for-granted assumptions about gendered roles in heterosexual relationships, particularly after the advent of children, and challenge men and women's investment in the continuation of the status quo. This is not simply about education or consciousness raising with individual women and men – it is about questioning our very constructions of gender and gendered roles. Men are sold a story of conquest, machismo and emotional independence, as well as being taught that women look after the home, the children, and men's emotional well-being. In the majority of families this is what happens – women in cohabiting heterosexual relationships still do 70 per cent of the housework and childcare, even if they are working full time,[66] as well as taking on the emotional management of the family, as discussed in Chapter 5.[ii] At the same time, women are taught to wait for Prince Charming, who will sweep them off their feet (if they are slim and attractive enough) to make them happy ever after. Despite a century of feminism, young women today say that marriage and motherhood are major goals in life, alongside a fulfilling job or career.[67–69] For as Dana Jack has argued, 'even today, most girls are being socialized according to a slightly watered down version of the nineteenth century cult of true womanhood'.[70, p.87] This may be tempered somewhat by a discourse of equality, which leads young women to expect their partner to help in the home. As 25-year-old Linh Nguyen commented:

> I don't envisage working . . . for much longer than 10 years . . . [then] I would be ready to be a better mum and wife and be there for my family. However, I do still believe in splitting the housework and would expect my husband to contribute, so it's not entirely traditional.[71, p.57]

If we look to the statistics on sharing of responsibility, Linh may be disappointed, and then distressed – understandably so.

Nancy Chodorow has argued that 'families organised around women's mothering and male dominance create incompatibilities in women's and men's relational needs'. She believes that men are unlikely to provide for women the 'needs that their mothering by women and the social organisation of gender have produced. The less that men participate in the domestic sphere, and especially in parenting, the more this will be the case'.[72, p.199] There have been some changes since 1978, when Chodorow wrote these words, but only minimally so – even in countries, such as Sweden, where men are eligible for full parental leave. We thus need to understand why this is so, before Nancy Chodorow's hopeful vision of gendered equality can come about.

Some women appear reluctant to adopt non-gendered parenting, perhaps because of the intrapsychic investment they have in the mothering role, the physical relationship between mother and child, and the positioning of the father as the 'third term',[73, p.123] in Wendy Hollway's words. The reluctance may also be because we are continuously told that being a 'good mother' is central to our fulfilment and identity as women, with all the self-sacrifice and subjugation that this entails. This is not simply about gendered roles in relation to parenting. The social expectation that women will provide care extends way beyond the mothering role, with women also taking on the greater burden of care in relation to elderly relatives and the sick, described as an 'invisible tax' that can erode health and well-being.[5, p.37] This burden of care is located in the material contexts of women's lives and gendered divisions of labour; the discursive construction of women as natural carers;[19] and women's intrapsychic and intersubjective negotiation of care and responsibility. For example, in a study I conducted with informal cancer carers, women gave accounts of being positioned as 'all encompassing expert carers', leading to over-responsibility and self-sacrifice, which in turn led to physical costs of caring, overwhelming emotions and self-silencing. In contrast, men who were carers positioned caring as a competency task, which had positive consequences in terms of self-mastery, with the primary negative consequence being difficulties in dealing with the emotional side of cancer.[74] Change needs to happen at each of these material-discursive-intrapsychic levels for women to be able to renegotiate caring responsibilities and avoid the physical and psychological consequences of overburden and lack of self-care.

A challenge to gendered roles and movement towards a more egalitarian relationship is also good for heterosexual men, as women who are in supportive empathic relationships experience less distress, and are more able to cope with the vicissitudes of life, which is good for both partners, and for the relationship. However, the findings of the PMS and Relationships Study, combined with previous research on lesbian relationships,[iii] suggests that for a woman, the odds of being in an egalitarian, empathic, supportive relationship are higher if your partner is a woman than if he is a man – regardless of the presence of children. These findings are not unique to PMS. In other areas of women's reproductive health, such as perinatal depression,[78] and menopausal distress,[79] having a woman partner has been found to ameliorate distress,[iv] as discussed in Chapter 5. This is not to suggest that women forsake men in the interests of their mental health, tempting as this suggestion might be. But it does reinforce the importance of gendered roles and patterns of relational interconnection and support.

At the same time, accounts of support from male partners in the PMS and Relationships Study contradict the belief held by many of our interviewees that 'men can't understand'. It is clearly possible for men to be supportive and respectful towards their partners premenstrually (or at any other time), which can facilitate a reduction in distress, and avoidance of the escalation of conflict, or the spiral of guilt and self-blame which many women engage in. Taking up an empathic, supportive position can also have positive benefits for men, as men who gave accounts of being able to talk to their partner about her needs premenstrually (or indeed, at any time in the month), and who reported acceptance and some understanding of the reality of premenstrual change, were less likely to give accounts of experiencing distress or anger themselves. Communication about premenstrual change between couples appears to be central to men's recognition and understanding,[84] which previous research has suggested can be assisted by men's involvement in monitoring of their partner's premenstrual change.[85] This suggests that the involvement of male partners in therapeutic interventions for severe premenstrual distress may be beneficial,[85] acting to inform men about the nature and course of premenstrual change, as well as engaging their involvement in strategies of support for their partner.[v]

What of individual solutions for women's misery? Women's accounts of survival and resistance centre on acknowledgement of the reality of distress, awareness of factors that might precipitate it, relational change, rejection of the 'good woman' discourse, and increased self-care. These are all important strategies that can be adopted. Women also talk of support from family, friends, or health professionals. Indeed, social support is widely recognised to be a major protective factor for mental health, acting as a buffer against the stresses and strains of life.[87] Therapy or counselling can be central to survival, providing a supportive context for the exploration and expression of women's distress, as well as a forum for developing strategies for coping. For despite the feminist criticisms outlined in Chapter 3, the majority of therapy modalities focus on enhancing insight and personal agency, as well as providing a supportive 'holding' relationship for women, described by Carl Rogers as 'unconditional positive regard'.[88] This is not to say that all therapies are the same – they are not, with major theoretical divisions existing between psychoanalytic, cognitive-behavioural and interpersonal therapies, in particular. However, effective psychotherapies have more in common than they do in opposition,[89] and if the particular therapy (and therapist) is matched to the needs and preferences of the individual woman, therapy can be very effective in reducing distress.

For example, while psychoanalysis may have borne the brunt of much feminist critique,[90] Janet Sayers has argued that Kleinian psychotherapy has the potential to help women to address and manage their anger and anxiety without adopting self-defeating coping strategies, because of the way in which Klein addressed issues of anger and destructiveness.[91] Sayers acknowledges the social location of women's self-silencing and resultant anger, and believes that Kleinian psychotherapy can address the double bind of women's outward expression of anger being a source of guilt and distress, whereas outwardly projected anger positions women as victims. Louise Gyler goes further in her espousal of a Kleinian approach, arguing that it 'may in practice hold more radical possibilities for the interests of women than the practices derived from psychoanalytic feminist-informed gender theory'.[92, p.171]

Feminist therapists also directly acknowledge women's individual life experience, as well as the cultural and political context wherein distress is constructed and lived,[e.g. 93–95] adopting a range of approaches, including systemic, narrative, cognitive-behavioural or psychodynamic techniques.[e.g. 58; 86; 96–99] Feminist therapists are also more likely to focus on a critical examination of taken-for-granted gender roles, and the need for women to stop self-policing as 'good women', in order to engage in relationship change and self-care. The goal is the empowerment of women and the development of a feminist consciousness. Laura Brown, a renowned exponent of feminist therapy, encapsulates it thus:

> Feminist therapists are interested in creating 'feminist conscious-ness', that is, the understanding that one's difficulties in life are not a reflection of personal deficits or failures to sufficiently strive, but rather derive from systemic forms of culturally based oppression. Developing personal power, defined in a very broad manner, is an overarching goal of feminist therapy.[93, p.337]

Thus in a women-centred therapy for moderate to severe premenstrual distress that I was involved in developing, which draws on both narrative and cognitive therapy,[86] we encourage women to re-author their premenstrual distress as an understandable response to their life circumstances and relationship context, at a time when they are sensitive because of embodied changes that take place across the menstrual cycle. This process is influenced by the discursive resources that women draw on to make sense of their distress; the patterns of thinking used in coping, which women are encouraged to explore. Empowering strategies for coping are facilitated, including diet and exercise, taking time for self-care, assertiveness and relationship communication, as well as re-authored thinking and challenging negative constructions of PMS. After taking part in this therapy, women reported greater awareness of premenstrual change and of their needs premenstrually, increased self-care, better communication with their partner, and a change in their understanding of premenstrual distress.[9; 14]

As Ellen said, 'I had started to believe I was kind of a victim of my pre-menstrual symptoms . . . but now feel more in charge of my life, which is quite liberating'.

Likewise, Lisa said that she is better able to 'manage' things, feeling that she is better equipped to 'get my head around it a lot easier' when things are going wrong for her. She described being able to say 'No' to people and doesn't feel so guilty if she does – that 'it's not the end of the world' and people won't 'hate me' for it.

In tolerating and normalising premenstrual change, women were able to move away from self-pathologisation, and rather than positioning themselves as victims of their hormones, were able to develop the agentic coping strategies outlined earlier in this chapter. This model of therapy has been found to be more effective than SSRIs in 'treating' women's premenstrual distress,[28; 100] so it clearly works.

In a similar vein, Sam Warner has developed what she describes as 'Visible Therapy',[101] which challenges the language of diagnosis, symptoms, normality, and pathology associated with child sexual abuse. As discussed in Chapter 4, Warner argues that women's 'symptoms' are better understood as coping strategies, which serve to make sense of the abuse that they have endured. Thus behaviour such as self-harm are conceptualised as 'a viable coping strategy that, when used in this way, has life affirming qualities'.[101, p.250] When the roots of distress are 'made visible' in therapy the woman is empowered, recognising herself as a 'survivor' rather than a 'victim' of sexual abuse. The therapy then focuses on exploring and developing women's positive coping strategies, and facilitating control over the more harmful strategies she might previously have employed. This is a recovery focused model of feminist therapy that enhances a woman's ability to effect change in her own life, by helping her to understand the multiple factors that impact upon her feelings and thoughts associated with the abuse, and on the coping strategies she has adopted to work through her thoughts and feelings. Visible Therapy thus avoids diagnosis and value judgements about behaviours, instead making sense of experiences that have shaped the life of the woman.

There has also been a considerable development of feminist support groups,[e.g. 102] or self-help groups,[e.g. 103] which allow women to 'explore collectively lived subjectivities and emerging social contexts'.[103, p.207] For example, in a study of self-help groups for Finnish women diagnosed with depression, women reported joining such groups to heal themselves and to share their feelings with others. In the group they discussed the relational context within which their distress had evolved, in particular the absence of partner support or relationship breakdown; their existential experience of life as a struggle; chronic health difficulties and limited social lives; their feelings of depression; and strategies of coping and resistance. The majority of women said that 'helping oneself' was more helpful than psychiatric treatment or medication,[103, p. 214] even though the majority were taking psychotropic drugs and had been for at least three years.

Equally, in spite of my stringent critique of the medicalisation of madness, and the role of Big Pharma in the pathologisation of women's distress, it is important to acknowledge that psychotropic medication, particularly when used alongside therapy, may be beneficial for alleviating some cases of 'extreme mental turmoil',[104, p.308] when the distress has not been reduced by time, the greatest cure of all – 'spontaneous remission'.[105]vi However, drugs are not necessary or appropriate for the 'problems in everyday living' that are positioned as 'depression' or 'anxiety' in pharmaceutical advertising.[106, p.19] As placebo effects account for approximately 75 per cent of the positive outcomes in antidepressant trials,[107] as discussed in Chapter 2, there is also a persuasive argument for greater utilisation of the placebo as an active treatment alongside psychological support,[105] rather than simply as a control condition in clinical trials. A 'sugar pill' would certainly produce fewer side effects than psychotropic medication, a significant issue for women, as we have already seen.[108, p.195] Medical treatments should also never stand alone as solutions for women's misery. In a clinical setting they need to be part of a multidisciplinary approach that involves 'consumers/survivors and recovering persons in a meaningful way', in Marina Morrow's words,[3, p.154] where women have *choice* in the treatments they receive, as well as a choice to have no treatment at all. And *any* individual treatment always needs to be part of a broader project that addresses the social, relational and political causes of women's suffering, where the individual woman is not the sole focus of intervention.

I will end as I began, with the personal. My own lived experience of prolonged misery was alleviated by many years of supportive and empathic psychotherapy, which acted to change the way I saw myself, and in many ways, the way I interact with the world. I've learnt to stop being a 'good girl' (to a degree) and no longer worry so much about pleasing others, or working as hard as I can, trying to find a sense of self-worth in both. I've also stopped looking to my intimate relationship to provide a sense of self, having learnt that I can be happy on my own, although paradoxically I am now more content in my relationship than I could ever have previously imagined. These changes act as protection from future despair – and provide a strong buffer when the abyss opens up again, as difficulties arise in life, as they inevitably do. The pharmacological route is one I have never followed: I once tried SSRIs, when I felt that I could not cope in any other way, but after two days the side effects were worse than the despair that drove me to seek medical help, so I stopped. I knew that the pain was a response to my situation, so I faced it, and survived. It wasn't easy, but I am not afraid that I won't cope if (or when) it happens again.

This is not a recipe for recovery. For other women, the problems, and the solutions, will be different, depending on their social and relational circumstances, their intrapsychic and embodied experiences, and the cultural context within which they live – as well as the availability of support. However, this material-discursive-intrapsychic analysis does illustrate that misery is not madness, and as such does not need to mark us as 'Other', as needing to be locked away or shunned, as has been the case with so many women across the centuries, as we have seen throughout this book. We thus need to unravel the myths of women's madness, exposing the fantasies and fears (as well as the misogyny) that these myths reflect, yet at the same time recognise and address the lived experience of misery that afflicts so many women. This is the answer to the conundrum of women's madness – the only possible one.

APPENDIX

PMS and Relationships Study

Summary

The construction and lived experience of premenstrual change within a relational context was examined, through a survey and in-depth interviews with self-defined PMS (premenstrual syndrome) sufferers, and a number of their partners. Negative constructions of PMS on the part of a woman's partner, more common in heterosexual relationships, exacerbated distress and resulted in women being pathologised premenstrually. Conversely, support and understanding offered by partners, more common in lesbian relationships, reduced guilt and self-blame, allowing women to engage in coping strategies premenstrually, such as taking time out to be alone, or engage self-care. These patterns of relational negotiation of women's premenstrual change need to be contextualised within broader cultural representation of hetero-normativity, which provide the context for gendered roles and coping.

Method

Survey participants were 321 Australian women aged 17 to 49 (average age 37) who were recruited through advertisements placed in local media and women's health centres asking for women who experienced PMS to take part in a research project on premenstrual experiences and relationships. Most participants were partnered (63 per cent), heterosexual (59.5 per cent), and reported having no children (55 per cent). Of the 44 per cent that reported having children, 92 per cent indicated that their children lived with them. Of the 76.6 per cent of the sample that reported being employed, 61 per cent were engaged in full-time employment. Interviews were also conducted with 60 Australian women aged 22 to 48 (average age 34), drawn from the survey sample, as well as 23 of their partners, 10 women and 15 men (average age 39). Most women were partnered (80 per cent), with 66 per cent currently in an intimate relationship with a man and 33 per cent currently in a relationship with a woman. Half the women interviewed reported having children (47 per cent), with heterosexual women more likely to have children (60 per cent) than lesbian women (25 per cent). The majority of participants were Anglo-Australian, in full-time education, part-time or full-time employment, and were resident in an urban location in Australia's largest city. Women were purposefully selected for interview, to ensure the inclusion of participants across a range of relationship types (lesbian/heterosexual) and contexts (presence of children; living alone vs. cohabitation). Women were recruited from a range of contexts: advertisement in the media and women's health centres; online chat-rooms and email lists; Relationships Australia (counselling organisation); and a lesbian mother–baby network. Ethics approval was received from the University Human Ethics Committee and pseudonyms have been allocated to all participants.

Survey results

Levels of self-silencing among this sample, assessed by the Silencing the Self Scale (STSS),[1] were significantly higher than previously published levels for non-clinical populations, for example, the means for an undergraduate sample.[2] In particular, this PMS sample had significantly higher global, 'Silencing the Self' and 'Divided Self' STSS scores than the comparison undergraduate sample.[see 3] Premenstrual distress, measured in response to the item 'to what extent is PMS distressing', was high for the sample, with most participants falling within one standard deviation of the maximum response 'extremely distressing'. Rates of psychological distress were assessed on the Hospital Anxiety and Depression Scale (HADS).[4] While not used to formally diagnose participants, 20.8 per cent and 40.8 per cent of this PMS sample met the criteria for borderline and abnormal anxiety caseness respectively. Rates for depression, while high for non-clinical samples, with 14.5 per cent and 11.8 per cent meeting the cut-offs for borderline and abnormal caseness respectively, revealed 72.9 per cent of the sample scoring in the normal range for depression.

The relationship between self-silencing, premenstrual and psychological distress was also examined, using correlational analyses. Expected findings were that all STSS scales were positively and significantly correlated with each other and with HADS anxiety, depression and total scores. Externalised Self-Perception, Divided Self and Global STSS scales correlated positively and significantly with PMS distress, whereas these scales and 'Silencing the Self' were negatively and significantly correlated with PMS coping. 'Care as Self-Sacrifice' was unrelated to PMS distress. HADS depression, anxiety and total scores were also found to significantly correlate with PMS distress. To further explore how levels of self-silencing and premenstrual distress are associated, predictive regression analyses were performed. Externalised Self-Perception ($b = 0.13$, t (236) = 4.22, $p <$ 0.001), Silencing the Self ($b = -0.10$, t (236) = -2.74, $p = 0.007$), and Divided Self ($b = 0.08$, t (236) = 2.51, $p = 0.013$) were found to be significant predictors of PMS distress, whereas Care as Self-Sacrifice was not ($b = -0.02$, t (236) = -0.49, $n.s$). Following variable reduction, three variables were tested for exploratory predictive modelling with a stepwise multiple regression where elimination of the least significant variable from the regression model was chosen as the selection criterion. A significant regression model with all variables in the equation was identified in one step. Externalised Self-Perception, Silencing the Self, and Divided Self accounted for 14 per cent of the variance in PMS distress ($R^2 = 0.14$; $F(3, 237) = 12.56, p < 0.001$), Externalised Self-Perception (t (237) = 4.34, $p < 0.001$) and Divided Self (t (237) = 2.50, $p = 0.013$) made significant positive contributions, whereas Silencing the Self (t (238) = -3.20, $p = 0.002$) was a significant negative predictor.

The inverse relationship between the 'Silencing the Self' subscale and premenstrual distress suggests that women are distressed, and position their distress as PMS, partly because of their inability to self-silence premenstrually. This may explain the relatively low level of depression in this sample, when compared to population norms,[4] and to women who score similarly on global self-silencing,[5–6] as women who position themselves as PMS sufferers are directing their anger outwards once a month, rather than internalising it and becoming depressed. However, this is not a beneficial outcome for women, as rates of anxiety in this study were significantly higher than population norms, and women adopted a position of self-pathologisation in relation to their anger and distress, through positioning it as a disorder, PMS.

Interviews

One-to-one semi-structured interviews were conducted to examine women's subjective experience of premenstrual change, and the negotiation of PMS in the context of relationships. The interviewer began by asking the woman, or the partner, to describe how the woman was when she 'had PMS', then describe a typical experience of PMS, and explore how this varied across relational contexts. The interviews ranged in duration from 45 to 90 minutes. After transcription, the interviews were read and reread by two researchers in order to identify themes relating to the construction and experience of PMS. Themes were grouped, checked for emerging patterns, variability and consistency, commonality across women, and for uniqueness within cases, and thematic coding of the interviews was conducted. Each coded theme was then read through by both authors, to identify patterns in the data, and differences across heterosexual and lesbian relationships. This process follows what Stenner has termed a 'thematic decomposition',[7,p.114] a close reading which attempts to separate a given text into coherent themes which reflect subject positions allocated to, or taken up by, a person.[8] Positioning theory, which posits that identity is constructed and negotiated in relation to the subject positions taken up by an individual, or the positions within which they are put by others,[9] was used to interpret the data.

An overarching theme 'PMS as a relational experience' was identified, wherein women positioned PMS as irritation, intolerance and insensitivity in reaction to others, or as a response to relational demands. A secondary theme described partner reactions to premenstrual change, consisting of accounts of rejection and absence of support, associated pathologisation and absence of relational communication; and accounts of support, understanding and conflict avoidance, associated with greater acceptance of premenstrual change. Each of these themes is outlined in Chapters 5 and 6, with commonalities and differences across lesbian and heterosexual interviews identified. Many of the lesbian women interviewed as a 'PMS sufferer' also discussed their partner's PMS, and one-third of the women interviewed as partners discussed their own PMS. In the analysis, women were be identified as 'partners' when they are talking about PMS in their partner.

Research funding

This study was funded by a Discovery grant from the Australian Research Council, *An examination of the development, experience and construction of premenstrual symptoms*, awarded to Jane Ussher and Janette Perz, in partnership with Relationships Australia, and Kerrie James. Emily May, Margaret Boulos, Julie Mooney-Somers, Lee Shepard, and Helen Vidler provided research support and assistance. The data were collected between 2005 and 2007.

Positive Premenstrual Experiences Study

Summary

This study examined the ways in which women experience and negotiate psychological, embodied and/or behavioural premenstrual changes, which come to be positioned as positive. Drawing on in-depth interviews and focus groups conducted with 47 female psychology students aged 18–42, it was found that 38 women experienced at least one embodied, psychological or behavioural change which they positioned as positive. The most commonly reported positive changes are: elevated moods, increased sexual arousal, more attractive breasts and satisfaction of food cravings. A thematic analysis identified that women position their changes positively due to a number of factors: 'Feeling good', 'Releasing tension', 'Increased perceived attractiveness', 'Legitimacy of self-care' and 'Indication for menstruation'. Factors that mediate the positioning of premenstrual changes were identified, emphasising the intersubjective context of women's negotiation of premenstrual change. The findings suggest that women position their changes in accordance to how it affects their relationships, their ability to function and how they feel, both emotionally and physically.

Method

Participants were 47 Australian women aged 18 to 42 (M = 21.89 years, SD = 40.01) who were primarily recruited through the School of Psychology Research Participation Scheme via an online Experiment Management System (EMS). Of the 47 women, 41 (87 per cent) were undergraduate, first year psychology students of the University of Western Sydney who were participating for course credit. The remaining 6 women were fourth year psychology students. One woman was excluded from the study as she was in the later stages of menopause. At the time of the study, 19 women (40 per cent) were taking some form of the oral contraceptive pill and 28 women (60 per cent) were not. Most participants were partnered (79 per cent), and reported having no children (68 per cent). Of the 17 per cent who reported having children, all indicated that at least one of their children lived with them. Of the sample, 46 reported being a full-time student, with one participant reporting being a part-time student and 66 per cent reported being employed.

Nine focus groups were conducted with group numbers ranging from five to seven. From the focus groups, two participants volunteered to partake in a further one-to-one in-depth semi-structured interview. The aim of the focus groups and interviews was to explore women's subjective experiences of premenstrual change. In order to elicit personal accounts of premenstrual change, open-ended questions were asked such as: 'Do you experience any changes during the premenstrual phase of your cycle? If so, what are they?' The interviewer employed the use of prompts to gain clarification and to explore issues in depth. At the beginning of the interview, the interviewer provided a list of changes (both positive and negative) to provide participants with a vocabulary by which they can describe their changes, to aid recollection of their changes and to inform them of the changes that women have been known to report.

Data analysis

Interviews were transcribed verbatim, taking note of laughs, emphasis and pauses. Participants' names were replaced with pseudonyms to ensure anonymity on their transcript and in any published material. Following transcription, a thematic analysis was used to determine what changes women positioned as positive.[10] Data gathered from the interviews were read and reread to allow in-depth familiarisation, and all stages of analysis discussed in detail with the supervisor to ensure consistency of emerging patterns, and plausibility of analysis. Analysis began with open coding, or identifying 'meaning units' through line-by-line examination, to generate naturally occurring themes. Reported premenstrual changes were grouped together according to women's positioning (negative, positive, neutral). Positive changes were further categorised into three major themes: 'Embodied change', 'Psychological change' and 'Coping strategy'. A secondary thematic analysis was conducted in order to examine the function of these themes, through investigating how and why women position such changes as positive (or negative). Positive changes were further themed according to participants' reasoning for their positioning, which were 'Indication for periods', 'Release of tension', 'Legitimacy of self-care', 'Perceived attractiveness' and 'Feeling good'. 'Deviant' cases (such as those participants who positioned a change differently from the rest of the participants) were considered, compared and contrasted to other cases and integrated into the wider context of premenstrual change to gain a wider understanding of the experience of premenstrual change. Finally, factors that mediated the positioning of premenstrual changes were also thematically analysed, in order to examine the intersubjective context of women's negotiation of premenstrual experience, described under the two themes 'Context' and 'Reactions of others'.

Funding

This study was conducted as a Psychology Honours research project by Marlee King, under the supervision of Jane Ussher, in 2008.[11]

Women at Midlife Study

Summary

The regimes of knowledge produced by science and medicine which act to circulate 'truths' about menopausal women tell us that decay, atrophy, and psychological distress are the inevitable outcome of the end of fecundity. Hormone replacement therapy (HRT) is portrayed as legitimate, or even necessary, medical management for the rest of a woman's life. However, a significant proportion of women resist these negative discourses as they are at odds with their lived experience. In interviews with 21 Australian women, midlife experiences were positioned as positive, with reports of increased confidence and wisdom from experience, greater time for self, and increased self-awareness and self-worth. A number of women reported feeling some sadness in relation to time passing and the physical markers of ageing, but this was not presented as a matter of serious concern. It is concluded that this reflects women's ability to negotiate and resist medical discourses associated with menopause, positioning midlife a time of change and positive development.

Method

Women were recruited through advertisements placed in local women's health centres and GP surgeries, asking for women aged 40–65 to volunteer to take part in a study of 'women's midlife transitions', where we were interested in 'how women view themselves at midlife, and how they deal with the challenges and changes of this period of life'. Snowballing was also used, with interviewees asked to pass the study advertisement onto other women they thought might be interested. In-depth interviews were conducted with 21 Australian women, living in both rural and urban locations. The age range was 41–56 years, with an average age of 49; 19 of the women were married or living with a partner; 5 identified as lesbian, the remainder as heterosexual; 16 had children, the average number being 2 (range 1–6); and all women were currently employed, with 13 in full-time employment. Semi-structured narrative interviews, lasting between 45 and 90 minutes, were conducted by a trained interviewer, in a place convenient to the interviewee: home, work, or an interview room at the University of Western Sydney. The aim of the interviews was to examine women's subjective accounts of midlife, focusing on women's experience of the body, meaning of life, and reflections on change. An open-ended question was asked at the beginning of the interview:

In this study we want to explore women's experiences of midlife. We're interested in women's understanding of the midlife transition and any changes that occur at that time. Can you tell me about your experience of this stage in your life?

The interviewer then followed the woman's lead, asking questions of clarification as and when necessary.

All of the interviews were transcribed verbatim. After transcription, the interviews were independently read by three members of the research team, in order to ascertain the major themes emerging, and to develop a coding frame, based on notions of consistency, commonality, and the function and effects of specific themes. The whole data set was then coded, line by line, by two of the researchers, after which a group meeting was held to discuss any new or unforeseen themes, and to re-evaluate the inclusion of themes which appeared with low frequency. The interpretation of these themes was conducted by a process of reading and rereading, as well as reference to relevant literature. This process follows what Stenner has termed a 'thematic decomposition'.[7, p.114] The interpretation of the data was conducted from within the framework of positioning theory,[8] outlined above.

Funding

This study was conducted by Janette Perz and Jane Ussher, with funding from the Gender, Culture and Health Research Unit, at the University of Western Sydney. Georgia Ovenden provided research assistance and support. The data were collected in 2008.

Gender and Therapy Referrals Study

Summary

The aim of this study was to explore gender and indigenous issues in general practitioner referral and treatment for psychological problems, as well as patients' perceptions and experiences of their referral and treatment through the 'Link Project', a government funded scheme of psychological services, in New South Wales, Australia. Additionally, the study provides a more detailed examination of the perspectives of service providers who participated in the Link Project by examining their perceptions of referral and treatment processes, as well as issues impacting on the effectiveness of the Link Project.

Method

A total of 22 GPs from the Nepean and Hawkesbury Divisions of General Practice, 23 Allied Mental Health Providers (AMHPs) who were involved in the Link Project, and 96 patients who were referred for treatment, took part in a survey-based evaluation. Data from three purpose-designed questionnaires and eight individual interviews were analysed to address three evaluation questions:

1 Examination of gender issues in the presentation of problems and in patterns of referral for treatment.
2 Patient preferences for intervention, levels of engagement, and satisfaction with the project and with treatment.
3 Examination of participants' perceptions of the effectiveness and implementation of the Link Project.

On average, GPs had 19 years of experience in medical practice (minimum 5, maximum 31 years), and AMHPs had an average of 9 years in practice (minimum 1, maximum 27 years). Of the 96 patients who returned questionnaires, 83 per cent (80) were female and 17 per cent (16) were male.

Patients ranged in age from 12 to 80 years, with an average age of 44. Nearly a quarter (24 per cent) of patients were aged between 35 and 44 years, and the rest were spread relatively evenly across the age range.

Funding

This study was conducted by Jane Ussher and Janette Perz, funded by the Nepean Division of General Practitioners. Beverly Johnson provided research support and assistance. The data were collected and analysed in 2007–2008.

Long Term Effects of Child Sexual Abuse Study

Summary

The overall objective of this study was to identify the mechanisms of negative long term effects of child sexual abuse (CSA), and the factors which may protect against such effects in a non-clinical population of women survivors, and second, to examine psychological well-being and sexual identity development in CSA survivors and a comparison group of women who have not experienced CSA, using a combination of psychological questionnaires and in-depth interviews. As much of the existing research in this area has been conducted in North America, this research was also designed to address the question of whether theories and findings from North America can be generalised to understanding CSA in Britain.

A subsidiary aim which developed during the research was to produce a method of analysing qualitative data for exploring both CSA and women's sexual identity, which would incorporate an investigation of both the material aspects of women's lives (such as economic factors, sexual violence, mental health problems, or reproductive issues), and the way in which these issues, and sexuality itself, is socially or linguistically/discursively constructed. Many existing methods of qualitative analysis focus solely on one or other of these levels of experience – the material or the social/discursive – we felt it was important to recognise and examine both.

Method

For this survey, 369 women who had experienced child sexual abuse were recruited through gynaecology clinics for problems other than CSA, at University College Hospital, London, local support groups for CSA, and advertising in the media. These were women who met the definition of CSA which was used: that they had been under 16 years of age, and the abuser was more than five years older than they were, when the abuse occurred. A further 238 women who had not experienced CSA were recruited through notices placed in two general practices and two family planning clinics in London; and advertisements placed in national women's magazines and in a local newspaper, asking for 'women who are willing to take part in research on sexuality and sexual identity' to contact us.

Survey

To examine levels of psychological well-being we used three standardised self-report questionnaires, which provided a comprehensive analysis of psychological and somatic symptom reporting, sexual well-being, and social and behavioural functioning. We also collected information on demographic variables, the nature of early sexual experiences, family support and relationships, as well as on the nature of childhood sexual abuse (where relevant), using a detailed questionnaire which was specifically developed for this study. A group of 369 UK women who were CSA survivors and a comparison group of 238 non-CSA women completed these questionnaires. There was no significant difference between the groups on demographic factors such as age, parity, social class or marital status. However, there was a significant difference between groups on all of the measures of psychological and physical well-being, with the CSA group reporting lower quality of life and higher rates of psychological problems. The CSA group were also significantly more likely to report having experienced hospitalisation for an emotional problem, having run away from home, having been arrested, having had an eating disorder, having been significantly overweight, having been raped as an adult, having had a sexual problem, and having been 'sexually promiscuous'. These results confirm previous findings that child sexual abuse is associated with long term problems.

We also found a difference between the groups on early childhood experiences, with the CSA survivors reporting more negative and less positive experiences with their parents, being significantly less happy while growing up, being significantly less likely to have had an adult or a friend to confide in, to have had good friends, or to have had a person to turn to in times of stress. The CSA survivors also reported significantly higher rates of family violence. This confirms previous suggestions that family discord and lack of social support are important factors in the aetiology of the long term effects of CSA. We carried out a multiple regression analysis which examined which factors were the most significant in accounting for current levels of psychological and physical well-being. For the CSA group, the major predictors of psychological well-being were friend and family support in childhood, followed by age, then marital status and occupation. When the different aspects of CSA were examined on their own, having received psychological therapy or counselling was the major predictor of positive outcome, with age of onset being the second most important factor. For the non-CSA group, the major predictor was negative experience of mother in childhood, followed by friend and family support. This confirms the positive role of social and family support in mental health, and suggests that professional psychological services can ameliorate the long term effects of CSA.

Interviews

In-depth interviews, lasting for between one and two hours, were carried out on up to four separate occasions each with 25 women survivors of CSA, and with 24 women who had not experienced CSA (the final participant failed to attend four appointments). Using narrative interviewing methods,[12] women were asked to explore the development of sexual identity, focusing on their sexual relationships from childhood through to adulthood. The method of narrative accounting allows women to examine their subjective experience of sexuality and relationships, and the subjective construction of identity across the lifespan. Up to four separate interviews with each woman were conducted in order to allow a careful discussion of the lifespan, and reflection on earlier discussion in later interviews. A number of women chose not to attend for four interviews as they felt that they had discussed everything they had to discuss in the earlier interviews; the average number of interviews attended was 2.5.

Each interview was transcribed immediately, and read by the interviewer, the participant, and a third party before subsequent interviews, in order to identify issues to be followed up at a second, third or fourth interview. All names of interviewees were changed, to protect anonymity. The results of in-depth qualitative interviews with 25 CSA survivors and 24 non-CSA women were examined using thematic decomposition. This allowed us to identify the ways in which childhood and current relationships impact upon women's sexual identity and psychological well-being, and to address in more detail the question of why sexual abuse and family discord is associated with long term problems in adulthood. It also allowed us to examine the continuities and discontinuities between women who have and have not been sexually abused in childhood in terms of general sexual identity development, and to gain a deeper understanding of women's subjective experiences of sexuality and sexual identity.

Funding

This study was funded by a UK Economic and Social Sciences Research Council grant, R000221434, where Jane Ussher was the chief investigator and Alison Dixon the researcher employed on the project. Data analysis was further supported by a grant from the College of Arts at University of Western Sydney. Lindsay Fraser, Rita Shackel, Erica Lewin and Shirley Kent also provided support in research coding. The data were collected in 1996 and coded and analysed between 1997 and 2008.

NOTES

1 THE MADNESS OF WOMEN: MYTH OR EXPERIENCE?

i   As Elaine Showalter has outlined, prior to the 1850 Lunatics Act, in the UK, male asylum patients outnumbered women by 30 per cent. However, after the Act women outnumbered men consistently for the remainder of the century.[3, p.52] The only asylums where men outnumbered women at the end of the nineteenth century were asylums for the criminally insane.

ii   Laura Brown has written a similar account of her own mother's depression, which was also treated with hospitalisation and ECT, and which abated when she engaged in paid work and political activity.[7] Laura took a similar route to myself, training as a therapist, and is now a strong proponent of feminist therapy.[8]

iii   Following Foucault,[14] Nikolas Rose has argued that the psy-professions, 'psychology, psychiatry and their cognates', play a key role in 'constituting our current regime of the self'[13, p.2] – both the self that represents reason or sanity, and the unreasoned 'mad' self.

iv   The *International Classification of Diseases* (ICD) is also used in some clinical contexts, and is now up to its tenth edition. I focus on the DSM in this book, as this is predominantly used for diagnosis in Australia, the USA and the UK, the contexts where my empirical research is drawn from.

v   At the time of writing, late 2010, DSM-V is in preparation.

vi   Foucault described discourse as 'an entity of sequences of signs in that they are enouncements (enoncés)'.[17, p.141] This includes language, talk, visual representations, and cultural beliefs and norms. Discursive practices are the associated actions and tactics of regulation. In the context of madness, this would include beliefs and representations of what constitutes dysfunctional feelings or behaviour, and the forms of treatment and intervention offered to women who are given a psychiatric diagnosis.

vii   The Mad Pride movement was launched in the late 1990s alongside a book of the same name *Mad Pride: A celebration of mad culture*, and has now become an international movement. However, the psychiatric users movement has a much longer history, as is documented by the US publication *Dendron* and the Canadian publication *Phoenix Rising*, both produced by consumers – those deemed mad.

viii   Neurasthenia was first described by G.M. Beard in 1869, and was characterised by an 'ill defined set of symptoms – a form of nervous exhaustion'.[43, p.130]

ix   Depression is reported to account for 41.9 per cent of the burden of disability related to neurological and psychiatric disorders for women, compared to 29.3 per cent in men.[53, p.143] It has also been described as the fifth greatest burden for women and the seventh for men across all physical and mental illnesses.[54] Diagnosis of depression is also more likely to be accompanied by diagnosis of other psychological disorders, such as anxiety.[55, p.32]

x   For example, in Australia in 2007, 26 per cent of men and 41 per cent of women who experienced mental health symptoms in the previous twelve months used mental health services, a ratio of 1.6.[57]

xi   For example, in Australia in 2007, 21 per cent of men compared to 32 per cent of women who experienced mental health symptoms in the previous twelve months had used antidepressants, a ratio of 1.5.[57]

xii For example, in Massachusetts in 1974, 69 per cent of those shocked were women,[62] as were 68 per cent of cases in Ontario, Canada in 2001.[63]

xiii Epistemology is the study of knowledge and justified belief. As the study of knowledge, epistemology is concerned with the following questions: What are the necessary and sufficient conditions of knowledge? What are its sources? What is its structure, and what are its limits? As the study of justified belief, epistemology aims to answer questions such as: How we are to understand the concept of justification? What makes justified beliefs justified? Is justification internal or external to one's own mind? Understood more broadly, epistemology is about issues having to do with the creation and dissemination of knowledge in particular areas of inquiry. http://plato.stanford.edu/entries/epistemology/

xiv In recent years, considerable attention has been given to the issue of depression in men, as it is recognised that men are often reluctant to express their distress, or to ask for help (discussed further in Chapter 3, pp. 77–78), and that suicide rates are higher for women than for men. This is a reversal of the practice of seeing depression as solely a 'woman's problem', and indeed, partly a reaction to this practice – which can have the effect of making men's depression or distress invisible.

2 THE DAUGHTER OF HYSTERIA: DEPRESSION AS A 'WOMAN'S PROBLEM'?

i   Women do not predominate in all categories of depression, however. For example, the findings on bipolar depression are equivocal, with some reviews reporting higher rates in women,[10] and others reporting no gender differences.[8] Gender differences in the course and nature of bipolar depression have been reported, however, with women reporting later age of onset, more depressive symptoms, a more rapidly cycling disorder, and greater comorbidity with medical disorders, in comparison to men.[10] There is also little evidence for significant differences in rates of psychosis across women and men,[3; 11] which can include psychotic depression.

ii   For example, in a National Comorbidity Survey of 8,098 respondents living in the USA,[12] Kessler and colleagues reported that 12.7 per cent of men and 21.3 per cent of women reported a lifetime prevalence of depression, with 19.2 per cent of men and 30.5 per cent of women reporting a lifetime prevalence of anxiety. Lifetime rates of 'major depressive disorder' (the formal DSM diagnosis) reported in other cultural contexts include: Paris (10.5 per cent men, 21.9 per cent women); Puerto Rico (3.1 per cent men, 5.5 per cent women); Munich (4.9 per cent men, 17 per cent women); Florence (6.1 per cent men, 18.1 per cent women); Edmonton (6.6 per cent men, 12.3

per cent women); Christchurch (7.5 per cent men, 15.5 per cent women); Seoul (1.9 per cent men, 3.8 per cent women); and Taiwan (1.1 per cent men, 1.8 per cent women).[13] Depression rates of two to one for women to men have also been reported in developing countries, including Cuban Americans in the Hispanic Health and Nutrition Examination Survey (HHANES),[14] and in Tijuana, Mexico.[15] Thus while the proportion of the population meriting diagnosis of depression may vary across cultures, the gender disparity appears to remain a constant.

iii   At the same time, men are more likely to experience substance abuse (including abuse of drugs and alcohol) than women. For example, 18 per cent of women compared to 35 per cent of men (a ratio of 1.9) reported a lifetime prevalence in the 1993 US National Comorbidity Survey.[3] In the 2003 US National Comorbidity Survey, the ratio was 1.4.[7] Similarly, in a national survey conducted in Australia in 2007, 7 per cent of men and 3 per cent of women reported a substance use disorder in the previous twelve months (a ratio of 2.1).[16] In a UK national survey conducted in 2000, 38 per cent of men and 15 per cent of women reported hazardous drinking (ratio of 2.3), 12 per cent of men and 3 per cent of women alcohol dependence (a ratio of 4), and 5.4 per cent of men compared with 2 per cent women drug dependence (a ratio of 2.7).[11] Men are also more likely to be diagnosed with antisocial personality – 5.8 per cent of men compared to 1.2 per cent of women (a ratio of 4.8) in the 1994 US National Comorbidity Survey,[3] and of 'impulse control disorder' – at a ratio of 1.7 in the 2003 US National Comorbidity Survey.[7]

iv   Bethlem Hospital, created in 1247 in Bishopsgate, London, was known as 'Bedlam', and is the orgin of the term which has subsequently been used to connote madness.[23]

v   Charcot later introduced the practice of hypnosis (in 1878), arguing that the capacity to be hynotised was a symptom of hysteria.[35, p.34]

vi   It was only in the 1970s that the reality and magnitude of child sexual abuse became widely recognised.

vii   For example, one study examining the genetic linkage in 81 families reported a greater number of genetic mechanisms in the causal pathway to depression in women,[43] with the variant of the CREB1 gene linked to depression in 80 per cent of women who developed it. In a study of rodents, the CREB1 gene was found to be linked to oestradiol,[44] leading to the conclusion that sex hormones and genetics may combine to produce depression in women.[45, p.152] An alternative hypothesis was presented by Abkevich and colleagues,[46, p.1271] who argued there was 'strong evidence for the existence of a sex-specific predisposition gene to major depression at 12q22-q23.2'.

viii   For example, in one community study of 11 year olds, 2.5 per cent of the boys and 0.5 per cent of the girls met the criteria for depressive disorder,[54] whereas in a study of 14–16 year olds 13 per cent of the girls and 3 per cent of the boys met the same criteria (a ratio of 4.3).[55]

ix   For example, in the UK study, which involved 9,792 individuals, women's rates of mixed anxiety and depression fell from 10.8 per cent to 5.2 per cent, and depression from 2.7 to 1.1 per cent after the age of 55. In contrast, men reported a slight increase in both mixed depression and anxiety (from 5.3 to 6 per cent), and in depression (from 1.7 to 2 per cent) after age 55.[60, p.13] Confirmation of a post-menopausal decrease in depression is also provided by more recent analyses of levels of psychological distress in Australia, based on a sample of 20,789 adults.[16] Rates of moderate to high distress fell from

48 per cent of women aged 18–24, to 35 per cent of women aged 55–64 (men's rates were consistently around 30 per cent across the two age groups).

x   Somewhat paradoxically, Maudsley also believed that the expenditure of intellectual energy through education would also be an 'excessive mental drain' on women, producing a 'delicate and ailing woman, whose future life is one of more or less suffering'.[65, p.467]

xi   The possibility of adrenarcheal effects in boys was not ruled out, however, as Angold and colleagues suggested that the pubertal fall in depression observed in boys is consistent with the negative association between levels of androstenedione and testosterone and depression.[52, p.59]

xii   The term 'self-in-relation theory' was used to describe a body of work that had developed from the work of Jean Baker Miller,[160] and the writings of the Stone Center psychologists,[161] whose aim was to examine how developmental psychology could be used to understand the psychological well-being, and distress, experienced by women. Following criticisms that the term 'self-in-relation' suggested an individualistic, separate self perspective, the theory was renamed 'relational cultural theory'.[162, p.55]

xiii   Nancy Chodorow has distanced herself from relational theories, however, writing 'I find myself uncomfortable with and resistant toward the post-modern locutions and word play that have entered into relational feminist writing'.[167, p.104]

xiv   Many who engage in cosmetic surgery have little say in how their transformed bodies will appear, as is evidenced by women interviewed by Kathy Davis.[181] This suggests that surgeons are defining what is an ideal body shape.

xv   However, in contrast, Herek and Garnets reviewed the evidence on sexual identity and mental health, concluding that while the minority stress model is a useful way of understanding heightened risks for depression in non-heterosexual women and men, a number of studies have 'not found statistically significant differences among sexual orientation groups when relevant demographic factors were statistically controlled for'.[216, p.359] Thus, gender, lifestyle, social support, and the presence of other factors (such as poverty, powerlessness, relationship conflict) can add to minority stress to increase the likelihood of depression (or protect against).

xvi   Intersectionality suggests that the classical models of oppression within society, such as those based on race/ethnicity, gender, religion, nationality, sexual orientation, class, or disability do not act independently of one another; instead, these forms of oppression interrelate creating a system of oppression that reflects the 'intersection' of multiple forms of discrimination.

xvii   Conversely, masculinity is not a necessarily positive trait for men: research has demonstrated an association between traditional characteristics of masculinity and risk taking or self-destructive behaviour, stress, increased anxiety and anger, emotional expressiveness, and poor health related behaviours.[236] Male gender role conflict, the strain resulting from attempting to adhere to ideals of masculinity, such as success, power and restricted emotionality, accompanied by fear of qualities deemed feminine,[237] has also been reported to be associated with 'personal restriction, devaluation, or violation of others or self'.[238, p.25] Men who report high levels of gender role conflict also report higher levels of depression,[239] and are also more reluctant to seek help for psychological problems,[240] than men with low gender role conflict. At the same time, the higher rates of youth suicide recorded in men have been reported to be associated with individualism, with indices of personal freedom and control, which has been seen to reflect a failure of Western societies to provide appropriate sites or sources of male social identity and attachment, combined with the tendency to promote unrealistic or inappropriate expectations of individual freedom and autonomy.[241]

xviii   Conversely, masculinity as a trait has been deemed to protect against depression, operating through perceived competence.[242] However, Bebbington has argued that as masculinity remains fairly stable throughout adolescence for girls, it cannot explain the gender difference in depression which emerges at this time.[4]

xix   Yet in a UK survey of 4,430 individuals, single women reported significantly better mental health than single men, and comparable to that of women who had remained in their first partnership.[256]

xx   The limitations of hypothetico-deductive methodologies have been well rehearsed elsewhere: the artificiality of controlled studies; the limited number of variables able to be studied at any one time; the limitations of quantitative analysis; the assumption that the individual can and should be studied separately from cultural and historical factors; the assumption that the individual should be the sole focus of attention at all; the notion that objectivity is possible, in either theory, analysis or the conduct of research; the limitations of predictive models of cause and effect.[296–300]

xxi   A disjunctive concept looks at whether individual attributes create a whole, and is therefore useful in creating a concept of something. Depression could be described as a disjunctive concept as a range of different individual 'symptoms' are considered to signify the unitary disorder 'depression'.

xxii   There is evidence, however, that more women than men from all ethnic backgrounds with unrecognised depression present to services with physical problems.[340] A further study reported no difference in somatic presentation between Asian and White patients.[341]

xxiii   Academic assessment exercises are conducted by government bodies, where the research of university departments is rated and ranked. In the UK this is the Research Assessment Exercise (RAE), in Australia it is the Excellence in Research for Australia (ERA) Initiative, and in New Zealand it is described as 'performance based research' (involving ranking and rating of individual staff members).

xxiv   For an example of this in relation to PMS research, see Koeske.[361]

xxv   For an excellent overview of this particular time in the history of psychiatry, see Metzl, 2003 (Chapter 2).[366; see also 367]

xxvi   The common brands of SSRIs are: Celexa (citalopram); Lexapro (escitalopram oxalate); Luvox (fluvoxamine); Paxil (paroxetine); Prozac (fluoxetine); Zoloft (sertraline).

xxvii   In the 1997 population based study by Kendler and colleagies, 75 per cent of women diagnosed with depression recovered after twelve weeks.[384]

xxviii   This is also the case with psychological therapy offered under Medicare in Australia (funded by the government) where a formal diagnosis is needed before a GP referral can be made.

3 LABELLING WOMEN AS MAD: REGULATING AND OPPRESSING WOMEN

i   All of the cases above are drawn from narratives produced by women incarcerated in the asylum, in the book *Women of the asylum*, edited by Jeffrey Geller and Maxine Harris.[7]

ii   This experience was immortalised in *The yellow wallpaper*, Gilman's auto-biographical account of the bed-rest cure.

iii   First hand accounts from each of these women are documented by Geller and Harris.[7]

iv   Graeme Clifford's film *Frances* (1982), starring Jessica Lang, documented this hospitalisation, and the role of Frances Farmer's mother.

v   Olivia Brown is a pseudonym, as are all the cases of women committed to Glenside hospital, discussed by Jill Matthews.[28] Olivia was an individual I worked with in the late 1980s when I was in training as a clinical psychologist, at Shenley Hospital.

vi   The Broverman paper has been described as a 'citation classic', one of the most cited papers in the field of mental health, which has impacted on the thinking of a generation of mental health professionals.[37]

vii   This is not an incontrovertible finding – other research has reported that items on depression inventories, such as the Goldberg Anxiety and Depression Scale, are not gender biased.[47]

viii   The study was an evaluation of the Link Project, a government funded project that provided funding for psychological therapy, and encouraged GPs and allied mental health professionals to collaborate in the diagnosis and treatment of mental health problems. There were 746 patient referrals through the Link Project in the 2004–2005 period. The evaluation canvassed GPs' perceptions of the factors contributing to these referrals. Out of the total of 746 referrals during 2004 and 2005, 70 per cent (522) were female and the remaining 30 per cent (224) were male. Around 91 per cent of GPs indicated that they refer more women than men for psychological treatment. Similarly, 91 per cent of AMHPs reported that they receive more female than male referrals. The evaluation examined the perceptions of GPs and AMHPs regarding the factors influencing this pattern of referral.

ix   Ashworth (at Maghull, Merseyside) is in a class now known as a high security hospital, having previously been known as a special hospital – a place where criminally insane women and men are committed, after having committed a crime.

x   In Rosenhan's study, researchers feigned hearing voices in order to gain hospital admission, then desisted from any symptom reporting once admitted. Their note taking behaviour (to record observations) and protestations of sanity were seen as symptoms of psychiatric illness.[87]

xi   The first ECT was 'Probably administered by a French physician, J.B. Leroy, in 1755 on a patient with a psychogenic blindness',[89, p.285] but its modern incarnation was in the 1930s in Italy, following the observation that schizophrenia and epilepsy didn't coincide.

xii   Lucy Johnstone specifically interviewed individuals who had had a negative experience of ECT.

xiii   Similarly, in a study of drug advertisements in medical journals in the mid 1980s, women were depicted as suffering from a range of family and housework related problems, whereas men were portrayed as being stressed at work.[112]

xiv   Valium was being taken by one in ten Americans, three-quarters of whom were women.[107, p.145]

xv   Sackett blames the medical "experts", who 'gain private profit (from their industry affiliations), to satisfy a narcissistic need for public acclaim or in a misguided attempt to do good, advocate "preventive" manoeuvres that have never been validated in rigorous randomized trials'.[140, pp.363–364]

xvi   Suttee (sometimes called Sati) is a religious funeral practice among some Hindu communities in which a recently widowed Hindu woman either voluntarily or by use of force and coercion immolates herself on her husband's funeral pyre. This practice is rare and has been outlawed in India since 1829. The term is derived from the original name of the goddess Sati, also known as Dakshayani, who self-immolated because she was unable to bear her father Daksha's humiliation of her (living) husband Shiva.

xvii   Prozac was first released in 1987.

xviii   A similar position is often adopted by parents of individuals with mental health problems, who find 'solace in therapists' announcements that their children suffer from brain diseases that are not the parents' fault'.[45, p.19]

xix   In this study, the women accepted the drug treatments prescribed by their physicians, as they believed they provided alleviation for their symptoms. However, they also wanted additional support, in terms of therapy, or help in developing new coping skills.[178]

xx   Positivist/realist approaches have been challenged in many areas of health and illness;[153; 181–186] these critiques are not unique to madness. Alternative models of conceptualising, researching, and, if necessary, treating symptomatology have been developed from within a broadly social constructionist perspective.[e.g. 187] Social constructionist approaches take a critical stance towards taken-for-granted knowledge; they acknowledge cultural and historical specificity; agree that knowledge is sustained by social practices; and that knowledge and social action go together.[188] Social constructionists challenge the realist assumptions of traditional biomedical and psychological research, arguing instead that subjectivity, behaviour, and the very definition and meaning of what is 'health' and what is 'illness' is constructed within social practices and rules, language, relationships, and roles; it is always shaped by culture and history. Science is seen as part of this constructive process, and as a consequence, research or clinical intervention can never be seen as objective or neutral; it is a social practice that partly shapes and constructs knowledge. Social constructionism has also been used as the epistemological basis of research where the gaze of the researcher is on the 'social' rather than on the individual, and where methodological naturalism is explicitly rejected. For example, there has been a move towards the use of discursive theories and methods, which focus specifically on the role of language, and its relation to cultural practices. These discourse analytic approaches draw upon principles from ethnomethodology,[189] post-structuralism,[190] and conversation analysis and linguistics,[191] in viewing discourse as constructive of reality and action-oriented.[192] The term 'discourse' refers to a set of shared cultural beliefs and practices, which are utilised in everyday life in order to construct meaning and interpretation about the world.[193] It is also argued that discourses are constitutive of subjectivity, and that the meanings of objects and events are inseparable from the way in which they are constituted within particular discourses.[192; 194] This stands in direct contrast to traditional psychological research that conceptualises factors such as cognitions as fixed entities that can be reliably measured. Here, the very notion of *a* cognitive style is dismissed, as interpretation and meaning is continuously negotiated within discourse. From a methodological point of view, this leads to the use of qualitative methods, and to reflexivity in research practice.[e.g. 160; 178; 195]

xxi   There are social constructionists who acknowledge the reality of women's distress – such as Kathleen Kendall,[25, p.43] or Vivian Burr and Trevor Butt.[146, p.187]

xxii   This is because a constructionist perspective is essentially relativist, claiming that material objects (including bodies) do not exist independently from perception or cultural discourse.[200] This is exemplified by the oft cited paper by Edwards, Ashmore and Potter,[201] where both death and furniture are deemed not real things in themselves, but social constructions, leaving discourse as the only valid unit of analysis. This results in the marginalisation of any experience outside of the realm of language, in particular embodiment.[202]

xxiii   'Mainstream' research is the term used by many feminist critics (such as Janet Stoppard) in their critiques of positivist research.[153]

xxiv   Many feminist accounts do, however, acknowledge women's subjective experiences of distress.[153; 160]

xxv   There are exceptions. For example, the feminist psychoanalyst Karen Horney (1935) developed theories of sexuality and gender relationships which encapsulated material, discursive and intrapsychic levels of experience.

xxvi   More specifically, Victoria Grace draws on this body of psychosocial theorising, in combination with Lacanian psychoanalysis, to explain women's depression, arguing that 'the subject experiencing the reality of a depressive state in*corp*orates the social (the 'outside') fully within the very possibility of its existence. These unconscious processes are traversed by desire and its depressive potential'.[212, p.276] She also argues that the '"cause" of "depression" [is] simultaneously unique to each individual and at the same time fully social as the subject ex-sists (is decentred in its existence) through an incorporation of the Other'.[212, p.276] She believes that this is consistent with a critical realist epistemology, as it 'foregrounds the inevitability of confronting unconscious dynamics of desire and loss as these are figured uniquely in each individual history in relation to the socially situated and invested construct of feminine subjectivity'.[212, p.277; see also 225]

xxvii   Relational psychoanalysis, that focuses on adult subjectivity and relationships, is one notable exception.[228–229]

4 WOMAN AS OBJECT, NOT SUBJECT: MADNESS AS RESPONSE TO OBJECTIFICATION AND SEXUAL VIOLENCE

i   As Jane Stein has argued,[13] 'there is a direct effect on health where one stands in the scale of things in society . . . it is no longer physical causes but social and cognitively mediated processes.[cited by 9, p.32]'

ii   For example, in the National Comorbidity Study of a representative sample of 5,877 US citizens, child sexual abuse was reported by 13 per cent of women and 2.5 per cent of men.[30] Similarly, in the UK, a study of 2,019 individuals reported that 12 per cent of women and 8 per cent of men had been sexually abused as children.[51] In a study of 1,411 adult women twins living in the USA, 30.4 per cent reported child sexual abuse, with 8.4 per cent reporting abuse that involved intercourse.[52] Two UK studies reported rates of 21 per cent (of 1,236 women) and 46 per cent (of 600 women) respectively.[53–54] Several studies also suggest that children with a disability are twice as likely to be sexually abused as those who do not have a disability.[55]

iii   Supporting this view, in what was described as a 'corrective meta-analysis', Rebecca Bolen and Maria Scannapieco estimated that 30–40 per cent of women, and 13 per cent of men, had experienced sexual abuse as children.[58] Diana Russell and Rebecca Bolen analysed nine representative US studies and concluded that 38 per cent of women had experienced sexual abuse before the age of 18, made up of 16 per cent of women who had been incestuously abused and 31 per cent of women who had experienced extra-familial sexual abuse.[59] They still consider this an underestimate, as homeless women and those in institutions are not included in the studies they analysed, as previously acknowledged by Molnar and colleagues.[30]

iv   In each instance the first study cited is the Ussher and Dewberry 1997 study,[63] and the second study is the Long Term Effects of Child Sexual Abuse Study that is described in detail in this chapter.

v   Other means of silencing the child reported in the Long Term Effects of Child Sexual Abuse Study were by telling the child: it was 'our secret' (55 per cent); no one would believe them if they disclosed (32 per cent); it was love (27 per cent); it was a game to teach about sex (28 per cent); they would be put in a home if they disclosed (14 per cent); or through bribery and blackmail (25 per cent).

vi   Both of the child sexual abuse cases (Valerie and Elizabeth) are drawn from the Long Term Effects of Child Sexual Abuse Study I conducted in the UK.

vii   The percentage of women with lifetime depression was 39.3 per cent in survivors of child sexual abuse, compared to 21.3 per cent in the general population, and 78 per cent of abused women met the criteria for one lifetime disorder, compared to 48.5 per cent of non-abused women.[30]

viii   These findings were confirmed in a meta-analysis of 27 studies which examined the effects of child sexual abuse, involving 25,367 individuals, where sexual abuse survivors were found to have a 20 per cent greater likelihood of experiencing depression, PTSD and suicide, regardless of the nature or type of the abuse.[131]

ix   Research by Cortina and Kubiak has disputed this theory, providing convincing evidence that sexual abuse history accounts for gender differences in PTSD diagnoses, not women's vulnerability.[155]

x   An alternative model, offered by Mary Koss and colleagues,[29] is to adopt an approach similar to that used in bereavement, where a diagnosis of depression is not given to those in the early stages of grief, even if all the major symptoms are present, as these symptoms are considered normal. Thus the 94 per cent of women diagnosed with PTSD immediately after being sexually assaulted, in one study,[139] would not receive a psychiatric diagnosis; indeed, neither would the 46 per cent who met the criteria three months later, if we consider distress experienced three months after a sexual assault to be 'normal' or 'reasonable'.

xi   Psychologists have taken issue with the notion that memories can be repressed, and are particularly sceptical about 'recovery' of memory in therapy, where encouragement to remember is given. However, most now accept the suppression of memory as a fact.

xii   Only 51 of the 369 (14 per cent) survey participants who disclosed the abuse were offered support by the person they disclosed to and girls were often punished for 'telling lies', or made to maintain their silence in order to protect the abuser – his status as a good, upstanding father/grandfather/uncle/brother.

xiii   In a case in 1973, a Sicilian girl was abducted in Italy. Her father would have been culturally obliged to kill her if she did not marry her kidnapper, but the Australian court annulled the marriage on the ground of duress.[193]

xiv   For example, one study by Gidycz and colleagues reported that 32 per cent of child sexual abuse survivors experienced adult victimisation compared with 14 per cent of non-abused women.[207] Other studies have reported that between 37 and 68 per cent of women who have been sexually abused in childhood experience physical, sexual or emotional victimisation as adults.[208–212]

xv Recent highly publicised cases in Australia of footballers engaging in group sex, with the women later describing it as rape,[223] or footballers hitting (or 'glassing') their girlfriends,[224] have received widespread condemnation in the press. However, these men are quickly welcomed back into the fold of their football team, or their television career, once an 'appropriate' length of time has passed.

xvi This includes the refusal of adults to take seriously girls' reports of sexual abuse, and the refusal of courts to take women's claims of rape seriously.

5 THE CONSTRUCTION AND LIVED EXPERIENCE OF WOMEN'S DISTRESS: POSITIONING PREMENSTRUAL CHANGE AS PSYCHIATRIC ILLNESS

i I have discussed the genealogy of PMS elsewhere.[1]

ii In this chapter I use the term 'PMS' when referring to women's accounts of moderate to severe premenstrual distress, as this is the colloquial term used by many women.

iii As Lisa Cosgrove and Paula Caplan have argued, Eli Lilly repatented Prozac as Sarafem at a time when its patent for Prozac was about to run out, which would result in a significant loss of revenue.[6]

iv In order to examine the association between self-silencing and PMS systematically, as part of the PMS and Relationships Study, Janette Perz and I gave 257 women who self-reported PMS Dana Jack's 'Silencing the Self Scale' (STSS) to complete.[40; 70] Jack identified four distinct facets underpinning self-silencing behaviour, which make up the subscales of the survey: 'Externalised Self-Perception' reflecting the tendency to judge the self by external standards; 'Care as Self-Sacrifice' assessing propensity to put needs of others before the self; 'Silencing the Self' involving the inhibition of thoughts, feelings and behaviours in order to avoid relationship conflict or loss; and 'Divided Self' assessing the tendency to behave in a compliant manner while feeling angry and resentful inside. We found that women who report PMS scored high on the 'Silencing the Self' and 'Divided Self' subscales – as well as high on Self-Silencing overall.[40; 70] This suggested that women were inhibiting feelings, and were experiencing a division between inner feelings and those presented to the world, as has previously been reported with women who are depressed.[71–72] 'Externalised Self-Perception', 'Divided Self' and Global STSS scales correlated positively and significantly with levels of premenstrual distress, whereas these scales and 'Silencing the Self' were negatively and significantly correlated with PMS coping. This suggested that judging the self by the standards of others, and putting on a false front to the world, was linked to higher levels of distress, and to lower levels of coping.

Conversely, there was an inverse relationship between the 'Silencing the Self' subscale and premenstrual distress, suggesting that women are distressed, and position their distress as PMS, partly because of their inability to self-silence premenstrually. This may explain the relatively low level of depression we found in this sample, when compared to women who score similarly on global self-silencing,[72–73] as women who position themselves as PMS sufferers are directing their anger outwards once a month, rather than internalising it and becoming depressed. However, this is not a beneficial outcome for women, as rates of anxiety in our study were significantly higher than population norms, and women adopted a position of self-pathologisation in relation to their anger and distress, through positioning it as a pathological disorder, PMS.

v   PMSBuddy is a website ostensibly aimed at men, which reminds them when their partner's period is due. It also contains 'stories' about PMS, posted by both women and men.

vi   For example, see the YouTube videos: http://www.youtube.com/watch?v=mCwKbUVyHLY; http://www.youtube.com/watch?v=_uuzPsigAyM&feature=fvw; http://www.youtube.com/watch?v=MfmgQDJZ7g0&feature=related; http://www.youtube.com/watch?v=8m9uEN9Xlwc

vii   Natasha Mauthner has made similar arguments in relation to post-partum depression.[88]

6 WOMEN'S MADNESS: RESISTANCE AND SURVIVAL

i   Rachel Perkins, who describes herself as a 'radical lesbian feminist and a psychologist' and is a vociferous critic of therapy for lesbians, as discussed in Chapter 3,[26] has written about 'choosing E.C.T' to alleviate her depression.[25, p.623] This is how she describes it:

> I was two months into my second bout of severe depression. The first had prevented me from working (or doing anything very much) for about six months, and now I was back in the same situation. Although I was profoundly miserable, this misery that characterises popular uses of the term 'depression' is not what bothers me most. More important to me is being unable to think properly. Although I was receiving medication, I was still unable to work, read, drive my car, make even the simplest decisions or look after myself. I had all the classic symptoms: early morning wakening, loss of appetite, diurnal variation and amenorrhea. And I was terrified. Could I, like last time, face months of this? . . . I had ECT – the standard six treatments. Two a week for three weeks and within a week of the sixth I was back at work.[25, p.623]

ii   Even when men do contribute to housework or childcare, it is invariably constructed as 'help' for women, rather than both partners negotiating responsibilities on an equal basis, so even the 30 per cent of housework that men are estimated to conduct could be questioned.

iii   In previous research, lesbian couples have been found to demonstrate a greater capacity for mutual empathy, empowerment and relational authenticity than heterosexual couples,[75] to resolve conflict more effectively,[76] being more likely to report open exploration of feelings, empathic attunement to non-verbals, negotiation, and the conscious avoidance of contempt.[77]

iv   Yet the implications of this research are far broader than the positioning and experience of the reproductive body. A growing body of research has reported that lesbian relationships are experienced as more satisfying than heterosexual relationships,[80–82] with predictors of this satisfaction being greater emotional companionship,[80] greater liking, trust and equality,[81] cohesion and flexibility,[82] as well as intimacy, equity and autonomy.[83]

The findings of the PMS and Relationships Study thus provide insight into the high levels of satisfaction reported in many lesbian relationships, and have broader implications for understanding and facilitating women's mental health and well-being.

v   In conjunction with Janette Perz, Edith Weisberg and Yasmin Hawkins, I am currently involved in a research study comparing one-to-one and couple psychological interventions for premenstrual distress, using an adaptation of the women centred intervention described previously.[86]

vi   As Gavin Andrews argues:

> Spontaneous remission accounts for a considerable amount of the improvement observed (in treatment studies). There are two naturalistic studies in which people have been interviewed on two occasions and the duration of intervening depressive episodes noted. McLeod *et al* (1992) reported from a sample of married persons that the median duration of DSM-III-R (American Psychiatric Association, 1987) episodes of depression was 10 weeks, with 75 per cent having episodes of under 22 weeks. Kendler *et al* (1997) studied a population sample of women and found a median time to recovery of 6 weeks, with 75 per cent recovering in 12 weeks. If the population time to recovery were a median of 8 weeks and 75 per cent recovered within 16 weeks, then people recruited into a trial after being depressed for 8 weeks would have a 50 per cent chance of remitting during the conduct of the usual 8-week trial. These two factors, response to encouragement and a 50 per cent probability of spontaneous remission during the trial, could account for the considerable progress of placebo control groups in depression trials.[105, p. 193]

REFERENCES

1 THE MADNESS OF WOMEN: MYTH OR EXPERIENCE?

1 Martin, P. (1987) *Mad women in romantic writing*. Brighton: Harvester.
2 Caplan, P.J. (1995) *They say you're crazy: How the world's most powerful psychiatrists decide who's normal*. Reading, MA: Addison-Wesley.
3 Showalter, E. (1987) *The female malady: Women, madness and English culture 1830–1940*. London: Virago.
4 Foucault, M. (1978) *The history of sexuality. Volume 1: An introduction*. London: Penguin.
5 Ussher, J.M. (1991) *Women's madness: Misogyny or mental illness?* Amherst, MA: University of Massachusetts Press.
6 Ussher, J.M. (2006) *Managing the monstrous feminine: Regulating the reproductive body*. London: Routledge.
7 Brown, L.S. (2010) Empowering depressed women: The importance of a feminist lens, in D.C. Jack and A. Ali (eds) *The depression epidemic: International perspectives on women's self-silencing and psychological distress*. Oxford: Oxford University Press, pp. 333–342.
8 Brown, L.S. (2010) *Feminist therapy*. Washington, DC: American Psychological Association.
9 Baruch, G.K. and A. Treacher (1978) *Psychiatry observed*. London: Routledge.
10 Goffman, E. (1961) *Asylums: Essays on the social situation of mental patients and other inmates*. New York: Doubleday.
11 Szasz, T. (1971) *The manufacture of madness: A comparative study of the inquisition and the mental health movement*. London: Routledge.
12 Conrad, P. (1982) On the medicalisation of deviance and social control, in D. Ingleby (ed.) *Critical Psychology*. Harmondsworth: Penguin, pp. 102–119.
13 Rose, N.S. (1996) *Inventing our selves: Psychology, power, and personhood*. New York: Cambridge University Press.
14 Foucault, M. (1979) *Discipline and punish: The birth of the prison*. London: Penguin.
15 American Psychiatric Association (APA) (2000) *Diagnostic and statistical manual of mental disorders*, 4th edn (DSM-IV). Washington, DC: APA.
16 Foucault, M. (1987) *Mental illness and psychology*. Berkeley, CA: University of California Press (first published 1976).
17 Foucault, M. (1969) *L'Archéologie du savoir*. Paris: Gallimard.

18 Foucault, M. (1972) *The archeology of knowledge and the discourse on language*, ed. T.A. Sheridan. New York: Pantheon.

19 Malson, H. (1996) *The thin women: Anorexia nervosa*. London: Routledge.

20 Burr, V. (1999) The extra-discursive in social constructionism, in D.J. Nightingale and J. Cromby (eds) *Social constructionist psychology: A critical analysis of theory and practice*. Buckingham: Open University Press, pp. 113–126.

21 Bhaskar, R. (1989) *Reclaiming reality: A critical introduction to contemporary philosophy*. London: Verso.

22 Brand, J. (2007) Glad to be mad? *Guardian*, 8 May. www.guardian.co.uk/society/2007/may/08/health.healthandwellbeing.

23 Mad Pride Blog (2009) *Hey ho – Let's go*. http://madpride.org.uk/blogs/madprideblog/index.php.

24 Szasz, T. (1996) *My madness saved me: The madness and marriage of Virginia Woolf*. New Brunswick, NJ: Transaction.

25 Caplan, P.J. and L. Cosgrove (2004) Is this really necessary?, in P.J. Caplan and L. Cosgrove (eds) *Bias in psychiatric diagnosis*. Lanham, MD: Jason Aronson, pp.xiv–xxxiii.

26 Laing, R.D. (1969) *The divided self*. New York: Random House.

27 Kaysen, S. (1993) *Girl, interrupted* (extract), in R. Shannonhouse (ed.) (2003) *Out of her mind: Women writing on madness*. New York: Modern Library, pp. 116–119.

28 Cosgrove, L. and B. Riddle (2004) Gender bias in sex distribution of mental disorders in the DSM-IV-TR, in P.J. Caplan and L. Cosgrove (eds) *Bias in psychiatric diagnosis*. Lanham, MD: Jason Aronson, pp. 127–140.

29 Olff, M., W. Langeland, N. Draijer and B.P.R. Gersons (2007) Gender differences in post-traumatic stress disorder. *Psychological Bulletin*, **133**(2): 183–204.

30 Harré, R. and L. van Langenhov (1999) *Positioning theory*. London: Blackwell.

31 Davies, B. and R. Harré (1990) Positioning: The discursive production of selves. *Journal of the Theory of Social Behaviour*, **20**: 43–65.

32 Foucault, M. (1967) *Madness and civilisation: A history of insanity in the age of reason*. London: Tavistock.

33 Sydenham, T. (1843[1679]) Epistolary dissertation to Dr. Cole, in *The works of Thomas Sydenham, Volume 2*. London: Sydenham Society.

34 Bronfen, E. (1998) *The knotted subject: Hysteria and its discontents*. Princeton, NJ: Princeton University Press.

35 Slavney, P.R. (1990) *Perspectives on hysteria*. Baltimore, MD: Johns Hopkins University Press.

36 Showalter, E. (1997) *Hystories: Hysterical epidemics and modern culture*. New York: Columbia University Press.

37 Laycock, T. (1840) *An essay on hysteria*. Philadelphia, PA: Haswell, Barrington and Haswell.

38 Smith-Rosenberg, C. (1986) *Disorderly conduct: Visions of gender in Victorian America*. Oxford: Oxford University Press.

39 Weininger, O. (1980[1903]) *Geschlecht und Charakter*. Munich: Matthes and Seitz.

40 Showalter, E. (1993) Hysteria, feminism and gender, in S.L. Gilman, H. King,

REFERENCES

R. Porter, G.S. Rousseau and E. Showalter, *Hysteria beyond Freud*. Berkeley, CA: University of California Press, pp. 286–344.

41 Donkin, H.B. (1892) Hysteria, in D.H. Tuke (ed.) *Dictionary of psychological medicine*. Philadelphia, PA: P. Blakiston, pp. 619–621.

42 Mitchell, S.W. (1885) *Lectures on diseases of the nervous system especially in women*. London: Churchill.

43 Busfield, J. (1996) *Men, women and madness: Understanding gender and mental disorder*. New York: New York University Press.

44 Playfair, W.S. (1892) Functional neurosis, in D.H. Tuke (ed.) *Dictionary of psychological medicine*. Philadelphia, PA: P. Blakiston, p. 851.

45 Becker, D. (2000) When she was bad: Borderline personality disorder in a posttraumatic age. *American Journal of Orthopsychiatry*, **70**(4): 422–432.

46 Micale, M.S. (1995) *Approaching hysteria: Disease and its interpretations*. Princeton, NJ: Princeton University Press.

47 Porter, R. (1993) The body and the mind, the doctor and the patient: Negotiating hysteria, in S.L. Gilman, H. King, R. Porter, G.S. Rousseau and E. Showalter, *Hysteria beyond Freud*. Berkeley, CA: University of California Press, pp. 225–285.

48 Shorter, E. (1992) *From paralysis to fatigue*. New York: Free Press.

49 Metcalfe, W.R. and P.J. Caplan (2004) Seeking 'normal' sexuality on a complex matrix, in P.J. Caplan and L. Cosgrove (eds) *Bias in psychiatric diagnosis*. Lanham, MD: Jason Aronson, pp. 121–126.

50 Malson, H. (1998) *The thin woman: Feminism, post-structuralism and the social psychology of anorexia nervosa*. London: Routledge.

51 Bordo, S. (1993) *Unbearable weight: Feminism, culture and the body*. Berkeley, CA: University of California Press.

52 Gardner, P. (2003) Distorted packaging: Marketing depression as illness, drugs as cure. *Journal of Medical Humanities*, **24**(1–2): 105–130.

53 Blehar, M.C. (2006) Women's mental health research: The emergence of a biomedical field. *Annual Review of Clinical Psychology*, **2**: 135–160.

54 Desjarlais, R., L. Eisenberg, B. Good and A. Kleinman (1996) *World mental health: Problems and priorities in low income countries*. Oxford: Oxford University Press.

55 World Health Organization (WHO) (2000) *Women's mental health: An evidence based review*. Geneva: WHO.

56 Bebbington, P.E. (1996) The origins of sex differences in depressive disorder: Bridging the gap. *International Review of Psychiatry*, **8**(4): 295–332.

57 Australian Bureau of Statistics (2008) *National Survey of Mental Health and Well-being: Summary of Results, 2007*. Canberra: Australian Bureau of Statistics.

58 Hamilton, J.A., M. Grant and M.F. Jensvold (1996) Sex and treatment of depressions: When does it matter?, in M.F. Jensvold, U. Halbreich and J.A. Hamilton (eds) *Psychopharmacology and women: Sex, gender and hormones*. Washington, DC: American Psychiatric Press, pp. 241–260.

59 Ashton, H. (1997) Psychotropic drug prescription for women. *British Journal of Psychiatry*, **158**(suppl. 10): 30–35.

60 Ettore, E. and E. Riska (1995) *Gendered moods: Psychotropics and society*. London: Routledge.

61 Currie, J. (2005) *The marketization of depression: The prescribing of SSRI antidepressants to women*, for Women and Health Protection. www.whp-apsf.ca/pdf/SSRIs.pdf

62 Burstow, B. (2006) Understanding and ending ECT: A feminist imperative. *Canadian Women's Studies*, **25**(1–2): 115–122.

63 Weitz, D. (2009) *Ontario ECT statistics 2000–2002*. www.ect.org/ontario-ect-statistics-2000-2002/

64 Ussher, J.M. (2000) Women's madness: A material-discursive-intrapsychic approach, in D. Fee (ed.) *Psychology and the postmodern: Mental illness as discourse and experience*. London: Sage, pp. 207–230.

65 Sayer, A. (2000) *Realism and social science*. London: Sage.

66 Williams, S. (2003) Beyond meaning, discourse and the empirical world: Critical realist reflections on health. *Social Theory and Health*, **1**: 42–71.

67 Grace, V. (2010) The desiring, gendered speakingbeing: Going a bit further with Ussher on women and depression. *Feminism and Psychology*, **20**(2): 272–277.

68 Batty, Z. (2006) *Masculinity and depression: Men's subjective experience of depression, coping and preferences for therapy and gender role conflict*. Thesis, School of Psychology, University of Western Sydney.

69 Australian Government Department of Health and Aging (2008) *Development of a national men's health policy: Summary of men's health issues*. www.drinkingnightmare.gov.au/internet/main/publishing.nsf/Content/18C92B67F5A5C423CA25750B000E6C6C/$File/issues-2.pdf, accessed 8 October 2009.

70 Irish Minister for Health and Children (2008) *National men's health policy 2008–2013*. www.dohc.ie/publications/pdf/mens_health_policy.pdf/, accessed 8 October 2009.

71 Rutter, M., A. Caspi and T.E. Moffit (2003) Using sex differences in psychopathology to study causal mechanisms: Unifying issues and research strategies. *Journal of Child Psychology and Psychiatry*, **44**: 1092–1115.

2 THE DAUGHTER OF HYSTERIA: DEPRESSION AS A 'WOMAN'S PROBLEM'?

1 American Psychiatric Association (APA) (2000) *Diagnostic and statistical manual of mental disorders*, 4th edn (DSM-IV). Washington, DC: APA.

2 Beyond Blue (2009) *What is depression?* www.beyondblue.org.au/index.aspx?link_id=1.3.

3 Kessler, R.C., K.A. McGonagle, S. Zhao et al. (1994) Lifetime and 12-month prevalence of DSM-II-R psychiatric disorders in the United States: Results from the National Comorbidity Survey. *Archives of General Psychiatry*, **5**(1): 8–19.

4 Bebbington, P.E. (1996) The origins of sex differences in depressive disorder: Bridging the gap. *International Review of Psychiatry*, **8**(4): 295–332.

5 Weissman, M.M., R.C. Bland and G.J. Canino (1996) Cross national epidemiology of major depression and bipolar disorder. *Journal of the American Medical Association*, **276**: 293–299.

6 Maier, W., M. Gänsicke, R. Gater et al. (1999) Gender differences in the

prevalence of depression: A survey in primary care. *Journal of Affective Disorders*, **53**: 241–252.

7 Kessler, R.C., P. Berglund, O. Demler et al. (2005) Lifetime prevalence and age-of-onset distributions of DSM-IV disorders in the National Comorbidity Survey Replication. *Archives of General Psychiatry*, **62**(6): 593–602.

8 Kuehner, C. (2003) Gender differences in unipolar depression: An update of epidemiological findings and possible explanations. *Acta Psychiatrica Scandinavica*, **108**: 163–174.

9 Perugi, G., L. Musetti, E. Simonini et al. (1990) Gender mediated clinical features of depressive illness: The importance of temperamental differences. *British Journal of Psychiatry*, **157**: 435–441.

10 Arnold, L.M. (2003) Gender differences in bi-polar disorder. *Psychiatric Clinics of North America*, **26**: 595–620.

11 Singleton, N., R. Bumpstead, M. O'Brien et al. (2001) *Psychiatric morbidity among adults living in private household, 2000*. London: TSO. www.statistics. gov.uk/downloads/theme_health/psychmorb.pdf.

12 Kessler, R.C., K.A. McGonagle, M. Swartz et al. (1993) Sex and depression in the National Comorbidity Survey I: Lifetime prevalence, chronicity and recurrence. *Journal of Affective Disorders*, **29**: 85–96.

13 Cross National Collaborative Group (1992) The changing rate of major depression: Cross national comparisons. *Journal of the American Medical Association*, **268**: 3098–3105.

14 Narrow, W.E., D.S. Rae, E.K. Mościcki et al. (1990) Depression among Cuban Americans: The Hispanic health and nutrition examination survey. *Social Psychiatry and Psychiatric Epidemiology*, **25**: 260–268.

15 Vega, W.A., B. Kolody, R.L. Hough and G. Figueroa (1987) Depressive symptomatology in northern Mexico adults. *American Journal of Public Health*, **77**: 1215–1218.

16 Australian Bureau of Statistics (2008) *National Survey of Mental Health and Well-being: Summary of results, 2007*. Canberra: Australian Bureau of Statistics.

17 Treichler, P. (1992) AIDS and HIV infection in the third world: A first world chronicle, in E. Fee and D. Fox (eds) *AIDS and the making of a chronic disease model*. Berkeley, CA: University of California Press, pp. 377–412.

18 Gardner, P. (2003) Distorted packaging: Marketing depression as illness, drugs as cure. *Journal of Medical Humanities*, **24**(1–2): 105–130.

19 Morison, A. and Morison, T.C. (1848) *Outlines of lectures on the nature, causes and treatment of insanity*, 4th edn. London.

20 Small, H. (1996) *Love's madness: Medicine, the novel and female insanity 1800–1865*. Oxford: Clarendon.

21 Wiltibank, J. (1854) *Introductory lecture for the session, 1853–54*. Philadelphia, PA: Edward Gratten.

22 Smith-Rosenberg, C. (1986) *Disorderly conduct: Visions of gender in Victorian America*. Oxford: Oxford University Press.

23 Showalter, E. (1987) *The female malady: Women, madness and English culture 1830–1940*. London: Virago.

24 Haslam, J. (1809) *Observations on madness and melancholy*, 2nd edn. London: J. Callow.

25 Burrows, G.M. (1828) *Commentaries on the causes, forms, symptoms and treatment, moral and medical, of insanity*. London: Underwood.

26 Tilt, E.J. (1882) *The change of life in health and disease: A clinical treatise on the diseases of the ganglionic nervous system incidental to women at the decline of life*. New York: Bermingham.

27 Bronfen, E. (1998) *The knotted subject: Hysteria and its discontents*. Princeton, NJ: Princeton University Press.

28 Borossa, J. (2001) *Hysteria*. Cambridge: Icon.

29 Foucault, M. (1967) *Madness and civilisation: A history of insanity in the age of reason*. London: Tavistock.

30 Foucault, M. (1978) *The history of sexuality. Volume 1: An introduction*. London: Penguin.

31 Munde, P.F. (1886) Clinical observations in reflex genital neurosis in the female. *Journal of Nervous and Mental Disease*, **13**: 129–139.

32 Rousseau, G.S. (1993) A strange pathology: Hysteria in the early modern world 1500–1800, in S.L. Gilman, H. King, R. Porter, G.S. Rousseau and E. Showalter, *Hysteria beyond Freud*. Berkeley, CA: University of California Press, pp. 91–221.

33 Carter, R.B. (1853) *On the pathology and treatment of hysteria*. London: Churchill.

34 Bloch, A.J. (1894) Sexual perversions in the female. *New Orleans Medical Journal*, **22**(1): 1–7.

35 Showalter, E. (1997) *Hystories: Hysterical epidemics and modern culture*. New York: Columbia University Press.

36 Conrad, P. (1992) Medicalization and social control. *Annual Review of Sociology*, **18**: 209–232.

37 National Institute of Mental Health (NIMH) (2008) *Women and depression: Discovering hope*. Bethesda, MD: NIMH.

38 Angold, A., E.J. Costello, A. Erkanli and C.M. Worthman (1999) Pubertal changes in hormones levels and depression in girls. *Psychological Medicine*, **29**: 1043–1053.

39 Sullivan, P.F., M.C. Neale and K.S. Kendler (2000) Genetic epidemiology of major depression: Review and meta-analysis. *American Journal of Psychiatry*, **157**(10): 1552–1562.

40 Nestler, E.J., M. Barrot, R.J. DiLeone et al. (2002) Neurobiology of depression. *Neuron*, **34**(1): 13–25.

41 Klein, D.F. and P.H. Wender (1993) *Understanding depression*. Oxford: Oxford University Press.

42 Fee, D. (2000) The project of pathology: Reflexivity and depression in Elizabeth Wurtzel's Prozac Nation, in D. Fee (ed.) *Pathology and the postmodern: Mental illness as discourse and experience*. London: Sage, pp. 74–99.

43 Zubenko, G.S., H.B. Hughes, B.S. Maher et al. (2002) Genetic linkage of region containing the CREB1 gene to depressive disorders in women from families with recurrent, early-onset, major depression. *American Journal of Genetics*, **114**: 980–987.

44 Abraham, I.M. and A.E. Herbison (2005) Major sex differences in non-

249

genomic estrogen actions in intracellular signaling in mouse brain in vivo. *Neuroscience*, **131**(4): 945–951.

45 Blehar, M.C. (2006) Women's mental health research: The emergence of a biomedical field. *Annual Review of Clinical Psychology*, **2**: 135–160.

46 Abkevich, V., N.J. Camp, C.H. Hensel et al. (2003) Predisposition locus for major depression at chromosome 12q22–12q23.2. *American Journal of Human Genetics*, **73**(6): 1271–1281.

47 Seaman, M.V. (1997) Psychopathology in women and men: Focus on female hormones. *American Journal of Psychiatry*, **154**(12): 1641–1647.

48 Studd, J. (1997) Depression and the menopause. *British Medical Journal*, **314**: 977.

49 Group for the Advancement of Psychiatry, APA (1999) *In the long run. . . . Longitudinal studies of psychopathology in children.* GAP report 143. Washington, DC: American Psychiatric Press.

50 Cosgrove, L. and B. Riddle (2004) Gender bias in sex distribution of mental disorders in the DSM-IV-TR, in P.J. Caplan and L. Cosgrove (eds) *Bias in psychiatric diagnosis.* Lanham, MD: Jason Aronson, pp. 127–140.

51 Nolen-Hoeksema, S., J.S. Girgus and M.E.P. Seligman (1991) Sex differences in depression and explanatory style in children. *Journal of Youth and Adolescence*, **20**: 233–245.

52 Angold, A., E.J. Costello and C.M. Worthman (1998) Puberty and depression: The roles of age, pubertal status and pubertal timing. *Psychological Medicine*, **28**: 51–61.

53 Kashani, J.H., D.P. Cantwell, W.O. Shekim and J.C. Reid (1982) Major depressive disorder in children admitted to an inpatient community mental health centre. *American Journal of Psychiatry*, **139**: 671–672.

54 Anderson, J.C., S. Williams, R. McGee and P.A. Silva (1987) DSM-III disorders in preadolescent children. *Archives of General Psychiatry*, **44**: 69–76.

55 Kashani, J.H., N.C. Beck, E.W. Hoeper et al. (1987) Psychiatric disorders in a community sample of adolescents. *American Journal of Psychiatry*, **144**: 584–589.

56 Dr Porter (1855) *Book of men, women and babies.* New York: De Witt and Davenport.

57 Peterson, A.C., P.A. Sarigiani and R.E. Kennedy (1991) Adolescent depression: Why more girls? *Journal of Youth and Adolescence*, **20**: 247–271.

58 Beekman, A.T., J.R. Copeland and M.J. Prince (1999) Review of community prevalence of depression in later life. *British Journal of Psychiatry*, **174**: 307–311.

59 Copeland, J.R., A.T. Beekman and M.E. Dewey (1999) Depression in Europe: Geographical distribution among older people. *British Journal of Psychiatry*, **174**: 312–321.

60 Bebbington, P., G. Dunn, R. Jenkins et al. (1998) The influence of age and sex on the prevalence of depression conditions: Report from the National Survey of Psychiatric Morbidity. *Psychological Medicine*, **28**(1): 9–19.

61 Bebbington, P.E. (1998) Sex and depression. *Psychological Medicine*, **28**(1): 1–8.

62 Cyranowski, J.M., E. Frank, E. Young and M.K. Shear (2000) Adolescent

onset of the gender difference in lifetime rates of major depression. *Archives of General Psychiatry*, **57**: 21–27.

63 Liebert, R. (2010) Feminist psychology, hormones and the raging politics of medicalization. *Feminism and Psychology*, **20**(2): 278–283.

64 Maudsley, H. (1879) *The pathology of mind*. London: Macmillan.

65 Maudsley, H. (1874) Sex in mind and education. *Fortnightly Review*, **15**: 466–483.

66 Mitchell, S.W. (1885) *Lectures on diseases of the nervous system especially in women*. London: Churchill.

67 Herndl, D.P. (1988) The writing cure. *NWSA Journal*, **1**(1): 52–74.

68 Gallop, J. (1983) *Nurse Freud: Class struggle in the family*. Miami University.

69 Showalter, E. (1993) Hysteria, feminism and gender, in S.L. Gilman, H. King, R. Porter, G.S. Rousseau and E. Showalter, *Hysteria beyond Freud*. Berkeley, CA: University of California Press, pp. 286–344.

70 Cixous, H. and C. Clement (1987) *The newly born women*, trans. B. Wing. Minneapolis, MN: University of Minnesota Press.

71 Bernheimer, C. and C. Kahane (1990) *In Dora's case: Freud–hysteria–feminism*, 2nd edn. New York: Columbia University Press.

72 Freud, S. (1964) *Dora: An analysis of a case of hysteria*. New York: Collins.

73 Brumberg, J.J. (1988) *Fasting girls: The emergence of anorexia nervosa as a modern disease*. Cambridge, MA: Harvard University Press.

74 Paikoff, R.L., J. Brooks-Gunn and M.P. Worren (1991) Effects of girls' hormonal status on depressive and aggressive symptoms over the course of one year. *Journal of Youth and Adolescence*, **20**: 1912–1915.

75 Susman, E.J., E.D. Nottelmann, G. Inoff-Germain et al. (1987) Hormonal influences on aspects of psychological development during adolescence. *Journal of Adolescent Health Care*, **8**: 492–504.

76 Brooks-Gunn, J. and M.P. Warren (1989) Biological and social contributions to negative affect in young adolescent girls. *Child Development*, **60**: 40–55.

77 Worthman, C.M. (1995) Hormones, sex and gender. *Annual Review of Anthropology*, **24**: 593–616.

78 Stoppard, J. (2000) *Understanding depression: Feminist social constructionist approaches*. London: Routledge.

79 Uchino, B.N., J.T. Cacioppo and J.K. Kiecolt-Glaser (1996) The relationship between social support and physiological processes: A review with emphasis on underlying mechanisms and implications for health. *Psychological Bulletin*, **119**: 499–531.

80 Frank, R. (1931) The hormonal causes of premenstrual tension. *Archives of Neurological Psychiatry*, **26**: 1053–1057.

81 Parry, B. (1994) Biological correlates of premenstrual complaints, in J.H. Gold and S.K. Severino (eds) *Premenstrual dysphoria: Myths and realities*. London: American Psychiatric Press, pp. 47–66.

82 Nolen-Hoeksema, S. (1990) *Sex differences in depression*. Stanford, CA: Stanford University Press.

83 Popay, J., M. Bartley and C. Owen (1993) Gender inequalities in health: Social position, affective disorders and minor psychiatric morbidity. *Social Science and Medicine*, **36**(1): 21–32.

84 Mira, M., S. Abraham, D. McNeil et al. (1995) The interrelationship of premenstrual symptoms. *Psychological Medicine*, **25**(5): 947–955.

85 Chrisler, J.C. and P. Caplan (2002) The strange case of Dr. Jekyll and Ms. Hyde: How PMS became a cultural phenomenon and a psychiatric disorder. *Annual Review of Sex Research*, **13**: 274–306.

86 Ussher, J.M. (2002) Processes of appraisal and coping in the development and maintenance of Premenstrual Dysphoric Disorder. *Journal of Community and Applied Social Psychology*, **12**: 1–14.

87 Ussher, J.M. (2006) *Managing the monstrous feminine: Regulating the reproductive body*. London: Routledge.

88 Ussher, J.M. (2003) The ongoing silencing of women in families: An analysis and rethinking of premenstrual syndrome and therapy. *Journal of Family Therapy*, **25**: 388–405.

89 Ussher, J.M. (2004) Premenstrual syndrome and self-policing: Ruptures in self-silencing leading to increased self-surveillance and blaming of the body. *Social Theory and Health*, **2**(3): 254–272.

90 Ussher, J.M., J. Perz and J. Mooney-Somers (2007) The experience and positioning of affect in the context of intersubjectivity: The case of premenstrual syndrome. *Journal of Critical Psychology*, **21**: 145–165.

91 Ussher, J.M. (2008) Challenging the positioning of premenstrual change as PMS: The impact of a psychological intervention on women's self-policing. *Qualitative Research in Psychology*, **5**(1): 33–44.

92 Ussher, J.M. and J. Perz (2008) Empathy, egalitarianism and emotion work in the relational negotiation of PMS: The experience of lesbian couples. *Feminism and Psychology*, **18**(1): 87–111.

93 Ussher, J.M. (2004) Postnatal depression: A critical feminist perspective, in M. Stewart (ed.) *Pregnancy, birth and maternity care: Feminist perspectives*. London: Books for Midwives.

94 Whiffen, V.E. (1992) Is postpartum depression a distinct diagnosis? *Clinical Psychology Review*, **12**(5): 485–508.

95 Williamson, G.L. (1993) Postpartum depression syndrome as a defence to criminal behaviour. *Journal of Family Violence*, **8**(2): 151–165.

96 Albright, A. (1993) Postpartum depression: An overview. *Journal of Counseling and Development*, **71**(3): 316–320.

97 Nazroo, J.Y., A.C. Edwards and G.W. Brown (1998) Gender differences in the prevalence of depression: Artefact, alternative disorders, biology or roles? *Sociology of Health and Illness*, **20**(3): 312–330.

98 Gotlib, I.H., V.E. Whiffen, J.H. Mount et al. (1989) Prevalence rates and demographic characteristics associated with depression in pregnancy and the postpartum. *Journal of Consulting and Clinical Psychology*, **57**(2): 269–274.

99 Bell, A.J., N.M. Land, S. Milne and F. Hassanyeh (1994) Long-term outcome of post-partum psychiatric illness requiring admission. *Journal of Affective Disorders*, **31**(1): 67–70.

100 O'Hara, M.W. and A.M. Swain (1996) Rates and risk of post-partum depression: A meta-analysis. *International Review of Psychiatry*, **8**: 37–54.

101 Swendsen, J.D. and C.M. Mazure (2000) Life stress as a risk factor for postpartum depression: Current research and methodological issues. *Clinical Psychology: Science and Practice*, **7**: 17–31.

102 Boyce, P. and A. Hickey (2005) Psychosocial risk factors to major depression after childbirth. *Social Psychiatry and Psychiatric Epidemiology*, **40**: 605–612.

103 Boyce, P., I. Hickie and G. Parker (1991) Parents, partners or personality? Risk factors for post-natal depression. *Journal of Affective Disorders*, **21**(4): 245–255.

104 Mauthner, N. (1998) 'It's a woman's cry for help': A relational perspective on post-natal depression. *Feminism and Psychology*, **8**(3): 325–355.

105 Mauthner, N. (2010) 'I wasn't being true to myself': Women's narratives of postpartum depression, in D.C. Jack and A. Ali (eds) *The depression epidemic: International perspectives on women's self-silencing and psychological distress.* Oxford: Oxford University Press, pp. 459–484.

106 Mauthner, N. (2000) Feeling low and feeling really bad about feeling low: Women's experience of motherhood and post-partum depression. *Canadian Psychology*, **40**(2): 143–161.

107 Harwood, K., N. McLean and K. Durkin (2007) First time mothers' expectations of parenthood: What happens when optimistic expectations are not matched by later experiences? *Developmental Psychology*, **43**(1): 1–12.

108 Miller, L.J. (2002) Postpartum depression. *Journal of the American Medical Association*, **287**: 762–765.

109 Patel, V., M. Rodrigues and N. DeSouza (2002) Gender, poverty, and postnatal depression: A study of mothers in Goa, India. *American Journal of Psychiatry*, **159**(1): 43–47.

110 Hollway, W. (2006) *The capacity to care: Gender and ethical subjectivity.* London: Routledge.

111 Deeks, A.A. (2003) Psychological aspects of menopause management. *Best Practice and Research in Clinical Endocrinology and Metabolism*, **17**(1): 17–31.

112 Yonkers, K.A., K.D. Bradshaw and U. Halbriech (2000) Oestrogens, progestins and mood, in M. Steiner, K.A. Yonkers and E. Eriksson (eds) *Mood disorders in women.* London: Martin Dunitz, pp. 207–232.

113 Avis, N.E., D. Brambilla, S.M. McKinlay and K. Vass (1994) A longitudinal analysis of the association between menopause and depression: Results from the Massachusetts women's health study. *Annals of Epidemiology*, **4**(3): 214–220.

114 Dennerstein, L. (1996) Well-being, symptoms and the menopausal transition. *Maturitas*, **23**: 147–157.

115 Perz, J. and J.M. Ussher (2008) The horror of this living decay: Women's negotiation and resistance of medical discourses around menopause and midlife. *Women's Studies International Forum*, **31**: 293–299.

116 McQuaide, S. (1998) Women at midlife. *Social Work*, **43**(1): 21–31.

117 Kaufert, P.A., P. Gilbert and R. Tate (1992) The Manitoba project: A re-examination of the link between menopause and depression. *Maturitas*, **14**: 143–155.

118 Earle, J.R., M.H. Smith, C.T. Harris and C.F. Longino, Jr (1998) Women, marital status, and symptoms of depression in a midlife national sample. *Journal of Women and Aging*, **10**(1): 41–57.

119 Robinson Kurpius, S.E., M. Foley Nicpon and S.E. Maresh (2001) Mood, marriage, and menopause. *Journal of Counseling Psychology*, **48**(1): 77–84.

120 Avis, N.E, P.A. Kaufert, M. Lock et al. (1993) The evolution of menopause symptoms. *International Practice and Research*, **7**(1): 17–32.

121 Maccaro, J. (2007) *Fabulous at 50*. Lake Mary, FL: Siloam.

122 Wilson, R. (1966) *Feminine forever*. New York: M. Evans.

123 Beck, A.T. (1987) Cognitive models of depression. *Journal of Cognitive Psychotherapy: An International Quarterly*, **1**: 5–37.

124 Bowlby, J. (1969) *Attachment and loss. Volume 1: Attachment*. New York: Basic Books.

125 Stolorow, R.D. and G.E. Atwood (1992) *Contexts of being: The intersubjective foundations of psychological life*. Hillsdale, NJ: Analytic Press.

126 Mitchell, S.A. (2000) *Relationality: From attachment to intersubjectivity*. Hillsdale, NJ: Analytic Press.

127 Bryant Waugh, R. (2000) Developmental-systemic-feminist therapy, in K.J. Miller and J.S. Mizes (eds) *Comparative treatments for eating disorders*. New York: Springer, pp. 160–181.

128 Jones, E. and E. Asen (2000) *Systemic couple therapy and depression*. New York: Karnac.

129 Becvar, D.S. and R.J. Becvar (2009) *Family therapy: A systemic integration*. Boston, MA: Allyn and Bacon/Pearson.

130 Miller, S.M. and N. Kirsch (1987) Sex differences in cognitive coping with stress, in R.C. Barnett, L. Biener and G.K. Baruch (eds) *Gender and stress*. New York: Free Press, pp. 278–307.

131 Nolen-Hoeksema, S. and J.S. Girgus (1994) The emergence of gender differences in depression during adolescence. *Psychological Bulletin*, **115**: 424–443.

132 Nolen-Hoeksema, S., J. Larson and C. Grayson (1999) Explaining the gender difference in depressive symptoms. *Journal of Personality and Social Psychology*, **77**(5): 1061–1072.

133 Jose, P.E. and I. Brown (2008) When does gender difference in rumination begin? Gender and age differences in the use of rumination by adolescents. *Journal of Youth and Adolescence*, **37**: 180–192.

134 Tamres, L.K., D. Janicki and V.S. Helgeson (2002) Sex differences in coping behavior: A meta-analytic review and an examination of relative coping. *Personality and Social Psychology Review*, **6**(1): 2–30.

135 Leach, L.S., H. Christensen, A.J. Mackinnon et al. (2008) Gender differences in depression and anxiety across the adult lifespan: The role of psychosocial mediators. *Social Psychiatry and Psychiatric Epidemiology*, **43**: 983–998.

136 Hankin, B.J. and L.Y. Abramson (2001) Development of gender differences in depression: An elaborated cognitive vulnerability-transactional stress theory. *Psychological Bulletin*, **127**(6): 773–796.

137 Abramson, L.Y., G.I. Metalsky and L.B. Alloy (1989) Hopelessness depression: A theory based sub-type of depression. *Psychological Review*, **96**: 358–372.

138 Goodwin, R.D. and I.H. Gotlib (2004) Gender differences in depression: The role of personality factors. *Psychiatry Research*, **126**: 135–142.

139 Pomerantz, E.M. and D.N. Ruble (1998) The role of maternal control in the development of sex differences in child-self-evaluative factors. *Child Development*, **69**: 458–478.

140 Nolen-Hoeksema, S. and B. Jackson (2001) Mediators of the gender difference in rumination. *Psychology of Women Quarterly*, **25**: 37–47.

141 Mazure, C.M., M.L. Bruce, P.K. Maciejewski and S.C. Jacobs (2000) Adverse life events and cognitive-personality characteristics in the prediction of major

depression and antidepressant response. *American Journal of Psychiatry*, **157**(6): 896–903.

142 Whitley, B.E. (1985) Sex role orientation and psychological well-being: Two meta-analyses. *Sex Roles*, **12**: 207–225.

143 Coyne, J.C. and V.E. Whiffen (1995) Issues in personality diatheses for depression: The case of sociotropy-dependency and autonomy-self-criticism. *Psychological Bulletin*, **111**: 358–378.

144 Fengold, A. (1994) Gender differences in personality: A meta-analysis. *Psychological Bulletin*, **116**: 429–456.

145 Cooper, M.L., P.R. Shaver and N.L. Collins (1998) Attachment styles, emotion regulation and adjustment in adolescence. *Journal of Personality and Social Psychology*, **74**: 1380–1397.

146 Jack, D.C. (1991) *Silencing the self: Women and depression*. Cambridge, MA: Harvard University Press.

147 Jack, D.C. and A. Ali (2010) Introduction: Culture, self-silencing, and depression – A contextual-relational perspective, in D.C. Jack and A. Ali (eds) *The depression epidemic: International perspectives on women's self-silencing and psychological distress*. Oxford: Oxford University Press, pp. 3–17.

148 Duarte, L.M. and J.M. Thompson (1999) Sex differences in self-silencing. *Psychological Reports*, **85**: 145–161.

149 Thompson, J.M. (1995) Silencing the self: Depressive symptomatology in close relationships. *Psychology of Women Quarterly*, **19**: 337–353.

150 Jack, D.C. and D. Dill (1992) The silencing the self scale: Schemas of intimacy with depression in women. *Psychology of Women Quarterly*, **16**: 97–106.

151 Whiffen, V.E., M.L. Foot and J.M. Thompson (2007) Self-silencing mediates the link between marital conflict and depression. *Journal of Social and Personal Relationships*, **24**(6): 993–1006.

152 Frank, J.B. and C. Thomas (2003) Externalized self-perceptions, self-silencing and the prediction of eating pathology. *Canadian Journal of Behavioural Science*, **35**(3): 219–228.

153 Ussher, J.M. and J. Perz (2010) Disruption of the silenced-self: The case of premenstrual syndrome, in D.C. Jack and A. Ali (eds) *The depression epidemic: International perspectives on women's self-silencing and psychological distress*. Oxford: Oxford University Press, pp. 435–458.

154 Perz, J. and J.M. Ussher (2006) Women's experience of premenstrual change: A case of silencing the self. *Journal of Reproductive and Infant Psychology*, **24**(4): 289–303.

155 Eaker, E.D. and M. Kelly-Hayes (2010) Self-silencing and the risk of heart disease and death in women: The Framingham offspring study, in D.C. Jack and A. Ali (eds) *The depression epidemic: International perspectives on women's self-silencing and psychological distress*. Oxford: Oxford University Press, pp. 399–414.

156 Carr, J.G., F.D. Gilroy and M.F. Sherman (1996) Silencing the self and depression among women. *Psychology of Women Quarterly*, **20**: 375–392.

157 Jack, D.C. (1987) Silencing the self: The power of social imperatives in women's depression, in R. Formanek and A. Gurian (eds) *Women and depression: A lifespan perspective*. New York: Springer, pp. 161–181.

158 Jack, D.C. (1999) Silencing the self: Inner dialogues and outer realities, in T.E.

Joiner and J.C. Coyne (eds) *The interactional nature of depression: Advances in interpersonal approaches.* Washington, DC: American Psychological Association, pp. 221–246.

159 Freud, S. (1933) *New introductory lectures in psychoanalysis: Standard edition.* New York: Norton.

160 Miller, J.B. (1986) *Towards a new psychology of women.* New York: Beacon.

161 Jordan, J.V., A.G. Kaplan, J.B. Miller et al. (1991) *Women's growth in connection: Writings from the Stone Center.* New York: Guilford.

162 Jordan, J.V. and L.M. Hartling (2002) New developments in relational-cultural theory, in M.B. Ballou and L.S. Brown (eds) *Rethinking mental health and disorder: Feminist perspectives.* New York: Guilford, pp. 48–70.

163 Chodorow, N. (1978) *The reproduction of mothering: Psychoanalysis and the sociology of gender.* Berkeley, CA: University of California Press.

164 Kaplan, A. (1986) The 'self-in-relation': Implications for depression in women. *Psychotherapy*, **23**: 234–242.

165 Marecek, J. (2006) Social suffering, gender, and women's depression, in C.L. Keyes and S.H. Goodman (eds) *Women and depression: A handbook for the social, behavioral and biomedical sciences.* Cambridge: Cambridge University Press, pp. 283–308.

166 Gilligan, C. (1982) *In a different voice: Psychological theory and women's development.* Cambridge, MA: Harvard University Press.

167 Chodorow, N. (2004) Beyond sexual difference: Clinical individuality and same-sex cross generation relations in the creation of feminine and masculine, in I. Mattis (ed.) *Dialogues on sexuality, gender and psychoanalysis.* London: Karnac, pp. 181–204.

168 Surrey, J. (1991) The self-in-relation: A theory of women's development, in J.V. Jordan, A.G. Kaplan, J.B. Miller, I.P. Stiver and J.L. Surrey, *Women's growth in connection: Writings from the Stone Center.* New York: Guilford, pp. 51–66.

169 Jack, D.C. (2001) Understanding women's anger: A description of relational patterns. *Health Care for Women International*, **22**: 385–400.

170 Kostanski, M. and E. Gullone (1998) Adolescent body image dissatisfaction: relationships with self-esteem, anxiety, and depression controlling for body mass. *Journal of Child Psychology and Psychiatry*, **39**: 255–262.

171 Stattin, H. and D. Magnusson (1990) *Paths through adult life: Pubertal maturation and female development.* Hillsdale, NJ: Lawrence Erlbaum Associates.

172 Bordo, S. (1993) *Unbearable weight: Feminism, culture and the body.* Berkeley, CA: University of California Press.

173 Harris, D.L. and A.T. Carr (2001) Prevalence of concern about physical appearance in the general population. *British Journal of Plastic Surgery*, **54**(3): 223–226.

174 Neighbors, L.A. and J. Sobal (2007) Prevalence and magnitude of body weight and shape dissatisfaction among university students. *Eating Behaviors*, **8**: 429–439.

175 Swami, V., D.A. Frederick, T. Aavik et al. (2010) The attractive female body weight and female body dissatisfaction in 26 countries across 10 world regions: Results of the International Body Project I. *Personality and Social Psychology Bulletin*, **36**(3): 309–325.

176 Schick, V.R., S.K. Calabrese, B.N. Rima and A.N. Zucker (2010) Genital

appearance dissatisfaction: Implications for women's genital image self-consciousness, sexual esteem, sexual satisfaction and sexual risk. *Psychology of Women Quarterly*, **34**: 394–404.

177 Braun, V. and L. Tiefer (2010) The 'designer vagina' and the pathologisation of female genital diversity: Interventions for change. *Radical Psychology*, **8** www.radicalpsychology.org/vol8-1/brauntiefer.html

178 Tiefer, L. (2008) Female genital cosmetic surgery: Freakish or inevitable? Analysis from medical marketing, bioethics, and feminist theory. *Feminism and Psychology*, **18**: 466–479.

179 Elliot, A. (2008) *Making the cut: How cosmetic surgery is transforming our lives.* London: Reaktion.

180 Elliot, A. (2003) *Better than well: American medicine meets the American dream.* New York: Norton.

181 Davis, K. (1995) *Reshaping the female body: The dilemma of cosmetic surgery.* New York: Routledge.

182 Hayward, C., I.H. Gotlib, P.K. Schraedley and I.F. Litt (1999) Ethnic differences in the association between pubertal status and symptoms of depression in adolescent girls. *Journal of Adolescent Health*, **25**: 143–149.

183 Nichter, M. (2000) *Fat talk: What girls and their parents say about dieting.* Cambridge, MA: Harvard University Press.

184 Grabe, S., L.M. Ward and J.S. Hyde (2008) The role of the media in body image concerns among women: A meta-analysis of experimental and correlational studies. *Psychological Bulletin*, **134**(3): 460–476.

185 Stoppard, J.M. (1999) Why new perspectives are needed for understanding depression in women. *Canadian Psychology*, **40**(2): 79–90.

186 Stoppard, J.M. (2010) Moving towards an understanding of women's depression. *Feminism and Psychology*, **20**(2): 267–271.

187 Taylor, S.E. (2006) Tend and befriend: Biobehavioral bases of affiliation under stress. *Current Directions in Psychological Science*, **15**: 273–277.

188 Becker, D. (2010) Women's work and the societal discourse of stress. *Feminism and Psychology*, **20**(1): 36–52.

189 Contratto, S. (2002) A feminist critique of attachment theory and evolutionary psychology, in M.B. Ballou and L.S. Brown (eds) *Rethinking mental health and disorder: Feminist perspectives*. New York: Guilford, pp. 32–47.

190 Gilligan, C. (2010) Introduction, in D.C. Jack and A. Ali (eds) *The depression epidemic: International perspectives on women's self-silencing and psychological distress*. Oxford: Oxford University Press, pp.ix–xvi.

191 Cowan, G., M. Bommersbach and S. Curtis (1995) Codependency, loss of self and power. *Psychology of Women Quarterly*, **19**: 221–236.

192 Remen, A.L., D.L. Chambless and T.L. Rodebaugh (2002) Gender differences in the construct validity of the silencing the self scale. *Psychology of Women Quarterly*, **26**: 151–159.

193 Ussher, J.M. and J. Perz (2010) Gender differences in self-silencing and psychological distress in informal cancer carers. *Psychology of Women Quarterly*, **34**(2): 228–242.

194 World Health Organization (1998) *The World Health Report: Executive summary*. Geneva: WHO.

195 United Nations Development Program (1997) *Human Development Report.* New York: Oxford University Press.

196 World Health Organization (2000) *Women's mental health: An evidence based review.* Geneva: WHO.

197 Barko, N. (2000) The other gender gap. *The American Prospect*, June 19–July 3: 61–63.

198 Desjarlais, R., L. Eisenberg, B. Good and A. Kleinman (1996) *World mental health: Problems and priorities in low income countries.* Oxford: Oxford University Press.

199 Patel, V., R. Araya, M. de Lima et al. (1999) Women, poverty and common mental disorders in four restructuring societies. *Social Science and Medicine*, **49**(11): 1461–1471.

200 Patel, V., C. Todd, M. Winston et al. (1998) Outcome of common mental disorders in Harare, Zimbabwe. *British Journal of Psychiatry*, **172**(1): 53–57.

201 Chen, Y.Y., S.V. Subramanian, D. Acevedo-Garcia and I. Kawachi (2005) Women's status and depressive symptoms: A multilevel analysis. *Social Science and Medicine*, **60**: 49–60.

202 Pezzini, S. (2005) The effect of women's rights on women's welfare: Evidence from a natural experiment. *Economic Journal*, **115**: C208–C227.

203 Kawachi, I., B.P. Kennedy, V. Gupta and D. Prothrow-Smith (1999) Women's status and the health of women and men: A view from the States. *Social Science and Medicine*, **48**: 21–32.

204 Frasure-Smith, N. and F. Lesperance (2005) Reflections on depression as a cardiac risk factor. *Psychosomatic Medicine*, **67**: S19–S25.

205 Molnar, B.E., S.L. Buka and R.C. Kessler (2001) Child sexual abuse and subsequent pathology: Results from the National Comorbidity Survey. *American Journal of Public Health*, **91**(5): 753–760.

206 Cortina, L.M. and S.P. Kubiak (2006) Gender and post-traumatic stress: Sexual violence as an explanation for women's increased risk. *Journal of Abnormal Psychology*, **115**(4): 753–759.

207 Kendler, K.S., C.M. Bulik, J. Silberg, J.M. Hettema et al. (2000) Childhood sexual abuse and adult psychiatric and substance use disorders in women. *Archives of General Psychiatry*, **57**: 953–959.

208 Kendall-Tackett, K.A. (2007) Inflammation, cardiovascular disease, and metabolic syndrome as sequelae of violence against women: The role of depression, hostility and sleep disturbance. *Trauma, Violence and Abuse*, **8**(2): 117–126.

209 Koss, M.P., Bailey, J.A., Yuan, N.P., Herrera, V.A. and Lichter, E.L. (2003) Depression and PTSD in survivors of male violence: Research and training initiatives to facilitate recovery. *Psychology of Women Quarterly*, **27**: 130–142.

210 Cutler, S.E. and S. Nolen-Hoeksema (1991) Accounting for sex differences in depression through female victimisation: Childhood sexual abuse. *Sex Roles*, **24**: 425–438.

211 Klonoff, E.A., H. Landrine and R. Campbell (2000) Sexist discrimination may account for well-known gender differences in psychiatric symptoms. *Psychology of Women Quarterly*, **24**: 93–99.

212 Dambrun, M. (2007) Gender differences in mental health: The mediating role

of perceived personal discrimination. *Journal of Applied Social Psychology*, **37**(5): 1118–1129.

213 Belle, D. and J. Doucet (2003) Poverty, inequality, and discrimination as sources of depression among US women. *Psychology of Women Quarterly*, **27**: 101–113.

214 Landrine, H., E.A. Klonoff, J. Gibbs et al. (1995) Physical and psychiatric correlates of gender discrimination. *Psychology of Women Quarterly*, **19**: 473–492.

215 Meyer, I.H. (2003) Prejudice, social stress, and mental health in lesbian, gay, and bisexual populations: Conceptual issues and research evidence. *Psychological Bulletin*, **129**: 674–697.

216 Herek, G.M. and L.D. Garnets (2007) Sexual orientation and mental health. *Annual Review of Clinical Psychology*, **3**: 353–375.

217 Gilman, S.E., D. Cochran, V.M. Mays et al. (2001) Risk of psychiatric disorders among individuals reporting same-sex sexual partners in the National Comorbidity Survey. *American Journal of Public Health*, **91**: 933–939.

218 Landrine, H. and E.A. Klonoff (1996) The schedule of racist events: A measure of racial discrimination and a study of its negative physical and mental health consequences. *Journal of Black Psychology*, **22**(2): 144–168.

219 Blanchflower, D. and A. Oswald (2004) Well-being over time in Britain and the USA. *Journal of Public Economics*, **88**(7–8): 1359–1386.

220 Taylor, J., D. Henderson and B.B. Jackson (1991) A holistic model for under-standing and predicting depressive symptoms in African American women. *Journal of Community Psychology*, **19**: 306–321.

221 Lester, D. and A. DeSimone (1995) Depression and suicidal ideation in African American and Caucasian students. *Psychological Reports*, **77**(1): 18–20.

222 Munford, M.B. (1994) Relationship of gender, self-esteem, social class, and racial identity to depression in blacks. *Journal of Black Psychology*, **20**: 157–174.

223 Jackson-Triche, M.E., J. Greer Sullivan, K.B. Wells et al. (2000) Depression and health-related quality of life in ethnic minorities seeking care in general medical settings. *Journal of Affective Disorders*, **58**: 89–97.

224 Alegría, M., G. Canino, P.E. Shrout et al. (2008) Prevalence of mental illness in immigrant and non-immigrant US Latino groups. *American Journal of Psychiatry*, **165**(3): 359–369.

225 Stevenson, B. and J. Wolfers (2009) The paradox of declining female happiness. *American Economic Journal: Economic Policy*, **1**(2): 190–225.

226 Brown, C., J. Abe-Kim and C. Barrio (2003) Depression in ethnically diverse women: Implications for treatment in primary care settings. *Professional Psychology: Research and Practice*, **34**(1): 10–19.

227 Ali, A. (2010) Exploring the immigrant experience through self-silencing theory and the full-frame approach: The case of Caribbean immigrant women in Canada and the United States, in D.C. Jack and A. Ali (eds) *The depression epidemic: International perspectives on women's self-silencing and psychological distress*. Oxford: Oxford University Press, pp. 227–240.

228 Takeuchi, D.T., R.C. Chung, K.M. Lin et al. (1998) Lifetime and twelve-month prevalence rates of major depressive episodes and dysthymia among Chinese

Americans in Los Angeles. *American Journal of Psychiatry*, **155**(10): 1407–1414.

229 Nazroo, J.Y. (1997) *Ethnicity and mental health*. London: Policy Studies Institute.

230 Shorter, E. (1992) *From paralysis to fatigue*. New York: Free Press.

231 Hussain, F. and R. Cochrane (2004) Depression in South Asian women living in the UK: A review of the literature with implications for service provision. *Transcultural Psychiatry*, **41**(2): 253–270.

232 Marshall, H. and A. Yazdani (2000) Young Asian women and self-harm, in J. Ussher (ed.) *Women's health: Contemporary international perspectives*. Leicester: British Psychological Society, pp. 60–69.

233 Davis, K. (2008) Intersectionality as buzzword: A sociology of science perspective on what makes a feminist theory successful. *Feminist Theory*, **9**(1): 67–85.

234 Hankivsky, O. and R. Cormier (2009) *Intersectionality: Moving women's health research and policy forward*. Vancouver, BC: Women's Health Research Network, www.whrn.ca/intersectionality-download.php.

235 Woolf, V. (1957) *A room of one's own*. New York: Harcourt, Brace and World.

236 Batty, Z. (2006) *Masculinity and depression: Men's subjective experience of depression, coping and preferences for therapy and gender role conflict*. Thesis, School of Psychology, University of Western Sydney.

237 O'Neil, J.M., B.J. Helms, R.K. Gable et al. (1986) Gender Role Conflict Scale: College men's fear of femininity. *Sex Roles*, **14**: 335–350.

238 O'Neil, J.M. (1990) Assessing men's gender role conflict, in D. Moore and F. Leafgren (eds) *Men in conflict: Problem solving strategies and interventions*. Alexandria, VA: American Counselling Association.

239 Cormoyer, R.J. and J.R. Mahalik (1995) Cross-sectional study of gender role conflict examining college-aged and middle aged men. *Journal of Counseling Psychology*, **42**: 11–19.

240 Good, G.E., D.M. Dell and L.B. Mintz (1989) Male role and male gender role conflict: Relations to help seeking in men. *Journal of Counseling Psychology*, **36**: 295–300.

241 Eckersley, R. and K. Dear (2002) Cultural correlates of youth suicide. *Social Science and Medicine*, **55**(11): 1891–1904.

242 Wilson, R. and E. Cairns (1988) Sex role attributes, perceived competence and the development of depression in adolescence. *Journal of Child Psychology and Psychiatry*, **29**: 635–650.

243 Eagley, A.H., M.G. Makhijani and B.G. Klonsky (1992) Gender and the evaluation of leaders: A meta-analysis. *Psychological Bulletin*, **111**: 3–22.

244 Brown, G.W. and T.O. Harris (eds) (1989) *Life events and illness*. New York: Guilford.

245 Bifulco, A., G.W. Brown, P. Moran et al. (1998) Predicting depression in women: The role of past and present vulnerability. *Psychological Medicine*, **28**: 39–50.

246 Turner, R.J. and D.A. Lloyd (1995) Lifetime traumas and mental health: The significance of cumulative adversity. *Journal of Health and Social Behaviour*, **36**(4): 360–376.

247 Gore, S., R.H. Aseltine and M.E. Colton (1992) Social structure, life stress and

depressive symptoms in a high school aged population. *Journal of Health and Social Behaviour*, **33**: 97–113.

248 Kessler, R.C. and J.D. McLeod (1984) Sex differences in vulnerability to undesirable life events. *American Sociological Review*, **49**: 620–631.

249 Belle, D. (1990) Poverty and women's mental health. *American Psychologist*, **45**: 385–389.

250 Maciejewski, P.K., H.G. Prigerson and C.M. Mazure (2001) Sex differences in event-related risk for major depression. *Psychological Medicine*, **31**(4): 593–604.

251 Brown, G.W. and T. Harris (1978) *Social origins of depression: A study of psychiatric disorders in women*. London: Tavistock.

252 Dalgard, O.S., C. Dowrick, V. Lehtinen et al. (2006) Negative life events, social support and gender difference in depression. *Social Psychiatry and Psychiatric Epidemiology*, **41**: 444–451.

253 Kessler, R.C., J.D. McLeod and E. Wethington (1985) The costs of caring: A perspective on the relationship between sex and psychological distress, in I.G. Sarason and B. Sarason (eds) *Social support: Theory, research and applications*. Boston, MA: Martinus Nijhoff, pp. 491–506.

254 Kendler, K.S., L.M. Thornton and C.A. Prescott (2001) Gender differences in the rates of exposure to stressful life events and sensitivity to their depressogenic effects. *American Journal of Psychiatry*, **158**(4): 587–593.

255 Turner, R.J. and W.R. Avison (1989) Gender and depression: Assessing exposure and vulnerability to life events in a chronically strained population. *Journal of Nervous and Mental Disease*, **177**(8): 443–445.

256 Willitts, M., Benzeval, M. and Stansfeld, S. (2004) Partnership history and mental health over time. *Journal of Epidemiology and Community Health*, **58**: 53–58.

257 Kiecolt-Glaser, J.K. and T.L. Newtown (2001) Marriage and health: His and hers. *Psychological Bulletin*, **127**: 472–503.

258 Bebbington, P., J. Hurry, C. Tennant et al. (1981) The epidemiology of mental disorders in Camberwell. *Psychological Medicine*, **11**: 561–579.

259 Sachs-Ericsson, N. and J.A. Ciarlo (2000) Gender, social roles and mental health: An epidemiological perspective. *Sex Roles*, **43**(9–10): 605–628.

260 Bebbington, P., T. Brugha, B. MacCarthy et al. (1988) The Camberwell Collaborative Depression Study, I. Depressed probands: Adversity and the form of depression. *British Journal of Psychiatry*, **152**: 754–765.

261 World Health Organization (1995) The World Health Organization Quality of Life assessment (WHOQOL) position paper. *Social Science and Medicine*, **41**: 1403–1409.

262 Brown, G.W., T.O. Harris and C. Hepworth (1995) Loss, humiliation and entrapment among women developing depression: A patient and non-patient comparison. *Psychological Medicine*, **25**: 7–21.

263 Nicolson, P. (1998) *Post-natal depression: Psychology, science and the transition to motherhood*. London: Routledge.

264 Whisman, M.A. and M.L. Bruce (1999) Marital distress and incidence of major depressive episode in a community sample. *Journal of Abnormal Psychology*, **108**: 674–678.

265 Byrne, M., A. Carr and M. Clark (2004) Power in relationships of women with depression. *Journal of Family Therapy*, **26**: 407–429.

266 Doyle, L. (1995) *What makes women sick? Gender and the political economy of health*. New Brunswick, NJ: Rutgers University Press.

267 Brown, G.W., B. Andrews, T. Harris et al. (1986) Social support, self-esteem and depression. *Psychological Medicine*, **16**(4): 813–831.

268 Byrne, M. and A. Carr (2000) Depression and power in marriage. *Journal of Family Therapy*, **22**: 408–427.

269 Price, J.S. (1991) Change or homeostasis? A systems theory approach to depression. *British Journal of Medical Psychology*, **64**: 331–344.

270 Bateson, G., D.D. Jackson, J. Haley and J. Weakland (1956) Toward a theory of schizophrenia. *Behavioral Science*, **1**: 251–264.

271 Lidz, T. and S. Fleck (1985) *Schizophrenia and the family*, 2nd edn. New York: International Universities Press.

272 Wirth-Cauchon, J. (2001) *Women and borderline personality disorder: Symptoms and stories*. New Brunswick, NJ: Rutgers University Press.

273 Penney, D. and P. Woodward (2005) Family perspectives on borderline personality disorder, in J.G. Gunderson and P.D. Hoffman (eds) *Understanding and treating borderline personality disorder: A guide for professionals and families*. Arlington VA: American Psychiatric Publishing, pp. 117–130.

274 Ballash, N.G., M.K. Pemble, W.M. Usui et al. (2006) Family functioning, perceived control, and anxiety: A mediational model. *Journal of Anxiety Disorders*, **20**(4): 486–497.

275 Cole-Detke, H. and R. Kobak (1996) Attachment processes in eating disorder and depression. *Journal of Consulting and Clinical Psychology*, **64**(2): 282–290.

276 McKinley, N.M. and L.A. Randa (2005) Adult attachment and body satisfaction: An exploration of general and specific relationship differences. *Body Image*, **2**(3): 209–218.

277 Ward, A., R. Ramsay and J. Treasure (2000) Attachment research in eating disorders. *British Journal of Medical Psychology*, **73**(1): 35–51.

278 Bebbington, P., C. Dean, G. Der et al. (1991) Gender, parity and the prevalence of minor affective disorder. *British Journal of Psychiatry*, **158**: 40–45.

279 Goldberg, A.E. and M. Perry-Jenkins (2004) Division of labor and working-class women's well-being across the transition to parenthood. *Journal of Family Psychology*, **18**(1): 225–236.

280 Meltzer, H., B. Gill, M. Petticrew and K. Hinds (1995) *The prevalence of psychiatric morbidity among adults living in private households*, Report 1. *OPCS surveys of psychiatric morbidity in Great Britain*. London: HMSO.

281 Arrindell, W.A., A. Steptoe and J. Wardle (2003) Higher levels of state depression in masculine than in feminine nations. *Behaviour Research and Therapy*, **41**: 809–817.

282 Gavey, N. (2005) *Just sex? The cultural scaffolding of rape*. London: Routledge.

283 Vine, S. and T. Kindersley (2009) *Backwards in high heels: The impossible art of being female*. London: Fourth Estate.

284 Sirianni, C. and C. Negrey (2000) Working time as gendered time. *Feminist Economics*, **6**(1): 59–76.

285 Western, M.C., J.H. Baxter, J. Pakulski et al. (2007) Neoliberalism, inequality and politics: The changing face of Australia. *Australian Journal of Social Issues*, **42**(3): 401–418.

286 Gray, J. (2008) *Why Mars and Venus collide: Improving relationships by*

understanding how men and women cope differently with stress. New York: HarperCollins.

287 Gove, W. (1972) Sex, marital status, and mental illness. *Social Forces*, **51**: 34–55.

288 Gove, W. and J. Tudor (1973) Adult sex roles and mental illness. *American Journal of Sociology*, **78**: 812–835.

289 Brown, G.W. and T.O. Harris (1989) Depression, in G.W. Brown and T.O. Harris (eds) *Life events and illness.* New York: Guilford, pp. 49–93.

290 Pilgrim, D. and R.P. Bentall (1999) The medicalisation of misery: A critical realist analysis of the concept of depression. *Journal of Mental Health*, **8**(3): 261–274.

291 Engel, G. (1977) The need for a new medical model: A challenge for biomedicine. *Science*, **196**: 129–136.

292 Mischel, W. (1973) Toward a cognitive social learning theory of depression. *Psychological Review*, **80**: 252–283.

293 Kessler, R.C. (2003) Epidemiology of women and depression. *Journal of Affective Disorders*, **74**: 5–13.

294 Cosgrove, L. (2000) Crying out loud: Understanding women's emotional distress as both lived experience and social construction. *Feminism and Psychology*, **10**(2): 247–267.

295 Keat, R. (1979) Positivism and statistics in social science, in J. Irvine, I. Miles and J. Evans (eds) *Demystifying social statistics.* London: Routledge.

296 Harré, R. and P.F. Secord (1972) *The explanation of social behaviour.* Oxford: Basil Blackwell.

297 Ingleby, D. (ed.) (1982) *Critical psychiatry: The politics of mental health.* Harmondsworth: Penguin.

298 Henriques, J., W. Hollway, C. Urwin et al. (1998) *Changing the subject: Psychology, social regulation and subjectivity*, 2nd edn. London: Routledge.

299 Hollway, W. (1989) *Subjectivity and method in psychology: Gender, meaning and science.* London: Sage.

300 Ussher, J.M. (1996) Premenstrual syndrome: Reconciling disciplinary divides through the adoption of a material-discursive epistemological standpoint. *Annual Review of Sex Research*, **7**: 218–251.

301 Shotter, K. and K.J. Gergen (eds) (1989) *Texts of identity.* London: Sage.

302 Lerman, H. (2005) Women's misery: Continuing pigeonholes into the twenty-first century, in R. Menzies, D.E. Chunn and W. Chan (eds) *Women, madness and the law: A feminist reader.* London: Glasshouse, pp. 99–114.

303 Keller, E.F. (1985) *Reflections on gender and science.* New Haven, CT: Yale University Press.

304 Smith, D. (1990) *The conceptual practice of power: A feminist sociology of knowledge.* Boston, MA: Northeastern University Press.

305 Marecek, J. (2002) Unfinished business: Postmodern feminism in personality psychology, in M.B. Ballou and L.S. Brown (eds) *Rethinking mental health and disorder: Feminist perspectives.* New York: Guilford, pp. 3–28.

306 Fausto-Sterling, A. (2000) *Sexing the body: Gender politics and the construction of sexuality.* New York: Basic Books.

307 Butler, J.P. (1990) *Gender trouble: Feminism and the subversion of identity.* New York: Routledge.

308 Ussher, J.M. (1997) *Fantasies of femininity: Reframing the boundaries of sex.* London/New York: Penguin/Rutgers.

309 Metcalfe, W.R. and P.J. Caplan (2004) Seeking 'normal' sexuality on a complex matrix, in P.J. Caplan and L. Cosgrove (eds) *Bias in psychiatric diagnosis.* Lanham, MD: Jason Aronson, pp. 121–126.

310 Rose, N.S. (1996) *Inventing our selves: Psychology, power, and personhood.* New York: Cambridge University Press.

311 Shive, B.M. (2008) Cello speak: Exploring new language for madness, in S. Chapadjiev (ed.) *Live through this: On creativity and self-destruction.* New York: Seven Stories Press, pp. 175–186.

312 Littlewood, R. and M. Lipsedge (1982) *Aliens and alienists: Ethnic minorities and psychiatry.* Harmondsworth: Penguin.

313 Ussher, J.M. (1991) *Women's madness: Misogyny or mental illness?* Amherst, MA: University of Massachusetts Press.

314 Kirk, S. and H. Kutchins (1992) *The selling of DSM: The rhetoric of science in psychiatry.* New York: A. de Gruyter.

315 Sedgewick, P. (1987) *Psychopolitics.* London: Pluto.

316 Fee, D. (ed.) (2000) *Pathology and the postmodern: Mental illness as discourse and experience.* London: Sage.

317 Scheff, T.J. (1966) *Being mentally ill.* London: Weidenfeld and Nicolson.

318 Rosenhan, D. (1973) On being sane in insane places. *Science,* **179**: 250–257.

319 Cosgrove, L. and P.J. Caplan (2004) Medicalizing menstrual distress, in P.J. Caplan and L. Cosgrove (eds) *Bias in psychiatric diagnosis.* Lanham, MD: Jason Aronson, pp. 221–232.

320 Szasz, T. (1961) *The myth of mental illness: Foundations of a theory of personal conduct.* London: Secker.

321 Goffman, E. (1961) *Asylums: Essays on the social situation of mental patients and other inmates.* New York: Doubleday.

322 Foucault, M. (1979) *Discipline and punish: The birth of the prison.* London: Penguin.

323 Burr, V. and T. Butt (2000) Psychological distress and postmodern thought, in D. Fee (ed.) *Pathology and the postmodern: Mental illness as discourse and experience.* London: Sage, pp. 186–206.

324 Scull, A.T. (1979) *Museums of madness: The social organisation of insanity in nineteenth century England.* London: Allen Lane.

325 Laing, R.D. (1969) *The divided self.* New York: Random House.

326 Gordon, C. (1980) *Power/Knowledge: Selected interviews and other writings, 1972–1977.* Brighton: Harvester.

327 Robinson, I. and A. Rodrigues (2009) *'Mad Pride' activists say they're unique, not sick.* ABC News, 24 August. http://abcnews.go.com/Health/story?id=8382903.

328 Mad Pride Blog (2009) *Hey Ho – let's go.* http://madpride.org.uk/blogs/madprideblog/index.php.

329 Burstow, B. (2005) Feminist antipsychiatry praxis – women and the movement(s): A Canadian perspective, in R. Menzies, D.E. Chunn and W. Chan (eds) *Women, madness and the law: A feminist reader.* London: Glasshouse, pp. 245–258.

330 Skov, J. (1985) Recovering from psychiatry: How I got myself back. *Phoenix Rising*, **5**(4): 5–8.

331 Berrios, G.E. (1995) Mood disorders: Clinical section, in G.E. Berrios and R. Porter (eds) *A history of clinical psychiatry: The origins and history of psychiatric disorders*. London: Athlone, pp. 384–408.

332 Murray, J.L. and A.D. Lopez (1996) *The global burden of disease: A comprehensive assessment of mortality and disability from diseases, injuries and risk factors in 1990 and projected to 2020. Summary*. Boston, MA: Harvard School of Public Health and World Health Organization.

333 Keller, M.V., M.C. Neale and K.S. Kendler (2007) Association of different adverse life events with distinct patterns of depressive symptoms. *American Journal of Psychiatry*, **164**: 1521–1529.

334 Marsella, A. (1981) Depressive experience and disorder across cultures, in H. Triadis and J. Draguns (eds) *Handbook of cross cultural psychiatry*. Boston, MA: Allyn and Bacon, pp. 237–289.

335 Jadhav, S. (1996) The cultural origins of Western depression. *International Journal of Social Psychiatry*, **42**: 269–286.

336 Fenton, S. and A. Sadiq (1991) *Asian women and depression*. London: Commission for Racial Equality.

337 Javed, N. (2004) Clinical cases and the intersection of sexism and racism, in P.J. Caplan and L. Cosgrove (eds) *Bias in psychiatric diagnosis*. Lanham, MD: Jason Aronson, pp. 77–79.

338 Wilson, K. and B. McCarthy (1994) Consultation as a factor in the low rate of mental health service use by Asians. *Journal of Psychological Medicine*, **20**: 113–119.

339 Brown, C., H.C. Schulberg and M.J. Madonia (1996) Clinical presentations of major depression by African Americans and Whites in primary medical care practice. *Journal of Affective Disorders*, **41**(3): 181–191.

340 Betrus, P.A., S.K. Elmore and R.A. Hamilton (1995) Women and somaticisation: Unrecognised depression. *Health Care for Women International*, **16**(4): 287–297.

341 Bhatt, A., B. Tomenson and S. Benjamin (1988) Transcultural patterns of somaticisation in primary care: A preliminary report. *Journal of Psychosomatic Research*, **33**: 671–681.

342 Chapman, T. and J. Burr (2004) Contextualising experiences of depression in women from South Asian communities: A discursive approach. *Sociology of Health and Illness*, **26**(4): 433–452.

343 Russell, J.A. (1991) Culture and categorization of emotions. *Psychological Bulletin*, **110**: 426–450.

344 Leff, J. (1973) Culture and differentiation of emotions. *British Journal of Psychiatry*, **123**: 299–306.

345 Giorgi, A. (1985) *Phenomenology and psychological research*. Pittsburgh, PA: Duquesne University Press.

346 Chesler, P. (2005) *Women and madness*, 2nd edn. New York: Doubleday.

347 LaFrance, M.N. (2009) *Women and depression: Recovery and resistance*. London: Routledge.

348 Hamilton, J.A. and S. Gallant (1990) Problematic aspects of diagnosing

premenstrual phase dysphoria: Recommendations for psychological research and practice. *Professional Psychology: Research and Practice*, **21**(1): 60–68.

349 Henwood, K. and N. Pigeon (1994) Beyond the qualitative paradigm: A framework for introducing diversity within qualitative psychology. *Journal of Community and Applied Psychology*, **4**: 225–238.

350 Fee, D. (2000) The broken dialogue: Mental illness as discourse and experience, in D. Fee (ed.) *Pathology and the postmodern: Mental illness as discourse and experience*. London: Sage, pp. 1–17.

351 Malson, H. (1998) *The thin woman: Feminism, post-structuralism and the social psychology of anorexia nervosa*. London: Routledge.

352 Payer, L. (1988) *Medicine and culture*. New York: Henry Holt.

353 Tiefer, L. (2001) The selling of 'female sexual dysfunction'. *Journal of Sex and Marital Therapy*, **27**(5): 625–628.

354 Oudshoorn, N. (1990) On measuring sex hormones: The role of biological assays in sexualizing chemical substances. *Bulletin of History of Medicine*, **64**: 243–261.

355 Walker, A. (1997) *The menstrual cycle*. London: Routledge.

356 Menkes, D.B., E. Taghavi, P.A. Mason and R.C. Howard (1993) Fluoxetine's spectrum of action in premenstrual syndrome. *International Clinical Psychopharmacology*, **8**(2): 95–102.

357 Watson, N.R., J.W. Studd, M. Savvas et al. (1989) Treatments of severe premenstrual syndrome with oestradiol patches and cyclical oral norethisterone. *British Medical Journal*, **297**: 900–901.

358 Hunter, M.S., C. Swann and J.M. Ussher (1995) Seeking help for premenstrual syndrome: Women's self-reports and treatment preferences. *Sexual and Marital Therapy*, **10**(3): 253–262.

359 Billig, M. (1991) *Ideologies and beliefs*. London: Sage.

360 Harding, S. (ed.) (1987) *Feminism and methodology*. Indianapolis, IN: Indiana University Press.

361 Koeske, R. (1983) Sociocultural factors in the premenstrual syndrome: Review, critiques and future directions, in National Institute of Mental Health, *Premenstrual Syndrome Workshop*. Rockville, MD: NIMH.

362 Foucault, M. (1989) *Birth of the clinic*. London: Penguin.

363 Currie, J. (2005) *The marketization of depression: The prescribing of SSRI antidepressants to women*, for Women and Health Protection. www.whp-apsf.ca/pdf/SSRIs.pdf

364 McPherson, S. and D. Armstrong (2006) Social determinants of diagnostic labels in depression. *Social Science and Medicine*, **62**(1): 50–58.

365 Kutchins, H. and S. Kirk (1997) *Making us crazy: DSM. The psychiatric bible and the creation of mental disorders*. New York: Free Press.

366 Metzl, J.M. (2003) *Prozac on the couch: Prescribing gender in the era of wonder drugs*. Durham, NC: Duke University Press.

367 Metzl, J.M. and J. Angel (2004) Assessing the impact of SSRI antidepressants on popular notions of women's depressive illness. *Social Science and Medicine*, **58**: 577–584.

368 Butler, S. and M. Meegan (2008) Recent developments in the design of antidepressive therapies: Targeting the serotonin transporter. *Current Medicinal Chemistry*, **15**(17): 1737–1761.

369 Zoloft (2009) www.zoloft.com/common_questions.asp

370 Moncrieff, J. (2009) Deconstructing psychiatric treatment, in J. Reynolds, T. Heller and R. Muston (eds) *Mental health still matters*. Basingstoke: Palgrave Macmillan, pp. 301–309.

371 Breggin, P.B. and G.R. Breggin (1991) *Toxic psychiatry: Why therapy, empathy and love must replace the drugs, electroshock and biochemical theories of the 'New Psychiatry'*. New York: St Martins Press.

372 Medawar, C. and A. Hardon (2004) *Medicines out of control? Antidepressants and the conspiracy of goodwill*. Netherlands: Aksant.

373 Andrews, G. (2001) Placebo response in depression: Bane of research, boon to therapy. *British Journal of Psychiatry*, **178**(3): 192–194.

374 Moncrieff, J. and I. Kirsch (2005) Efficacy of antidepressants in adults. *British Medical Journal*, **331**: 155–157.

375 Kramer, P. (1993) *Listening to Prozac: A psychiatrist explores antidepressant drugs and the remaking of the self*. New York: Viking Penguin.

376 Marcia, A. (2004) *The truth about the drug companies: How they deceive us and what to do about it*. New York: Random House.

377 Liebert, R. and N. Gavey (2008) 'I didn't just cross a line I tripped over an edge': Experiences of serious adverse side effects with selective serotonin reuptake inhibitor use. *New Zealand Journal of Psychiatry*, **37**(1): 38–48.

378 Gunnell, D., J. Saperia and D. Ashby (2005) Selective serotonin reuptake inhibitors (SSRIs) and suicide in adults: Meta-analysis of drug company data from placebo controlled randomized controlled trials submitted to MHRA's safety review. *British Medical Journal*, **330**: 385–388.

379 Gregorian, R., K. Golden and A. Bahce (2002) Antidepressant induced sexual dysfunction. *Annals of Pharmacotherapy*, **36**: 1577–1589.

380 VanderKooy, J.D., S. Kennedy and R. Bagby (2002) Antidepressant side effects in depression patients treated in a naturalistic setting: A study of bupropien, moclobemide paroxetine, sertraline and venlafaxine. *Western Canada Journal of Psychiatry*, **47**(2): 174–180.

381 Spigset, O. (1999) Adverse reactions of selective serotonin reuptake inhibitors – response from a spontaneous reporting system. *Drug Safety*, **20**: 277–287.

382 Healy, D. (2003) Lines of evidence on the risk of suicide with selective serotonin reuptake inhibitors. *Psychotherapy and Psychosomatics*, **72**: 71–79.

383 Andrews, G. (2001) Should depression be managed as a chronic disease? *British Medical Journal*, **322**(7283): 419–421.

384 Kendler, K.S., E.E. Walters and R.C. Kessler (1997) The prediction of length of major depressive episodes: Results from an epidemiological survey of female twins. *Psychological Medicine*, **27**: 107–117.

385 Dunn, A., M.H. Trivedi, J.B. Kampert et al. (2005) Exercise treatment for depression: Efficacy and dose response. *American Journal of Preventative Medicine*, **28**(1): 1–8.

386 Williams, J.M.G. (1992) *The psychological treatment of depression*. London: Routledge.

387 Hales, D.R. and R.E. Hales (1995) *Caring for the mind: The comprehensive guide to mental health*. New York: Bantam.

388 Brown, C. and T. Augusta-Scott (2007) *Narrative therapy: Making meaning, making lives*. Thousand Oaks, CA: Sage.

389 McWilliams, N. (2004) *Psychoanalytic psychotherapy: A practitioner's guide.* New York: Guilford.

390 Brown, L.S. (2010) *Feminist therapy.* Washington, DC: American Psychological Association.

391 Ussher, J.M., M. Hunter and M. Cariss (2002) A woman-centred psychological intervention for premenstrual symptoms, drawing on cognitive-behavioural and narrative therapy. *Clinical Psychology and Psychotherapy*, **9**: 319–331.

392 Liebert, R. and N. Gavey (2009) 'There are always two sides to these things': Managing the dilemma of serious side effects from SSRIs. *Social Science and Medicine*, **68**: 1882–1891.

393 Moynihan, R., I. Heath and D. Henry (2002) Selling sickness: The pharmaceutical industry and disease mongering. *British Medical Journal*, **324**: 886–890.

394 Double, D. (2002) The limits of psychiatry. *British Medical Journal*, **324**: 900–904.

395 Pilgrim, D. and A. Rogers (2005) The troubled relationship between psychiatry and sociology. *International Journal of Social Psychiatry*, **51**(3): 228–241.

396 Ussher, J.M. (2000) Women's madness: A material-discursive-intrapsychic approach, in D. Fee (ed.) *Psychology and the postmodern: Mental illness as discourse and experience.* London: Sage, pp. 207–230.

397 Pilgrim, D. (2007) The survival of psychiatric diagnosis. *Social Science and Medicine*, **65**: 536–547.

398 Kleinman, A. and B. Good (eds) (1986) *Culture and depression: Studies in the anthropology and cross-cultural psychiatry of affect and disorder.* Berkeley, CA: University of California Press.

399 Caplan, P.J. and W.E. Profit (2004) Some future considerations, in P.J. Caplan and L. Cosgrove (eds) *Bias in psychiatric diagnosis.* Lanham, MD: Jason Aronson, pp. 249–253.

400 American Psychiatric Association (APA) (1980) *Diagnostic and statistical manual of mental disorders*, 3rd edn (DSM-III). Washington, DC: APA.

401 Caplan, P.J. and L. Cosgrove (2004) Is this really necessary?, in P.J. Caplan and L. Cosgrove (eds) *Bias in psychiatric diagnosis.* Lanham, MD: Jason Aronson, pp.xiv–xxxiii.

402 Caplan, P.J. (1995) *They say you're crazy: How the world's most powerful psychiatrists decide who's normal.* Reading, MA: Addison-Wesley.

403 Cosgrove, L., S. Krimsky, M. Vijayaraghavan and L. Schneider (2006) Financial ties between DSM-IV panel members and the pharmaceutical industry. *Psychotherapy and Psychosomatics*, **75**(3): 154–160.

404 Cosgrove, L. and H.J. Bursztajn (2009) Toward credible conflict of interest policies in clinical psychiatry. *Psychiatric Times*, **26**(1): 40–41. www.psychiatric times.com

405 Cosgrove, L., H.J. Bursztajn, S. Krimsky et al. (2009) Conflicts of interest and disclosure in the American Psychiatric Association's Clinical Practice Guidelines. *Psychotherapy and Psychosomatics*, **78**: 228–232.

406 Shorter, E. (1997) *A history of psychiatry.* New York: Wiley.

407 Healy, D. (2003) *Let them eat Prozac.* Toronto: James Lorimer.

3 LABELLING WOMEN AS MAD: REGULATING AND OPPRESSING WOMEN

1 Kaplan, A. (1986) The 'self-in-relation': Implications for depression in women. *Psychotherapy*, **23**: 234–242.

2 Ettore, E. and E. Riska (1995) *Gendered moods: Psychotropics and society*. London: Routledge.

3 Menzies, R. and D.E. Chunn (2005) Charlotte's web: Historical regulation of 'insane' women murderers, in R. Menzies, D.E. Chunn and W. Chan (eds) *Women, madness and the law: A feminist reader*. London: Glasshouse, pp. 80–100.

4 Chesler, P. (1972) *Women and madness*. New York: Doubleday.

5 Weissten, N. (1973) Psychology constructs the female: Or the fantasy life of male psychologists, in P. Brown (ed.) *Radical psychology*. London: Tavistock.

6 Ussher, J.M. (1991) *Women's madness: Misogyny or mental illness?* Amherst, MA: University of Massachusetts Press.

7 Geller, J.L. and M. Harris (eds) (1994) *Women of the asylum: Voices from behind the walls 1840–1945*. New York: Anchor.

8 Showalter, E. (1987) *The female malady: Women, madness and English culture 1830–1940*. London: Virago.

9 Porter, R. (2002) *Madness: A brief history*. Oxford: Oxford University Press.

10 Gill, R. (2007) *Gender and the media*. Cambridge: Polity.

11 Bronfen, E. (1998) *The knotted subject: Hysteria and its discontents*. Princeton, NJ: Princeton University Press.

12 Veith, I. (1964) *Hysteria: The story of a disease*. Chicago, IL: University of Chicago Press.

13 Wilson, M.I. (1940) *Borderline minds* (excerpt), in J.L. Geller and M. Harris (eds) (1994) *Women of the asylum: Voices from behind the walls 1840–1945*. New York: Anchor, pp. 275–282.

14 Smith-Rosenberg, C. (1986) *Disorderly conduct: Visions of gender in Victorian America*. Oxford: Oxford University Press.

15 Barker, F. (1883) *The puerperal diseases: Clinical lectures delivered at Bellevue Hospital*. New York: Appleton.

16 Mitchell, S.W. (1877) Massage. *Journal of Nervous and Mental Disease*, **4**: 636–638.

17 Gilman, C.P. (1935) *The living of Charlotte Perkins Gilman*. New York: Arno.

18 Stubbs, J. and J. Tolmie (2005) Defending battered women on charges of homicide: The structural and systematic versus the personal and particular, in R. Menzies, D.E. Chunn and W. Chan (eds) *Women, madness and the law: A feminist reader*. London: Glasshouse, pp. 191–209.

19 Bingham-Russell, A. (1898) *A plea for the insane* (excerpt), in J.L. Geller and M. Harris (eds) (1994) *Women of the asylum: Voices from behind the walls 1840–1945*. New York: Anchor, pp. 192–202.

20 Gilman, C.P. (1935) *The living of Charlotte Perkins Gilman* (excerpt), in J.L. Geller and M. Harris (eds) (1994) *Women of the asylum: Voices from behind the walls 1840–1945*. New York: Anchor, pp. 161–168.

21 Labrum, B. (2005) The boundaries of femininity: Madness and gender in New

Zealand 1870–1910, in R. Menzies, D.E. Chunn and W. Chan (eds) *Women, madness and the law: A feminist reader*. London: Glasshouse, pp. 60–77.

22 Martin, P. (1987) *Mad women in romantic writing*. Brighton: Harvester.

23 Gilbert, S.M. and S. Gubar (2000) *The madwoman in the attic: The woman writer and the nineteenth century literary imagination*, 2nd edn. New Haven, CT: Yale University Press.

24 Rigney, B.H. (1978) *Madness and sexual politics in the feminist novel: Studies in Brontë, Woolf, Lessing and Atwood*. Madison, WI: University of Wisconsin Press.

25 Kendall, K. (2005) Beyond reason: Social constructions of mentally disordered offenders, in R. Menzies, D.E. Chunn and W. Chan (eds) *Women, madness and the law: A feminist reader*. London: Glasshouse, pp. 41–57.

26 Menzies, R. and D.E. Chunn (1999) The gender politics of criminal insanity: 'Order in council' women in British Columbia 1888–1950. *Histoire sociale / Social History*, **31**: 241–279.

27 Millett, K. (1990) *The loony-bin trip*. Urbana, IL: University of Illinois Press.

28 Matthews, J.J. (1984) *Good and mad women: The historical construction of femininity in twentieth century Australia*. Sydney: Allen and Unwin.

29 Kaysen, S. (1993) *Girl, interrupted*. New York: Turtle Bay.

30 Gilman, S.L. (1988) *Disease and representation: Images of illness from madness to AIDS*. Ithaca, NY: Cornell University Press.

31 Halleck, S.L. (1971) *The politics of therapy*. New York: Science House.

32 Herman, J. (1992) *Trauma and recovery*. New York: Basic Books.

33 Caplan, E.J. (2004) Psychiatric diagnosis in the legal system, in P.J. Caplan and L. Cosgrove (eds) *Bias in psychiatric diagnosis*. Lanham, MD: Jason Aronson, pp. 49–59.

34 Ainsley, J.N. (2000) 'Some mysterious agency': Women, violent crime, and the insanity acquittal in the Victorian courtroom. *Canadian Journal of History*, **35**(1): 37–55.

35 Williams, J. (1996) Social inequalities and mental health: Developing services and developing knowledge. *Journal of Community and Applied Social Psychology*, **6**(5): 311–316.

36 Lloyd, A. (2005) The treatment of women in secure hospitals, in R. Menzies, D.E. Chunn and W. Chan (eds) *Women, madness and the law: A feminist reader*. London: Glasshouse, pp. 227–244.

37 Kelley, L.P. and R.K. Blashfield (2009) An example of psychological science's failure to self-correct. *Review of General Psychology*, **13**(2): 122–129.

38 Broverman, I.K., D.M. Broverman, F.E. Clarkson et al. (1970) Sex-role stereotypes and clinical judgements of mental health. *Journal of Consulting and Clinical Psychology*, **34**(1): 1–7.

39 Widiger, T.A. and S.A. Settle (1987) Broverman et al. revisited: An artifactual sex bias. *Journal of Personality and Social Psychology*, **53**(3): 463–469.

40 Sherman, J.A. (1980) Therapist attitudes and sex role stereotyping, in A.M. Brodsky and R.T. Hare-Mustin (eds) *Women and psychotherapy*, New York: Guilford, pp. 35–66.

41 Waisberg, J. and S. Page (1988) Gender role conformity and the perception of mental illness. *Women and Health*, **14**(1): 3–16.

42 Rosenfield, S. (1982) Sex roles and societal reactions to mental illness: Labelling of 'deviant' deviance. *Journal of Health and Social Behaviour*, **23**: 18–24.

43 Potts, M.K., M.A. Burnam and K.B. Wells (1991) Gender differences in depression detection: A comparison of clinician diagnosis and standardized assessment. *Psychological Assessment: A Journal of Consulting and Clinical Psychology*, **3**(4): 609–615.

44 Loring, M. and B. Powell (1988) Gender, race and DSM-III: A study of the objectivity of psychiatric diagnostic behavior. *Journal of Health and Social Behaviour*, **29**(1): 1–22.

45 Poland, J. and P.J. Caplan (2004) The deep structure of bias in psychiatric diagnosis, in P.J. Caplan and L. Cosgrove (eds) *Bias in psychiatric diagnosis*. Lanham, MD: Jason Aronson, pp. 9–24.

46 Salokangas, R.K., K. Vaahtera, S. Pacriev et al. (2002) Gender differences in depressive symptoms: An artefact caused by measurement instruments. *Journal of Affective Disorders*, **68**: 215–220.

47 Leach, L.S., H. Christensen and A.J. Mackinnon (2008) Gender differences in the endorsement of symptoms for depression and anxiety: Are gender-biased items responsible? *Journal of Nervous and Mental Disease*, **196**(2): 128–135.

48 Nazroo, J.Y. (1997) *Ethnicity and mental health*. London: Policy Studies Institute.

49 Caplan, P.J. and L. Cosgrove (2004) Is this really necessary?, in P.J. Caplan and L. Cosgrove (eds) *Bias in psychiatric diagnosis*. Lanham, MD: Jason Aronson, pp.xiv–xxxiii.

50 Siegal, R.J. (2004) Ageism in psychiatric diagnosis, in P.J. Caplan and L. Cosgrove (eds) *Bias in psychiatric diagnosis*. Lanham, MD: Jason Aronson, pp. 89–97.

51 Metcalfe, W.R. and P.J. Caplan (2004) Seeking 'normal' sexuality on a complex matrix, in P.J. Caplan and L. Cosgrove (eds) *Bias in psychiatric diagnosis*. Lanham, MD: Jason Aronson, pp. 121–126.

52 Hollingshead, A.B. and F.C. Redlich (1958) *Social class and mental illness: A community study*. New York: Wiley.

53 Jenkins-Hall, K. and W.P. Sacco (1991) Effect of client race and depression on evaluations by white therapists. *Journal of Social and Clinical Psychology*, **38**: 322–333.

54 Jones, E.E. (1982) Psychotherapists' impressions of treatment outcome as a function of race. *Journal of Clinical Psychology*, **38**: 722–731.

55 Burr, J. (2002) Cultural stereotypes of women from South Asian communities: Mental health care professionals' explanations for patterns of suicide and depression. *Social Science and Medicine*, **55**(5): 835–845.

56 Williams, P.E., G. Turpin and G. Hardy (2006) Clinical psychology service provision and ethnic diversity within the UK: A review of the literature. *Clinical Psychology and Psychotherapy*, **13**: 324–338.

57 Hussain, F. and R. Cochrane (2004) Depression in South Asian women living in the UK: A review of the literature with implications for service provision. *Transcultural Psychiatry*, **41**(2): 253–270.

58 Ginter, G.G. (1995) Differential diagnosis in older adults: Dementia, depression and delirium. *Journal of Counseling and Development*, **73**: 346–351.

59 Davis, K. (2008) Intersectionality as buzzword: A sociology of science

perspective on what makes a feminist theory successful. *Feminist Theory*, **9**(1): 67–85.

60 Parks, C.L., T.L. Hughes and A.K. Matthews (2004) Race/ethnicity and sexual orientation: Intersecting identities. *Cultural Diversity and Ethnic Minority Psychology*, **10**(3): 241–254.

61 Newman, J.P. (1984) Sex differences in symptoms of depression: Clinical disorder or normal distress? *Journal of Health and Social Behaviour*, **25**: 136–159.

62 Craig, T.J. and P.A. Van Notta (1979) Influence of two demographic characteristics on two measures of depressive symptoms. *Archives of General Psychiatry*, **36**: 149–154.

63 Kessler, R.C., K.A. McGonagle, M. Swartz et al. (1993) Sex and depression in the National Comorbidity Survey I: Lifetime prevalence, chronicity and recurrence. *Journal of Affective Disorders*, **29**: 85–96.

64 Wilhelm, K. and G. Parker (1994) Sex differences in lifetime depression rates: Fact or artifact? *Psychological Medicine*, **24**(1): 97–11.

65 Johnson, B., J. Perz and J.M. Ussher (2006) *Examining access to allied mental health services through general practice – consumer perspectives. The Link project evaluation report*. University of Western Sydney.

66 Kessler, R.C., R.L. Brown and C.L. Broman (1981) Sex differences in psychiatric help-seeking: Evidence from four large-scale surveys. *Journal of Health and Social Behaviour*, **22**: 49–64.

67 Warren, L.W. (1983) Male intolerance of depression: A review with implications for psychotherapy. *Clinical Psychology Review*, **3**: 147–156.

68 Batty, Z. (2006) *Masculinity and depression: Men's subjective experience of depression, coping and preferences for therapy and gender role conflict*. Thesis, School of Psychology, University of Western Sydney.

69 Padesky, C.A. and C.L. Hammen (1981) Sex differences in depressive symptom expression and help-seeking among college students. *Sex Roles*, **7**: 309–320.

70 Wirth-Cauchon, J. (2000) A dangerous symbolic mobility: Narratives of borderline personality disorder, in D. Fee (ed.) *Pathology and the postmodern: Mental illness as discourse and experience*. London: Sage, pp. 141–162.

71 Jimenez, M.A. (1997) Gender and psychiatry: Psychiatric conceptions of mental disorders in women. *Affilia*, **12**(2): 154–175.

72 American Psychiatric Association (APA) (1968) *Diagnostic and statistical manual of mental disorders*, 2nd edn (DSM-II). Washington, DC: APA.

73 American Psychiatric Association (APA) (1980) *Diagnostic and statistical manual of mental disorders*, 3rd edn (DSM-III). Washington, DC: APA.

74 Ussher, J.M. (1997) *Fantasies of femininity: Reframing the boundaries of sex*. London/New York: Penguin/Rutgers.

75 Becker, D. (1997) *Through the looking glass: Women and borderline personality disorder*. Boulder, CO: Westview.

76 Becker, D. and S. Lamb (1994) Sex bias in the diagnosis of Borderline Personality Disorder and Posttraumatic Stress Disorder. *Professional Psychology: Research and Practice*, **25**: 55–61.

77 Widiger, T. and M. Weissman (1991) Epidemiology of borderline personality disorder. *Hospital and Community Psychiatry*, **42**: 1015–1019.

78 Becker, D. (2000) When she was bad: Borderline personality disorder in a posttraumatic age. *American Journal of Orthopsychiatry*, **70**(4): 422–432.

79 American Psychiatric Association (APA) (1987) *Diagnostic and statistical manual of mental disorders*, 3rd revised edn (DSM-IIIR). Washington, DC: APA.

80 Barrett, L.F. and E. Bliss-Moreau (2009) She's emotional: He's having a bad day. Attributional explanations for emotion stereotypes. *Emotion*, **9**(5): 649–658.

81 Bedell Smith, S. (1999) *Diana in search of herself: Portrait of a troubled princess.* New York: Times Books.

82 Hall-Flavin, D. (2009) *Borderline personality disorder: A clinical perspective.* www.bpdfamily.com/bpdresources/nk_a103.htm.

83 Akema, P. (1981) The borderline personality disorder and transitional relatedness. *American Journal of Psychiatry*, **138**: 45–60.

84 Wirth-Cauchon, J. (2001) *Women and borderline personality disorder: Symptoms and stories.* New Brunswick, NJ: Rutgers University Press.

85 Bryer, J.B., B.A. Nelson, J.B. Miller and P.A. Krol (1987) Childhood sexual and physical abuse as factors in adult psychiatric illness. *American Journal of Psychiatry*, **144**: 1426–1430.

86 Morrow, M. (2008) Women, violence and mental illness: An evolving feminist critique, in C. Patton and H. Loshny (eds) *Global science / Women's health.* New York: Cambria, pp. 147–162.

87 Rosenhan, D. (1973) On being sane in insane places. *Science*, **179**: 250–257.

88 Frame, J. (1961) *Faces in the water.* New York: Women's Press.

89 Warren, C. (1988) Electroconvulsive therapy, the self and family relations. *Research in the Sociology of Health Care*, **7**: 283–300.

90 Walter, C. (2009) Shock therapy forced on parents. *Sydney Morning Herald*, 6 June. www.smh.com.au/national/shock-therapy-forced-on-patients-20090605-byi6.html.

91 Weitz, D. (2009) *Ontario ECT statistics 2000–2002.* www.ect.org/ontario-ect-statistics-2000-2002/.

92 Freeman, C.P.L. and R.E. Kendall (1980) ECT: Patients' experiences and attitudes. *British Journal of Psychiatry*, **137**: 8–16.

93 Burstow, B. (2006) Understanding and ending ECT: A feminist imperative. *Canadian Women's Studies*, **25**(1–2): 115–122.

94 Johnstone, L. (1999) Adverse psychological effects of ECT. *Journal of Mental Health*, **8**(1): 69–85.

95 Ward, M.J. (1946) *The snake pit* (extract), in R. Shannonhouse (ed.) (2003) *Out of her mind: Women writing on madness.* New York: Modern Library, pp. 60–69.

96 Sareceno, B. (2005) Document actions WHO opposes involuntary electroshock, in WHO, *WHO resource book on mental health, human rights and legislation.* Geneva: WHO. www.mindfreedom.org/kb/mental-health-abuse/electroshock/who-opposes-forced-ect.

97 Feld, D. (2007) *Attorney loses battle to stop Simone D forced electroshock.* MindFreedom, 2 July. www.mindfreedom.org/kb/mental-health-abuse/electroshock/simone-d/200707.

98 Skov, J. (1985) Recovering from psychiatry: How I got myself back. *Phoenix Rising*, **5**(4): 5–8.

99 UK Advocacy Network (1996) Electroshock survey: The UK experience (excerpt), *Dendron*, 37–38.

100 Browne, A. and D. Finkelhor (1986) Impact of child sexual abuse: A review of the research. *Psychological Bulletin*, **99**(1): 66–77.

101 Lambourne, J. and D. Gill (1978) A controlled comparison of simulated and real ECT. *British Journal of Psychiatry*, **113**: 514–519.

102 Black, D. and G. Winoker (1989) Does treatment influence mortality of depressives? *Annals of Clinical Psychiatry*, **1**: 165–173.

103 Templer, D. and D. Veleber (1982) Can ECT permanently harm the brain? *Clinical Neuropsychology*, **4**(2): 62–66.

104 Robitscher, J. (1980) *The powers of psychiatry*. Wilmington, MA: Houghton Mifflin.

105 Funk, W. (1998) *What difference does it make?* Cranbrook, BC: Wild Flower.

106 Perkins, R.E. (1994) Choosing ECT. *Feminism Psychology*, **4**(4): 623–627.

107 Metzl, J.M. (2003) *Prozac on the couch: Prescribing gender in the era of wonder drugs*. Durham, NC: Duke University Press.

108 Mant, A. and D.B. Darroch (1975) Media images and medical images. *Social Science and Medicine*, **9**: 613–618.

109 Hansen, F.J. and D. Osborne (1995) Portrayal of women and elderly patients in psychotropic drug advertisements. *Women and Therapy*, **16**: 129–141.

110 Leppard, W., S.M. Olgetree and E. Wallen (1993) Gender stereotyping in medical advertising: Much ado about something? *Sex Roles*, **29**: 829–838.

111 Munce, S.E., E.K. Robertson, S.N. Sansom and D.E. Stewart (2004) Who is portrayed in psychotropic drug advertisements? *Journal of Nervous and Mental Disease*, **192**(4): 284–288.

112 Hawkins, J.W. and C.S. Aber (1988) The content of advertisements in medical journals: Distorting the image of women. *Women and Health*, **14**: 43–59.

113 Small, H. (1996) *Love's madness: Medicine, the novel and female insanity 1800–1865*. Oxford: Clarendon.

114 Metzl, J.M. and J. Angel (2004) Assessing the impact of SSRI antidepressants on popular notions of women's depressive illness. *Social Science and Medicine*, **58**: 577–584.

115 Cooley, D. (1956) The new nerve pills and your health, *Cosmopolitan*, January: 70–75.

116 Metzl, J. (in press) The relationship with this man has been a source of conflict: Gender stereotypes in the diagnosis of depression. *Gender and Society*, in press.

117 Blum, L.M. and N.F. Stracuzzi (2004) Gender in the Prozac nation: Popular discourse and productive femininity. *Gender and Society*, **18**(3): 269–286.

118 Metzl, J.M. (2002) Prozac and the pharmacokinetics of narrative form. *Signs*, **27**(2): 347–380.

119 Kramer, P. (1993) *Listening to Prozac: A psychiatrist explores antidepressant drugs and the remaking of the self*. New York: Viking Penguin.

120 Zita, J. (1998) *Body talk: Philosophical reflections on sex and gender*. New York: Columbia University Press.

121 Bordo, S. (1993) *Unbearable weight: Feminism, culture and the body*. Berkeley, CA: University of California Press.

122 Showalter, E. (1997) *Hystories: Hysterical epidemics and modern culture*. New York: Columbia University Press.

123 Gottlieb, D. (2008) Lady Lazarus: Uncoupleting suicide and poetry, in S. Chapadjiev (ed.) *Live through this: On creativity and self-destruction*. New York: Seven Stories Press, pp. 27–35.

124 Kolata, G. and M. Petersen (2002) Hormone replacement study a shock to the medical system, *New York Times*, 10 July.

125 Vines, G. (1993) *Raging hormones: Do they rule our lives?* Berkeley, CA: University of California Press.

126 Wilson, R. (1966) *Feminine forever*. New York: M. Evans.

127 Coupland, J. and A. Williams (2002) Conflicting discourses, shifting ideologies: Pharmaceutical, 'alternative' and feminist emancipatory texts on the menopause. *Discourse and Society*, **13**(4): 419–445.

128 Utian, W. (1989) Renewing our commitment to the remaining 85 per cent. *Menopause Management*, **1**(2): 2–6.

129 Wells, R.G. (1989) Should all post-menopausal women receive hormone replacement therapy? *Senior Patient*, **6**(1): 65–70.

130 New York Times (2002) Editorial: Hormone therapy woes. *New York Times*, 11 July. www.nytimes.com/2002/07/11/opinion/hormone-therapy-woes.html.

131 BBC (2000) *Teresa Gorman: Thatcherite maverick*. BBC News, 1 March. http://news.bbc.co.uk/2/hi/uk_news/politics/662353.stm.

132 Whittaker, R. (1998) Re-framing the representation of women in advertisements for hormone replacement therapy. *Nursing Enquiry*, **5**: 77–86.

133 Ussher, J.M. (2006) *Managing the monstrous feminine: Regulating the reproductive body*. London: Routledge.

134 Canadian Medical Association Journal (2002) Editorial: One conclusion may hide another. *Canadian Medical Association Journal*, **167**(4): 329.

135 Beral, V. and Million Women Study collaborators (2003) Breast cancer and hormone-replacement therapy in the Million Women Study. *Lancet*, **362**(9382): 419–447.

136 Investigators, WGftWsHI (2002) Risks and benefits of estrogen plus progesterone in healthy menopausal women: Principal results from the Women's Health Initiative randomized controlled trial. *Journal of the American Medical Association*, **288**(3): 321–333.

137 Yusuf, S. and S. Anand (2002) Hormone replacement therapy: A time for pause. *Canadian Medical Association Journal*, **167**(4): 357–359.

138 Beral, V. and Million Women Study collaborators (2007) Ovarian cancer and hormone replacement therapy in the Million Women Study. *Lancet*, **369**(9547): 1703–1710.

139 Petersen, M. (2002) Company sends letter to retain hormone sales. *New York Times*, 11 July: Section A:21.

140 Sackett, D.L. (2002) The arrogance of preventative medicine. *Canadian Medical Association Journal*, **167**(4): 363–364.

141 Warren, M.P. and S. Halpert (2004) Hormone replacement therapy: Controversies, pros and cons. *Best Practice and Research in Clinical Endocrinology and Metabolism*, **18**(3): 317–332.

142 Machens, K. and K. Schmidt-Gollwitzer (2003) Issues to debate on the

Women's Health Initiatives Study: An epidemiological dilemma? *Human Reproduction*, **18**(10): 1992–1999.

143 RANZCOG (2004) Advice to medical practitioners regarding the use of postmenopausal hormone therapy. www.jeanhailes.org.au/issues/hrt_benefits_con.htm.

144 Sibbald, B. (2002) Fallout from *JAMA*'s HRT study continuing to land in MDs' offices. *Canadian Medical Association Journal*, **167**(4): 387.

145 Wilson, D. (2009) Maker of hormonal drug must pay $113m. *Sydney Morning Herald*, 25 November: 15.

146 Burr, V. and T. Butt (2000) Psychological distress and postmodern thought, in D. Fee (ed.) *Pathology and the postmodern: Mental illness as discourse and experience.* London: Sage, pp. 186–206.

147 Daly, M. (1979) *Gyn/ecology: The metaethics of radical feminism.* London: Women's Press.

148 Fulani, L. (ed.) (1987) *The psychopathology of everyday racism and sexism.* New York: Harrington Park.

149 Chesler, P. (2005) *Women and madness*, 2nd edn. New York: Doubleday.

150 Pope, K. (2001) Sex between therapists and clients, in J. Worell (ed.) *Encyclopedia of women and gender: Sex similarities and differences and the impact of society on gender.* London: Academic Press, pp. 955–962.

151 Marecek, J. (2006) Social suffering, gender, and women's depression, in C.L. Keyes and S.H. Goodman (eds) *Women and depression: A handbook for the social, behavioral and biomedical sciences.* Cambridge: Cambridge University Press, pp. 283–308.

152 Stoppard, J.M. (1999) Why new perspectives are needed for understanding depression in women. *Canadian Psychology*, **40**(2): 79–90.

153 Stoppard, J. (2000) *Understanding depression: Feminist social constructionist approaches.* London: Routledge.

154 LaFrance, M.N. (2009) *Women and depression: Recovery and resistance.* London: Routledge.

155 Holmes, J. (2009) All you need is cognitive behaviour therapy?, in J. Reynolds, T. Heller and R. Muston (eds) *Mental health still matters.* Basingstoke: Palgrave Macmillan, pp. 311–315.

156 Stoppard, J. (1989) An evaluation of the adequacy of cognitive/behavioural theories for the understanding of depression in women. *Canadian Psychology*, **30**(1): 39–47.

157 Miller, S.M. and N. Kirsch (1987) Sex differences in cognitive coping with stress, in R.C. Barnett, L. Biener and G.K. Baruch (eds) *Gender and stress.* New York: Free Press, pp. 278–307.

158 Perkins, R.E. (1991) Therapy for lesbians? The case against. *Feminism and Psychology*, **1**(3): 325–338.

159 Gattuso, S., S. Fullagar and I. Young (2005) Speaking of women's 'nameless misery': The everyday construction of depression in Australian women's magazines. *Social Science and Medicine*, **61**: 1640–1648.

160 LaFrance, M.N. (2007) A bitter pill: A discursive analysis of women's medicalized accounts of depression. *Journal of Health Psychology*, **12**(1): 127–140.

161 Layard, R. (2006) *The case for psychological treatment centres.* http://cep.lse.

ac.uk/textonly/research/mentalhealth/DEPRESSION_REPORT_LAYARD. pdf, accessed 9 August 2009.

162 Ussher, J.M. (2003) The role of premenstrual dysphoric disorder in the subjectification of women. *Journal of Medical Humanities*, **24**(1–2): 131–146.

163 Rittenhouse, C.A. (1991) The emergence of premenstrual syndrome as a social problem. *Social Problems*, **38**(3): 412–425.

164 Gardner, P. (2003) Distorted packaging: Marketing depression as illness, drugs as cure. *Journal of Medical Humanities*, **24**(1–2): 105–130.

165 National Institute of Mental Health (NIMH) (2008) *Women and depression: Discovering hope.* Bethesda, MD: NIMH.

166 Emmons, K. (2008) Narrating the emotional woman, in H. Clark (ed.) *Depression and narrative: Telling the dark.* New York: State University of New York Press, pp. 111–126.

167 McKenzie-Mohr, S. and M. LaFrance (forthcoming) Telling stories without the words: 'Tightrope talk' in women's accounts of coming to live well after rape or depression. *Feminism and Psychology*.

168 Rose, N.S. (1996) *Inventing our selves: Psychology, power, and personhood.* New York: Cambridge University Press.

169 Becker, D. (2010) Women's work and the societal discourse of stress. *Feminism and Psychology*, **20**(1): 36–52.

170 Human Rights and Equal Opportunities Commission (2000) *Striking the balance: Women, men, work and family.* www.hreoc.gov.au/sex_discrimination/publication/strikingbalance/docs/STB_Final.pdf: Sydney.

171 Lyons, A.C. and C. Griffin (2003) Managing menopause: A qualitative analysis of self-help literature for women at midlife. *Social Science and Medicine*, **56**(8): 1629–1642.

172 Sundquist, K. (1992) *Menopause made easy: How to turn a change into a change for the better.* London: Robinson.

173 Guilleman, M. (2000) Blood, bone, women and HRT: Co-constructions in the menopause clinic. *Australian Feminist Studies*, **15**(32): 191–203.

174 Foucault, M. (1987) *Mental illness and psychology.* Berkeley, CA: University of California Press (first published 1976).

175 Cosgrove, L., M. Pearrow and M. Anaya (2009) Toward a new paradigm for psychiatric diagnosis and clinical research in sexology. *Feminism and Psychology*, **18**(4): 457–465.

176 Cooperstock, R. and H. Lennard (1979) Some social meanings of tranquilliser use. *Sociology of Health and Illness*, **1**: 331–347.

177 Hemminki, E. (1975) Review of literature on factors affecting drug prescribing. *Social Science and Medicine*, **9**: 111–115.

178 Gammell, D.J. and J.M. Stoppard (1999) Women's experiences of treatment of depression: Medicalization or empowerment? *Canadian Psychology*, **40**(2): 112–128.

179 Gardiner, J.K. (1995) Can Ms. Prozac talk back? Feminism, drugs, and social constructionism. *Feminist Studies*, **21**(3): 501–517.

180 Thompson, T. (1996) *The beast: A journey through depression.* New York: Penguin.

181 Ingleby, D. (ed.) (1982) *Critical psychiatry: The politics of mental health.* Harmondsworth: Penguin.

182 Foucault, M. (1967) *Madness and civilisation: A history of insanity in the age of reason.* London: Tavistock.

183 Nicolson, P. (1986) Developing a feminist approach to depression following childbirth, in S. Wilkinson (ed.) *Feminist social psychology.* Milton Keynes: Open University Press, pp. 135–148.

184 Stainton-Rogers, W. (1996) *Explaining health and illness.* Hemel Hempstead: Harvester Wheatsheaf.

185 Yardley, L. (ed.) (1997) *Material discourses of health and illness.* London: Routledge.

186 Ussher, J.M. (1997) *Body talk: The material and discursive regulation of sexuality, madness and reproduction.* London: Routledge.

187 Fee, D. (ed.) (2000) *Pathology and the postmodern: Mental illness as discourse and experience.* London: Sage.

188 Burr, V. (1995) *An introduction to social constructionism.* London: Routledge.

189 Garfinkle, H. (1967) *Studies in ethnomethodology.* New York: Prentice Hall.

190 Henriques, J., W. Hollway, C. Urwin et al. (1998) *Changing the subject: Psychology, social regulation and subjectivity,* 2nd edn. London: Routledge.

191 Wetherall, A. (2002) *Gender, language and discourse.* London: Routledge.

192 Potter, J. and M. Wetherall (1986) *Discourse and social psychology.* London: Sage.

193 Parker, I. (1992) *Discourse dynamics: Critical analysis for social and individual psychology.* London: Sage.

194 Foucault, M. (1979) *Discipline and punish: The birth of the prison.* London: Penguin.

195 Mauthner, N. (2000) Feeling low and feeling really bad about feeling low: Women's experience of motherhood and post-partum depression. *Canadian Psychology,* **40**(2): 143–161.

196 Hollway, W. (2006) *The capacity to care: Gender and ethical subjectivity.* London: Routledge.

197 Nightingale, D.J. and J. Cromby (eds) (1999) *Social constructionist psychology: A critical analysis of theory and practice.* Buckingham: Open University Press.

198 Speer, S. (2000) Let's get real? Feminism, constructivism and the realism/relativism debate. *Feminism and Psychology,* **10**(4): 519–530.

199 Williams, S. (2003) Beyond meaning, discourse and the empirical world: Critical realist reflections on health. *Social Theory and Health,* **1**: 42–71.

200 Cromby, J. and D.J. Nightingale (1999) What's wrong with social constructionism?, in D.J. Nightingale and J. Cromby (eds) *Social constructionist psychology: A critical analysis of theory and practice.* Buckingham: Open University Press, pp. 1–21.

201 Edwards, D., M. Ashmore and J. Potter (1995) Death and furniture: The rhetoric, politics and theology of bottom-line arguments against relativism. *History of the Human Sciences,* **8**(2): 25–49.

202 Sims-Schouten, W., S.C.E. Riley and C. Willig (2007) Critical realism in discourse analysis: A presentation of a systematic method of analysis using women's talk of motherhood, childcare and female employment as an example. *Theory and Psychology,* **17**(1): 101–124.

203 Wurtzel, E. (1995) *Prozac nation.* New York: Riverhead.

204 Malson, H. (2009) Appearing to disappear: Postmodern femininities and self-

starved subjectivities, in H. Malson and M. Burns (eds) *Critical feminist approaches to eating disorders*. London: Routledge, pp. 135–155.

205 Bornstein, K. (2008) Art as prayer, in S. Chapadjiev (ed.) *Live through this: On creativity and self-destruction*. New York: Seven Stories Press, pp. 207–218.

206 Yalom, I.D. and G. Elkin (1974) *Every day gets a little closer: A twice told therapy*. New York: Basic Books.

207 Ussher, J.M. (2003) The ongoing silencing of women in families: An analysis and rethinking of premenstrual syndrome and therapy. *Journal of Family Therapy*, **25**: 388–405.

208 Ussher, J.M. and J. Perz (2006) Evaluating the relative efficacy of a self-help and minimal psycho-educational intervention for moderate premenstrual distress conducted from a critical realist standpoint. *Journal of Reproductive and Infant Psychology*, **24**(2): 347–362.

209 Mauthner, N. (2000) Feeling low and feeling really bad about feeling low: Women's experience of motherhood and post-partum depression. *Canadian Psychology*, **40**(2): 143–161.

210 Kirmeyer, L.J. (1988) Mind and body as metaphors: Hidden values in bio-medicine, in M. Lock and D. Gordon (eds) *Biomedicine examined*. Dordecht: Kluwer.

211 Yardley, L. (1996) Reconciling discursive and materialist perspectives on health and illness: A reconstruction of the biopsychosocial approach. *Theory and Psychology*, **6**(3): 485–508.

212 Grace, V. (2010) The desiring, gendered speakingbeing: Going a bit further with Ussher on women and depression. *Feminism and Psychology*, **20**(2): 272–277.

213 Schore, A. (1994) *Affect regulation and the origin of the self: The neurobiology of emotional development*. Hillsdale, NJ: Lawrence Erlbaum Associates.

214 Siegal, D.J. (1999) *The developing mind: How relationships and the brain interact to shape who we are*. New York: Guilford.

215 Jordan, J. (2010) On the critical importance of relationships for women's well-being, in D.C. Jack and A. Ali (eds) *The depression epidemic: International perspectives on women's self-silencing and psychological distress*. Oxford: Oxford University Press, pp. 99–106.

216 Pilgrim, D. and R.P. Bentall (1999) The medicalisation of misery: A critical realist analysis of the concept of depression. *Journal of Mental Health*, **8**(3): 261–274.

217 Bhaskar, R. (1989) *Reclaiming reality: A critical introduction to contemporary philosophy*. London: Verso.

218 Pilgrim, D. (2007) The survival of psychiatric diagnosis. *Social Science and Medicine*, **65**: 536–547.

219 Sayer, A. (2000) *Realism and social science*. London: Sage.

220 Yardley, L. (1999) Understanding embodied experience: Beyond mind–body dualism in health research, in M. Murray and K. Chamberlain (eds) *Qualitative health psychology*. London: Sage, pp. 31–46.

221 LaFrance, M. and J. Stoppard (2007) Re-storying women's depression: A material-discursive approach, in C. Brown and T. Augusta-Scott (eds) *Narrative therapy: Making meaning, making lives*. Thousand Oaks, CA: Sage, pp. 23–37.

222 Burr, V. (1999) The extra-discursive in social constructionism, in D.J. Nightingale and J. Cromby (eds) *Social constructionist psychology: A critical analysis of theory and practice*. Buckingham: Open University Press, pp. 113–126.

223 Frosh, S. and L. Baraitser (2008) Psychoanalysis and psychosocial studies. *Psychoanalysis, Culture and Society*, **13**(4): 346–365.

224 Hollway, W. (2006) Paradox in the pursuit of a critical theorization of the development of self in family relationships. *Theory and Psychology*, **16**: 465–482.

225 Grace, J., K.K. Lee, C. Ballard and M. Herbert (2001) The relationship between post-natal depression, somatization and behaviour in Malaysian women. *Transcultural Psychiatry*, **38**(1): 27–34.

226 Walkerdine, V. (2008) Contextualizing debates about psychosocial studies. *Psychoanalysis, Culture and Society*, **13**(4): 341–345.

227 Wetherell, M. (2003) Paranoia, ambivalence and discursive practices: Concepts of position and positioning in psychoanalysis and discursive psychology, in R. Harré and F. Moghaddam (eds) *The self and others: Positioning individuals and groups in personal, political and cultural contexts*. New York: Praeger, pp. 99–120.

228 Mitchell, S. (1988) *Relational concepts in psychoanalysis*. Cambridge, MA: Harvard University Press.

229 Mitchell, S.A. (2000) *Relationality: From attachment to intersubjectivity*. Hillsdale, NJ: Analytic Press.

230 Gyler, L. (2010) *The gendered unconscious*. London: Routledge.

231 Shorter, E. (1992) *From paralysis to fatigue*. New York: Free Press.

232 Engel, G. (1977) The need for a new medical model: A challenge for bio-medicine. *Science*, **196**: 129–136.

4 WOMAN AS OBJECT, NOT SUBJECT: MADNESS AS RESPONSE TO OBJECTIFICATION AND SEXUAL VIOLENCE

1 Gardner, R. (1993) A theory about the variety of human sexual behaviour. *Issues in Child Abuse Accusations*, **5**(2): 295–306.

2 Tjaden, P. and N. Thoennes (2006) *Extent, nature, and consequences of rape victimization: Findings from the National Violence Against Women Survey*. Washington, DC: National Institute of Justice, Office of Justice Programs, US Department of Justice and Centers for Disease Control and Prevention (NCJ 210346). www.ojp.usdoj.gov/nij

3 Warner, S. (2009) *Understanding the effects of child sexual abuse: Feminist revolutions in theory, research and practice*. London: Routledge.

4 de Beauvoir, S. (1949) *The second sex*, trans. H.M. Parshley, 1953. New York: Knopf.

5 Astbury, J. (2010) The social causes of women's depression: A question of rights violated, in D.C. Jack and A. Ali (eds) *The depression epidemic: International perspectives on women's self-silencing and psychological distress*. Oxford: Oxford University Press, pp. 19–46.

6 Kristof, N.D. and S. Wudunn (2010) *Half the sky: How to change the world*. London: Virago.

7 Sen, A. (1990) More than 100 million women are missing. *New York Review*, 20 December: 61–66.

8 World Health Organization (2009) *Mental health aspects of women's reproductive health: A global review of the literature*. Geneva: WHO.

9 World Health Organization (2000) *Women's mental health: An evidence based review*. Geneva: WHO.

10 Barko, N. (2000) The other gender gap. *The American Prospect*, June19–July 3: 61–63.

11 Loewenson, R.H. (1999) Women's occupational health in globalization and development. *American Journal of Industrial Medicine*, **36**: 34–42.

12 LeQuesne, C. (1996) From GATT to WTO: The results of the Uruguay Round, in B. Coote (ed.) *The trade trap: Poverty and the global commodity markets*. Oxford: Oxfam, pp. 192–215.

13 Stein, J. (1997) *Empowerment and women's health: Theory, methods and practice*. London: Zed Books.

14 American Psychological Association Task Force on the Sexualization of Girls (2007) *Report of the APA Task Force on the Sexualization of Girls*. Washington, DC: American Psychological Association. www.apa.org/pi/wpo/sexualization. html

15 Ussher, J.M. (1997) *Fantasies of femininity: Reframing the boundaries of sex*. London/New York: Penguin/Rutgers.

16 Alan, M., K. Albury and L. Catharine (2008) *The porn report*. Carlton, Vic.: Melbourne University Publishing.

17 Segal, L. (1992) Sweet sorrows, painful pleasures: Pornography and the perils of heterosexual desire, in L. Segal and M. Mackintosh (eds) *Sexuality and the pornography debate*. London: Virago, pp. 65–91.

18 Brongersma, E. (1984) Aggression against pedophiles. *International Journal of Law and Psychiatry*, **7**: 79–87.

19 Chiswick, D. (1983) Sex crimes. *British Journal of Psychiatry*, **143**: 236–242.

20 Sandfort, T., E. Brongersma and A. van Naerssen (1990) Man–boy relations: Different concepts for a diversity of phenomenon. *Journal of Homosexuality*, **20**(1–2): 5–12.

21 Wilson, D.R. (1981) *The man they called a monster*. North Ryde, NSW, Australia: Cassell.

22 Armstrong, L. (2000) What happened when women said 'incest', in C. Itzen (ed.) *Home truths about child sexual abuse influencing policy and practice: A reader*. London: Routledge, pp. 2–48.

23 Camps, F.E. (1962) The medical aspects of the investigation of sexual offences. *The Practitioner*, **189**(1129): 31–35.

24 Tait, R.L. (1989) *Diseases of women and abdominal surgery*. Leicester: Richardson.

25 Adler, Z. (1987) *Rape on trial*. London: Routledge and Kegan Paul.

26 Whiffen, V.E. and S. Clarke (1997) Does victimisation account for sex differences in depressive symptoms? *British Journal of Clinical Psychology*, **36**: 185–193.

27 Bebbington, P.E. (1998) Sex and depression. *Psychological Medicine*, **28**(1): 1–8.

28 Cutler, S.E. and S. Nolen-Hoeksema (1991) Accounting for sex differences in

depression through female victimisation: Childhood sexual abuse. *Sex Roles*, **24**: 425–438.

29 Koss, M.P., Bailey, J.A., Yuan, N.P., Herrera, V.A. and Lichter, E.L. (2003) Depression and PTSD in survivors of male violence: Research and training initiatives to facilitate recovery. *Psychology of Women Quarterly*, **27**: 130–142.

30 Molnar, B.E., S.L. Buka and R.C. Kessler (2001) Child sexual abuse and subsequent pathology: Results from the National Comorbidity Survey. *American Journal of Public Health*, **91**(5): 753–760.

31 Grauerholz, E. and A. King (1997) Primetime sexual harassment. *Violence Against Women*, **3**: 129–148.

32 Ward, L.M. and R. Rivadeneyra (1999) Contributions of entertainment television to adolescents' sexual attitudes and expectations: The role of viewing amount versus viewer involvement. *Journal of Sex Research*, **36**: 237–249.

33 Andsager, J. and K. Roe (2003) 'What's your definition of dirty, baby?' Sex in music videos. *Sexuality and Culture: An Interdisciplinary Quarterly*, **7**(3): 79–97.

34 Greenberg, B.S., M. Siemecki, S. Dorfman et al. (1993) Sex content in R-rated films viewed by adolescents, in B.S. Greenberg, J.D. Brown and N.L. Buerkel-Rothkuss (eds) *Media, sex, and the adolescent*. Cresskill, NJ: Hampton, pp. 45–58.

35 Kelly, J. and S.L. Smith (2006) *Where the girls aren't: Gender disparity saturates G-rated films* [Research brief]. www.thriveoncreative.com/clients/

36 Garner, A., H.M. Sterk and S. Adams (1998) Narrative analysis of sexual etiquette in teenage magazines. *Journal of Communication*, **48**: 59–78.

37 Duffy, M. and J.M. Gotcher (1996) Crucial advice on how to get the guy: The rhetorical vision of power and seduction in the teen magazine. *Journal of Communication Inquiry*, **20**: 32–48.

38 Lin, C. (1997) Beefcake versus cheesecake in the 1990s: Sexist portrayals of both genders in television commercials. *Howard Journal of Communications*, **8**: 237–249.

39 Reichert, T., J. Lambiase, S. Morgan et al. (1999) Cheesecake and beefcake: No matter how you slice it, sexual explicitness in advertising continues to increase. *Journalism and Mass Communication Quarterly*, **76**: 7–20.

40 Gill, R. (2007) *Gender and the media*. Cambridge: Polity.

41 Lindner, K. (2004) Images of women in general interest and fashion advertisements from 1955 to 2002. *Sex Roles*, **51**: 409–421.

42 Rudman, W.J. and P. Verdi (1993) Exploitation: Comparing sexual and violent imagery of females and males in advertising. *Women and Health*, **20**: 1–14.

43 Sullivan, G.L. and P.J. O'Connor (1988) Women's role portrayals in magazine advertising, 1958–1983. *Sex Roles*, **18**: 181–188.

44 Reichert, T. and C. Carpenter (2004) An update on sex in magazine advertising, 1983 to 2003. *Journalism and Mass Communication Quarterly*, **81**: 823–837.

45 Mooney Somers, J. (2005) *The construction and negotiation of hegemonic discourses of heterosexual male sexuality*. Unpublished doctoral thesis, University of Western Sydney.

46 Jackson, P., S. Stevenson and K. Brooks (2001) *Making sense of men's magazines*. London: Wiley-Blackwell.

47 Taylor, M., E. Quayle and G. Holland (2001) Child pornography: The internet and offending. *Canadian Journal of Policy Research*, **2**(2): 94–100.

48 Taylor, M. and E. Quayle (2003) *Child pornography: An internet crime.* London: Routledge.

49 Itzen, C. (2000) Child sexual abuse and the radical feminist endeavour: An overview, in C. Itzen (ed.) *Home truths about child sexual abuse influencing policy and practice: A reader.* London: Routledge, pp. 1–24.

50 Wyatt, G. (1985) The sexual abuse of Afro-American and White American women in childhood. *Child Abuse and Neglect,* **9**: 507–519.

51 Baker, A.W. and S.P. Duncan (1985) Child sexual abuse: A study of prevalence in Great Britain. *Child Sexual Abuse and Neglect,* **9**: 457–467.

52 Kendler, K.S., C.M. Bulik, J. Silberg et al. (2000) Childhood sexual abuse and adult psychiatric and substance use disorders in women. *Archives of General Psychiatry,* **57**: 953–959.

53 Hall, R.E. (1985) *Ask any woman: A London inquiry into rape and sexual assault.* Bristol: Falling Wall Press.

54 West, D. (1985) *Sexual victimisations.* New York: Gower.

55 Petersilia, J. (1998) *Report by the California Senate Public Safety Committee hearings on persons with developmental disabilities in the criminal justice system.* Washington, DC: National Center on Child Abuse and Neglect, Administration on Child, Youth and Families.

56 Gorey, K. and D. Leslie (1997) The prevalence of child sexual abuse: Integrative review adjustment for potential response and measurement biases. *Child Abuse and Neglect,* **21**: 391–398.

57 Finkelhor, D. (1994) Current information on the scope and nature of child sexual abuse: The future of children. *Child Sexual Abuse,* **4**(2): 31–53.

58 Bolen, R.M. and M. Scannapieco (1999) Prevalence of child sexual abuse prevalence: A corrective meta-analysis. *Child Maltreatment,* **3**(2): 157–170.

59 Russell, D.L. and R.M. Bolen (2000) *The epidemic of rape and child sexual abuse in the United States.* Thousand Oaks, CA: Sage.

60 Bolen, R.M., D.L. Russell and M. Scannapieco (2000) Child sexual abuse prevalence: A review and re-analysis of relevant studies, in C. Itzen (ed.) *Home truths about child sexual abuse influencing policy and practice: A reader.* London: Routledge, pp. 169–196.

61 Finkelhor, D. (1994) The international epidemiology of child sexual abuse. *Child Abuse and Neglect,* **18**: 409–417.

62 Finkelhor, D., G. Hotaling, I.A. Lewis and C. Smith (1990) Sexual abuse in a national survey of adult men and women: Prevalence, characteristics, and risk factors. *Child Abuse and Neglect,* **14**(1): 19–28.

63 Ussher, J.M. and C. Dewberry (1995) The nature and long-term effects of childhood sexual abuse: A survey of adult women survivors in Britain. *British Journal of Clinical Psychology,* **34**(2): 177–192.

64 Observer (2010) Editorial: The Catholic church should free its priests from celibacy. *Observer,* 10 March. www.guardian.co.uk/commentisfree/2010/mar/14/editorial-catholic-priests-celibacy

65 Lamb, S. (1996) *The trouble with blame: Victims, perpetrators and responsibility.* Cambridge, MA: Harvard University Press.

66 World Health Organization (2002) *World report on violence and health.* Geneva: WHO. www.who.int/violence_injury_prevention/violence/world_report/en/

67 UNICEF Innocenti Research Center (2001) Early marriage: Child spouses. *Innocenti Digest*, 7. Florence, Italy: Innocenti Research Center.

68 Mounassar, H. (2010) Dead Yemeni child bride's family calls for husband's death. *Sydney Morning Herald*, 12 April: 8.

69 Sagarone (2009) *The brides of death*. http://sagarone.blogspot.com/2009/09/brides-of-death.html

70 Muhsen, Z. (1994) *Sold: Story of modern-day slavery*. London: Little Brown Book Group.

71 Halcón, L., T. Beuhring and R.A. Blum (2000) *A portrait of adolescent health in the Caribbean*. Minneapolis, MN: University of Minnesota and Pan American Health Organization.

72 Caceres, C., M. Vanoss and E. Sid Hudes (2000) Sexual coercion among youth and young adolescents in Lima, Peru. *Journal of Adolescent Health*, **27**: 361–367.

73 Jewkes, R., C. Vundule, F. Maforah and E. Jordaan (2001) Relationship dynamics and teenage pregnancy in South Africa. *Social Science and Medicine*, **52**(5): 733–744.

74 Gavey, N. (2005) *Just sex? The cultural scaffolding of rape*. London: Routledge.

75 Kilpatrick, D.G., C.N. Edmunds and A.K. Seymour (1992) *Rape in America: A report to the nation*. Arlington, VA: National Victim Center.

76 Resnick, H.S., D.G. Kilpatrick, B.S. Dansky et al. (1993) Prevalence of civilian trauma and posttraumatic stress disorder in a representative national sample of women. *Journal of Consulting and Clinical Psychology*, **61**: 984–991.

77 Tjaden, P. and N. Thoennes (1998) *Prevalence, incidence and consequences of violence against women: Findings from the National Violence Against Women Survey*. Washington, DC: National Institute of Justice and Centers for Disease Control and Prevention.

78 Weiss, P. and J. Zverina (1999) Experiences with sexual aggression within the general population in the Czech Republic. *Archives of Sexual Behavior*, **28**: 265–269.

79 Russell, D.E.H. (1982) *Rape in marriage*. New York: Macmillan.

80 Ellsberg, M., L. Heise and E. Shrader (1999) *Researching violence against women: A practical guide for researchers and advocates*. Washington, DC: Center for Health and Gender Equity.

81 Kelly, L., J. Lovett and L. Regan (2005) *A gap or a chasm? Attrition in reported rape cases*. Home Office Research Study 293. London: Child and Women Abuse Studies Unit, Home Office.

82 Wood, L.A. and H. Rennie (1994) Formulating rape: The discursive construction of victims and villains. *Discourse and Society*, **5**(1): 125–148.

83 Campbell, J. and K. Soeken (1999) Forced sex and intimate partner violence: Effects on women's risk and women's health. *Violence Against Women*, **5**: 1017–1035.

84 Granados Shiroma, M. (1996) *Salud reproductiva y violencia contra la mujer: un análisis desde la perspectiva de género*. [Reproductive health and violence against women: A analysis from the gender perspective.] Nuevo León, Mexico: Asociación Mexicana de Población, Colegio de México.

85 Yoshihama, M. and S. Sorenson (1994) Physical, sexual, and emotional abuse

by male intimates: Experiences of women in Japan. *Violence and Victims*, **9**: 63–77.

86 Plichta, S. and C. Abraham (1996) Violence and gynecologic health in women less than 50 years old. *American Journal of Obstetrics and Gynecology*, **996**(174): 903–907.

87 Tjaden, P. and N. Thoennes (2000) *Full report of the prevalence, incidence, and consequences of violence against women: Findings from the National Violence Against Women Survey.* Washington, DC: National Institute of Justice, Office of Justice Programs, US Department of Justice and Centers for Disease Control and Prevention (NCJ 183781).

88 McKenzie-Mohr, S. and M. LaFrance (in press) Telling stories without the words: 'Tightrope talk' in women's accounts of coming to live well after rape or depression. *Feminism and Psychology*, in press.

89 Greenfeld, L. (1997) *Sex offenses and offenders: An analysis of data on rape and sexual assault.* Washington, DC: Office of Justice Programs, Bureau of Justice Statistics, US Department of Justice (NCJ 163392).

90 Swiss, S. and J.E. Giller (1993) Rape as a crime of war: A medical perspective. *Journal of the American Medical Association*, **270**: 612–615.

91 Pacific Women Against Violence (2000) Violence against East Timor women. *Pacific Women's Network Against Violence Against Women*, **5**: 1–3.

92 Stiglmayer, A. (1994) *Mass rape: The war against women in Bosnia Herzgovina.* Lincoln, NE: University of Nebraska Press.

93 Mollica, R.F. and L. Son (1989) Cultural dimensions in the evaluation and treatment of sexual trauma: An overview. *Psychiatric Clinics of North America*, **12**: 363–379.

94 Morrell, R. (ed.) (2001) *Changing men in Southern Africa.* Pietermaritzburg, South Africa: University of Natal Press.

95 Benninger-Budel, C. (1999) *Violence against women: A report.* Geneva: World Organization Against Torture.

96 Richard, A.O. (1999) *International trafficking in women to the United States: A contemporary manifestation of slavery and organized crime.* Washington, DC: Center for the Study of Intelligence.

97 Migration Information Programme (1996) *Trafficking in women to Italy for sexual exploitation.* Geneva: International Organization for Migration.

98 Migration Information Programme (1995) *Trafficking and prostitution: The growing exploitation of migrant women from central and eastern Europe.* Geneva: International Organization for Migration.

99 Bagley, C., F. Bolitho and L. Bertrand (1997) Sexual assault in school, mental health and suicidal behaviors in adolescent women in Canada. *Adolescence*, **32**: 361–366.

100 Lipson, J. (2001) *Hostile hallways: Bullying, teasing, and sexual harassment in school.* Washington, DC: American Association of University Women Educational Foundation.

101 International Helsinki Federation for Human Rights Women (2000) *An investigation into the status of women's rights in Central and South-Eastern Europe and the Newly Independent States.* Helsinki: International Helsinki Federation for Human Rights Women.

102 Australian Human Rights Commission (2008) *Sexual harassment: Serious*

business. Results of the 2008 Sexual Harassment National Telephone Survey. Sydney: Australian Human Rights Commission. www.hreoc.gov.au/sexual harassment/serious_business/index.html

103 Child and Woman Abuse Studies Unit (2010) *Sexual harassment statistics (EOC 2000).* London: London Metropolitan University. www.cwasu.org/page_display.asp?pageid=STATS&pagekey=107&itemkey=122

104 Ilies, R., N. Hauserman, S. Schwochau and J. Stibal (2003) Reported incidence rates of work-related sexual harassment in the United States: Using meta-analysis to explain reported rate disparities. *Personnel Psychology*, **56**(3): 607–631.

105 Lundgren, E., G. Heimer, J. Westerstrand and A. Kalliokoski (2002) *Captured queen: Men's violence against women in 'equal' Sweden – A prevalence study.* Stockholm: Offentliga Publikationer.

106 Walby, S. and J. Allen (2004) *Domestic violence, sexual assault and stalking: Findings from the British Crime Survey.* London: Home Office.

107 Stanko, E.A. (1985) *Intimate intrusions: Women's experience of sexual violence.* London: Routledge and Kegan Paul.

108 VicHealth (2009) *National Survey on Community Attitudes to Violence Against Women: Changing cultures, changing attitudes – preventing violence against women.* Carlton, Vic.: Victorian Health Promotion Foundation. www.facsia. gov.au/sa/women/.../violence/...survey/.../VHP_NCAS_report.pdf: Carlton, South Australia.

109 Russell, D.E.H. (1988) Pornography and rape: A causal model. *Political Psychology*, **9**(1): 41–73.

110 Itzin, C. (1997) Pornography and the organization of intrafamilial and extrafamilial child sexual abuse: Developing a conceptual model. *Child Abuse Review*, **6**(2): 94–106.

111 Segal, L. and M. Mackintosh (eds) (1992) *Sexuality and the pornography debate.* London: Virago.

112 Landsburg, S.E. (2006) *How the web prevents rape.* www.slate.com/id/2152487/

113 Fredrickson, B.L. and T.A. Roberts (1997) Objectification theory: Toward understanding women's lived experiences and mental health risks. *Psychology of Women Quarterly*, **21**(2): 173–206.

114 Tolman, D.L., E.A. Impett, A. Tracy and A. Michael (2006) Looking good, sounding good: Femininity ideology and adolescent girls' mental health. *Psychology of Women Quarterly*, **30**: 85–95.

115 Fredrickson, B.L., T.A. Roberts, S.M. Noll et al. (1998) That swimsuit becomes you: Sex differences in self-objectification, restrained eating, and math performance. *Journal of Personality and Social Psychology*, **75**: 269–284.

116 Tiggemann, M. and J.E. Lynch (2001) Body image in adult women across the life span: The role of self-objectification. *Developmental Psychology*, **37**: 243–253.

117 Botta, R.A. (2003) For your health? The relationship between magazine reading and adolescents' body image and eating disturbances. *Sex Roles*, **48**: 389–399.

118 Grabe, S., L.M. Ward and J.S. Hyde (2008) The role of the media in body image concerns among women: A meta-analysis of experimental and correlational studies. *Psychological Bulletin*, **134**(3): 460–476.

119 Tiggemann, M. and J.K. Kuring (2004) The role of body objectification in disordered eating and depressed mood. *British Journal of Clinical Psychology*, **43**: 299–311.

120 Rosenfeld, A.A., C.C. Nadelson, M. Krieger and J.H. Backman (1977) Incest and sexual abuse of children. *Journal of the American Academy of Child Psychiatry*, **16**: 327–339.

121 Spencer, J. (1978) Father–daughter incest: A clinical view for the correction field. *Child Welfare*, **57**: 581–590.

122 Palmer, R.L., D.A. Chaloner and R. Oppenheimer (1992) Childhood sexual experiences with adults reported by female psychiatric patients. *British Journal of Psychiatry*, **160**: 261–265.

123 Browne, A. and D. Finkelhor (1986) Impact of child sexual abuse: A review of the research. *Psychological Bulletin*, **99**(1): 66–77.

124 Putman, F.W. (2003) Ten-year research update review: Child sexual abuse. *Journal of the American Academy of Child and Adolescent Psychiatry*, **42**(3): 269–278.

125 Jumper, S.A. (1995) A meta-analysis of the relationship of child sexual abuse to adult psychological adjustment. *Child Abuse and Neglect*, **19**(6): 715–728.

126 Beitchman, J.H., K.J. Zucker, J.E. Hood et al. (1992) A review of the long term effects of child sexual abuse. *Child Abuse and Neglect*, **16**(1): 101–118.

127 Saunders, B.E., D.G. Kilpatrick, R.F. Hanson et al. (1999) Prevalence, case characteristics, and long-term psychological correlates of child rape among women: A national survey. *Child Maltreatment*, **4**: 187–200.

128 Kessler, R.C., A. Sonnega, E. Bromet et al. (1995) Posttraumatic stress disorder in the National Comorbidity Survey. *Archives of General Psychiatry*, **52**: 1048–1060.

129 Wiederman, M.W., R.A. Sansone and L.A. Sansone (1998) History of trauma and attempted suicide among women in a primary care setting. *Violence and Victims*, **13**: 3–9.

130 Davidson, J.R., D.C. Hughes, L.K. George and D.G. Blazer (1996) The association of sexual assault and attempted suicide within the community. *Archives of General Psychiatry*, **53**(6): 550–555.

131 Paolucci, E.O., M.L. Genuis and C. Violato (2001) A meta-analysis of the published research on the effects of child sexual abuse. *Journal of Psychology*, **135**(1): 17–36.

132 Bryer, J.B., B.A. Nelson, J.B. Miller and P.A. Krol (1987) Childhood sexual and physical abuse as factors in adult psychiatric illness. *American Journal of Psychiatry*, **144**: 1426–1430.

133 Becker, D. (2000) When she was bad: Borderline personality disorder in a posttraumatic age. *American Journal of Orthopsychiatry*, **70**(4): 422–432.

134 Kimerling, R. and K. Calhoun (1994) Somatic symptoms, social support and treatment seeking among sexual assault victims. *Journal of Consulting and Clinical Psychology*, **62**: 333–340.

135 Koss, M.P. and T. Mukai (1993) Recovering ourselves: The frequency, effects and resolution of rape. Research on battered women and their assailants, in F. Denmark and M. Paludi (eds) *Psychology of women: A handbook of issues and theories*. Westport, CT: Greenwood, pp. 478–512.

136 Campbell, J.C. and K. Soeken (1999) Forced sex and intimate partner violence: Effects on women's health. *Violence Against Women*, 5: 1017–1035.

137 Creamer, M., P. Burgess and A. McFarlane (2001) Post-traumatic stress disorder: Findings from the Australian National Survey of Mental Health and Well-being. *Psychological Medicine*, 31: 1237–1247.

138 Dickinson, L.M., F.V. deGruy, W.P. Dickinson and L.M. Candib (1999) Health related quality of life and symptom profiles of female survivors of sexual abuse in primary care. *Archives of Family Medicine*, 8: 35–43.

139 Rothbaum, B.O., E.B. Foa, D.S. Riggs et al. (1992) A prospective examination of post-traumatic stress disorder in rape victims. *Journal of Traumatic Stress*, 5: 455–475.

140 Breslau, N., G.C. Davis, P. Andreski and E. Peterson (1991) Traumatic events and posttraumatic stress disorder in an urban population of young adults. *Archives of General Psychiatry*, 48: 216–222.

141 Goodman, L.A., S.D. Rosenberg, K.T. Mueser and R.E. Drake (1997) Physical and sexual assault history in women with serious mental illness: Prevalence, correlates, treatment, and future directions. *Schizophrenia Bulletin*, 23(4): 685–696.

142 Mullen, P.E., S.E. Romans-Clarkson, V.A. Walton and G.P. Herbison (1988) Impact of sexual and physical abuse on women's mental health. *Lancet*, 16(8590): 841–84.

143 Golding, J.M. (1999) Intimate partner violence as a risk factor for mental disorders. *Journal of Family Violence*, 14: 99–132.

144 Woods, S. (2001) Prevalence and patterns of posttraumatic stress in abused and postabused women. *Issues in Mental Health Nursing*, 21: 309–324.

145 Anderson, D.K., D.G. Saunders, M. Yoshihama et al. (2003) Long term trends in depression among women separated from abusive partners. *Violence Against Women*, 9(7): 807–838.

146 Fry, R. (1993) Adult physical illness and childhood sexual abuse. *Journal of Psychosomatic Research*, 37(2): 89–103.

147 Kendall-Tackett, K.A. (2007) Inflammation, cardiovascular disease, and metabolic syndrome as sequelae of violence against women: The role of depression, hostility and sleep disturbance. *Trauma, Violence and Abuse*, 8(2): 117–126.

148 Street, A.E., J.L. Gradus, J. Stafford and K. Kelly (2007) Gender differences in experiences of sexual harassment: Data from a male-dominated environment. *Journal of Consulting and Clinical Psychology*, 75(3): 464–474.

149 Putnam, F.W. (2003) Ten-year research update review: Child sexual abuse. *Journal of American Academy of Child and Adolescent Psychiatry*, 42(3): 269–278.

150 Johnstone, L. (2003) Prescription rights peer commentary: Back to basics. *The Psychologist*, 16(4): 186–187.

151 Williams, J. (1996) Social inequalities and mental health: Developing services and developing knowledge. *Journal of Community and Applied Social Psychology*, 6(5): 311–316.

152 Baker, C.D. (2002) *Female survivors of sexual abuse*. London: Routledge.

153 Putnam, F.W. and P. Trickett (1997) The psycho-biological effects of sexual abuse: A longitudinal study. *Annals of New York Academy*, 821: 150–159.

154 Breslau, N., H.D. Chilcoat, R.C. Kessler et al. (1999) Vulnerability to assaul-

tive violence: Further specifications of the sex difference in post-traumatic stress disorder. *Psychological Medicine*, **29**: 813–821.

155 Cortina, L.M. and S.P. Kubiak (2006) Gender and post-traumatic stress: Sexual violence as an explanation for women's increased risk. *Journal of Abnormal Psychology*, **115**(4): 753–759.

156 Wolfe, J. and R. Kimerling (1997) Gender issues in the assessment of posttraumatic stress disorder, in J.P. Wilson and T.M. Keane (eds) *Assessing psychological trauma and PTSD*. New York: Guilford, pp. 192–237.

157 Olff, M., W. Langeland, N. Draijer and B.P. Gersons (2007) Gender differences in posttraumatic stress disorder. *Psychological Bulletin*, **133**(2): 183–204.

158 Carmen, E.H., P.P. Rieker and T. Mills (1984) Victims of violence and psychiatric illness. *American Journal of Psychiatry*, **141**: 378–383.

159 Stein, J.A., J.M. Golding, J.M. Siegel et al. (1988) Long-term psychological sequelae of child sexual abuse, in G.E. Wyatt and G.J. Powell (eds) *Lasting effects of child sexual abuse*. Beverly Hills, CA: Sage, pp. 135–154.

160 Finkelhor, D. and A. Browne (1985) The traumatic impact of sexual abuse: A conceptualisation. *American Journal of Orthopsychiatry*, **66**: 530–541.

161 Linehan, M.M. (1993) *Cognitive-behavioral treatment of borderline personality disorder*. New York: Guilford.

162 Reavey, P. (2003) When past meets present to produce a sexual other: Examining professional and everyday narratives about child sexual abuse and sexuality, in P. Reavey and S. Warner (eds) *New Feminist stories about women and child sexual abuse: Sexual scripts and dangerous dialogues*. London: Taylor and Francis, pp. 148–166.

163 Steuve, A., B.P. Dohrenwend and A.E. Skodal (1998) Relationship between stressful life events and episodes of major depression and nonaffective psychotic disorders: Selected results from a New York risk factor study, in B.P. Dohrenwend (ed.) *Adversity, stress and psychopathology*. New York: Oxford University Press, pp. 341–357.

164 Herman, J. (1992) *Trauma and recovery*. New York: Basic Books.

165 American Psychiatric Association (APA) (1980) *Diagnostic and statistical manual of mental disorders*, 3rd edn (DSM-III). Washington, DC: APA.

166 American Psychiatric Association (APA) (2000) *Diagnostic and statistical manual of mental disorders*, 4th edn (DSM-IV). Washington, DC: APA.

167 Kutchins, H. and S. Kirk (1997) *Making us crazy: DSM – The psychiatric bible and the creation of mental disorders*. New York: Free Press.

168 Marecek, J. (1999) Trauma talk in feminist clinical practice, in S. Lamb (ed.) *New versions for victims: Feminists struggle with concept*. New York: New York University Press, pp. 158–182.

169 Bachar, K. and M.P. Koss (2001) From prevalence to prevention: Closing the gap between what we know about rape and what we do, in J. Renzetti, L. Edleson and R.K. Bergen (eds) *Sourcebook on violence against women*. Thousand Oaks, CA: Sage, pp. 117–142.

170 Brewin, C.R., B. Andrews and J. Valentine (2000) Meta-analysis of risk factors for posttraumatic stress disorder in trauma-exposed adults. *Journal of Consulting and Clinical Psychology*, **6**: 748–766.

171 Briere, J. (1984) The effects of childhood sexual abuse on later psychological

functioning: Defining a post-sexual abuse syndrome. Third National Conference on Sexual Victimization of Children, Washington, DC.

172 Morrow, M. and M. Chappell (1999) *Hearing women's voices: Mental health care for women*. Vancouver, BC: British Columbia Centre of Excellence for Women's Health.

173 Reavey, P. and B. Gough (2000) Dis/locating blame: Survivors' constructions of self and sexual abuse. *Sexualities*, **3**(3): 325–346.

174 Goldberg, D. (1996) A dimensional model for common mental disorders. *British Journal of Psychiatry*, **168**(suppl. 30): 44–39.

175 Briere, J. (1992) *Child sexual abuse trauma: Theory and lasting effects*. London: Sage.

176 Spiegel, D. (1997) Foreword, in D. Spiegel (ed.) *Repressed memories*. Washington, DC: American Psychiatric Press, pp. 5–11.

177 Schacter, D.L. (1995) Memory wars. *Scientific American*, **272**: 135–139.

178 Loftus, E.F., M. Garry and H. Hayne (2008) Repressed and recovered memory, in E. Borgida and S.T. Fiske (eds) *Beyond common sense: Psychological science in the courtroom*. Malden, MA: Blackwell, pp. 177–194.

179 Conway, M. (ed.) (1997) *Recovered memories and false memories*. Oxford: Oxford University Press.

180 Geraerts, E., L. Raymaekers and H. Merckelbach (2008) Recovered memories of childhood sexual abuse: Current findings and their legal implications. *Legal and Criminological Psychology*, **13**(2): 165–176.

181 McNally, R.J. and E. Geraerts (2009) A new solution to the recovered memory debate. *Perspectives on Psychological Science*, **4**(2): 126–134.

182 Clancy, S.A. and R.J. McNally (2005–2006) Who needs repression? Normal memory processes can explain 'forgetting' of childhood sexual abuse. *Scientific Review of Mental Health Practice*, **4**: 66–73.

183 Ceci, S.J. and E.F. Loftus (1994) 'Memory work': A royal road to false memories? *Applied Cognitive Psychology*, **8**: 351–364.

184 Wirth-Cauchon, J. (2001) *Women and borderline personality disorder: Symptoms and stories*. New Brunswick, NJ: Rutgers University Press.

185 Itzen, C. (2000) The experience and effects of child sexual abuse involving pornography, in C. Itzen (ed.) *Home truths about child sexual abuse influencing policy and practice: A reader*. London: Routledge, pp. 123–140.

186 hooks, b. (1991) Interview, in A. Juno and V. Vale (eds) *Angry women*. San Francisco, CA: Re/search publications.

187 Jack, D.C. (1991) *Silencing the self: Women and depression*. Cambridge, MA: Harvard University Press.

188 Shackel, R.L. (2008) The beliefs commonly held by adults about children's behavioral responses to sexual victimization. *Child Abuse and Neglect*, **32**(4): 485–495.

189 Shackel, R.L. (2009) How child victims respond to perpetrators of sexual abuse. *Psychiatry, Psychology and Law*, **16**(suppl. 1): 55–63.

190 Coffey, P., H. Leitenberg, K. Henning et al. (1996) Mediators of the long term impact of child sexual abuse: Perceived stigma, betrayal, powerlessness and self-blame. *Child Abuse and Neglect*, **20**(5): 447–455.

191 Ussher, J.M. (2009) Sexual science and the law, in A.L. Ferber, K. Holcomb

and T. Wentling (eds) *Sex, gender and sexuality*. New York: Oxford University Press, pp. 377–416.

192 The Havens (2009) *Wake up to rape*. www.thehavens.co.uk/docs/Havens_ Wake_Up_To_Rape_Report_Summary.pdf

193 Gibson, J. (2010) Sexist migrants create legal problem. *Sydney Morning Herald*, 16 April.

194 Musico, I.M. (2008) Slash an' burn, in S. Chapadjiev (ed.) *Live through this: On creativity and self-destruction*. New York: Seven Stories Press, pp. 79–90.

195 Anonymous (2008) Silent body, speaking body, in S. Chapadjiev (ed.) *Live through this: On creativity and self-destruction*. New York: Seven Stories Press, pp. 199–205.

196 Babiker, G. and L. Arnold (1997) *The language of injury: Comprehending self-mutilation*. Leicester: British Psychological Society.

197 Bordo, S. (1993) *Unbearable weight: Feminism, culture and the body*. Berkeley, CA: University of California Press.

198 Cixous, H. and C. Clement (1987) *The newly born women*, trans. B. Wing. Minneapolis, MN: University of Minnesota Press.

199 Blackman, N. (2008) She's lost control again (or how Alice learned to drive), in S. Chapadjiev (ed.) *Live through this: On creativity and self-destruction*. New York: Seven Stories Press, pp. 92–104.

200 Jehu, D., C. Klassen and M. Gazan (1986) Cognitive restructuring of distorted beliefs associated with childhood sexual abuse. *Journal of Social Work and Human Sexuality*, 4(1–2): 25–45.

201 Simons, R.L. and L.B. Whitbeck (1991) Sexual abuse as a precursor to prostitution and victimization among adolescent and adult homeless women. *Journal of Family Issues*, 12(3): 361–379.

202 Tyler, K.A. (2002) Social and emotional outcomes of childhood sexual abuse: A review of recent research. *Aggression and Violent Behavior*, 7(6): 567–589.

203 Davis, J.L. and P.A. Petretic-Jackson (2000) The impact of child sexual abuse on adult interpersonal functioning: A review and synthesis of the empirical literature. *Aggression and Violent Behavior*, 5(3): 291–328.

204 Mullen, P.E., J.L. Martin, J.C. Anderson et al. (1994) The effect of child sexual abuse on social, interpersonal, and sexual function in adult life. *British Journal of Psychiatry*, 165: 35–47.

205 Banyard, V.L., L.M. Williams and J.A. Siegel (2004) Childhood sexual abuse: A gender perspective on context and consequences. *Child Maltreatment*, 9(3): 223–238.

206 DiLillo, D., D. Giuffre, G.C. Tremblay and L. Peterson (2001) A closer look at the nature of intimate partner violence reported by women with a history of child sexual abuse. *Journal of Interpersonal Violence*, 16(2): 116–132.

207 Gidycz, C.A., C.N. Coble, L. Latham and M.J. Layman (1993) Sexual assault experience in adulthood and prior victimization experiences: A prospective analysis. *Psychology of Women Quarterly*, 17(2): 151–168.

208 Classen, C.C., O.G. Palesh and R. Aggarwal (2005) Sexual revictimization: A review of the empirical literature. *Trauma, Violence, and Abuse*, 6(2): 103–129.

209 Breitenbecher, K.H. (2001) Sexual revictimization among women: A review of the literature focusing on empirical investigations. *Aggression and Violent Behavior*, 6(4): 415–432.

210 Chu, J.A. (1992) The revictimization of adult women with histories of child-hood abuse. *Journal of Psychotherapy Practice and Research*, **1**: 259–269.

211 Arata, C.M. (2002) Child sexual abuse and sexual revictimization. *Child Maltreatment*, **9**: 28–38.

212 Messman, T.L. and P.J. Long (1996) Child sexual abuse and its relationship to revictimization in adult women: A review. *Clinical Psychology Review*, **16**(5): 397–420.

213 Schloredt, K.A. and J.R. Heiman (2003) Perceptions of sexuality as related to sexual functioning and sexual risk in women with different types of childhood abuse histories. *Journal of Traumatic Stress*, **16**(3): 275–284.

214 Maltz, W. (2002) Treating the sexual intimacy concerns of sexual abuse survivors. *Sexual and Relationship Therapy*, **17**(4): 321–327.

215 Van Bruggen, L.K., M.G. Runtz and H. Kadlec (2006) Sexual revictimization: The role of sexual self-esteem and dysfunctional sexual behaviors. *Child Maltreatment*, **11**(2): 131–145.

216 Salter, A.E. (1995) *Transforming trauma: A guide to understanding and treating adult survivors of child sexual abuse.* London: Sage.

217 Sgroi, S. (1986) *Vulnerable populations: Sexual abuse treatment for children, adult survivors, offenders and persons with mental retardation.* New York: Lexington.

218 Messman-Moore, T.L. and P.J. Long (2003) The role of childhood sexual abuse sequelae in the sexual revictimization of women: An empirical review and theoretical reformulation. *Clinical Psychology Review*, **23**(4): 537–571.

219 Finney, L.D. (1990) *Reach for the rainbow: Advanced healing for survivors of sexual abuse.* Park City, UT: Changes.

220 Merrill, L.L., J.M. Guimond, C.J. Thomsen and J.S. Milner (2003) Child sexual abuse and number of sexual partners in young women: The role of abuse severity, coping style, and sexual functioning. *Journal of Consulting and Clinical Psychology*, **71**(6): 987–996.

221 Watkins, B. and A. Bentovim (1992) The sexual abuse of male children and adolescents: A review of current research. *Journal of Clinical Psychology and Psychiatry*, **33**(10): 197–248.

222 Banyard, V.L., L.M. Williams and J.A. Siegel (2004) Childhood sexual abuse: A gender perspective on context and consequences. *Child Maltreatment*, **9**(3): 223–238.

223 Barrett, R. (2009) *Matthew Johns in group sex scandal.* ABC News, 9 May. www.abc.net.au/news/stories/2009/05/07/2563957.htm

224 Jensen, E., B. Walter, G. Jackson and D. Welch (2008) The footballer, the glassed girlfriend and his fall guy. *Brisbane Times*, 26 August. www.brisbane times.com.au/news/national/the-footballer-the-glassed-girlfriend-and-his-fall-guy/2008/08/25/1219516406609.html

225 Kellogg, N. and R. Huston (1995) Unwanted sexual experiences in adolescents: Patterns of disclosure. *Clinical Pediatrics*, **34**: 306–318.

226 Nicolson, P. (2010) *Domestic violence and psychology: A critical perspective.* London: Routledge.

227 Social Trends (2009) Households and families. www.statistics.gov.uk/down loads/theme_social/Social-Trends40/ST40_Ch02.pdf

228 Shail, J., M. Montgomery and O. Agius (2004) Household, family and living

arrangements of the population of Australia, 1986 to 2026, in *Population and society: Issues, research, policy*. Australian Population Association Twelfth Biennial Conference. Canberra, ACT: ACSPRI Centre for Social Research, Australian National University.

5 THE CONSTRUCTION AND LIVED EXPERIENCE OF WOMEN'S DISTRESS: POSITIONING PREMENSTRUAL CHANGE AS PSYCHIATRIC ILLNESS

1 Ussher, J.M. (2006) *Managing the monstrous feminine: Regulating the reproductive body*. London: Routledge.
2 Figert, A.E. (2005) Premenstrual syndrome as cultural artifact. *Integrative Physiological and Behavioral Science*, **40**(2): 102–113.
3 Frank, R. (1931) The hormonal causes of premenstrual tension. *Archives of Neurological Psychiatry*, **26**: 1053–1057.
4 Dalton, K. (1959) Menstruation and acute psychiatric illness. *British Medical Journal*, **1**: 148–149.
5 American Psychiatric Association (APA) (2000) *Diagnostic and statistical manual of mental disorders*, 4th edn (DSM-IV). Washington, DC: APA.
6 Cosgrove, L. and P.J. Caplan (2004) Medicalizing menstrual distress, in P.J. Caplan and L. Cosgrove (eds) *Bias in psychiatric diagnosis*. Lanham, MD: Jason Aronson, pp. 221–232.
7 Fawcett, J. (2010) *Report of the DSM-5 Mood Disorders Work Group*. Washington, DC: American Psychiatric Association. www.dsm5.org/progress reports/pages/0904reportofthedsm-vmooddisordersworkgroup.aspx
8 Steiner, M. and L. Born (2000) Advances in the diagnosis and treatment of premenstrual dysphoria. *CNS Drugs*, **13**(4): 287–304.
9 Rittenhouse, C.A. (1991) The emergence of premenstrual syndrome as a social problem. *Social Problems*, **38**(3): 412–425.
10 Chrisler, J.C. and K.B. Levy (1990) The media construct a menstrual monster: A content analysis of PMS articles in the popular press. *Women and Health*, **16**(2): 89–104.
11 Rodin, M. (1992) The social construction of premenstrual syndrome. *Social Science and Medicine*, **35**(1): 49–56.
12 Epstein, M. (1995) *Thoughts without a thinker: Psychotherapy from a Buddhist perspective*. New York: Basic Books.
13 Chang, A.M., E. Holroyd and J.P. Chau (1995) Premenstrual syndrome in employed Chinese women in Hong Kong. *Health Care for Women International*, **16**(6): 551–561.
14 Yu, M., X. Zhu, J. Li et al. (1996) Perimenstrual symptoms among Chinese women in an urban area of China. *Health Care for Women International*, **17**: 161–172.
15 Chrisler, J.C. and I. Johnston-Robledo (2002) Raging hormones? Feminist perspectives on premenstrual syndrome and postpartum depression, in M.B. Ballou and L.S. Brown (eds) *Rethinking mental health and disorder: Feminist perspectives*. New York: Guilford, pp. 174–197.
16 Johnson, T.M. (1987) Premenstrual syndrome as a Western culture-specific disorder. *Culture, Medicine and Psychiatry*, **11**(3): 337–356.

17 Martin, E. (1987) *The woman in the body*. Milton Keynes: Open University Press.
18 Chrisler, J.C. and P. Caplan (2002) The strange case of Dr. Jekyll and Ms. Hyde: How PMS became a cultural phenomenon and a psychiatric disorder. *Annual Review of Sex Research*, **13**: 274–306.
19 Parlee, M. (1973) The premenstrual syndrome. *Psychological Bulletin*, **80**: 454–465.
20 Ussher, J.M. (2004) Blaming the body for distress: Premenstrual dysphoric disorder and the subjectification of women, in A. Potts, N. Gavey and A. Wetherall (eds) *Sex and the body*. Palmerstone North, NZ: Dunmore, pp. 183–202.
21 Lichten, E. (2009) *PMS information*. www.usdoctor.com/pms.htm
22 Cosgrove, L. and B. Riddle (2003) Constructions of femininity and experiences of menstrual distress. *Women and Health*, **38**(3): 37–58.
23 Zoloft (2009) www.zoloft.com/common_questions.asp
24 Caplan, P.J. and W.E. Profit (2004) Some future considerations, in P.J. Caplan and L. Cosgrove (eds) *Bias in psychiatric diagnosis*. Lanham, MD: Jason Aronson, pp. 249–253.
25 Bayer Healthcare (2009) *What is PMDD?* www.yaz-us.com/consumer/about_pmdd/index.jsp
26 US Food and Drug Administration (FDA) (2008) *Warning letter*. www.fda.gov/downloads/Drugs/GuidanceComplianceRegulatoryInformation/EnforcementActivitiesbyFDA/WarningLettersandNoticeofViolationLettersto PharmaceuticalCompanies/ucm053993.pdf
27 Kissling, E. (2009) *Cycling*, 26 September. http://menstruationresearch.org/blog/
28 Zoloft (2009) www.zoloft.com/pmdd_symptoms.aspx
29 Cosgrove, L., M. Pearrow and M. Anaya (2009) Toward a new paradigm for psychiatric diagnosis and clinical research in sexology. *Feminism and Psychology*, **18**(4): 457–465.
30 Medawar, C. and A. Hardon (2004) *Medicines out of control? Antidepressants and the conspiracy of goodwill*. Netherlands: Aksant.
31 Andrews, G. (2001) Placebo response in depression: Bane of research, boon to therapy. *British Journal of Psychiatry*, **178**(3): 192–194.
32 Hunter, M.S., C. Swann and J.M. Ussher (1995) Seeking help for premenstrual syndrome: Women's self-reports and treatment preferences. *Sexual and Marital Therapy*, **10**(3): 253–262.
33 Moody Mommy (2009) *PMDD made me do it*. http://moodymommy.word press.com/category/zoloft/
34 Bordo, S. (1993) *Unbearable weight: Feminism, culture and the body*. Berkeley, CA: University of California Press.
35 Ussher, J.M. (2003) The role of premenstrual dysphoric disorder in the subjectification of women. *Journal of Medical Humanities*, **24**(1–2): 131–146.
36 Ussher, J.M. (2004) Premenstrual Syndrome and self-policing: Ruptures in self-silencing leading to increased self-surveillance and blaming of the body. *Social Theory and Health*, **2**(3): 254–272.
37 Koeske, R.K. and G.F. Koeske (1975) An attributional approach to moods and the menstrual cycle. *Personality and Social Psychology*, **31**: 473–481.

38 Brooks, J., D.N. Ruble and A. Clarke (1977) College women's attitudes and expectations concerning menstrual-related change. *Psychosomatic Medicine*, **39**(5): 288–298.

39 Chrisler, J.C. (2008) 2007 presidential address: Fear of losing control: power, perfectionalism and the psychology of women. *Psychology of Women Quarterly*, **32**: 1–12.

40 Ussher, J.M. and J. Perz (2010) Disruption of the silenced-self: The case of pre-menstrual syndrome, in D.C. Jack and A. Ali (eds) *The depression epidemic: International perspectives on women's self-silencing and psychological distress.* Oxford: Oxford University Press, pp. 435–458.

41 Sabin Farrell, R. and P. Slade (1999) Reconceptualizing pre-menstrual emotional symptoms as phasic differential responsiveness to stressors. *Journal of Reproductive and Infant Psychology*, **17**(4): 381–390.

42 Ussher, J.M. and J.M. Wilding (1992) Interactions between stress and performance during the menstrual cycle in relation to the premenstrual syndrome. *Journal of Reproductive and Infant Psychology*, **10**(2): 83–101.

43 Coughlin, P.C. (1990) Premenstrual syndrome: How marital satisfaction and role choice affect symptom severity. *Social Work*, **35**(4): 351–355.

44 Fontana, A.M. and T.G. Palfaib (1994) Psychosocial factors in premenstrual dysphoria: Stressors, appraisal, and coping processes. *Journal of Psychosomatic Research*, **38**(6): 557–567.

45 Walker, A. (1997) *The menstrual cycle.* London: Routledge.

46 Woods, N.F., M.J. Lentz, E.S. Mitchell et al. (1998) Perceived stress, physiologic stress arousal, and premenstrual symptoms: Group differences and intra-individual patterns. *Research in Nursing and Health*, **21**(6): 511–523.

47 Slade, P. and F.A. Jenner (1980) Performance tests in different phases of the menstrual cycle. *Journal of Psychosomatic Research*, **24**: 5–8.

48 Ussher, J.M. (2002) Processes of appraisal and coping in the development and maintenance of Premenstrual Dysphoric Disorder. *Journal of Community and Applied Social Psychology*, **12**: 1–14.

49 Siegel, J. (1986) Marital dynamics of women with premenstrual tension syndrome. *Family Systems Medicine*, **4**(4): 358–366.

50 Kuczmierczyk, A.R., A.H. Labrum and C.C. Johnson (1992) Perception of family and work environments in women with premenstrual syndrome. *Journal of Psychosomatic Research*, **36**(8): 787–795.

51 Steege, J.F., A.L. Stout and S.L. Rupp (1988) Clinical features, in W.R. Keye (ed.) *The premenstrual syndrome.* Philadelphia, PA: Saunders, pp. 113–127.

52 Ryser, R. and L.L. Feinauer (1992) Premenstrual syndrome and the marital relationship. *American Journal of Family Therapy*, **20**(2): 179–190.

53 Frank, B., D.N. Dixon and H.J. Grosz (1993) Conjoint monitoring of symptoms of premenstrual syndrome: Impact on marital satisfaction. *Journal of Counseling Psychology*, **40**(1): 109–114.

54 Clayton, A.H., G.J. Clavet, E.L. McGarvey et al. (1999) Assessment of sexual functioning during the menstrual cycle. *Journal of Sex and Marital Therapy*, **25**(4): 281–291.

55 Brown, M.A. and P.A. Zimmer (1986) Personal and family impact of premenstrual symptoms. *Journal of Obstetric, Gynecologic, and Neonatal Nursing*, **15**(1): 31–38.

56 Stout, A.L. and J.F. Steege (1985) Psychological assessment of women seeking treatment for premenstrual syndrome. *Journal of Psychosomatic Research*, **29**(6): 621–629.

57 Ussher, J.M. (2003) The ongoing silencing of women in families: An analysis and rethinking of premenstrual syndrome and therapy. *Journal of Family Therapy*, **25**: 388–405.

58 Halbreich, U., J. Borenstein, T. Pearlstein and L.S. Kahn (2003) The prevalence, impairment, impact, and burden of premenstrual dysphoric disorder (PMS/PMDD). *Psychoneuroendocrinology*, **28**(suppl. 3): 1–23.

59 Robinson, R.L. and R.W. Swindle (2000) Premenstrual symptom severity: Impact on social functioning and treatment-seeking behaviors. *Journal of Women's Health and Gender Based Medicine*, **9**(7): 757–768.

60 Schwartz, C.B. (2001) The relationship between partner social support and premenstrual symptoms. *Abstracts International: Section B: The Sciences and Engineering*, **61**(10-B): 5580.

61 Smith-Martinez, K.L. (1995) Premenstrual symptomatology and its impact on marital communication. *Abstracts International: Section B: The Sciences and Engineering*, **56**(6-B): 2887.

62 Welthagen, N. (1995) *The influence of premenstrual symptoms on marital communication*. Unpublished PhD thesis; University of Pretoria.

63 Sveinsdottir, H., B. Lundman and A. Norberg (2002) Whose voice? Whose experiences? Women's qualitative accounts of general and private discussion of premenstrual syndrome. *Scandinavian Journal of Caring Sciences*, **16**(4): 414–423.

64 Koch, P. (2006) Women's bodies as a 'puzzle' for college men. *American Journal of Sexuality Education*, **1**(3): 51–72.

65 Cortese, J. and M.A. Brown (1989) Coping responses of men whose partners experience premenstrual symptomatology. *Journal of Obstetric, Gynecologic and Neonatal Nursing*, **18**(5): 405–412.

66 Ussher, J.M., J. Perz and J. Mooney-Somers (2007) The experience and positioning of affect in the context of intersubjectivity: The case of premenstrual syndrome. *Journal of Critical Psychology*, **21**: 145–165.

67 Jones, A., V. Theodos, W.J. Canar et al. (2000) Couples and premenstrual syndrome: Partners as moderators of symptoms?, in K.B. Schmaling (ed.) *The psychology of couples and illness: Theory, research, and practice*. Washington, DC: American Psychological Association, pp. 217–239.

68 McDaniel, S.H. (1988) The interpersonal politics of premenstrual syndrome. *Family Systems Medicine*, **6**(2): 134–149.

69 Cosgrove, L. (2000) Crying out loud: Understanding women's emotional distress as both lived experience and social construction. *Feminism and Psychology*, **10**(2): 247–267.

70 Perz, J. and J.M. Ussher (2006) Women's experience of premenstrual change: A case of silencing the self. *Journal of Reproductive and Infant Psychology*, **24**(4): 289–303.

71 Duarte, L.M. and J.M. Thompson (1999) Sex differences in self-silencing. *Psychological Reports*, **85**: 145–161.

72 Thompson, J.M. (1995) Silencing the self: Depressive symptomatology in close relationships. *Psychology of Women Quarterly*, **19**: 337–353.

73 Jack, D.C. (1991) *Silencing the self: Women and depression*. Cambridge, MA: Harvard University Press.

74 Jack, D.C. (2001) Understanding women's anger: A description of relational patterns. *Health Care for Women International*, **22**: 385–400.

75 Gottman, J.M. and L.J. Krokoff (1989) Marital interaction and satisfaction: A longitudinal view. *Journal of Consulting and Clinical Psychology*, **57**(1): 47–52.

76 Jack, D.C. (1999) Silencing the self: Inner dialogues and outer realities, in T.E. Joiner and J.C. Coyne (eds) *The interactional nature of depression: Advances in interpersonal approaches*. Washington, DC: American Psychological Association, pp. 221–246.

77 Jack, D.C. and D. Dill (1992) The silencing the self scale: Schemas of intimacy with depression in women. *Psychology of Women Quarterly*, **16**: 97–106.

78 Elson, J. (2002) Menarche, menstruation, and gender identity: Retrospective accounts from women who have undergone premenopausal hysterectomy. *Sex Roles*, **46**: 37–48.

79 Hammond, D.C. (1988) The psychosocial consequences, in W.R. Keye (ed.) *The premenstrual syndrome*. Philadelphia, PA: Saunders, pp. 128–144.

80 MsQ (2009) *Can't help it*. PMSBuddy, 31 August. http://pmsbuddy.com/index.php?view=story&action=display_single_story&story_id=271.

81 Chodorow, N. (1978) *The reproduction of mothering: Psychoanalysis and the sociology of gender*. Berkeley, CA: University of California Press.

82 O'Grady, H. (2005) *Women's relationship with herself: Gender, Foucault, therapy*. London: Routledge.

83 Grimshaw, J. (1986) *Philosophy and feminist thinking*. Minneapolis, MN: University of Minnesota Press.

84 Ussher, J.M., M. Hunter and S.J. Browne (2000) Good, bad or dangerous to know: Representations of femininity in narrative accounts of PMS, in C. Squire (ed.) *Culture and psychology*. New York: RoutledgeFalmer, pp. 87–99.

85 Sexton, L.G. (1994) *Searching for Mercy Street: My journey back to my mother, Anne Sexton* (extract), in R. Shannonhouse (ed.) (2003) *Out of her mind: Women writing on madness*. New York: Modern Library, pp. 120–129.

86 Bassin, D., M. Honey and M.M. Kaplan (1994) *Representations of motherhood*. New Haven, CT: Yale University Press.

87 Berggren-Clive, K. (1998) Out of the darkness and into the light: Women's experiences with depression after childbirth. *Canadian Journal of Community Mental Health*, **17**: 103–120.

88 Mauthner, N. (2010) 'I wasn't being true to myself': Women's narratives of postpartum depression, in D.C. Jack and A. Ali (eds) *The depression epidemic: International perspectives on women's self-silencing and psychological distress*. Oxford: Oxford University Press, pp. 459–484.

89 Rich, A. (1977) *Of woman born*. London: Virago.

90 Feeney, J.A. (2002) Allocation and performance of household tasks: A comparison of new parents and childless couples, in P. Noller and J.A. Feeney (eds) *Understanding marriage: Developments in the study of couple interaction*. New York: Cambridge University Press, pp. 411–436.

91 Meleis, A.I. and T.G. Lindgren (2002) Man works from sun to sun but women's work is never done: Insights on research and policy. *Health Care for Women International*, **23**: 742–753.

92 Western, M.C., J.H. Baxter, J. Pakulski et al. (2007) Neoliberalism, inequality and politics: The changing face of Australia. *Australian Journal of Social Issues*, **42**(3): 401–418.

93 Woolf, V. (1957) *A room of one's own*. New York: Harcourt, Brace and World.

94 Forssen, A.S.K. and G. Carlstedt (2006) 'It's heavenly to be alone!' A room of one's own as a health promoting resource for women: Results from a qualitative study. *Scandinavian Journal of Public Health*, **34**: 175–181.

95 Foucault, M. (1979) *Discipline and punish: The birth of the prison*. London: Penguin.

96 Benjamin, J. (1999) Recognition and destruction: An outline of intersubjectivity, in S.A. Mitchell and L. Aron (eds) *Relational psychoanalysis: The emergence of a tradition*. Hillsdale, NJ: Analytic Press, pp. 181–209.

97 Mooney-Somers, J., J. Perz and J.M. Ussher (2008) A complex negotiation: Women's experiences of naming and not naming premenstrual distress in couple relationships. *Women and Health*, **47**(3): 57–77.

98 Yosho (2009) *Insane*, 21 August. http://pmsbuddy.com/index.php?view=story&action=display_single_story&story_id=269

99 Rui (2009) *Trust*, 10 November. http://pmsbuddy.com/index.php?view=story&action=display_single_story&story_id=281

100 Stolorow, R.D. and G.E. Atwood (1992) *Contexts of being: The intersubjective foundations of psychological life*. Hillsdale, NJ: Analytic Press.

101 Mitchell, S. (1988) *Relational concepts in psychoanalysis*. Cambridge, MA: Harvard University Press.

102 Coward, R. (1993) *Our treacherous hearts: Why women let men get their way*. London: Faber and Faber.

103 Duncombe, J. and D. Marsden (1998) Stepford wives and hollow men? Doing emotion work, doing gender and authenticity in heterosexual relationships, in G. Bendelow and S. Williams (eds) *Emotions in social life: Critical themes and contemporary issues*. London: Routledge, pp. 211–227.

104 Perz, J. and J.M. Ussher (2009) Connectedness, communication and reciprocity in lesbian relationships: Implications for women's construction and experience of PMS, in P. Hammock and B.J. Cohler (eds) *Life course and sexual identity: Narrative perspectives on gay and lesbian identity*. Oxford: Oxford University Press, pp. 223–250.

105 Ussher, J.M. and J. Perz (2008) Empathy, egalitarianism and emotion work in the relational negotiation of PMS: The experience of lesbian couples. *Feminism and Psychology*, **18**(1): 87–111.

106 Perz, J. and J.M. Ussher (2009) The experience and positioning of premenstrual mood change in the context of intersubjectivity: Differences between lesbian and heterosexual women. Society for Menstrual Cycle Research, Spokane, WA, June.

107 Ross, L.E. (2005) Perinatal mental health in Lesbian mothers: A review of potential risk and protective factors. *Women and Health*, **41**(3): 113–128.

108 Winterich, J.A. (2003) Sex, menopause and culture: Sexual orientation and the meaning of menopause for women's lives. *Gender and Society*, **17**(4): 627–642.

109 Bailey, J.M. and K.J. Zucker (1995) Childhood sex-typed behavior and sexual orientation: A conceptual analysis and quantitative review. *Developmental Psychology*, **31**: 43–55.

110 Kurdek, L.A. (1987) Sex-role self schema and psychological adjustment in coupled homosexual and heterosexual men and women. *Sex Roles*, **17**: 549–562.

111 Green, R.J., M. Bettinger and E. Zacks (1996) Are lesbian couples fused and gay male couples disengaged? Questioning gender straightjackets, in J. Laird and R.-J. Green (eds) *Lesbians and gays in couples and families: A handbook for therapists*. San Francisco, CA: Jossey Bass, pp. 185–230.

112 Metz, M.E., B.R.R. Rosser and N. Strapko (1994) Differences in conflict-resolution styles among heterosexual, gay, and lesbian couples. *Journal of Sex Research*, **31**(4): 293–308.

113 Koepke, L., J. Hare and P. Moran (1992) Relationship quality in a sample of lesbian couples with children and child-free couples. *Family Relations*, **41**: 224–229.

6 WOMEN'S MADNESS: RESISTANCE AND SURVIVAL

1 Kaysen, S. (1993) *Girl, interrupted*. New York: Turtle Bay.

2 Wirth-Cauchon, J. (2001) *Women and borderline personality disorder: Symptoms and stories*. New Brunswick, NJ: Rutgers University Press.

3 Morrow, M. (2008) Women, violence and mental illness: An evolving feminist critique, in C. Patton and H. Loshny (eds) *Global science / Women's health*. New York: Cambria, pp. 147–162.

4 McKenzie-Mohr, S. and M. LaFrance (in press) Telling stories without the words: 'Tightrope talk' in women's accounts of coming to live well after rape or depression. *Feminism and Psychology*, in press.

5 LaFrance, M.N. (2009) *Women and depression: Recovery and resistance*. London: Routledge.

6 Schreiber, R. (1996) (Re)defining my self: Women's process of recovery from depression. *Qualitative Health Research*, **6**(4): 469–491.

7 Laing, R.D. (1969) *The divided self*. New York: Random House.

8 Mauthner, N. (2010) 'I wasn't being true to myself': Women's narratives of postpartum depression, in D.C. Jack and A. Ali (eds) *The depression epidemic: International perspectives on women's self-silencing and psychological distress*. Oxford: Oxford University Press, pp. 459–484.

9 Ussher, J.M. and J. Perz (2006) Evaluating the relative efficacy of a self-help and minimal psycho-educational intervention for moderate premenstrual distress conducted from a critical realist standpoint. *Journal of Reproductive and Infant Psychology*, **24**(2): 347–362.

10 Slater, L. (1996) *Black swans* (extract), in R. Shannonhouse (ed.) (2003) *Out of her mind: Women writing on madness*. New York: Modern Library, pp. 138–150.

11 Ridge, D. and S. Ziebland (2006) 'The old me could never have done that': How people give meaning to recovery following depression. *Qualitative Health Research*, **16**(8): 1038–1053.

12 hooks, b. (2008) no more crying, in S. Chapadjiev (ed.) *Live through this: On creativity and self-destruction*. New York: Seven Stories Press, pp. 187–192.

13 Musico, I.M. (2008) Slash an' burn, in S. Chapadjiev (ed.) *Live through this: On creativity and self-destruction*. New York: Seven Stories Press, pp. 79–90.

14 Ussher, J.M. (2008) Challenging the positioning of premenstrual change as PMS: The impact of a psychological intervention on women's self-policing. *Qualitative Research in Psychology*, **5**(1): 33–44.

15 Ussher, J.M. (2006) *Managing the monstrous feminine: Regulating the reproductive body*. London: Routledge.

16 Perz, J. and J.M. Ussher (2008) The horror of this living decay: Women's negotiation and resistance of medical discourses around menopause and midlife. *Women's Studies International Forum*, **31**: 293–299.

17 Howden, S. (2010) Sixties libertine returns to critique sex lives of today's scantily clad young. *Sydney Morning Herald*, 22 May: 7.

18 Bebbington, P., T. Brugha, B. MacCarthy et al. (1988) The Camberwell Collaborative Depression Study, I. Depressed probands: Adversity and the form of depression. *British Journal of Psychiatry*, **152**: 754–765.

19 O'Grady, H. (2005) Women's relationship with herself: Gender, Foucault, therapy. London: Routledge.

20 Drew, S. and R. Paradice (1996) Time, women and well-being. *Feminism Psychology*, **6**(4): 563–568.

21 Woolf, V. (1957) *A room of one's own*. New York: Harcourt, Brace and World.

22 Forssen, A.S.K. and G. Carlstedt (2006) 'It's heavenly to be alone!' A room of one's own as a health promoting resource for women: Results from a qualitative study. *Scandinavian Journal of Public Health*, **34**: 175–181.

23 Forssen, A.S.K. and G. Carlstedt (2007) Health-promoting aspects of a paid job: Findings in a qualitative interview study with elderly women in Sweden. *Health Care for Women International*, **28**(10): 909–929.

24 Brown, L.S. (2010) Empowering depressed women: The importance of a feminist lens, in D.C. Jack and A. Ali (eds) *The depression epidemic: International perspectives on women's self-silencing and psychological distress*. Oxford: Oxford University Press, pp. 333–342.

25 Perkins, R.E. (1994) Choosing ECT. *Feminism Psychology*, **4**(4): 623–627.

26 Perkins, R.E. (1991) Therapy for lesbians? The case against. *Feminism and Psychology*, **1**(3): 325–338.

27 Gammell, D.J. and J.M. Stoppard (1999) Women's experiences of treatment of depression: Medicalization or empowerment? *Canadian Psychology*, **40**(2): 112–128.

28 Hunter, M.S., J.M. Ussher, M. Cariss et al. (2002) Medical (fluoxetine) and psychological (cognitive-behavioural) treatment for premenstrual dysphoric disorder: A study of treatment process. *Journal of Psychosomatic Research*, **53**(3): 811–817.

29 Steiner, M. and L. Born (2000) Advances in the diagnosis and treatment of premenstrual dysphoria. *CNS Drugs*, **13**(4): 287–304.

30 Ussher, J.M. (2003) The ongoing silencing of women in families: An analysis and rethinking of premenstrual syndrome and therapy. *Journal of Family Therapy*, **25**: 388–405.

31 Perz, J. and J.M. Ussher (2006) Women's experience of premenstrual change: A case of silencing the self. *Journal of Reproductive and Infant Psychology*, **24**(4): 289–303.

32 Gottman, J.M. and L.J. Krokoff (1989) Marital interaction and satisfaction: A longitudinal view. *Journal of Consulting and Clinical Psychology*, **57**(1): 47–52.

33 Lee, S. (2002) Health and sickness: The meaning of menstruation and premenstrual syndrome in women's lives. *Sex Roles*, **46**(1–2): 25–35.

34 Ussher, J.M. (2002) Processes of appraisal and coping in the development and maintenance of Premenstrual Dysphoric Disorder. *Journal of Community and Applied Social Psychology*, **12**: 1–14.

35 Cosgrove, L. and B. Riddle (2003) Constructions of femininity and experiences of menstrual distress. *Women and Health*, **38**(3): 37–58.

36 Chrisler, J.C. and P. Caplan (2002) The strange case of Dr. Jekyll and Ms. Hyde: How PMS became a cultural phenomenon and a psychiatric disorder. *Annual Review of Sex Research*, **13**: 274–306.

37 King, M. (2009) *Women's subjective experiences of positive premenstrual changes*. Psychology Honours research project, School of Psychology, University of Western Sydney.

38 Stewart, D.E. (1989) Positive changes in the premenstrual period. *Acta Psychiatrica Scandinavica*, **79**: 400–405.

39 Chaturvedi, S.K. (1990) Stress-protective functions of positive experiences during the premenstrual period. *Stress Medicine*, **6**(1): 53–55.

40 Alagna, S.W. and J.A. Hamilton (1986) Social stimulus perception and self evaluation: Effects of menstrual cycle phase. *Psychology of Women Quarterly*, **20**: 327–338.

41 Shive, B.M. (2008) *Mad Skywriting*, in S. Chopodjiv (ed.) *Live through this: On creativity and self-destruction*. New York: Seven Stories Press, p. 184.

42 Cooper, D. (1974) *The grammar of living: An examination of political acts*. London: Penguin.

43 Gilbert, S.M. and S. Gubar (2000) *The madwoman in the attic: The woman writer and the nineteenth century literary imagination*, 2nd edn. New Haven, CT: Yale University Press.

44 Nochlin, L. (1988) *Women, art, power and other essays*. New York: Harper Row.

45 Geller, J.L. and M. Harris (eds) (1994) *Women of the asylum: Voices from behind the walls 1840–1945*. New York: Anchor.

46 Dix, D. (1843) *On behalf of the insane poor* (extract), in R. Shannonhouse (ed.) (2003) *Out of her mind: Women writing on madness*. New York: Modern Library, pp. 8–15.

47 Ward, M.J. (1946) *The snake pit* (extract), in R. Shannonhouse (ed.) (2003) *Out of her mind: Women writing on madness*. New York: Modern Library, pp. 60–69.

48 Millett, K. (1990) *The loony-bin trip*. Urbana, IL: University of Illinois Press.

49 Frame, J. (1961) *Faces in the water*. New York: Women's Press.

50 Wurtzel, E. (1995) *Prozac nation*. New York: Riverhead.

51 Chapadjiev, S. (ed.) (2008) *Live through this: On creativity and self-destruction*. New York: Seven Stories Press.

52 Savran, J. (ed.) (2004) *Hysteria: An anthology of poetry, prose, and visual art on the subject of women's mental health*. New York: LunaSea Press.

53 Shannonhouse, R. (ed.) (2003) *Out of her mind: Women writing on madness*. New York: Modern Library.

54 Ussher, J.M. (1991) *Women's madness: Misogyny or mental illness?* Amherst, MA: University of Massachusetts Press.

55 Sexton, L.G. (1994) *Searching for Mercy Street: My journey back to my mother, Anne Sexton* (extract), in R. Shannonhouse (ed.) (2003) *Out of her mind: Women writing on madness*. New York: Modern Library, pp. 120–129.

56 Gottlieb, D. (2008) Lady Lazarus: Uncoupleting suicide and poetry, in S. Chapadjiev (ed.) *Live through this: On creativity and self-destruction*. New York: Seven Stories Press, pp. 27–35.

57 Shive, B.M. (2008) Cello speak: Exploring new language for madness, in S. Chapadjiev (ed.) *Live through this: On creativity and self-destruction*. New York: Seven Stories Press, pp. 175–186.

58 Linehan, M.M. (1993) *Cognitive-behavioral treatment of borderline personality disorder*. New York: Guilford.

59 Kovel, J. (1988) A critique of the DSM-III. *Research in Law, Deviance and Social Control*, **9**: 127–146.

60 Johnstone, L. and R. Dallos (2006) *Formulation in psychology and psychotherapy: Making sense of people's problems*. London: Routledge.

61 Harper, D. and D. Moss (2003) A different type of chemistry? Reformulating formulations. *Clinical Psychology*, **25**: 6–10.

62 Bentall, R.P. (1992) *Reconstructing schizophrenia*. London: Routledge.

63 Koss Bailey, N.P. et al. (2003) Depression and PTSD in survivors of male violence: Research and training initiatives to facilitate recovery. *Psychology of Women Quarterly*, **27**: 130–142.

64 Gavey, N. (2005) *Just sex? The cultural scaffolding of rape*. London: Routledge.

65 Hollway, W. (1989) *Subjectivity and method in psychology: Gender, meaning and science*. London: Sage.

66 Western, M.C., J.H. Baxter, J. Pakulski et al. (2007) Neoliberalism, inequality and politics: The changing face of Australia. *Australian Journal of Social Issues*, **42**(3): 401–418.

67 Lees, S. (1993) *Sugar and spice: Sexuality and adolescent girls*. London: Penguin.

68 Tolman, D. (2002) *Dilemmas of desire: Teenage girls talk about sexuality*. Cambridge, MA: Harvard University Press.

69 Huntley, R. (2006) *The world according to Y: Inside the new adult generation*. Crows Nest, NSW: Allen and Unwin.

70 Jack, D.C. (1991) *Silencing the self: Women and depression*. Cambridge, MA: Harvard University Press.

71 Venuto, L. (2009) The return of the happy housewife, in *Notebook*. Sydney: News Magazines, pp. 55–57.

72 Chodorow, N. (1978) *The reproduction of mothering: Psychoanalysis and the sociology of gender*. Berkeley, CA: University of California Press.

73 Hollway, W. (2006) *The capacity to care: Gender and ethical subjectivity*. London: Routledge.

74 Ussher, J.M. and M. Sandoval (2008) Gender differences in the construction and experience of cancer care: The consequences of the gendered positioning of carers. *Psychology and Health*, **23**(8): 945–963.

75 Mencher, J. (1990) *Intimacy in lesbian relationships: A critical re-examination of fusion*. Work in Progress no. 42. Wellesley, MA: Stone Center for Women's Development, Wellesley College.

76 Kurdek, L.A. (2004) Gay men and lesbians: The family context, in M. Coleman

and L.H. Ganong (eds) *Handbook of contemporary families: Considering the past, contemplating the future*. Thousand Oaks, CA: Sage, pp. 96–105.

77 Connolly, C.M. and M.K. Sicola (2006) Listening to lesbian couples: Communication competence in long term relationships, in J.J. Bigner (ed.) *An introduction to GLBT family studies*. New York: Howarth, pp. 271–296.

78 Ross, L.E. (2005) Perinatal mental health in lesbian mothers: A review of potential risk and protective factors. *Women and Health*, **41**(3): 113–128.

79 Winterich, J.A. (2003) Sex, menopause and culture: Sexual orientation and the meaning of menopause for women's lives. *Gender and Society*, **17**(4): 627–642.

80 Metz, M.E., B.R.R. Rosser and N. Strapko (1994) Differences in conflict-resolution styles among heterosexual, gay, and lesbian couples. *Journal of Sex Research*, **31**(4): 293–308.

81 Kurdek, L.A. (2003) Differences between gay and lesbian cohabiting couples. *Journal of Social and Personal Relationships*, **20**: 411–436.

82 Green, R.J., M. Bettinger and E. Zacks (1996) Are lesbian couples fused and gay male couples disengaged? Questioning gender straightjackets, in J. Laird and R.-J. Green (eds) *Lesbians and gays in couples and families: A handbook for therapists*. San Francisco, CA: Jossey Bass, pp. 185–230.

83 Schreurs, K.M.G. and B.P. Buunk (1996) Closeness, autonomy, equity, and relationship satisfaction in lesbian couples. *Psychology of Women Quarterly*, **20**: 577–592.

84 Mooney-Somers, J., J. Perz and J.M. Ussher (2008) A complex negotiation: Women's experiences of naming and not naming premenstrual distress in couple relationships. *Women and Health*, **47**(3): 57–77.

85 Jones, A., V. Theodos, W.J. Canar et al. (2000) Couples and premenstrual syndrome: Partners as moderators of symptoms?, in K.B. Schmaling (ed.) *The psychology of couples and illness: Theory, research, and practice*. Washington, DC: American Psychological Association, pp. 217–239.

86 Ussher, J.M., M. Hunter and M. Cariss (2002) A woman-centred psychological intervention for premenstrual symptoms, drawing on cognitive-behavioural and narrative therapy. *Clinical Psychology and Psychotherapy*, **9**: 319–331.

87 Paykel, E.S. (1994) Life events, social support and depression. *Acta Psychiatrica Scandinavica*, **89**(suppl. 377): 50–58.

88 Rogers, C.R. (1961) *On becoming a person: A therapist's view of psychotherapy*. Boston, MA: Houghton Mifflin.

89 Lambert, M.J. and D.E. Barley (2001) Research summary on the therapeutic relationship and psychotherapy outcome. *Psychotherapy: Theory, Research, Practice, Training*, **38**(4): 357–361.

90 Mitchell, J. (1974) *Psychoanalysis and feminism*. London: Allen Lane.

91 Sayers, J. (1991) *Mothering psychoanalysis: Helen Deutsch, Karen Horney, Anna Frued and Melanie Klein*. London: Hamish Hamilton.

92 Gyler, L. (2010) *The gendered unconscious*. London: Routledge.

93 Brown, L.S. (2010) *Feminist therapy*. Washington, DC: American Psychological Association.

94 Worell, J. and P. Remer (2003) *Feminist perspectives in therapy: Empowering diverse women*. New York: Wiley.

95 Burstow, B. (1992) *Radical feminist therapy: Working in the context of violence*. Newbury Park, CA: Sage.

REFERENCES

96 Lee, J. (1997) Women re-authoring their lives through feminist narrative therapy. *Women and Therapy*, **20**(3): 1–22.
97 McQuaide, S. (1999) Using psychodynamic, cognitive-behavioral, and solution-focused questioning to co-construct a new narrative. *Clinical Social Work Journal*, **27**(4): 339–353.
98 Gremillion, H. (2004) Unpacking essentialisms in therapy: Lessons for feminist approaches from narrative work. *Journal of Constructivist Psychology*, **17**(3): 173–188.
99 Silverstein, L.B. and T.J. Goodrich (2003) *Feminist family therapy: Empowerment in social context*. Washington, DC: American Psychological Association.
100 Hunter, M.S., J.M. Ussher, S.J. Browne et al. (2002) A randomized comparison of psychological (cognitive behavior therapy), medical (fluoxetine) and combined treatment for women with premenstrual dysphoric disorder. *Journal of Psychosomatic Obstetrics and Gynaecology*, **23**: 193–199.
101 Warner, S. (2009) *Understanding the effects of child sexual abuse: Feminist revolutions in theory, research and practice*. London: Routledge.
102 Taylor, V. (1996) *Rock-a-by baby: Feminism, self-help, and postpartum depression*. New York: Routledge.
103 Laitinen, I. and E. Ettore (2004) The women and depression project: Feminist action research and guided self-help groups emerging from the Finnish women's movement. *Women's Studies International Forum*, **27**: 203–221.
104 Moncrieff, J. (2009) Deconstructing psychiatric treatment, in J. Reynolds, T. Heller and R. Muston (eds) *Mental health still matters*. Basingstoke: Palgrave Macmillan, pp. 301–309.
105 Andrews, G. (2001) Placebo response in depression: Bane of research, boon to therapy. *British Journal of Psychiatry*, **178**(3): 192–194.
106 Currie, J. (2005) *The marketization of depression: The prescribing of SSRI antidepressants to women*, for Women and Health Protection. www.whp-apsf.ca/pdf/SSRIs.pdf
107 Rief, W., Y. Nestoriuc, S. Weiss et al. (2009) Meta-analysis of the placebo response in antidepressant trials. *Journal of Affective Disorders*, **118**(1–3): 1–8.
108 Stoppard, J. (2000) *Understanding depression: Feminist social constructionist approaches*. London: Routledge.

APPENDIX

1 Jack, D.C. (2001) Understanding women's anger: A description of relational patterns. *Health Care for Women International*, **22**: 385–400.
2 Jack, D.C. and D. Dill (1992) The silencing the self scale: Schemas of intimacy with depression in women. *Psychology of Women Quarterly*, **16**: 97–106.
3 Ussher, J.M. and J. Perz (2010) Disruption of the silenced-self: The case of premenstrual syndrome, in D.C. Jack and A. Ali (eds) *The depression epidemic: International perspectives on women's self-silencing and psychological distress*. Oxford: Oxford University Press, pp. 435–458.
4 Zigmond, A.S. and R.P. Snaith (1983) The hospital anxiety and depression scale. *Acta Psychiatrica Scandinavica*, **67**(6): 361–370.
5 Jack, D.C. (1991) *Silencing the self: Women and depression*. Cambridge, MA: Harvard University Press.

6 Thompson, J.M. (1995) Silencing the self: Depressive symptomatology in close relationships. *Psychology of Women Quarterly*, **19**: 337–353.

7 Stenner, P. (1993) Discoursing jealousy, in E. Burman and I. Parker (eds) *Discourse analytic research*. London: Routledge, pp. 114–134.

8 Davies, B. and R. Harré (1990) Positioning: The discursive production of selves. *Journal of the Theory of Social Behaviour*, **20**: 43–65.

9 Harré, R. and L. van Langenhov (1999) *Positioning theory*. London: Blackwell.

10 Braun, V. and V. Clarke (2006) Using thematic analysis in psychology. *Qualitative Research in Psychology*, **3**: 77–101.

11 King, M. (2009) *Women's subjective experiences of positive premenstrual changes*. Psychology Honours research project, School of Psychology, University of Western Sydney.

12 Reissman, C.K. (1993) *Narrative analysis: Qualitative research methods, Volume 30*. London: Sage.

INDEX